PERGAMON INTERNATIONAL LIBRARY
of Science, Technology, Engineering and Social Studies
The 1000-volume original paperback library in aid of education,
industrial training and the enjoyment of leisure
Publisher: Robert Maxwell, M.C.

PARAPSYCHOLOGY: SCIENCE OR MAGIC?
A Psychological Perspective

Foundations and Philosophy of Science and Technology Series

General Editor: MARIO BUNGE,
McGill University, Montreal, Canada

Some Titles in the Series:

AGASSI, J.
The Philosophy of Technology

ANGEL, R.
Relativity: The Theory and its Philosophy

BUNGE, M.
The Mind–Body Problem

GIEDYMIN, J.
Science and Convention

HATCHER, W.
The Logical Foundations of Mathematics

SIMPSON, G.
Why and How: Some Problems and Methods in Historical Biology

WILDER, R.
Mathematics as a Cultural System

Pergamon Journals of Related Interest

STUDIES IN HISTORY AND PHILOSOPHY OF SCIENCE*

Editor: GERD BUCHDAHL, *Department of History and Philosophy of Science, University of Cambridge, England*

This journal is designed to encourage complementary approaches to history of science and philosophy of science. Developments in history and philosophy of science have amply illustrated that philosophical discussion requires reference to its historical dimensions and relevant discussions of historical issues can obviously not proceed very far without consideration of critical problems in philosophy. *Studies* publishes detailed philosophical analyses of material in history of the philosophy of science, in methods of historiography and also in philosophy of science treated in developmental dimensions.

* Free specimen copies available on request

PARAPSYCHOLOGY
Science or Magic?

A Psychological Perspective

by
JAMES E. ALCOCK
Glendon College, York University, Toronto, Canada

PERGAMON PRESS

OXFORD · NEW YORK · TORONTO · SYDNEY · PARIS · FRANKFURT

U.K.	Pergamon Press Ltd., Headington Hill Hall, Oxford OX3 0BW, England
U.S.A.	Pergamon Press Inc., Maxwell House, Fairview Park, Elmsford, New York 10523, U.S.A.
CANADA	Pergamon Press Canada Ltd. Suite 104, 150 Consumers Road, Willowdale, Ontario M2J 1P9, Canada
AUSTRALIA	Pergamon Press (Aust.) Pty. Ltd., P.O. Box 544, Potts Point, N.S.W. 2011, Australia
FRANCE	Pergamon Press SARL, 24 rue des Ecoles, 75240 Paris, Cedex 05, France
FEDERAL REPUBLIC OF GERMANY	Pergamon Press GmbH, 6242 Kronberg-Taunus, Hammerweg 6, Federal Republic of Germany

First edition 1981
British Library Cataloguing in Publication Data

Alcock, James E
  Parapsychology, science or magic? – (Foundations
  and philosophy of science and technology series) –
  (Pergamon international library).
  1. Psychical research
  I. Title
  II. Series
  133   BF1031   80–41254

ISBN   0 08 025773 9   hardcover
       0 08 025772 0   flexicover

Printed and bound in Great Britain by A. Wheaton & Co., Ltd., Exeter

This book is dedicated to three people to whom I am profoundly indebted for the indelible influence they have had on my learning:

D. WILLIAM CARMENT

J. CARSON BOCK

I. ARNOLD BERG

Entia non sunt multiplicanda praeter necessitatem
(Occam's Razor)

"Reason, of course, is weak, when measured against its never-ending task. Weak, indeed, compared with the follies and passions of mankind, which, we must admit, almost entirely control our human destinies, in great things and small."
Albert Einstein (1950)

"The straight path of reason is narrow, the tempting byways many and easier of access."
Joseph Jastrow (1935/1962)

Foreword

THIS book was written to provide the interested reader with a critical perspective on parapsychology. However, the parapsychologist who reads this book might be disturbed to find no mention of some of the celebrated star subjects of parapsychology such as Pavel Stepanek (who, according to Beloff (1980), is now "parapsychologically defunct"). Nor is there any mention of some of the more controversial figures, such as Ted Serios, who practices "thought photography" by supposedly concentrating his mental powers on a camera (through a small "gizmo" held between himself and the lens). Nor are most of the "classic" laboratory studies discussed. These omissions are deliberate, for this book attempts neither a comprehensive history of experimental parapsychology nor a detailed treatment of classic research and supposedly gifted individuals. Readers are directed to other works, such as Girden (1978) or Hansel's (1980) *ESP and parapsychology: A critical re-evaluation*, for such information.

Given the extensive literature on the subject, it will always be possible for anyone determined to believe in the paranormal to argue that such and such an experiment which was passed over in this work would answer all the criticisms I have raised. To such people I would respond that I should like to be able to perform, or at least to observe, such an experiment myself. Critics have been calling for such a repeatable, publicly verifiable demonstration ever since experimental parapsychology began, but even many leading parapsychologists admit that this has not been possible to provide. I have not omitted any reference which in my opinion could add something crucial to the case for the paranormal. However, rather than trust my judgment on this, the reader is invited to turn to the various works listed under Suggested Readings at the back of this book.

In preparing this book I have attempted to deal with two separate but related sets of questions: (1) What are the central problems with parapsychology, with its theoretical basis, its methodology, its data, that prevent it from achieving what many parapsychologists so dearly want: acceptance within the scientific community? As the reader shall see, I believe that these problems are so fundamental that, until they are overcome (if that were to prove possible), the basis for belief in the paranormal will continue to be faith rather than objective evidence. (2) If paranormal phenomena do not exist, how can one account for the persistence of belief in them? Why, generation after generation, do some young scholars turn to parapsychology and subsequently devote large portions of their professional careers to it? Why do some scientists advocate belief in the paranormal, while others sneer at it? Why do so many people have experiences which, for them, seem to demand paranormal explanations? What is it in the individual's psychological make-up, and in the fabric of society, that engenders and maintains such belief?

Keeping these two sets of questions always in mind, I have drawn on a wide range of interdisciplinary subject matter. I claim no expertise outside my own specialty of social psychology; my treatment of some subject matter pertaining to philosophy of science, to physics, to anthropology and to sociology has, of necessity, been brief and simplified. I beg the reader's indulgence if, where his own area of specialization is involved, I have seemed superficial in my treatment. Such simplification is not meant to mislead the reader into thinking that complex issues can be easily reduced to simple statements. However, a more profound analysis than that given here is not, in my opinion, necessary for the points being made. One does not have to grapple with emerging conceptions of philosophy of science to argue that parapsychology's *ad hoc* and *post hoc* explanations are not in keeping with scientific method. Although modern philosophers of science have moved away from the simplistic positivist viewpoint of the 1930s and early 1940s, the inability of parapsychologists to present testable hypotheses is as relevant and as serious a problem now as it was during that earlier period.

Each chapter in the book treats what I believe to be an important perspective from which parapsychology should be considered.

In Chapter 2, "Magic, Religion and Science", the reader is reminded that supernatural/transcendental/paranormal belief has been a part of every society throughout history. Efforts to explain the genesis of such belief have not been conclusive, and it is suggested that, rather than trying to understand the origins of the substance of the belief, or the specific reasons for the adoption of the belief, it is more appropriate to try to understand the *process* by which such beliefs can be generated. It is possible that this same process may contribute to the acquisition and maintenance of modern beliefs about the paranormal.

The theme of Chapter 3, "The Psychology of Belief", is that beliefs are not simply sets of presumed facts filed away in the individual's memory. Rather, each is typically part of a hierarchical network, and changes made in one belief may necessitate changes in many others. By understanding the characteristics of belief systems, we can more readily understand why belief about the paranormal often seems resistant to negative information.

In Chapter 4, "The Psychology of Experience", the nature of experience is considered in some depth. It is argued that, based on our knowledge of normal perceptual and cognitive processes, we should *expect* to have from time to time the kinds of "paranormal" experiences that people report.

In Chapter 5, "The Fallibility of Human Judgement", the human propensity to see causality and covariation where none exists is treated at length. Until we learn that our own judgements are highly unreliable, we will continue to read causality into situations where coincidental occurrence is responsible for what we observe.

Chapters 6, "Science or Pseudo-science: The Case of Parapsychology", and 7, "Parapsychology and Statistics", treat the subjects of scientific evidence and statistical evidence for parapsychology respectively.

Chapter 8, "The Public Debate Continues", provides some information about the ongoing debate between advocates and critics of parapsychology. The role of the media and popular literature also is examined.

I am a skeptic. My own skepticism about the paranormal is based on more than a decade of following the parapsychological literature and on my knowledge, as a social psychologist, of the many sources of error both in the interpretation of everyday experience and in the carrying out of experimentation involving human subjects. Were there any persuasive evidence for any of the various paranormal phenomena which are claimed to exist, I would, along with a large proportion of the psychological research community, leap to the study of what would be beyond doubt the most exciting, the most important psychological ability ever discovered. But, alas, the evidence is not there. Thousands of research reports and monographs and books attest to the strength of the evidence, but thousands of books and documents have attested to the reality of Satan, and I am not persuaded by either. I hope to show in the pages that follow that parapsychology (to paraphrase C. E. M. Hansel, 1971) is best described as being belief in search of data rather than data in search of explanation.

Acknowledgements

I wish to acknowledge my deep gratitude to each of the following people whose assistance was so important in the preparation of this book:

For their careful reading of the early manuscript and for their thoughtful comments, which have been of critical importance to me,

Thomas Gray, Concordia University
Michael Lacroix, Glendon College, York University
Ann MacKenzie, Glendon College, York University
Timothy Moore, Glendon College, York University
Laura Otis, York University
Harald Proppe, Concordia University
Page Westcott, Glendon College, York University

For manuscript typing, Jane Pham-Van Huyen and Lillian Facey. I am particularly grateful to Jane Pham-Van Huyen, upon whom the greatest burden fell. She was not only responsible for the entire final draft, but she cheerfully and unflinchingly put up with what seemed like an endless series of last-minute alterations.

For her excellent and indispensable editorial assistance, Susan Noakes.

In addition I wish to sincerely thank Mario Bunge of McGill University. Without his interest and enthusiasm this book would never have been written.

I reserve special thanks for Barnard Gilmore of the University of Toronto, not only for his very important comments on the early manuscript, but also for his unceasing encouragement and countless inspiring suggestions throughout the period during which this book was being written.

Finally, I wish to thank Herbert Jenkins of McMaster University who, although he has probably long since forgotten about it, was responsible for my initial involvement with the parapsychological literature. His encouragement with regard to the need to bring a critical evaluation of this literature to the attention of colleagues and public alike brought about the first step along the path which led to this manuscript.

Contents

CHAPTER 1

Introduction

What can we expect an astronomer to say when he is told that at least a thousand horoscopes are drawn today to one three hundred years ago? What will the educator and the advocate of philosophical enlightenment say to the fact that the world has not been freed of one single superstition since Greek antiquity?

Carl Jung[1]

We have seen an official blueprint for the construction of a British Rail metal divining rod, with a brass handle containing a steel rod, bent through a right angle and freely revolving in two ball races. The best amalgamation of modern technology with genuine old traditions.

Ravensdale and Morgan[2]

THIS is an age of wonders. The products of technology which we come so quickly to take for granted would have appeared to be miracles in any previous age. Imagine travelling back in time armed with a pair of walkie-talkies, a camera whose pictures develop before your eyes, a battery-powered wrist watch, or any of thousands upon thousands of products of the modern era. The wisest scholars of the day would be unable to begin to understand the functioning of such devices, and might very well treat them as contrivances of the devil himself.

To one suddenly awakened from a Van Winklean sleep, the marvels of our age would be nothing short of shocking. Careful perusal of a random selection of books and magazines would overwhelm one with the accomplishments and wonders of the latter part of the twentieth century. For example, cardiac pacemakers, organ transplants, brain scans and laser "scalpels" are all part of modern medicine, and all have contributed to saving countless lives. At the same time, one would read about the hundreds and even thousands of people caught in the grips of otherwise fatal diseases restored to the full bloom of health through the powers of the psychic surgeons of the Philippines, who operate without instruments and leave no scars.

The United States has landed men on the face of the moon and brought them back to tell about it. At the same time the media say that there is scientific evidence which demonstrates that a person's non-physical essence can leave the body and travel independently to various points on earth or even to the planets. The awesome power of the atom has been harnessed for use in peace and war; it is also argued that there is strong evidence that the mind itself can directly influence inanimate objects without the need for any physical contact or energy transfer. Almost instantaneous world-wide communication is now made possible by satellite relays, while studies of extrasensory perception are said to demonstrate that mind-to-mind communication is possible by means of a psychic process that is totally unaffected by considerations of time and space. Remote-sensing satellites are regularly employed in the search for minerals and the monitoring of the weather, while psychical research is reported to

---

[1] Jung (1933), p. 208.
[2] Ravensdale & Morgan (1974), p. 192.

have revealed that some gifted people can, by means of psychic powers, solve crimes, find lost children, and even see into the future.

The evidence of the bookstore and magazine stand is enough to convince many that all of the above reports are essentially correct. Some of these discoveries and developments involved the labours of people pursuing "normal" science, with its gradual accumulation of "facts" through carefully controlled research and the establishment of causal links among various variables so that by the time technology took over and constructed the satellite or built the nuclear reactor, the processes involved were "understood" in that one could accurately predict outcomes given specific initial conditions. The other examples involved processes which occur, if at all, mysteriously. They cannot be elicited on demand simply by arranging conditions in a specified way. They seem predisposed to appear only to people who believe in them, and not always to all of those. No causal chain linking outcomes to initial conditions has ever been established for these processes. Yet, since people believe that earth satellites exist without having direct experience of them, why not also believe the reports of psychic phenomena, especially since most people at some time in their lives have experiences which could easily be taken to be instances of the paranormal?

During this era of unprecedented scientific and technological accomplishment, there are many signs of a strong resurgence of interest in paranormal and occult phenomena. This is reflected not only in the obvious interest shown by the media in themes dealing with everything from the Bermuda Triangle to extrasensory perception to demonic possession, but also in the controversy about the paranormal that has reached into the ranks of the scientific community itself.

At the same time that interest in the paranormal is flourishing, new religious and quasi-religious cults, some of which have aroused considerable debate because of the tactics used to attract and influence members, have proliferated. Fundamentalist Christianity, too, is enjoying renewed popularity, and is beginning to once again make its presence felt in the secular world. For example, in some part of North America, California in particular, efforts are being made, with some degree of success, to compel educators to teach the Biblical account of creation in science classes as an alternative to the theory of evolution.

Some scholars view this situation with alarm, interpreting it as a wave of rebellion against science and rationality. Others view it as a reflection of the human desire to reassert the spiritual side of human existence which has, so it is argued, been too long neglected or suppressed by mechanistic science.

We ourselves are the "centuries ago" people of a few centuries hence. Will it be said of us that our knowledge was so limited, our image of nature so imperfect, that we were able to grasp but a small fragment of reality? Should this possibility give us pause when we are faced with accounts of the miraculous today? More importantly for the task at hand, do accounts of the paranormal reflect glimpses of hidden powers that lie within all of us, and that one day everyone will routinely use? It is a thought which appeals to many people. Consider, for example, what one journalist said of her experience in a Dick Sutphen "past life seminar" in which she was supposedly hypnotically regressed to lives past;

> A sense of life's infinite possibilities gives a zest to living that nothing else can match. What I got from the Dick Sutphen seminar has been reinforced by subsequent reading and living: a sense of the incredible potential powers of my own mind and a feeling of the intricate and fluid vastness of the universe. If the only real limits we have are those we impose on ourselves, then let's push them out as far as possible. (Kreps, 1979, p. 38.)

Was her regression to supposed earlier incarnations veridical? Or was it imaginary? And how can people learn to tell the difference? That is essentially what this book is about—the problems involved in trying to tell the difference between reality and fantasy in our own personal experiences, in the testimony of others, and in evidence which is presented in the name of science.

Before going any further, it is essential to define some of the basic terms that will be used throughout.[3]

The Paranormal: Basic Terminology

The term "paranormal" is used to describe putative phenomena which cannot be explained in terms of presently accepted theories of nature because they violate one or more of the basic assumptions, or axioms, of the current scientific worldview.[4] One such axiom is that an effect cannot precede its cause, and therefore precognition, or the ability to see into the future, is a paranormal concept, since it would involve "seeing" an event the cause of which has not yet occurred.

Such phenomena as precognition involve a supposed power of the mind, or "psyche", and hence they have come to be known as "psychic" phenomena, with the terms "paranormal" and "psychic", or simply "psi", being used interchangeably with each other. The term "parapsychology", which refers to the study of paranormal processes and events, was coined by the French mystic Boirac in 1893,[5] and was introduced to the English-speaking world by the eminent psychologist William McDougall who reserved its usage for that part of psychical investigation which is the domain of the academic researcher (Beloff, 1977). "Paraphysics" is a related term which refers to "the physics of paranormal phenomena" (Chaplin, 1976). It is usually used as a synonym for parapsychology, being preferred to the latter by students of the paranormal whose professional background is in the physical rather than the social sciences.

Psi phenomena are many and varied. *Extrasensory perception* or ESP, the acquisition of information about the external environment without use of the known sensory channels, is a basic concept. ESP includes (1) telepathy: the transference of thought between two people who are in "rapport", (2) clairvoyance: the ability to see or become aware of events and things which are not in sight, and (3) precognition: the perception of events before they occur. These three types of ESP are in principle difficult to separate from each other. A psychic may be able to determine the order and character of a set of cards which are viewed by a second person, a sender, but the researcher cannot determine whether there has been telepathy between the subjects, precognition of the order of the cards by the psychic, or spontaneous clairvoyant knowledge of them. This problem is so fundamental that even pre-eminent psychologist Joseph Banks Rhine argued;

> . . . it has not been possible to design a definitive experimental test of telepathy . . . and the suggestion is . . . that telepathy be indefinitely shelved until, if ever, a conclusive test design is discovered. (1974a, p. 137.)

Another psi concept is *psychokinesis* (PK), the ability to physically influence inanimate

---

[3] More extensive glossaries can be found in any issue of *The Journal of Parapsychology*, in the *Handbook of parapsychology* (Wolman, 1977) or in Chaplin's (1976) *Dictionary of the occult and paranormal*.

[4] The definition of the paranormal will be discussed in greater detail in Chapter 6.

[5] *The psychology almanac* (Wilkening, 1973).

objects without physical or other known forms of contact. The putative ability to influence the roll of dice by the power of one's mind is a typical example.

The notion that an individual's "mental" or "spiritual" being can leave the physical body and move about independently, while having at its disposal all the faculties and abilities usually associated with the physical brain and nervous system, is called the *out-of-body experience* (OOBE). The concept is not central to parapsychology, although many parapsychologists accept it. Again, Rhine (1974a) pointed to the inherent impossibility of distinguishing between an OOBE and forms of ESP. The subject could be using clairvoyance, for example, while imagining that he has left his body. Similar problems arise in the study of reincarnation and of mediumistic communication since

> Even if the evidence were acceptable by conclusive psi research standards (which is so far not at all the case) *it would still be alternatively explainable by means of psi contact with the sources used in the checking.* (Rhine, 1974a, p. 149, italics added.)

A great many other phenomena are also studied under the rubric of the paranormal, although a phenomenon accepted by one researcher may be considered totally without foundation by another. *Faith healing, pyramid power, psychic powers of plants, dowsing, auras, Kirlian photography,* and *poltergeists* are among the great many putative phenomena of the paranormal world. Further out on the fringes of parapsychology, leading an almost separate existence, are found such things as *astrology* and *biorhythm theory, Tarot cards,* and the *I Ching,* and a host of others.

Parapsychology: A Brief Historical Overview[6]

The history of formal parapsychological research began with the establishment of the Society for Psychical Research in London in 1882 and the American Society for Psychical Research in 1885. Early research focused on the study of mediums, who claimed to be receiving information from the souls of the departed, and on the investigation of spontaneous experiences of ESP.

Noted psychologist William McDougall, considered by many as the founder of modern social psychology, had a deep interest in the study of the paranormal. (He was at one time president of the Society for Psychical Research in England.) In 1927 he moved from Harvard University to Duke University, and was soon joined there by a young botanist he had met at Harvard, Joseph Banks Rhine. Rhine and his wife and co-worker Louisa were to become the predominant personages in American parapsychology for the next half-century. With McDougall's encouragement Rhine brought parapsychology into the laboratory.

Beloff (1977) saw Rhine's laboratory approach as representing two significant milestones in the history of parapsychology:

1. It was a bid to give parapsychology recognized academic status within university circles.
2. It replaced the earlier search for qualitative evidence based on personal accounts with a quantitative statistical approach.

---

[6] For a more detailed history, consult Beloff (1977), Hansel (1980), or Rogo (1975). Some aspects of the background of formal parapsychology will be discussed in more depth in Chapter 2.

In 1934 Rhine published his first research report in a monograph entitled "Extrasensory Perception" (a phrase he coined), which brought his laboratory approach to the attention of both friend and foe of parapsychology. In it he claimed that by means of experiments using a special deck of cards, the Zener deck, he had established the existence of psi beyond any reasonable doubt.[7] In 1935 the Parapsychology Laboratory became a separate unit from the psychology department, with Rhine as its director.[8]

Beloff (1977) noted that in the early days of the Duke Laboratory, parapsychologists were blessed with a good number of first-rate subjects who were able to consistently obtain above-chance scores, and sometimes very high scores, in ESP studies. As research conditions were tightened in response to critical commentary from those outside the field, consistent scorers virtually disappeared. Had it not been for the discovery of *negative* scoring (consistent below-chance scoring by some subjects), Beloff (1977) commented, the research at Duke might have come to an early end. Negative scoring suggested that attitude and/or personality might play a role in psi ability, and generated a new wave of research into both the effects of personality attributes and the differences between selected high scorers and low scorers.

Parapsychology has grown over the years, both in terms of the number of researchers interested in it, and in its organizational structure, which is modelled after that of other research disciplines. In 1937 *The Journal of Parapsychology*, founded by Rhine, began publication. It was intended to be a scientific journal dealing with research into the paranormal. By 1977 *Parapsychology Review* (May/June issue) listed fifty-four parapsychology periodicals published in fifteen different countries. The same periodical (January/February 1975), in what it described as "by no means an exhaustive" list named more than eighty parapsychological associations in the United States, six in Canada, and eighty-eight distributed among twenty-eight other countries.

In 1969 the Parapsychology Association in the United States was admitted as a member of the prestigious American Association for the Advancement of Science (A.A.A.S.), an action which has repeatedly been cited by parapsychologists as an indication of their growing stature in the eyes of the scientific community. (More will be said about this in a later chapter.)

Parapsychology courses (often non-credit) are being taught in an increasing number of universities around the world,[9] leading Beloff to comment,

> but whether this represents a tribute to [parapsychology's] achievements or a concession to the greater intellectual permissiveness of our age (the initiative usually comes from the student body for whom its unorthodoxy constitutes its principal recommendation!) is a debatable point. (1977, p. 20.)

Thus, parapsychology seems well established.

There have always been prominent skeptics such as Chester Kellogg, Joseph Jastrow, E. G. Boring, D. H. Rawcliffe, C. E. M. Hansel (all psychologists), Martin Gardner, and many others. One of these stands out from the rest, and that is Hansel, for he alone (Hansel, 1966) carried out a detailed examination of the conditions under which the most celebrated psi experiments were conducted (e.g. the Pearce–Pratt experiments (1933–1934), the Pratt–Woodruff experiments (1938–1939), the Soal–Goldney experiments (1941–1943)).

---

[7] See Hansel (1980), Chapter 8, for a critical discussion of the studies upon which Rhine's monograph was based.

[8] In 1965 when Rhine was due to retire, Duke University severed all connections with the Parapsychology Laboratory, which then became a private institution, the Institute for Parapsychology of the Foundation for Research on the Nature of Man (FRNM).

[9] *Parapsychology Review* regularly mentions new courses being offered.

In his investigations Hansel was struck by important differences between British and American investigations. While in the United States researchers were quick to find evidence of clairvoyance and telepathy (they conducted most of their research into clairvoyance since it only requires one subject and is easier to control experimentally), in Britain little or no evidence was forthcoming for clairvoyance. Hansel (1966) also noted that in the United States, high-scoring subjects, who were easily discovered in the 1930s, could not be found after 1939 following tightening up of experimental procedures. Similarly, S. G. Soal, who dominated British parapsychology in the 1930s, found that high-scoring subjects virtually disappeared when procedures were tightly controlled. When Soal loosened up his tight procedures, extraordinary performers were found once more.

Hansel found various demonstrable inadequacies in experimental design and controls and suggested that fraud may have played a part in some well-known studies. He concluded after his investigation that none of the studies had been conducted in such a way that the *possibility* of fraud had been eliminated:

> In the case of each of these conclusive experiments, the result could have arisen through a trick on the part of one or more of those taking part. In addition, closer examination of the experiments to see how far the hypothesis of trickery is consistent with information concerning the experiments in no case invalidates the hypothesis and in some cases strengthens it. (1966, p. 241.)

Hansel concluded that, while one cannot state categorically that trickery was responsible for the results of these experiments, as long as the possibility has not been eliminated, the experiments cannot be considered conclusive evidence for ESP.

In 1980 an updated version of Hansel's book, titled *ESP and parapsychology: A critical re-evaluation*, was published. In this work, Hansel examined more recent evidence, such as the Targ–Puthoff studies of Uri Geller at the Stanford Research Institute, the telepathic dream studies at Maimonides Medical Centre, and the Schmidt studies of psi using radioactive decay from random-event generators. Hansel reported that while much innovation had entered psi research, little had been done to provide the *conclusive* experiment. He found no more reason to believe that ESP had been demonstrated in 1980 than he had in 1966.

Thus, the lines are drawn. Many parapsychologists believe that there is conclusive evidence that psi exists. Skeptics such as Hansel do not. While most people in the scientific community take the position that the evidence for psi is not persuasive, there is widespread public and media acceptance of the paranormal. Many of the reasons for this will be elucidated in the chapters that follow.

CHAPTER 2

Magic, Religion and Science

God is dead. (Nietzsche)

The tribal gods are being worshipped once again, in substantial part as a protest against the hyper-rationalist society and the failures of that society.

Andrew M. Greeley[1]

IN THE name of religion human beings have committed genocide, toppled thrones, built gargantuan shrines, practiced ritual murder, forced others to conform to their way of life, eschewed the pleasures of the flesh, flagellated themselves, or given away all their possessions and become martyrs. Throughout history religious belief has had an awesome power to motivate individuals and whole societies. Although many nineteenth-century scholars predicted the decline and eventual disappearance of religion, viewing it as a system of erroneous beliefs which would founder in the face of advancing scientific knowledge disseminated through universal education, history has proven them wrong. Religion has continued to survive and flourish, even in totalitarian societies where governments have attempted to eradicate it. There are still many individuals willing to martyr themselves in defiance of secular laws in order to serve a kingdom not of this world.

While religion has had, in one way or another, a profound effect on virtually every individual in every society throughout history, it was only with the emergence of the social sciences around the turn of the century that empirical scholars began to interest themselves in the workings of religion. Since it was in vogue in the latter part of the nineteenth century to focus on the *origins* of human behaviour, whether one was interested in art or language or society, sociologists and historians concerned with the study of religion were obsessed with finding its primordial roots (Eliade, 1969). The beginnings of religious belief are lost in the dim recesses of prehistory, so scholars assumed that all religious belief is basically similar, and that the study of such belief among existing "primitive" peoples would elucidate the foundations of religion everywhere.

An examination of the origins and functions of religion, as viewed by twentieth- and late-nineteenth-century social scientists, is a useful starting-point for the study of modern parapsychology. By studying the problems that scholars have had in trying to learn the origins of religion, and by considering the eventual disposition of various hypotheses, we shall be in a better position to understand the difficulties involved in trying to find the roots of paranormal belief. At the same time, consideration shall be given to processes which might be capable of generating *both* religious and paranormal beliefs.

Not all supernatural belief is considered to be of a religious nature. Classic anthropological treatments of supernatural beliefs and practices distinguished between religion and magic; magic involves impersonal supernatural forces which can be harnessed and manipulated by the informed individual to serve his own purposes; religion is the belief in

---

[1] Greeley (1970), p. 206.

personified spirit entities which control various aspects of nature. Modern anthropology does not make such a sharp distinction. Instead, anthropologists believe that there is no clear dividing line between magic and religion, that they lie along a continuum. Some anthropologists argue that even that distinction cannot be made, and that *any* belief in superordinate agencies is religious. Magic, in this view, is a form of ritual behaviour which is part of religion (Hammond, 1970).

The reader should be aware that in the use of terms such as "magic", "religion", and "science" in the anthropological literature to be cited here, it is virtually impossible to find definitions for these terms that would allow one to say both that, (1) before the seventeenth century, when the modern conception of scientific method began to form, magical, religious and scientific beliefs and practices formed mutually exclusive categories, and (2) before the seventeenth century, beliefs such as astrology which are classified as magical today were less rational than other "scientific" beliefs. Before scientific evidence became available which rendered the astrological hypothesis extremely unlikely, such a belief was just as "rational" as many beliefs which later were confirmed by science. Rationality will be discussed in more detail later.

Thus, while the terms "magic", "religion", and "science" will be freely used in the discussion that follows to facilitate a review of the literature, these categories should not be considered rigid, nor should the terms be taken to imply that magic and religion can be identified directly with irrationality, and science with rationality.

Magic

The term "magic" has descended to us via Greek and Latin from a Persian word meaning "the work of priests or wise men" (Crow, 1968). Anthropologists, as was pointed out earlier, employ the word "magic" to refer to beliefs and practices based on the precept that there exist impersonal and intangible supernatural forces which are subject to invariant laws, which, once discovered, allow these powers to be harnessed and exploited. Magic, to many "primitive" peoples, depends on "mana", a form of supernatural power which is supposed to be an intrinsic property of certain "magical" objects.

The practitioner of magic believes that he can control objects or events by magical behaviour, although there is no objective causal link between the behaviour and the object or event. Crossing one's fingers to bring good fortune is a simple contemporary example of such behaviour. Alchemy, astrology, and faith healing, along with hypnosis, clairvoyance, and mental telepathy have all been considered at one time or another to be of a magical nature (Day, 1975).

Sometimes magical behaviour is not so much an attempt to control nature as an effort to fit into its mysterious workings. Ceremonies were held every year in ancient Egypt to make sure that the Nile would flood and irrigate the land. The ceremonies were held at a time when the Nile should flood naturally, and if it failed to do so, it was assumed that the correct procedure had not been followed. Rainmaking rituals still carried out in many primitive societies are not performed in the middle of the dry season as might be expected, but at the beginning of the rainy season. The ceremonies are viewed as the people's contribution to the order of things. To fail to carry out the appropriate ceremonies might disturb this order (Cavendish, 1977).

The rituals involved in these ceremonies are so elaborate that, should the desired effect not occur, people conclude that part of the ritual was performed incorrectly or that the person in charge was deficient in some respect. If the rain does not fall the rainmakers think the order of nature has been upset by their own mistakes. Magic has remained resistant to extinction because of men's ability to interpret the results in this way. If the prediction of a specific oracle was not accurate, the early Greeks assumed the magician (in this case, the oracle) had erred, but did not lose their belief in oracles.

The Scottish anthropologist and classicist Sir James Frazer (1854–1941) studied the magic and religion practiced in a number of "primitive" societies. In his now classic work, *The Golden Bough* (1896/1923), he described two fundamental types of magic, both of which still exist in some form in modern Western society. The first, "homeopathic magic" (or "imitative magic") is imitative and presumes a "law of similarity". The magic is practiced on an object similar to the one the magician wants to affect, and the law of similarity dictates that the same effect will occur on the remote object. Voodoo, practiced in some contemporary West Indian societies, is homeopathic magic. Pins stuck into the effigies of individuals are believed to bring pain or harm to the individuals themselves. A corollary belief is that objects similar in appearance share other properties beyond mere physical similarity. In the Middle Ages, the swollen roots of the mandrake plant were seen to have the approximate shape of human beings, and in consequence, this plant was believed to have a soul and to scream as it was being extracted from the ground. This scream was believed to be so magically powerful that it would cause the death of any person hearing it. Consequently European peasants in the Middle Ages used dogs to pull up these plants when their roots were needed for magic (Ravensdale and Morgan, 1974).

The second kind of magic identified by Frazer is "contagious magic" (or "sympathetic magic"). In this case, a "law of contact" is involved: objects having once been in contact with one another are thought to mutually influence each other after being separated. A magician who wanted to cast a spell on his enemy would use a piece of his clothing, or better still, some of his hair or his nail-clippings. People in societies where such practices flourished were careful to bury or burn both nail-clippings and discarded hair. This perhaps explains why in many parts of the world, nail-clippings and hair themselves came to be considered magical. It is likely that the Biblical story of Sampson's strength waning following the loss of his hair is related to this belief, as was the punishment of shaving off the hair of French women who had consorted with German soldiers during World War Two (Seligman, 1948).

Primitive magic, although it suffered somewhat at the hands of the Greek rationalists, came to Western society by means of Rome (Cavendish, 1977) and continues to this day in the form of both superstitious behaviours and certain "psychic" practices. Examples of the latter include the putative ability to discover water or minerals by observing the motion of a pendulum moved across a map of the area of interest (homeopathic magic) and the handling of clothing or other possessions of an individual in order to divine his past or future, or even his whereabouts should he be lost (contagious magic). Modern psychic sleuths who claim to solve crimes by using the impressions garnered from handling key bits of evidence are using the principles of contagious magic.

To the layperson, the term "magic" refers simply to stage-conjuring—"prestidigitation", "legère-de-main", etc. But this kind of magic, too, can be traced to the primitive magic we have been discussing. Even among the ancients, trickery was often used to convince nobleman and peasant alike of the powers of magic. The Persian priests, or magi, were steeped in both practical and medical knowledge, and they employed considerable ritual as well as outright deception to impress others with their powers (Vetter, 1973). (Originally the tutors of kings and the custodians of traditional wisdom, they eventually lost their high status and power and became itinerant fortune-tellers, jugglers, and diviners (Underwood, 1979)). Egyptian magicians 5000 years ago performed a cutting-off and restoring of a human head, a forerunner of the sawing-the-woman-in-half trick of modern magic (Gibson, 1967). Indeed,

> [magic] was an art cultivated by the Egyptian, Chaldean, Jewish, Roman, and Grecian priesthoods, being used to dupe the innocent masses. Weeping and bleeding statues, temple doors that flew open with thunderous sound and apparently by supernatural means, and perpetual lamps that flamed forever were some of the thaumaturgic feats of the pagan priests. Heron, a Greek mechanician and mathematician who lived in the second century before Christ, wrote several interesting treatises on automata and magical appliances used in the ancient temples . . . St. Hippolytus, one of the fathers of the early Christian Church, also described and exposed in his works many of these wonders. (Evans, 1975/1897, p. 2.)

The Biblical story of Aaron turning his staff into a serpent to demonstrate God's power to the Pharoah tells of the Pharoah's magicians doing likewise. Nineteenth-century magician Robert Heller reported having many times witnessed a similar demonstration by Egyptian magicians of his day (Evans, 1897). The Egyptian conjurers used the Egyptian cobra, which is peculiar in that it can be temporarily paralyzed, becoming rigid like a stick, by pressure just below the head. The magicians carried staffs of a similar shape and size, and then, by substituting a rigid snake at the right moment, made it appear that an ordinary stick had been thrown to the ground and turned into a snake, which then wriggled away (Gibson, 1967).

Thus, modern-day magic wands and "abracadabras" used by stage magicians reflect a history more ancient than that of virtually any other form of contemporary entertainment. More importantly, people are still capable of being duped, laymen and scientists alike, by the conjurer who pretends that his magic is "real".

Religion

Religion, simply defined, is a belief in superhuman beings, and man's socially patterned relationships with them (Spiro, 1966). While the supernatural powers fundamental to belief in magic can be manipulated by men, the gods or powers of religion require obedience; men do, not as they please, but as they believe the god or gods would wish. There have been a great many different and often conflicting explanations offered for the development of religion. Some of the more historically prominent ones merit some consideration at this point.[2]

1. Animism and nature-myth

Anthropologist Edward Tylor (1958/1871) suggested that dreams about dead acquaintances led people to believe that the dead still live in some form. This notion of an essence, or "soul", which survives death was gradually extended to other living and even non-living things, he argued. Tylor coined the word "animism" (from the Greek word *anima*, meaning soul) to refer to all such activating principles taken to underlie the activity of a body or object. Animism led to the conception that the sun, the moon, and other important aspects

---

[2] This survey is of necessity brief. More detailed information is available in such sources as Argyle and Beit-Hallahmi (1975), Budd (1973), Thomas (1971), and Vetter (1973).

of nature are deities with human attributes, according to this view. Sociologist Herbert Spencer (1820–1903) added to Tylor's interpretation by arguing that because of the respect accorded to ancestors in primitive societies, man turned the ghosts (the dreams) of his ancestors into gods. Spencer believed ancestor worship was one of the roots of all religion (Vetter, 1973).

Other nineteenth-century anthropologists, impressed with the commonness of religious symbols associated with the sun, the moon, fire, and so on, adopted a "nature-myth" approach (Comstock, 1971) and argued that religious belief grew out of the awe experienced by primitive peoples when confronted by nature's more spectacular features. However, this idea was discounted by Evans–Pritchard (1937), who said that primitive peoples in general tend not to react with awe to nature's spectaculars, and that the attribution of such inspiration to them reflects instead the awed reactions of the Western anthropologists.

Vetter (1973) suggested that the roots of animistic thought and religion lie in man's consciousness. Human beings feel that the mind in some way exists apart from the body and it is this feeling that gives rise to the idea of spirit entities:

> The prototype of all non-material forces or agencies conceived to exist is the subjective thought or the volitional process that is the common experience of all mankind. (p. 130.)

As Ravensdale and Morgan (1974) observed, the death of a fellow human must have always been an occasion for considerable awe, since the passing from a living state to that of a corpse has no immediate physical effect on the appearance of the body. The flesh is unchanged, the body organs remain in the same position, the body is still warm and there is no apparent change in weight, yet something awesome has happened: the person no longer moves or makes sounds. The "personality" has vanished. Only the physical being remains. The "personality" must have gone elsewhere.

Even in the early twentieth century there were serious attempts by some physicians to accurately weigh the body of a dying person to see if one could observe a loss of weight due to the "flight of the soul": Dr. Duncan MacDougall wrote in the 1907 volume of the *Journal of the American Society for Psychical Research* that he had placed dying patients on a light bed, mounted on a set of carefully balanced scales. He reported sudden weight losses at the time of death of between $\frac{3}{8}$ ounce and $1\frac{1}{2}$ ounces for six different patients (Christopher, 1975). MacDougall also carried out similar experiments with dying dogs, but observed no weight losses at death. This suggested to him that dogs may not have souls. These findings have not, as yet, been substantiated by other researchers!

However, the primitive notion of a spiritual essence of some sort does not involve a sharp separation between body and soul, flesh and spirit, matter and mind. The concept of a non-material "soul" and of abstract deities is a relatively recent one. The older Greek philosophers thought such an idea preposterous, and even though Plato, in some of his dialogues, described the soul as being totally non-material, this viewpoint was not accepted by most of his contemporaries (Vetter, 1973). Even the early Christians viewed God as a corporeal entity, thus displaying an animistic view which was little different from those of all primitive societies:

> . . . as late as four hundred years after Christ the conception of both God and the soul as it emerges from the writings of the church fathers is indistinguishable from that of the gaseous, vaporous, but still material substance of the ghost or soul of primitive animism. Both body and soul were still *material* to early church fathers. And immortality was not one of the attributes of this quasi-material soul. (Vetter, 1973, p. 81.)

How is it, then, that the idea of an abstract God and a non-material soul came to predominate? William McDougall (1938) argued that,

> The spiritualization of the soul seems to have been achieved by way of the refinement of the conception of God. This refining process consisted in successively denying Him all the distinctive attributes of matter, until the conception of an immaterial spirit was reached. And then the conception of the human soul was assimilated to this more refined conception of God. (p. 30.)

Vetter (1973) suggested that increasing knowledge of nature and of man makes it increasingly difficult for people to maintain their naïve anthropomorphic conception of a god of gods, and that the believer is forced to embrace a more and more abstract concept of his deities to maintain any belief in them.

It is interesting to note that children, like the people of primitive cultures, are not sharp mind–body dualists. Research indicates that they do not discriminate between subjective psychological events and objective physical events. Jean Piaget (1929) described how young children identify thought with the act of speaking, viewing it as a substantial, material event rather than an inner psychological process. The 6-year-old also believes that dreams have an objective, external reality and that they are viewed with the eyes. The dichotomy of subjective and objective, of mind and matter, develops gradually as the child matures (Flavell, 1963).

In summary, while the narrow nature-myth interpretation of the origins of religion has not had any continued importance, the role given to animism, the generalization of one's own subjective experience to objects and to aspects of nature, appears quite reasonable. The development of the concept of spirits from experiences such as dreams and hallucinations involving images of the dead, and the increasing abstraction of the nature of a God or gods as knowledge of the physical world accumulates are credible ideas which should not be too readily dismissed (even though they are totally untestable).

2. Society as the model for religion

French sociologist Emile Durkheim (1912) argued that the very ubiquity of religion suggests that there must be more going on than simply the acceptance of the existence of imaginary spirits. Durkheim[3] believed that religion must reflect aspects of society: Concepts of the supernatural evolved from the model provided by society itself. People, unaware of the extent to which their behaviour is shaped by social factors, felt themselves governed in part by mysterious forces. These forces seemed real, yet could not be objectively identified and so seemed to be not of this world. Durkheim suggested that these social forces were given objective reality by being personified as spirits and gods. Religion became the embodiment of society's most important laws, and it is always society itself, in the final analysis, that is the object of veneration. Society does possess the characteristics that typify the supernatural: It is powerful, ubiquitous, and immortal. Durkheim observed that the individual feels strong, confident, and at peace when he is carrying out society's mandate, and uneasy or guilty when he transgresses the rules. Religion is functional, Durkheim said, because among other things it produces compliance to society's laws without the need for constant surveillance.

Durkheim's theory engendered considerable criticism. The primary objection to his treatment of religious behaviour and belief is that it is too simplistic. This criticism can be

---

[3] I am following Swanson's (1960) summary of Durkheim's extensive writings on the subject.

applied to most theories of religion; the many and varied phenomena associated with religion cannot be explained in terms of one or two variables.

Swanson (1960) carried Durkheim's societal explanation further by documenting the relationship between political systems and the development of religion. A society's experience with a sovereign group (e.g. monarch, council) would affect the character of the religious spirits in which people believed, Swanson said. The areas of jurisdiction attributed to deities would correspond to those of the sovereign group. One would expect that in a loosely organized society with competing local chieftains, each unable to gain hegemony over the others, religious belief would be of a pantheistic nature, whereas in a highly structured, strictly hierarchical society, religious beliefs would centre on a single supreme god. Swanson made a specific prediction in this context: Belief in a high god, especially a monotheistic one, would be found in societies with three or more hierarchical levels of sovereign groups (e.g. monarch, parliament, local government). He tested this hypothesis by analyzing the religions of fifty societies and concluded that it was strongly but not consistently supported. Bowker (1973), however, argued that the data used by Swanson were of varying, often indeterminate, reliability, and that Swanson's definition of monotheism is open to serious question.

Durkheim's societal structuralism approach to religion, although no longer an important force in its own right, has contributed to the modern Western view of religion in terms of its functionalism for the individual and for society. Religion's primary function is seen as integrating the individual into society by defining his values and providing a set of ultimate goals (Budd, 1973). Religion is also functional in providing hope in the face of adversity, and giving people reason to fight on for their individual and collective survival even when their objective assessment of their situation provides little encouragement. From this perspective, the abandonment of religion without its replacement with some other system of belief which can provide the same integrative functions might well lead to social disorganization. Kingsley Davis (1949) has suggested that such disorganization as a result of increasing secularization would produce the formation of new religious sects in the attempt to erect a system of integrative beliefs. This is consistent with what seems to be happening today.

3. Psychological functionalism and religion

Psychologists and psychiatrists interested in the study of religion as a belief system and social system have typically focused on the ways in which magico-religious belief might satisfy the psychological needs of the individual.

(a) *Dependency needs.* In one of his discussions of the origins of religion, Sigmund Freud (1928) attempted to explain the concept of a god as the outgrowth of the child's dependency needs. The child, who relies on the parents for protection and nourishment, comes to view them as omnipotent and capable of exerting invisible control over him. When the child realizes that he is mistaken about his parents' and particularly his father's powers, he feels shorn of protection and support. He then invents the concept of God to embody both the omnipotent invisible power and the source of support that the father once seemed to provide. This happens to be functional for society, Freud added, since it makes more acceptable society's pressure on the individual to renounce or control personal needs so as to further the goals of the group, because the pressure seems to come from God.

Freud's idea is interesting but not very useful in understanding religion, since many peoples have never developed "high gods" (i.e. a single god or a small number of very powerful gods that might reflect the power once symbolized by the parents) (Swanson, 1960). Moreover, most people begin to acquire religion long before they are disabused about the omnipotence of their parents.

However, there is some evidence that the treatment of children by their parents and beliefs about the nature of the gods are related. In a study of sixty-two cultures, Lambert, Triandis, and Wolf (1959) found that societies which view supernatural beings as being primarily malevolent and aggressive are much more likely to employ punitive and harsh childrearing practices than are societies in which the gods and spirits are viewed as being primarily benevolent. This does not imply that there is a *causal* relationship between childrearing practices and the attributes given to the gods, however.

(b) *Need for meaning and purpose.* Carl Jung was fascinated by people's apparent need to believe in metaphysical ideas, and he believed that the need to find meaning in life was one of the principal factors in the development of religion. It is normal to wonder about immortality and abnormal to have no questions about it, Jung (1938) said. If a man ceases to exist at death, how can life have meaning? But if people continue to exist in some form after death, does not that imply that there must be a world of spirit-beings? These questions come naturally to human beings, in Jung's view. Jung also saw religion, particularly the belief in immortality, as being functional for a society: Societies or individuals with strong religious beliefs would draw strength from them in times of adversity, and thus might be expected to struggle longer and harder, eventually vanquishing enemies who do not have religion to sustain them.

(c) *Reduction of fear and uncertainty.* William James and Wilhelm Wundt, two prominent nineteenth-century psychologists, both emphasized the importance of emotional reactions such as *fear* in the development of religious belief. Uncertainty about how to react in unusual or dangerous circumstances creates stress and fear. Primitive peoples may attribute god-like qualities to aspects of nature that produce fear, thus allowing them to deal with a "known" fear, which is generally easier to cope with than an unknown one.

Anthropologist Bronislaw Malinowski argued that both supernatural *and* magical ideas arose in order to deal with situations which were anxiety-provoking and in which no natural course of action was efficacious. Where there is no anxiety, there is no magic, he contended. He supported his argument with evidence from his study of the Trobiand Islanders (Malinowski, 1948) in which he observed that fishermen who fished on an inner lagoon, where there was little danger, had no magical rites to protect them, unlike the ocean-going fishermen, who were steeped in magic to protect themselves from the perils of the open sea. Illusory control was preferable to no control. Religion, he said, not only counteracts the forces of fear, dismay, and demoralization, but also provides the most powerful means for the reestablishment of the morale and solidarity of a group shaken by crisis.

Malinowski also stressed the importance of the knowledge that one will die as a source of fear and uncertainty:

> . . . the belief in immortality is the result of a deep emotional revelation, standardized by religion, rather than primitive philosophic doctrine. Man's conviction of continued life is one of the supreme gifts of religion, which judges and selects the better of the two alternatives suggested by self-preservation—the hope of continued life and the fear of annihilation. The belief in spirits is the result of the belief in immortality. The substance of which the spirits are made is the full-blooded passion and desire for life, rather than the shadowy stuff which haunts his dreams and illusions. (1948, p. 51.)

Malinowski's ideas were heavily criticized. Contrary to what Malinowski suggested, some primitive groups lack supernatural explanations for spectacular and dangerous events, such as storms, and yet employ them for more prosaic events (Swanson, 1960). The Eskimos face much more danger than do the Trobiand Islanders, but have much less magic, and the Polynesians must deal with the same amount of danger as the Trobiand Islanders, but have less magic (Jahoda, 1969). The Karok and Yurok Indians of California suffer little anxiety, having plentiful food and no enemies or serious disease problems, yet they are steeped in magic (Kroeber, 1963).

Another problem with the anxiety-reduction hypothesis is that it cannot account for the fact that people in many cultures have created supernatural beliefs that serve to actually *increase* anxiety. Furthermore, is it not odd, if religious belief was invented to give comfort in times of stress or in face of death, that the "life after death" promised by many religions is not particularly attractive? If people were really inventing beliefs in order to assuage their anxieties, would they not invent more appealing fantasies? Why do some primitive peoples view "afterlife" as gray and disinteresting (Swanson, 1960)? Why do Christians fear terrible punishment after death if they lead a "bad" life, and yet hope to go to a heaven which judging by many Christian descriptions is far from idyllic, should they lead a "good" one? Mark Twain found this choice of afterlife very puzzling. In his *Letters from the Earth* (DeVoto, 1962) he described how, while most people dislike hymn-singing, are bored by church services, find monotony unpleasant, and so forth, they look forward to a Heaven which seems to be just the opposite to what they would enjoy. He went on to say of man's view of Heaven that

> . . . it has not a single feature in it that he *actually* values. It consists—utterly and entirely—of diversions which he cares next to nothing about, here on the earth, yet is quite sure he will like in heaven. (p. 16.)

> . . . he has imagined a heaven, and has left entirely out of it one of the supremest of all his delights . . . sexual intercourse! (p. 15.)

> . . . exalting intellect above all things else in his world, . . . this sincere adorer of intellect and prodigal rewarder of its mighty services here in the earth has invented a religion and a heaven which pay no compliments to intellect, offer it no distinctions, fling it no largess: in fact never even mention it. (p. 19.)

Kroeber (1963) argued that the claim that magico-religious belief arose from the need to reduce anxiety is quite simply incorrect. The origins of such belief cannot be determined, he said, but once established, it is transmitted to each new generation as part of the culture, regardless of what functional aspects it might have originally had. Kroeber's point is important. Many other aspects of our current cultural *modus vivendi* no longer serve any practical function, although they may have done so at one time. Handshakes, for example, supposedly originated as a method of indicating clearly to another that one was unarmed; the left hand carried the shield, the right hand carried the weapon.

There have been various other suggestions about the psychological functions served by religion.[4] However, it is relatively easy to make such suggestions, but quite impossible to substantiate them. Again, it is unlikely that magico-religious belief can be explained simply in terms of one or two variables. Nonetheless, the importance of anxiety reduction as a

---

[4] Other psychological treatments of religion have focused on its compensatory nature (i.e.—on the way religion helps people deal with deprivation). Even *sexual* deprivation has been proposed as a basis for religion (Leuba, 1925; Thouless, 1923).

function of religion should not be dismissed. With the promise of some sort of immortality, religion no doubt helps to make life meaningful and assuage the fear of death or sorrow of bereavement for many people. Perhaps it is because of this that people seem to deepen their interest in religion and belief in immortality after the age of 60 (see Argyle and Beit-Hallahmi, 1975). While they may very well increase anxiety in some situations, it is also very likely that magico-religious beliefs do help many people cope in times of crisis and social and personal disorganization. Such crises may make religion more appealing. Stress and anxiety tend to make people more suggestible and more willing to accept explanations that they might readily reject in other circumstances. Heightened suggestibility might in fact lead people to accept, to "convert" to, magico-religious interpretations of events (Sargant, 1973). In this vein, it has been observed that soldiers who have faced death under enemy fire are more religious than they were before such experiences (see Argyle and Beit-Hallahmi, 1975).

Operant conditioning and magico-religious belief

In the traditional psychological approaches to religion outlined above, supernormal agencies were assumed to meet a psychological need such as dependency, the need for meaning in life, or escape from anxiety and fear. Yet each anthropological or psychological theory put forward to explain religion and magic has had too many exceptions to be accepted as adequate. There will always be societies which do not follow the pattern proposed; two cultures with similar environmental conditions may have radically different belief systems.

However, when expressions such as "need reduction" or "escape from fear and anxiety" arise, it is difficult for an experimental psychologist not to think immediately of "operant conditioning": When an organism produces or "emits" a behaviour which is followed closely in time by something instrumental to its well-being (i.e. food if it is hungry, water if it is thirsty, escape from pain and suffering) it is more likely that the organism will repeat the behaviour pattern the next time similar conditions occur. The reduction of the organism's need is a "reinforcement", increasing the likelihood that the response will be repeated the next time the subject is hungry, thirsty, or in pain. In all likelihood, the same kind of conditioning underlies the development of belief in magic and religion, although the actual circumstances which give rise to such belief may vary enormously from culture to culture.

As a simple example, when a human being accepts, even partially, the belief that the soul survives after death, anxiety about death may be reduced, reinforcing acceptance of the belief, in that when the individual considers the concept of an important soul in the future, he may accept it more readily or with fewer reservations.

Before exploring in greater detail this approach to the origins of magico-religious belief, it is important to note that if a behaviour which at one time was followed by reinforcement is performed a number of times without being reinforced, the behaviour will tend to die out, or "extinguish". However, such behaviour will be considerably more resistant to extinction if it has been reinforced intermittently rather than on every occasion. A simple example should make this clear: If you did not know anything about slot machines, and you put a coin in the machine and immediately won several coins, and if you repeated this with similar success twenty times in a row, and then if on the next ten successive tries nothing happened, you would likely walk away thinking the machine to be broken or empty. On the other hand, again not knowing anything about slot machines, if you won money the first time, but not the second, you may be quite likely to try again a couple of times. Winning on the fourth occasion would teach you that non-success for a few tries does not mean that there will not be success in future.

The reinforcement need not be causally related to the response. All that is required is that the reinforcement follow the response closely in time. Skinner provided an illustration of non-contingent, or "superstitious", conditioning with pigeons. Pigeons were placed in a cage where food was mechanically delivered by a hopper at prechosen intervals without regard for the pigeon's ongoing behaviour.

> One bird was conditioned to turn counterclockwise about the cage, making two or three turns between reinforcements. Another repeatedly thrust its head into the upper corners of the cage. A third developed a "tossing" response, as if placing its head beneath an invisible bar and lifting it repeatedly, two birds developed a pendulum motion of the head and body, in which the head was extended forward and swung from right to left with a sharp movement followed by a somewhat slower return.
>
> The conditioning process is usually obvious. *The bird happens to be executing some response as the hopper appears; as a result it tends to repeat this response* (1948a, p. 168, original italics.)

Vetter, discussing this susceptibility to superstitious conditioning as it applies to magico-religious behaviour, wrote:

> In the normal course of events rains usually do fall, plagues run their course, and even if the crops are lost or the illness carries away many individuals of critical importance, *in the end*, either the crises are resolved in the material world or the individual finally adjusts himself to the loss of crops or family, which he must by one means or another anyhow. *And whatever activities were concomitants of this adjustive process that finally ended the stresses will again be the habits called out the next time similar crises arise.* (1973, p. 227, italics in original.)

Henslin (1967) provided a more direct example of superstitious conditioning of human behaviour. He was struck by the mixture of rationality and irrationality in the behaviour of players in a number of crap games in which he participated. While the players usually bet according to the known probabilities associated with the game ("rational" behaviour), they also engaged in many magical practices in their betting and shooting—snapping their fingers as the dice were rolling, talking to the dice, and so on. The players acted as if these actions influenced the outcome of the game ("irrational" behaviour). Henslin ascribed the development of these beliefs and the behaviour associated with them to operant conditioning. As the shooter throws the dice, he emits various behaviours not associated directly with dice-throwing. If the dice come up in a winning combination, the irrelevant behaviours, because of their temporal contiguity with the "reinforcement" (the win), are more likely to accompany future dice throws.

Adventitiously reinforced behaviours are adopted by other human beings in the social context and can become part of the culture. A particular act or word or gesture becomes part of expected crap-shooting behaviour and is transmitted to newcomers by more "fully socialized" players. The behaviour is maintained in new players both by intermittent adventitious reinforcement, and by the strength of social custom, since departure from custom can itself be anxiety-provoking, particularly when one's status in a group is low or uncertain.

The conditioning operates independently of the individual's "rational" self. The crap-shooter feels the need to perform the magical act, but may not express or feel a belief in its utility, just as the person with a phobia of dogs "knows" that his pronounced fear reaction in the presence of a small puppy is irrational, but cannot control it. Many people who carry lucky charms know "rationally" that the charms cannot help them. Similarly, Vetter described a fighter pilot who couldn't imagine going on a combat mission unless he was wearing a particular sweater:

> [He] was as surprised subjectively by the irrational attachment as was any non-combattant. It was not the product of an act of logic; he just *found* the attachment there. And there you have the psychological essence of all magic and fetishism. (1973, p. 227.)

Operant conditioning is a powerful process, one which is certainly capable of accounting for the development of magico-religious belief in all its varied forms. Whenever some kind of reinforcing event—rain to end a drought, or escape from danger, or reduction of anxiety—happens to follow a specific behaviour, verbal or otherwise, the behaviour is more likely to recur the next time similar hardship is experienced. Many behaviours will extinguish because they are not reinforced again, but some will be reinforced by chance several times running and then only occasional reinforcement may be enough to maintain the behaviour. Similarly, once a concept of spirits has developed, possibly because of dreams of the dead, appeals to departed loved ones for assistance or appeals to the gods will sometimes be adventitiously reinforced.

Behaviour which develops in a society may be reinforced without anyone being conscious of it. The persecution of the witches in medieval Europe was reinforced, Harris (1974) has argued, by the way it functioned to support the priesthood and the nobility. Harris gave this analysis:

Before A.D. 1000 the Roman Catholic Church insisted that there were no such things as witches flying through the air, and people were forbidden to harbour such a belief, since it would be based on an illusion created by Satan. Five hundred years later, around 1480, Catholics were forbidden to believe that witches *do not* fly through the air. While some people who called themselves witches (a very small minority of those so accused by the Inquisition), apparently *did* have "transcendent" experiences, likely through the use of psychoactive drugs, the real function of the witchcraft crisis, which generally spared those in the ranks of the powerful from condemnation, was to deal with increasing social ferment in European society. In effect, the clergy and nobility were operantly reinforced for their persecution of witches by the resulting decline in activities directed against them. The witch mania, said Harris, shifted the blame for social problems from the abuses and economic mismanagement of the Church and the nobility to imaginary demons. The Church and the nobility were not only exonerated in the minds of the public, but they became their very defenders. Far from being the reflection of an institutional structure found wanting, the witch mania was an integral part of the defense of that structure. It served, Harris argued, to demobilize the poor, fill them with internecine suspicions, heighten their feelings of insecurity, and increase their dependence on the ruling class. Yet, presumably, neither clergy nor nobility were conscious of these effects.

Another aspect of operant conditioning is important to the current discussion. When the reinforcement consists of the elimination or avoidance of an anxiety-inducing situation, the individual, e.g. someone who developed a strong fear reaction to dogs after being bitten, will experience relief each time he removes himself from a situation where this fear reaction is evoked. Such avoidance behaviour is self-maintaining, since anxiety-reduction reinforces it, and since extinction, which would occur over time if the individual were to have repeated exposure to dogs without being attacked by them, cannot occur.

People may pray in part because it reduces anxiety, but also in part because not praying will make them feel anxious and guilty. The anxiety caused by not praying will pressure the individual to pray. The distress will then be reduced, reinforcing the habit of prayer. (Prayer may also serve to reduce anxiety in times of stress insofar as it "fills in" time, distracting the individual from the anxiety he feels or from the danger he is in (Vetter, 1973).)

Prayer and other religious ritual is, of course, more directly reinforced if it is followed by "success"—for example, escape from danger. In fact, such behaviour may actually be efficacious in that if the individual, because of what he has been taught or what he has experienced in the past, links such actions to feelings of hope and confidence, his anxiety will be calmed, making possible effective action which might otherwise have been impossible (Jahoda, 1969; Vetter, 1973).

Yet, if operant conditioning accounts for the development of magico-religious behaviour and belief, why is there not considerable "drift" in specific practices? After all, each individual will experience adventitious reinforcement for all sorts of different acts. The answer to this is that, while individuals do develop their own specific magical acts based on their own experience, the culturally accepted *system* of magico-religious belief is not dependent on direct operant reinforcement for its maintenance. In any social group, there is always pressure towards uniformity and conformity. Some beliefs win out, not necessarily because of their inherent appeal, but because of the power of those who advocate them. (Think of the many widely divergent and competing viewpoints about the basic tenets of Christianity in the centuries immediately following Christ's crucifixion. Most of these viewpoints did not die natural deaths. They were expunged.) As Budd commented, men do not choose

> whether or not they want to adopt religious beliefs of a certain kind which correspond to personal needs or not, since they are born into a context where certain beliefs and behaviours are required of them, and very often, where other social roles and categories of thought are contingent upon religious ones. (1973, p. 33.)

Skinner, too, recognized this fact:

> The pigeon is not exceptionally gullible. Human behaviour is also heavily superstitious. Only a small part of the behaviour strengthened by accidental contingencies develops into ritualistic practices which we call "superstitious", but the same principle is at work. . . . Superstitious rituals in human society usually involve verbal formulae and are transmitted as part of the culture. To this extent they differ from the simple effect of accidental operant reinforcement. But they must have had their origin in the same process, and they are probably sustained by occasional contingencies which follow the same pattern. (1953, pp. 86–87.)

Before leaving the discussion of operant conditioning, it should be noted that magico-religious belief may be particularly responsive to operant conditioning because the human mind is fertile ground for it. One of the most important factors in the development of belief may be, as Professor Barnard Gilmore has put it,

> the normal, inevitable, magical psychology that all of us construct as we pass through three years of age and which rules us until we are approximately seven or eight years old. . . . Our unconscious remains confidently magical to this day. (Gilmore, 1980.)

The human mind is not born to logic; it learns it, just as it learns about cause and effect, what is "rational" and what "irrational". This will be discussed in greater detail in Chapter 5.

Although this has been but a brief review of some of the major theories of the origins and functions of religion, it should be obvious by this time that such belief is not something that can be explained by means of a single or a small group of variables. Religion in all likelihood sometimes helps to reduce anxiety and to quell the individual's existential fears, and in some societies it no doubt serves as an important foundation for the internalization of social norms and the integration of society. Yet none of these are the *sine qua non* of religion, or specific only to religion.

Viewing operant conditioning as the process which underlies religious belief and behaviour carries with it the possibility that a wide variety of variables are capable of giving rise to such activity. The developmental history of a given religion, going from its probable basis in simple operantly conditioned responses to highly complex beliefs and behaviour, is extremely difficult to determine. It cannot be proven that operant conditioning provided the basis; it is a defensible and not unlikely supposition that it did.

One puzzling question remains: Magic also performed the various functions claimed for religion. It formed an almost universal belief system, existing along with and shading into developing religious belief. How is it that behaviour at the magic end of the magico-religious continuum has declined so significantly in the modern Western world, while religion continues to flourish?

The Decline of Magic and the Rise of Science

The practice of magic has not died away entirely in modern society. Most newspapers still carry astrology columns, which are based on one of the earliest magical traditions. People still cross their fingers for "luck" and builders more often than not avoid having a "13th floor" in their office and apartment buildings. We still buy products, be it gasoline or toothpaste, mouth-wash or Little Liver Pills because their "secret ingredients" promise us better mileage, more popularity with the opposite sex or less indigestion. We buy not on the basis of scientific evaluation but on the basis of a magical belief that the product has some property that will bring us what we want. Yet, magical behaviour is much less prevalent than it once was.

It is impossible to draw a line and say that magic ended at such and such a time and then religion began. The two, as has been pointed out, are closely interconnected, and elements of magic are still evident in most modern religions. As Thomas said,

> Conversions to [Christianity], whether in the time of the primitive Church or under the auspices of the missionaries of more modern times, have frequently been assisted by the views of converts that they are acquiring not just a means of other-wordly salvation, but a new and more powerful magic. (1971, p. 27.)

Similarly, it is impossible to draw a boundary in time and say "This is when science began". Isaac Newton was an extraordinary scientist, and yet he devoted a considerable amount of time to the pursuit of alchemy, considered by many to belong to the realm of magic. The study of alchemy may be called "magical" now, but before knowledge of the periodic table of elements accumulated, the idea that base metals could be transmitted into gold was a reasonable hypothesis which required testing. It became solely "magic" once it was discarded by science.

Sir James Frazer, whose ideas had a profound effect on the thinking of scholars interested in the origins of religion, saw a connection among magic and religion and science. Magic, he observed, predominated over religion in primitive societies, but as societies developed, the inefficacy of magic came to be recognized. People faced with the failure of magic concluded that the invisible forces which they believed to underlie nature were not amenable to control by man, Frazer said. Instead, invisible spirit beings controlled the forces of nature and men would have to enlist their aid or cooperation if they wanted to change their environment. The failure of magic thus led to religious belief. Frazer believed that intelligent members of primitive societies were later disillusioned with religion as well, and began to closely observe the workings of nature and to attempt to exert control over the environment by natural means, thus laying the way open for the rise of science (Frazer, 1923).

Scientific thought, like magical thought, is based on the assumption that there are fixed laws of nature, Frazer said, and if man can discover these laws, he can exploit his environment. While scientific knowledge of nature's laws is seen as tentative, valid only until a better theory or interpretation is given, religion, unlike either magic or science, provides man with a set of absolute truths. These truths are binding on men, but not on gods.

Frazer's theory of the social evolution of science from religion and of religion from magic fell out of favour for several reasons. The argument that people turned to spirit belief because of the "failure" of magic suggests that religion was in some way *less* subject to failure, which is a doubtful claim. Secondly, one can observe in primitive societies (as in our own) evidence of the continued coexistence of magical, religious, and scientific thought (Lévy-Bruhl, 1926). Critics also have objected to the heavy emphasis on pragmatism associated with magic in the social-evolutionary approach, arguing that the chief functions of magic are symbolic and expressive, satisfying emotional needs, rather than directed towards the accomplishment of objective goals.

In the same spirit, Vetter (1973) contended that the label "magic" has always been attached to discarded practices involving the supernatural or arcane. These practices were not abandoned because they were magical, but discarded first and labelled afterwards (e.g. alchemy). The categorization of practices and beliefs as "magical" may reflect as much on the observer as on the observed:

> I would quite agree that your typical Christian observer, confronted with the diverse magico-religious practices in the world would cry "magic" far oftener than he would be moved to say "there is true religion". (Vetter, 1973, p. 166.)

Magical beliefs were shown earlier to be difficult to disprove in primitive societies; any outcome of a magical ritual can be interpreted in a way which supports the belief. Failure was taken to reflect errors on the part of the practitioner, rather than the weakness of the magic. Either the procedure was not followed precisely or someone unknown was practising counter-magic to nullify the effects of the magical rite. Religion is similarly difficult to disprove. Some religions teach, for example, that God answers all prayers but that since men are incapable of understanding His divine ways and purposes, they may not recognize or like His answers. Thus, people who pray for a medical cure but who experience no improvement will accept, if their faith is strong, that the lack of improvement is part of God's plan. Failure of the test of the belief does not weaken the belief.

If magical and religious beliefs are so difficult to disprove how and why did people abandon them? This is probably the most difficult question in the entire study of magic and religion. As Thomas (1971) observed, witchcraft, divination, ghosts, and fairies were all taken very seriously by intelligent and educated people in the sixteenth and seventeenth centuries. In Tudor and Stuart England, there were also many skeptics, but it is rare to find any documented instances of someone in those days actually *becoming* a skeptic and abandoning his prior beliefs. People spoke of their skepticism without explaining how they became skeptical. Thomas (1971) suggested that the desire for power through magical control and the search for magical mechanisms might have led to intellectual and environmental circumstances which were conducive to empirical research and inductive thought. While religion in the medieval period was of a "passive" nature, pushing people towards contemplative resignation, magic was "active". Astrological interest led to careful observation of the heavens. Interest in numerology, which was based on the belief that numbers are the key to all the mysteries of the universe, motivated the revival of mathematics. The alchemist's dream of turning base metals into gold led to greater understanding about chemical processes, and so on. Gradually, as a result of its relative superiority as a guide to controlling nature, the mechanistic philosophy of emerging science triumphed over magic. This led to the decline of animistic belief upon which magic was based. However, while magic no longer satisfied the intellectual appetite of the educated elite, such dissatisfaction took a long time to filter down to the general populace, according to Thomas.

The abandonment of magic could not have occurred simply on the basis of improved "understanding", nor simply as a result of the scientific-industrial revolution, since there were many skeptics before the revolution and many people who believed in magic after it. In fact, the decline in magic in England began even *before* appropriate technical solutions were found for problems that magic was directed at in the past (Thomas, 1971).

Thomas ultimately concluded that the changes that occurred in the late seventeenth century were not so much technological as attitudinal. There was a new faith in human initiative; people believed that they *could* solve problems without using magic. Even the Protestant Reformation reflected this, in teaching that "God helps those who help themselves", that people should seek solutions themselves before turning to God. Thomas' conclusion is, by his own admission, incomplete since it does not explain why this new confidence in human capabilities emerged. That question is still unanswered.

The birth of modern parapsychology

How could educated people of the nineteenth century who grew up with deeply held religious beliefs react to such compelling challenges to their faith as those implied by both Darwinian and Freudian theory? They would have found it difficult to summarily dismiss the evidence which supported Darwinian evolution.[5] If the Biblical account of creation is incorrect, can one trust the rest of the scriptures? Promised immortality by their faith, but led to doubt this by their logic, many people must have experienced considerable conflict and emotional turmoil. It was precisely such conflict that historian Lawrence Moore (1977) argued was responsible for the spectacular interest shown in spiritualism beginning in the mid-nineteenth century, an interest shared by people from all walks of life. Both spiritualism and the psychical research which grew out of it offered people, in Moore's words, "a 'reasonable' solution to the problem of how to accommodate religious and scientific interests" (p. xii). The popularity of spiritualism was one of the dominant cultural

---

[5] The stage was set for a real confrontation between religion and science. Even today there is opposition to the theory of evolution. Groups such as the Institute for Creation Research in the United States work to persuade or force school authorities and textbook editors to give the Biblical account of creation as much explication as is normally given the theory of evolution. The Institute of Creation Research lists twenty-one scientists, including a physicist, two biochemists and a biologist, on its staff and advisory board. Each of these people has stated that the Biblical theory of creation is a much better explanation (some of them say a better *scientific* explanation) than the theory of evolution. (Creation-Life Publishers, 1977.)

phenomena of the latter part of the nineteenth century, both in North America and in Europe. It began in the United States in the mid-1800s. Moore cited a study by Geoffrey Nelson which linked the growth of spiritualism to the unsettling social conditions in the United States at that time, brought about by a high rate of immigration, high social mobility, and rapidly increasing industrialization. Increased social stress might have fostered a greater dependence on religion, but for many, scientific thought rendered religion impotent to soothe their troubles and fears.

However, spiritualists were careful to argue that they were not basing their beliefs on a religious faith. They were dealing with observable phenomena, they claimed, and they rejected supernaturalism. They believed in the immutability of natural laws, and emphasized the importance of empirically derived knowledge. In Moore's view, they claimed to be on the side of science:

> For most of the 19th century, leading spiritualists had a childlike faith in empirical science as the only approach to knowledge. They tried to emulate the scientific method . . . they copied and helped popularize scientific language. (Moore, 1977, p. 7.)

Thus, spiritualists enabled people to believe that they could advance scientific knowledge by their interest in seances:

> Transforming a concern for man's inward spiritual nature into an empirical inquiry into the nature of spirits, they built a belief in an afterlife upon such physical signs as spirits from another realm could muster. (Moore, 1977, p. 19.)

Spiritualism shared, with most other "religions" that developed from the nineteenth century onwards, the conviction that it could be validated empirically and objectively. Moore (1977) observed that virtually every new American religion in the nineteenth or twentieth century—Mormonism, Christian Science, Scientology, Transcendental Meditation—has claimed to have an *objective* basis for its beliefs.

By the time spiritualism began to wane near the end of the nineteenth century, it had generated enough interest among some scholars to lead to the formal pursuit of psychical research, research dedicated to examining empirical evidence for the existence of spirits, thought transference, and other related phenomena. In 1882 a small group of British scholars formed the Society for Psychical Research,[6] which at heart was concerned with the scientific investigation of phenomena associated with seances and spiritualism. The founders of this group were unwilling to accept the implications of scientific materialism *vis-à-vis* the mortality of man. They sought to demonstrate the survival of the soul by means of scientific empiricism. The quest for evidence of post-mortem survival was also the "directing motive" underlying the establishment of Rhine's laboratory at Duke University (McVaugh and Mauskopf, 1974).

In one of his Presidential Addresses, Henry Sidgwick stated that when the Society was founded,

> . . . it appeared to us that there was an important body of evidence—tending *prima facie* to establish the independence of soul and spirit . . . (and) tending to throw light on the question of the action of mind either apart from the body or otherwise than through known bodily organs. (Cited by Flew, 1980.)

---

[6] This was an elite group. Its first President was Henry Sidgwick, a Cambridge philosopher. It included among others a past Prime Minister of England, W. E. Gladstone; a future Prime Minister, Arthur Balfour; eight fellows of the Royal Society, the most prestigious scientific body in the world at that time; essayist John Russell; poet Alfred, Lord Tennyson, and author Charles Dodgson (Lewis Carroll) (Cohen, 1973).

Frederick Myers, in his 1900 Presidential Address to the Society for Psychical Research (London), suggested that their goal was to provide a "preamble to all religions" and to reach a state where it would be possible to say,

> Thus we demonstrate that a spiritual world exists, a world of independent and abiding realities, not a mere 'epiphenomenon' or transitory effect of the material world. (Cited by Flew, 1980.)

These early parapsychologists and supporters of their research, such as the eminent psychologist/philosopher William James, had typically experienced a personal religious crisis earlier in life:

> Reared by evangelical parents who placed religion at the centre of things, they had been thrown badly off balance when their subsequent education brought their faith in conflict with their reason. (Moore, 1977, p. 141.)

> ... most parapsychologists, from the very time that they lapsed into agnosticism, began searching for evidence to sustain the view that individual life held meaning. (Moore, 1977, p. 239.)

Many modern parapsychologists have been drawn to parapsychology for similar reasons. Impressed with the power of scientific methodology as a means to knowledge, yet unable to accept either a mechanistic world view or the alternative offered by traditional religious belief, these men saw in parapsychology an attractive alternative—the scientific study of spirituality.

Charles Tart, a psychologist-become-parapsychologist and a Past-President of the Parapsychology Association, wrote,

> Because I was so impressed with the power and accomplishment of the scientific enterprise, I found it hard to believe that science could have *totally* ignored the spiritual dimensions of human existence. . . . (1977, p. xii.)

> I happened upon a partial resolution of my personal (and my culture's) conflict between science and religion. Parapsychology validated the existence of basic phenomena that could partially account for, and fit in with, some of the spiritual views of the universe. (1977, pp. xii–xiii.)

Randall in his book *Parapsychology and the Nature of Life* argued that we are witnessing, through parapsychology, the extension of scientific inquiry to the spiritual side of human existence:

> Parapsychology, once the despised outcast of a materialistically-oriented orthodoxy, may now claim pride of place among the spiritual sciences; for it was parapsychology which pioneered the exploration of the world beyond the senses. (1975, p. 241.)

Thus, one root of psychic research is the desire to refute the increasingly prevalent materialistic, mechanistic, atheistic, scientific worldview by proving scientifically that the soul survives the body.

Magic, religion and science in contemporary society

The last two decades have been marked by an apparent explosion of interest in the occult and paranormal. While comparative figures are difficult to come by, it certainly seems that astrology, numerology, possession, astral projection, extra-sensory perception and a host of related subjects have a much greater appeal to people and are subject to much more favourable treatment by the media today than they were, say, in the 1950s. Newspapers and

TABLE 1 PERCENTAGES OF STUDENTS AND PROFESSORS INDICATING BELIEF
AND SKEPTICISM WITH REGARD TO BASIC PARANORMAL PHENOMENA

	N	Believers	Undecideds	Skeptics
Psychology undergraduates, York (second-year courses)	222	83%	14%	3%
Psychology undergraduates, McGill (third-year courses)	80	73%	22%	5%
Science undergraduates, McGill (third-year courses)	115	79%	13%	8%
Professors of natural and social sciences, York	53	21%	49%	30%

magazines, films and television programs generally deal with occult/paranormal subjects in a non-critical fashion, much to the distress of many skeptics. The media seem more interested in entertaining and titillating their audience with the paranormal than giving complete, dispassionate information. (It is not fair to generalize too much; there have been important exceptions to this.)

One index of this growth of interest is the number of books listed under "occult and psychic" in *Books in Print*. This figure went from 131 in 1965 to 1071 in 1975 (Otis and Alcock, 1979). The formal pursuit of parapsychological investigation has experienced a similar growth. The number of North American journals devoted to parapsychology and the occult has increased from twelve to forty-six over the last 10 years, according to Ulrich's *International Periodical Directory, 1968–1978* (Otis and Alcock, 1979).

Just how widespread is belief in the paranormal in contemporary society? I have myself surveyed samples of social science and natural science undergraduates both at York University in Toronto and McGill University in Montreal with regard to belief in basic paranormal phenomena (telepathy, clairvoyance, precognition, psychokinesis).[7] In addition, I collected similar information from a sample of York University professors in the social and natural sciences. The distribution in terms of believers (those who believe in one or more of the basic paranormal phenomena), skeptics (those who rejected these beliefs), and undecideds (those who responded with a mixture of rejection and indecision) is shown in Table 1.

Most of these students expressed belief in the reality of at least some paranormal phenomena, while very few expressed disbelief across the board. Professors, however, expressed considerably greater skepticism. (There were no differences in the distribution of belief among either students or professors as a function of either academic area or sex.)

Similar findings were reported by Otis (1979). She surveyed undergraduate psychology students as well as professors and members of the general public and found that 80 percent of the 120 university undergraduates she sampled indicated that they believed that ESP is real, while 85 percent of 226 members of the general public expressed the same belief. However, only 33 percent of the 352 professors she surveyed indicated such belief.

---

[7] Items were simple: e.g. "Precognition, the ability to 'see into the future', occurs."
    "Psychokinesis, the ability to move or affect objects by the 'power of the mind', occurs."
Responses were made on a seven interval scale going from "strongly agree" to "strongly disagree". Those subjects described above as "believing" in a phenomenon are those who responded with "agree", "moderately agree", or "strongly agree" while those described as rejecting the beliefs responded with "disagree", "moderately disagree", or "strongly disagree".

A survey of attitudes towards parapsychology was also carried out by *New Scientist* magazine in Great Britain in 1972. Approximately 1400 replies to a questionnaire published in the magazine were returned by readers from the 70,000 copies of the magazine that had been printed. (This survey suffers from the possibility of response bias, as there is a possibility that believers had a stronger tendency to respond than non-believers.) Sixty-seven percent of the respondents expressed a favourable attitude towards the hypothesis that ESP exists, while 22 percent were clearly negative (Evans, 1973). A high proportion (63 percent) of the respondents had university degrees of one kind or another, and 29 percent had higher degrees suggesting, as Evans (1973) said, that this sample was not an "academically feeble fringe".

In a more recent study of university professors in general (Wagner and Monnet, 1979), 2400 questionnaires were mailed to faculty in the natural sciences, social sciences, humanities, arts and education at 120 colleges and universities across the United States. Eleven hundred and eighty-four replies were forthcoming. Attitudes towards ESP were divided: 66 percent were favourably predisposed to believe in ESP and 23 percent were negative. Eighty-four percent felt that the study of ESP is a legitimate field of scientific inquiry. There was a difference between scientists and non-scientists: Positive attitude toward ESP was expressed by 73 percent of the respondents from the humanities, the arts, and education, compared with only 55 percent of those in the natural sciences and 56 percent of those in the social sciences.[8]

Wagner and Monnet also cited a recent Gallup poll which found that only one-half of a sample of 1553 adult Americans believed in ESP. They concluded that college professors, as a group, have attitudes towards ESP that are much more positive than those of the American public in general.

It is interesting to note that experimental psychologists have traditionally been highly critical of the claims of the parapsychologists.[9] For example, Warner and Clark (1938) and Warner (1952) surveyed members of the American Psychological Association with regard to their views toward parapsychological research. Roughly two-thirds of the people they polled responded in each case. In 1938, 8 percent had favourable attitudes and 50 percent had unfavourable attitudes towards ESP (i.e. towards the likelihood that it exists), while in 1952, 17 percent had favourable attitudes and 49 percent had unfavourable attitudes. (In both instances, however, 89 percent stated that ESP research is of a legitimate scientific nature.)

In Wagner and Monnet's study mentioned above, psychologists were more skeptical than other social scientists, who in turn were more skeptical than natural scientists. Only 34 percent of psychologists were positive towards the possibility that ESP exists, while they accounted for over half[10] of all highly negative attitudes ("ESP is an impossibility").

Furthermore, Wagner and Monnet compared their data to that collected by Warner in 1952 and concluded that,

> While there is a generally positive attitude toward ESP, psychologist respondents not only remained skeptical but actually became less neutral and more hostile than was reported 25 years

---

[8] The percentages of social and natural scientists indicating a positive attitude are considerably higher than found either by myself or by Otis (1979) as described earlier. Examination of the questions used in each case does not suggest a reason for such a difference.

[9] Psychologists have also been found to have a stronger belief in strict determinism than members of other academic disciplines (Doyle, 1965).

[10] The proportion of psychologists in the Wagner and Monnet sample was not reported. However, they were included among the "social science" respondents, who made up 20.7 percent of the sample.

ago. . . . It is tempting to speculate that having read more [parapsychological] journal articles and books . . . and having a greater familiarity with research design and the potential pitfalls of experimental research . . . may account for this greater degree of negativity towards ESP. (1979, pp. 13–14.)

These and other similar studies indicate clearly that belief in the paranormal, psychologists aside, is currently very common. Various studies of university undergraduate and graduate students (Jahoda, 1968; Pasachoff, Cohen, and Pasachoff, 1970; Salter and Routledge, 1971) have indicated that amount of university education has virtually no effect on this.[11]

However, it is difficult to be sure that the current level of such belief really represents any change from years past. Without statistics on belief in the paranormal from the late nineteenth or early twentieth century with which to compare current statistics it is impossible to ascertain empirically if there has been any long-term trend. In one of my surveys of psychology undergraduates, I found that 46 percent of a sample of fifty-three students said they believed that one can make another person turn around by staring at his back. The same question was asked of psychology students at Columbia University in 1925 (Nixon, 1925). Nixon found that 44 percent of his sample of 359 students believed they could make a person turn towards them by staring, virtually the same percentage as in my sample. Perhaps had questions about ESP been asked at that time, one would have found a similar level of belief among students.

But if there *is* an upsurge in interests and belief in the paranormal (and it is my strong *impression* that such has been the case over the last 20 years), if the increases in books and periodicals and television programmes dealing with the subject mirror a genuine increase in such belief on the part of the general public, how can this be explained? Some accounts suggest that it reflects increasing social disintegration. It is often said that such belief flourished in the past during periods of decline, i.e. the final days of the Roman Empire, and during the Old Régime in France just prior to the Revolution. With regard to this latter period, it has been said that,

The mania for the supernatural, the rage for the marvelous, prevailed in the last days of the eighteenth century, which had wantonly derided every sacred thing. Never were the Rosicrucians, the adepts, sorcerers, and prophets so numerous and so respected. Serious and educated men, magistrates, courtiers, declared themselves eye-witnesses of alleged miracles. . . .[12]

Yet, it is impossible to say that such activity is a common concomitant of social decay. Many, many changes occur as societies disintegrate. It must be remembered, too, that equally fervent belief in the occult and psychic domains was evident during the social upheaval brought about by the Renaissance (Staude, 1972).

It is more likely that whatever upsurge there has been in paranormal belief has been brought about by one or more of four factors. (There is no well-developed way for assessing the accuracy of this kind of social analysis, so these factors should be taken as an expression of my own opinion, and the opinions of the people cited.)

1. *The "religious void" hypothesis.* If, as many people argue, religion satisfies man's existential needs, a loss of faith in traditional religion might well leave people facing a

---

[11] It has been reported that it is often the most intelligent and best educated students who become most involved with "extraordinary" phenomena such as astrology (Greeley, 1970; Tiryakian, 1972).

[12] Imbert Saint-Amand, *Marie Antoinette and the End of the Old Régime*, cited by Evans (1897).

"religious void". People without traditional religious beliefs may, it is suggested, substitute belief in parapsychology.

In the twentieth century, science and philosophy have questioned the tenets of traditional religion and debunked for most rational men the Christian explanation of creation and the rise of man. At the same time science has brought about rapid technological and social changes which may increase the anxiety people feel in facing the future. Nothing is sure; automation is capable of supplanting whole segments of the occupational ladder; the institutions of marriage and the family seem to be breaking down. The change in moral and ethical values is particularly distressing to some people. Birth-control, abortion, homosexuality, premarital and extra-marital sex, and euthanasia are meeting with an acceptance undreamed of at the beginning of the century. Computerization seems to rob man of his cherished individuality; he can be reduced to a mere number. The media bring a violent and demoralizing world into the living room. In the name of scientific advancement man is polluting his environment and has created weapons which can destroy the world with brief sudden violence.

Scientists and philosophers have inadvertently fostered existential fears by making it seem that there is no purpose to life:

> The senselessness and futility of the Universe are proclaimed . . . by many philosophers. . . . This being the judgement of some of the highest authorities in science and philosophy, it is only natural that many of the most intelligent of our young contemporaries become "turned off" and alienated from the meaningless world. (Dobzhansky, 1972, p. 377.)

Salvatore Maddi (1971), a psychotherapist, reported that the most frequent complaints brought to the psychotherapist's office are feelings of meaninglessness, apathy, and aimlessness. Distress over a failure to find meaning in life is rampant, he said. Fear of death by radiation, fear of cancer from pollution, fear of annihilation by atomic war or fear of violent social unrest is exacerbating the distress people feel. Separation and divorce, high mobility, and the decline of religion as an organizing force have served to rob many people of sources of social support (i.e. family, community, and the Church) during times of stress (Klerman, 1979).

Moreover, we are left without an adequate value system to face these traumatically changing times. Traditional Christian thought is based on the concept of "moral theism"; one should take God's authority (theism) for how we should live (morality). The Christian moral code, then, has as its basis and as its justification the commands of God; one strives to abide by this moral code because one wants to do God's will. Morality is tied directly to theology. It is interesting to note that the Christian Church under the guidance of St. Thomas tied theology (including the moral code) to Aristotelian science, or at least to Aquinas' Platonized version of it. This linking of theology to Aristotelian science perpetrated the warfare between science and theology in the sixteenth and seventeenth centuries.[13] In every area of overlap, whether biology, astronomy, or physics, science won the battle. Insofar as theology remained tied to the overthrown Aristotelian science, it, along with the basis for the Christian ethic, was discarded as well.

Although Aristotelian science has been supplanted by modern science, philosophy and jurisprudence have not kept pace by developing an understandable and acceptable moral theory, at least insofar as the layperson is concerned. Modern science offers an austere view of man and his place in nature, and people are left with nothing to replace God to give them a

---

[13] See Andrew Dickson White's *A history of the warfare of science with theology in Christendom* (1896; new edition, New York: Free Press, 1965).

sense of self-worth or value. Although people have a new science to replace the old, they have no real value system to replace the discarded one.[14]

Thus, simply put, the religious void hypothesis suggests that science has on the one hand produced rapid change which has increased existential anxiety, while on the other hand it has weakened religion to the point where it is of little help in dealing with this anxiety. People have been left without a system of values to guide them in this period of extraordinary technological and social change. They turn to occult/paranormal belief which may allow them, among other things, to believe that there is a harmony in the universe of which they are a part, that each individual has hidden inside him undeveloped powers of potentially staggering magnitude, that the soul survives death. Evans expressed this viewpoint bluntly. The weakening of the appeal for traditional religion has, he said, left the field wide open as never before for stop-gap, pseudo-scientific philosophies, quasi-technological cults, and new messiahs which can assuage the existential anxieties that lie within most people (Evans, 1974).

However, one problem with blaming the apparent resurgence in paranormal belief on a religious void is that it is not clear that traditional religious belief has really declined. *Organized* religion certainly does seem to be losing its power and influence. Surveys in both Canada[15] and the United States (Wuthnow and Glock, 1974) indicate that there has been a sharp decline in church attendance in recent years. Yet at the same time, basic religious belief still appears to be very strong; a Canadian survey in 1977[16] revealed that 88 percent of those sampled reported a belief in God or some other kind of supreme being, and 73 percent claimed to have very strong or somewhat strong religious beliefs. A Gallup poll[17] in the United States carried out at around the same time found that 94 percent of Americans expressed a belief in God.[18] Hunsberger (1978) surveyed Canadian university students and found little support for the idea that students become less religious during their years at university. Only their frequency of church attendance declined.

In my own survey of McGill University students I included questions dealing with (a) the belief in God/Supreme Being, (b) the belief in immortality, and (c) the belief that science and technology have failed to qualitatively improve the world. As can be seen in Table 2 one-half of the science students indicated that they believe in God or a Supreme Being, while 16 percent rejected such a belief. A significantly higher proportion of science students than psychology students indicated belief in God.[19] More importantly, the correlation between belief in parapsychological phenomena and the belief that science and technology have failed

---

[14] I am indebted to Professor Ann MacKenzie for her extremely helpful comments concerning the history and philosophy of science here and elsewhere in this book.

[15] For example, a large-scale survey carried out by Reginald Bibby and reported in the *Toronto Star*, May 4, 1976.

[16] Carried out by T. R. Bird, Data Laboratories Research Consultants Limited, for *Weekend Magazine*, December 24, 1977.

[17] Reported in *The Humanist*, January/February 1977, p. 36.

[18] Argyle and Beit-Hallahmi (1975) found that there has been a greater decline in the importance of religious activity in Great Britain than in the United States:

> "Religion in America has become an American religion, which is mostly secularized, middle-class, and supportive of an individual and national 'good image', while religion in Great Britain has maintained its traditional character, and changes in the world around it have brought about its decline" (p. 29).

They suggested that the existence of socialist parties in Great Britain partially explains the relative apathy towards religion of the British lower classes; the lowest percentage of church attenders in Britain is among those people who identify with both the working class and the Labour Party. Thus, socialism may fill some or many of the psychological needs filled in North America by organized religion.

[19] $chi^2 = 10.8$, 1 df, $p < .05$.

TABLE 2 PERCENTAGES OF STUDENTS IN THE McGILL SURVEY INDICATING BELIEF AND SKEPTICISM WITH REGARD TO A SUPREME BEING, IMMORTALITY, AND THE QUALITATIVE IMPROVEMENT BROUGHT BY SCIENCE AND TECHNOLOGY

	N	No	Undecided	Yes
Belief in God/Supreme Being				
Psychology students	80	36%	26%	38%
Science students	114	16%	32%	52%
Belief in immortal soul				
Psychology students	81	20%	23%	57%
Science students	116	15%	32%	53%
Belief that science and technology have *failed* to qualitatively improve the world				
Psychology students	80	77%	13%	10%
Science students	118	85%	9%	6%

to qualitatively improve the world was virtually zero.[20] Those who believe most strongly in parapsychology are no more inclined to see science as having failed to qualitatively improve our lives than are other students, thus suggesting that it is not a reaction against science that encourages paranormal belief.

There was also no relationship between belief in the paranormal and disbelief in God.[21] While only one-third to one-half of the students were sure about their belief in a Supreme Being, the near-zero correlations argue against the idea that parapsychological belief represents an attempt to fill a religious void, since one would expect, if this argument were true, that parapsychological belief would be strongest when belief in a Supreme Being is lowest. The data indicate that belief in the paranormal, which was held by most of the students, is *not* stronger in those people who have a weak belief in the existence of a deity. Further evidence in this regard comes from a survey mentioned earlier of natural and social science professors at York University. In all, 43 percent reported that they were atheists. Among those who rejected parapsychological phenomena, 65 percent were atheists, while among believers and undecideds, the figures were only 20 and 24 percent respectively. Among those who reported having had a religious upbringing, 73 percent of those skeptical about the paranormal and only 33 and 37 percent of the believers and undecideds respectively, said that they have abandoned their religious beliefs. This indicates that paranormal belief may be more appealing to those who have religious beliefs than to those who do not.

These data do not destroy the religious-void hypothesis. It could be argued that only among those who have had strong religious beliefs can a "void" occur: Those who do not "need" religion reject both it and its supposed surrogate, psychic belief. Yet, one must be careful before accepting at face value the idea that paranormal belief is always adopted because it is functional. That may be true for some people and quite untrue for others. It should also be noted that the moving away from participation in organized religion is not unique to the present time. During the early eighteenth century, a survey of the Diocese of St. David in Wales found that large numbers of people had lost interest in the Church (Greeley,

---

[20] Pearson $r = .06$, psychology, .04 science.
[21] Pearson $r = -.05$, psychology, $-.16$ science.

1970). Various religious geographers have also been able to trace low levels of religious participation in France back to the Middle Ages.

Ironically, at the same time that the movement away from organized religion has seemed to be so evident, there is also a movement *towards* two forms of religion: the fundamentalist churches and the new cults.

Fundamental religion is currently attracting large numbers of followers. The tremendous success of new-style religious "talk-shows" on North American television and the conversion of several leading entertainment figures such as folksinger Bob Dylan to "born-again" Christianity attest to the widespread appeal of fundamentalism. This kind of resurgence of fundamentalism is not new. During economic or social upheavals in the past in North America, similar movements away from traditional churches to fundamentalist ones have occurred (Sales, 1972). Paraphrasing Fromm (1941), alienation and dehumanization can result from too much political or social or ethical freedom. Some people escape this alienation by taking refuge in authoritarian social groups, which might be of a religious or political nature depending on the kind of freedom that is troubling them.

The new cults, like fundamentalist Christian groups, are typically highly authoritarian in nature. The rigid structure they provide for their members may help to reduce existential anxiety by removing the need to make moral/ethical decisions. As Maddi said,

> In subscribing to authoritarian religions and leaders, youngsters are reverting to a meaning orientation in which what is important is determined externally. This is clearly a form of conformity. (1971, p. 182.)

Although such cults have been attractive during times of uncertainty in the past, Levine (1979) believes that the current upsurge of cult popularity will not be short-lived:

> . . . never before have these movements been so popular and open; nor has there been such a concerted search for a new consciousness and life style. . . . Never have there been as many social philosophers offering rationales and encouragement to these movements . . . [and] never have so many of our youth experienced religious awakening with such obvious personal involvement . . . ." (Levine, 1979, pp. 593–594.)

Levine reported that most cult members come from stable homes, have been fairly well educated, and join the cult because of dissatisfaction with their lives. The religious cult provides them with a *raison d'être*—a collection of ideas and values which seems reasonably coherent—and a sense of belonging to a community:

> Alienation, demoralization, and low self-esteem are at least temporarily, but unequivocally alleviated or eradicated; their needs have been fulfilled. (Levine, 1979, p. 594.)

Levine's examination of such cults as the Hare Krishna, the Unification Church ("Moonies"), the Church of God, the Jesus People, the Process and Foundation churches, and Scientology led him to conclude that,

> The particular content of the theology is never as important as the trappings, and certainly not nearly as significant as believing and belonging, and the increase of self-esteem . . . they all give simple answers to the complexities of modern life; there are no longer any existential dilemmas; life becomes secure and comfortable. (pp. 594–595.)

Greeley (1970) observed that the new "faiths" have several characteristics in common:

1. They are non-rational, if not explicitly anti-rational.
2. They stress the basic "goodness" of human nature: If one is "oneself", if one can "get in touch with one's feelings", if one can escape the chains of materialistic, technological society, then one can do no wrong.

3. They are salvationist: "The hippie, the sensitivity enthusiast, the expert with horoscopes, has not the slightest doubt that he has found the answer for himself and for anyone who has the good faith to be willing to listen to him" (p. 209).
4. They are "millenialistic": cultists believe they can create a wonderful, new world in which people are "open" and "honest" with each other.
5. The leaders, gurus, trainers, and experts are usually highly charismatic.
6. They are liturgical: ritual, "sacred" instruments, and vestments, words, and phrases are of extreme importance.

Greeley suggested that the "new" sacralization is simply the reappearance of the old "tribal gods" of ecstatic emotion, superstition, and tribal consciousness dressed in new garb. While the tribal religions may never capture a large segment of the population, Greeley added, they will be around for a long time.

In summary, then, while the evidence to demonstrate a link among religious decline, social change, and existential needs is lacking, there are undoubtedly some people who adopt paranormal beliefs to fill a "void" as "religious void" theorists contend. However, it is unlikely that the widespread interest in the paranormal can be explained in this way.

2. *The "distrust of rationality/science" hypothesis.* Although the apparent growth of interest in the paranormal and occult seems to us to be a recent phenomenon, Carl Jung in 1933 was already writing about such an upsurge:

> The rapid and worldwide growth of a "psychological" interest over the last two decades shows unmistakably that modern man has to some extent turned attention from material things to his own subjective processes. . . . This psychological interest of the present time shows that man expects something from the psychic life that he has not received from the outer world.
> I am not thinking merely of the interest taken in psychology as a science . . . but of the widespread interest in all sorts of psychic phenomena as manifested in the growth of spiritualism, astrology, theosophy and so forth. The world has seen nothing like it since the end of the seventeenth century. (pp. 205–206.)

Beginning in the 1960s, the interest in self-exploration, "getting in touch with your feelings", communing with nature and the like mushroomed dramatically. A concomitant of this movement was an open distrust of rationality and science in many quarters. Science seemed to many to be "out-of-tune" with nature; pollution, defoliation, resource depletion, overpopulation, the threat of thermonuclear war were seen as the products of a society dominated by scientific thinking and crazed by technology. Science and technology came to be viewed as the enemy of individuality, of feeling, of human emotions. As Greeley (1970) said, "There are few better ways of rejecting science than turning to astrology; few more effective ways of snubbing the computer than relying on Tarot cards . . ." (p. 206). For people with this negative view of science, parapsychology offers a world of psychic powers which need not follow the limiting "laws of nature" which science presents. Science suggests men are but skin and sinew, blood and bone, fleshy automatons with the illusion of free will; parapsychology offers realms which defy definition.

Various reports and comments about a growing skepticism and suspiciousness about science among college undergraduates have appeared in the literature (e.g. Cotgrove, 1973; Frank, 1977; Frankel, 1973; McBurney, 1976). Yet the results of my survey that I discussed earlier (see Table 2) did not indicate that rejection of science is a concomitant of paranormal belief. (However, it would be premature to judge this issue only on the basis of one such question.) Moreover, while an examination of the origins of formal experimental parapsychology lend some support to the distrust of rationality idea, it was not so much a *rejection* of rationality and science that was involved, but rather the *use* of science to probe the putative spiritual dimension.

We pay considerable lip service to the ideal of rationality in Western society, and often brand people's "superstitious" beliefs as irrational. Yet, members of most primitive tribes consider their magical and supernatural beliefs to be quite rational, with no distinction being drawn between natural and supernatural (Swanson, 1960). On the other hand, we typically distinguish our religious beliefs from our "rational" beliefs, switching from one belief system to another.

What is a "rational" belief? It is not simply a "true" belief, for a belief can be true merely as the result of a lucky guess, while at the same time it can be quite rational to hold a belief that ultimately turns out to be false. The rationality of a belief must be measured in terms of whether the belief, once formed, can be subjected to a test, and whether the individual will continue to hold the belief even if the test refutes it.[22]

Are rationality and logic the same thing? No, they are not. Formal logic is a tool used to pursue the goals of rational inquiry, but rationality itself must be understood independently before one can address the question of how logical systems are used in, for example, scientific investigations (Toulmin, 1972). The decision to use logic is in itself a *part* of a rational approach.

Most people talk as though they *know* what rationality is. In general, they are referring to a decision process which is based on logic and objective data rather than on subjective feelings. In recent years there seems to have been a growing suspicion of such "rationality". Science, viewed by many as the quintessence of rational endeavour, is seen by some as having created as many or more problems as it has solved, and as having led to an erosion of the dignity and the spirituality of human beings. The myth of the scientist as the "hard-nosed", unemotional super-intellect, unconcerned with human values and driven by an unquenchable lust for knowledge and the excitement of wresting secrets away from nature, has long been disseminated by Hollywood movies and popular novels. Such a myth adds to popular suspicion of scientists. Well-known contemporary writers, such as Theodore Roszak, R. D. Laing, Charles Reich and Kurt Vonnegut, try to persuade their readers that conventional rationality is in many ways contemptible, and that the consequences of scientific and technological endeavour are for the most part evil (Holton, 1974). They put more emphasis on feelings, on direct experiences, and advocate closer integration with nature and the cosmos.

Inside and outside parapsychology, the transcendentalism of the seventies has led to increased attacks on science as a method for gaining knowledge about nature. Some people simply argue that scientific inquiry is not relevant to their new-found beliefs. However, many intelligent people find it unpalatable to accept that their beliefs have no scientific status, and a more sophisticated strategy is to argue that science itself, rather than being rational, is mystical and intuitive, thus making any discord between science and mysticism a superficial one (cf. Nisbett and Wilson, 1977; Albin and Montagna, 1977).

---

[22] The philosophical point here is that although reality is objective (in the sense that reality exists independently of the way we think about it and of the way we wish it to be) and so too is truth objective (a statement or belief is true if and only if it corresponds to what it is about—"it tells it like it is" as we say), what it is reasonable (or rational) to believe, however, *is* relative to lots of things: to the information available at the time, to the conceptual apparatus (logic, mathematics, etc.) available, and even to some extent, to the state of technology at the time the belief is held. Thus, in the Middle Ages it was reasonable (or at least not unreasonable) to believe that base metals might be transformed into gold; after the discovery of the periodic table of the elements such a belief became unreasonable (MacKenzie, 1980).

Reaction against rationality is not new. Philosopher Charles Frankel has written that it often occurs when cherished beliefs are threatened by new scientific "truths";

> the quarrel between supporters and opponents of rational methods represents an ancient division in the Western soul. . . . It rises to a fever pitch when scientific discovery accelerates and when the discoveries that science makes seem more and more subversive of inherited beliefs, social creeds, habits of action, laws, or the soundness of old and cherished hopes and hates. Under these circumstances, irrationality offers a promise of relief and immunity. . . . It is natural that science . . . should seem to be a Frankenstein to those who are threatened by it. (1973, p. 931)

In Frankel's view, the current "irrationalists" (among whom he includes Carlos Castañeda, R. D. Laing, and Norman Brown) share five fundamental propositions. First, the universe is divided into two realms, one of appearance, typified by coldness, doubt, uncertainty and alienation, and one of reality in which the world is in line with one's deepest desires and where there is harmony, coherence, immortality, and timelessness. Second, people mistake appearance for reality because society has inculcated them with biased pre-suppositions. Third, each individual mirrors this dualism between appearance and reality; within everyone is a battle between intellect and emotion, head and heart. When rationality manages to extend itself beyond its proper domain, the result is dehumanization and devaluation of nature. Fourth, when this dehumanization has occurred, people arrive at a state of consciousness where they can now distinguish between "subjective" and "objective" reality. Science is to be distrusted because its whole basis rests on this undesirable distinction. Finally, all human problems, social, emotional, or cognitive, result from a loss of harmony between man and nature, intellect and emotion. Encounter movements are an attempt to restore this harmony, to get people "in touch with their feelings". Astrology may help to make people feel that they are linked directly to the harmony of the universe. Parapsychology may bridge the gap between science and religion, objective and subjective.

Frankel was disturbed that proponents of "irrationality" promise a "good life" free from unease, and conflict, for people who abandon rationality. Science, he asserted, does *not* denude human experience. It has added immeasurably to our appreciation of the complexity of nature. However, the excitement of scientific discovery can only be shared by those who have made any effort to understand science. If science has in any way "denuded" human nature, Frankel argued, it is by introducing ideas that require effort and specialized knowledge to appreciate; ideas that are not readily comprehended by the "man on the run". Both the rational and irrational view of the world delineate a difference between appearance and reality, Frankel said, but irrationalism

> knows in advance that this "reality" must meet the human heart's desires. . . . In contrast, when scientific investigation distinguishes between what is "real" and what is only "apparent", the distinction is always specific, made in a particular context, and as a consequence of a particular inquiry. (1973, p. 929.)

While Frankel's "irrationalists" blame science for existential anxiety, for some people, including no less a man than Albert Einstein, the pursuit of scientific inquiry may be a *solution* to it:

> . . . one of the strongest motives that lead persons to art and science is flight from the everyday life with its painful harshness and wretched dreariness, and from the fetters of one's own shifting desires. One who is more finely tempered is driven to escape from personal existence into the world of objective observing and understanding. . . . A person seeks to form for himself, in whatever manner is suitable for him, a simplified and lucid image of the world, so to overcome the world of experience by striving to replace it to some extent by this image. . . . Into this image and its

formation he places the centre of gravity of his emotional life, in order to attain the peace and serenity that he cannot find within the narrow confines of swirling, personal experience. (Einstein, 1954, pp. 224–227, cited by Holton, 1974.)

The distrust of rationality hypothesis undoubtedly has some element of truth in it. It is unlikely that it can account for the general interest in parapsychology today, although it may well be important in explaining the attraction that parapsychology has for some dedicated workers in the field.

3. *The "unfettered mind" hypothesis.* Modern man is surrounded by technological magic: pictures that develop in seconds before our eyes, chess-playing computers for home use, virtually instantaneous colour television coverage of events from around the globe, and so on. Most people have little understanding of how these modern miracles work. Push a button and the miracle unfolds. It is "magic". However, the average man is aware that there is a causal process occurring that experts somewhere understand.

Most people are unable to get involved in science. It is too technical, too demanding; its apprenticeship is too long. In a real sense, the average man is estranged from science. When he reads about parapsychological claims, which are rarely presented in other than a positive light, why should he dispute them? If Professor X at such and such a university announces that he has developed a process to regenerate human limbs, most people would be inclined to believe him, since he is an "expert". So why be skeptical when physicists (e.g. Targ and Puthoff) at an important research centre report that they have demonstrated the existence of psi forces? Why doubt something that fits in so well with our own experience—after all, who has not from time to time had feelings of *déjà vu*, or been thinking of someone just a moment before that person called?

It is likely that the current upsurge in interest in the paranormal is, in part, motivated by curiosity about the unknown. Most of the curious cannot critically evaluate what they recall or hear because they are deprived of the specific information needed to weigh the claims. Moreover, nothing in their upbringing prepares them for the "psychic-like" experiences which may occur because of the way the nervous system works, or because of coincidence. When an explanation is provided for such experiences by authorities who claim to speak for science, would it not be foolhardy to dismiss them?

While most people may ridicule old magical beliefs, they would have difficulty in explaining why such beliefs are ridiculous. The individual who goes to a physician seeking relief from a painful swelling, accepts that the fluid injected into his body will have a beneficial effect. Yet his *knowledge* of the causal relationship is in most cases no greater than that of the person who goes to a witch-doctor and subjects himself to the application of magical unguents. In both cases, of course, the patient may experience some relief simply *because* of his faith in the "magic" (the "placebo" effect). (Given the complexity of modern pharmacology the modern physician sometimes may have little knowledge himself of "how" a treatment works.)

More than anything else, contemporary interest in the psychic realm may simply reflect uncritical acceptance of claims widely broadcast under the guise of being scientific. The danger lies not so much in the beliefs themselves, but in the absence of a critical evaluation of them.

4. *The role of personal experience.* While the hypotheses described above have a certain appeal to them, it is also important to ask what people who believe in parapsychology themselves see as the root of their belief. (Their responses are not necessarily correct, for the

TABLE 3 REASONS FOR BELIEF/DISBELIEF IN ESP (PRINCIPAL REASON FOR EACH SUBJECT)

Skeptics (23 responses)		Believers (134 responses)	
Would have to experience it; haven't done so	35%	Personal experience	31%
		Friends or relatives with personal experiences	10%
No adequate proof exists	39%	Media reports	16%
Fraud, etc.	26%	Demonstrations, people say they have it	20%
		Evidence is strong	6%
		Anything is possible, other spiritual realities exist	11%
		Other or don't know	6%

effects of a "religious void" and the like are not likely to be recognized by the individual.)

Consider first parapsychologists themselves: Most people engaged in formal parapsychology report that a *personal experience* was of very great importance in initiating their interest: McConnell (1977a) reported that a survey of the members of the Parapsychology Association, which he said comprises about 230 members and is the only professional association in the field, found that 71 percent (of the almost 90 percent of the membership who responded) reported that personal psychic experiences or those of people close to them contributed significantly to their belief in ESP.

Other studies, too, have found personal experience to be the most important reason that people give for their belief in the paranormal. In 1977 I surveyed a group of 272 introductory psychology students, 80 percent of whom indicated a belief in parapsychology. They were asked to state their major reason for belief or disbelief in ESP. The break-down of the results from the 156 students who responded with reasons is presented in Table 3.

As can readily be seen, most believers cited their own experience or the reports of others. Skeptics, too, seemed to consider experience important, in that it was lack of personal experience that they said was responsible for their skepticism.

Otis (1979) found a significant correlation ($r = .55$) between immediacy of personal experience (i.e. was the experience a personal one, or did it occur to a close relative, an acquaintance, etc.) and belief in the paranormal, but only among academics. Such a relationship did not exist for members of the general public. With regard to the *New Scientist* survey mentioned earlier, Evans (1973) reported that a majority of scientists and technicians who believed in paranormal phenomena said that their conviction arose because of a definite personal experience. Yet Wagner and Monnet (1979) found that among their sample of university professors, only 10.9 percent cited personal experience as the basis of their belief while 53.5 percent cited newspapers, 26.1 percent books by Joseph Banks Rhine, and 18.7 percent journal articles. (The authors did not separate the percentages for believers and skeptics.)

Thus, most of these studies have found that people consider their experiences to have been very important in bringing about their belief in the paranormal. However, I am frankly suspicious that many such reports only reflect an attribution process—people are asked to give a reason, and they provide one that is reasonable to them. It may also serve as a justification for their belief. We do not know how many people interpret their experience as paranormal because of prior belief or propensity to believe in the paranormal, and how many suddenly believe in the paranormal because of such an experience. I doubt that the latter occurs very often, for reasons to be discussed in the next chapter.

In summary, there are various reasons for the apparent growth of the belief in paranormal. Undoubtedly, some of these reflect the incredible pace of social change. However, just as it proved fruitless to try to identify one or two functions of or reasons for religious belief, so too it would be unwise to expect to find one explanation for interest in the paranormal.

Concluding Comments

Magic has, in many respects, paid its dues to the human species. Invented by humans and used by humans, it was a belief system which aided these same humans to deal with the vagaries of an unpredictable and often hostile environment. Seligman emphasized this point:

> The fact remains that magic upheld the great civilizations of the ancient world. Its predominance did not prevent man from leaving behind him works of continuing value, from tolerating his neighbour, cherishing his family, doing the adequate thing at the right time. Magic was a stimulus to thinking. It freed man from fears, endowed him with a feeling of his power to control the world, sharpened his capacity to imagine, and kept alive his dreams of higher achievement. (1948, p. 322.)

We shall likely never be without magico-religious thinking, for as Thomas and Hook have pointed out, respectively:

> If magic is to be defined as the employment of ineffective techniques to allay anxiety when effective ones are not available, then we must recognize that no society will ever be free from it. (Thomas, 1971, p. 800.)

> . . . so long as most human beings fear death and make survival in one form or another the greatest good and do not recognize and accept the naturalness of death in a well-ordered life, there will always be powerful religious sentiment and movements in the world. (Hook, 1977, p. 39.)

It is only when uncritical acceptance of magico-religious belief is coupled with a rejection of rationality and science that we should really become concerned. Some scholars warn that this danger is already with us. Philosopher D. B. McKown wrote that,

> In my view, the scientific outlook is potentially in deep trouble, whether scientists know it or not, in any social context in which fundamentalism becomes the most vital form of traditional religion; in which pseudo-scientific cults and magic . . . become booming, multi-million dollar businesses; in which the mastering of language and logic is spurned in favour of meditation and mysticism; in which masses of people confuse subjective certainty with changeable perceptions of reality. (1979, pp. 5–6.)

Indeed, it would seem that schools and universities may be in many cases failing to teach students how to become critical thinkers. In fact, some scholars themselves, charged with teaching the young, have openly expressed a distrust of rationality. Consider, for example, anthropologist Marvin Harris' comments about some of his fellow scholars:

> What now passes for wisdom among my own colleagues is that science is a Western disease; that alternative ways of knowing should never be compared; that Carlos Castañeda's hundred-foot gnats are as real as anything else; that all descriptions of social life are fabrications; that it is useless to seek for objective truth; and that empirical research is nothing but a dirty bourgeois trick. (1978, p. E21.)

Hook warned too that there has been a marked decline in American schools and universities in the development of curricula to strengthen ability to critically evaluate evidence, and insufficient emphasis upon the importance of methodological sophistication in both the logic and ethics of inquiry:

> In their absence, no amount of information is a safeguard against credulity, wishful thinking, and, in personal and political affairs, the will to illusion. It is not enough to stress the critical approach in some disciplines. It must be done in all disciplines in which claims to knowledge are made. . . . (1977, p. 38.)

While there has always been "irrationality" in the world, twentieth-century North American society may be entering one of those dangerous phases in history where the forces of irrationality and anti-rationality threaten science itself. While there is no need for undue alarm, the challenges to science that are being made should be recognized. When groups of people holding the titles of scientists organize themselves to try to compel schools and textbook editors to give the Biblical account of creation equal footing with the theory of evolution, when more and more universities are teaching courses in parapsychology, when television "documentary" after "documentary" attests to the reality of hauntings, mysterious "triangles" in the ocean near Bermuda, and the cures of the psychic surgeons of the Philippines, we must be careful to defend rationality and to teach the value of critical thinking. There is much more technological change and social upheaval to come. If we are wise, we shall be careful to guard our rational heritage jealously.

CHAPTER 3

The Psychology of Belief

Our reason is quite satisfied, in nine-hundred and ninety-nine cases out of every thousand of us, if it can find a few arguments that will do to recite in case our credulity is criticized by someone else. Our faith is faith in someone else's faith, and in the greatest matters this is most the case.

William James[1]

WE GENERALLY speak of our beliefs as though they were the end product of some careful analytical process. Yet if pressed, we would be able to present neither logical basis nor empirical evidence for many of our most cherished beliefs. We may believe democracy to be preferable to dictatorship, but a good debater could choose to defend dictatorships and attack democracy, and most of us would probably lose the debate, even though we would be unlikely to alter our belief. We simply are not skilled in defending the value of democracy. Our belief that it is the best system of government was inculcated in us as school children, and we accept it on faith. Likewise, we all believe the world to be round, and we may smile when we think of the ignorance of people 500 years ago who still believed it to be flat. But how do we *know* it's round? Not because of experience; not because of evidence. We accept it because it has been taught to us. We may cite the space flights around the earth as evidence, if we are challenged, but the television and still pictures that we have seen could easily have been produced on a Hollywood lot. No, we accept the roundness of the world on faith. And we do this despite what our everyday experience tells us: the world clearly *seems* to be flat.

We believe, too, that the earth revolves about the sun, and not vice versa. We believe this even though our senses tell us that the sun moves across our skies once every day. We believe this even though it would not at all be incorrect to assert that the sun revolves about the earth. (It all depends on the point of reference. By choosing the sun as the point of reference, the mathematical description of the various planetary loci is much simpler and more "elegant" than if the earth were arbitrarily chosen as the centre. But that is not why most of us have accepted the heliocentric view.)

Thus, beliefs can be and often are independent of our direct experience. One might even say that we do not choose them at all, for we are incapable of believing or disbelieving at will. Neither physical force nor material gain would be enough to make a person *really* believe the Biblical account of creation if he did not believe it in the first place. We can pretend to believe. We can act as though we believe, and maybe if we keep up the act long enough we will come to believe. But we do not believe something just because we "want" to believe it.

What is meant by the term "belief"? As for most other psychological constructs, the definitions of belief are as numerous as they are vague. In general, a belief can be thought of as "a *simple expectancy* regarding a property of an object or series of objects or events" (Rotter, 1972, p. 336). Thus, we believe (expect) water to be wet, fire to be hot, candy to be sweet.

---

[1] James (1896/1956), p. 9.

An individual's confidence about his beliefs varies. He might be quite certain about some beliefs (e.g. "Australia exists"), and quite uncertain about others (e.g. "regular jogging lowers the risk of heart attacks"). In principle, one can assign to each belief a number ranging from zero to one to indicate the subjectively held, or "psychological", probability that the belief is veridical (Scheibe, 1970). (Such numbers reflect not a scale of measurement so much as a way of communicating one's degree of confidence—e.g. "I am as confident that it will rain tomorrow as I am that I will get two heads if I toss two coins once.")

We can never be certain that what we believe to be true is true. Furthermore, we are not always able to verbalize our beliefs (Rokeach, 1960), and, in that sense, we don't "know" them, although others may be able to infer what they are by the way we behave. In the same way, we can only ever infer the nature of other people's beliefs on the basis of their overt behaviour, verbal and otherwise. People who proclaim their lack of racial prejudice may betray through their behaviour underlying beliefs which are at variance with their words. A person may "believe" one thing, and yet be "forced" to act contrary to that belief. A man with a phobia for dogs may "believe" with very high confidence that a particular little puppy that he encounters will not and cannot harm him, and yet the individual might demonstrate an uncontrollable fear reaction leading us to wrongly infer that he believes the animal to be dangerous. Which is the "real" belief—the belief that dogs are harmless, or the belief that one must try to escape them? In the final analysis, it is pointless to talk in terms of a person's "real" beliefs, as though they are independent of his actions and independent of time and situation, for beliefs are not "thing-like"; they do not have an independent existence (Scheibe, 1970).

Explanation

Human beings are always seeking explanations for events. We are struck by events for which we cannot assign causes—a burst of thunder on a cloudless day, a door that slowly opens by itself, a "disembodied" scream—and most of us do not rest easy until we can find an explanation for seemingly anomalous events. This, of course, can lead to error, for often we do not have enough information upon which to base an explanation. Most people seem to prefer not to categorize an event as inexplicable. They may prefer to conclude that a strange light in the sky was a spacecraft from another planet than to simply categorize it as a strange light which defies easy explanation. Moreover, as Quine and Ullian observed, the elimination of some possible explanations often unreasonably increases one's confidence that one of those that remain is correct:

> In general we tend to believe not only that explanations exist, but that ones that would enlighten us exist . . . it often happens that when we look for an explanation we reasonably believe that it will be found within certain narrow limits. . . . In this situation, elimination of some of the possibilities increases the plausibility of those that remain. Sometimes even an explanation that was initially held to be implausible is accepted because it explains something that can be explained in no other way. Men have been hanged for want of plausible alternatives. (1970, pp. 78–79.)

Explanation is a complicated concept. Have we *explained* how an electric light works if, in so doing we involve a more basic concept such as "electricity" which then itself requires explanation? We may say a stone plummets *because* of gravity. How many of us really understand "gravity"? However, most people seek, not a full explanation, but the feeling that the process or event is not a mystery. The layperson is often content that things which he cannot personally "explain" are "understood" by specialists. Perplexity about an event is often removed if the event can be subsumed under a general principle, even if the general principle is not itself understood. Television sets and micro-wave ovens are beyond the knowledge of the layperson to explain, yet he is content with a vague "explanation" which gives an analogy to some other more commonplace concept. He may believe that the functioning of the sensorimotor nervous system is like a telephone system and thus think that he understands it conceptually. Although he may be manifestly ignorant about telephone systems, there appears to be no "mystery".

Thus, many people, when confronted with an unusual experience, attempt to fit a simple explanation to it and failing in that, they sometimes conclude that no rational explanation is possible, and that paranormal processes must be involved. Unaware of the limitations of their own sensory-perceptual, memory, and judgemental processes, they cannot offer explanations based on normal psychological processes, and thus see no possible normal explanation. As Quine and Ullian said: "The reason . . . widespread misbeliefs can thrive is that the ignorance of relevant truths is often accompanied by ignorance of that ignorance" (1970, p. 39). Persinger (1976) spoke of the "analytical rigidity" of people who experience unusual events, and he extended this criticism to many researchers in parapsychology. If obvious possible explanations fail, people fall back on, or jump to, a paranormal explanation. "If not this, it has to be that", as Persinger said.

When a stage magician entertains by means of illusion, the spectator is in most cases likely to enjoy being fooled. The "impossible" is being performed before his eyes, but he knows that there is a normal explanation of which he is simply unaware. However, if the same conjurer were to pretend that his feats were done by means of paranormal forces, then (as the Uri Gellers of the world have shown only too well) many people will accept at face value this "explanation" because they have "seen it with their own eyes".

People sometimes accept the labelling of a behaviour or event as a substitute for an explanation. This is the "nominal fallacy". A person may be labelled "neurotic" by his friends because of his odd behaviour. Unfortunately, this gives the impression that the cause of the behaviour has been explained. "Why does he bite his nails and worry so much about nothing?" "Because he's neurotic." "How do you know he's neurotic?" "Because he's always worrying about trivialities and biting his nails." This nominal fallacy can have serious consequences. It may lead to the treatment of certain kinds of behaviour as though they were "caused" by some disease-like process; cure the "neuroticism" and the "neurotic" will regain normalcy.

The commission of the nominal fallacy often serves to choke off further inquiry because it seems to provide an explanation. For example, around the turn of the century, psychologists had "explained" a large number of behaviours by labelling them as 'instincts'. (One psychologist counted reference to 10,000 different instincts!) People strive to have children, psychologists said, because of a "reproductive instinct". A mother protects her babies because of her "maternal instinct". Birds migrate to the same places every year because of their "migratory instinct". Chicks peck their way out of their eggs because of instinct. "Instinct" really explains nothing, and it was only because some people refused to accept this simple "instinct" notion that a much better understanding of these "instinctual" phenomena was developed. Birds are sensitive to a variety of very subtle environmental cues which they use to guide their migratory flight. The growing chick, confined by the walls of the shell, reaches a point where a reflexive up and down motion of the head is triggered by the pressure of the shell on the nerves in the neck. This motion has the effect of breaking the shell. Human reproductive behaviour, we now realize, is greatly affected by our social learning experience. None of these things would have been understood had the instinct "explanation" been accepted.

A similar problem occurs when unusual phenomena are labelled "paranormal". People typically look no further for an explanation. Why did a subject in a telepathy experiment succeed to an extent greater than a statistical model would predict? "Because" of precognition or telepathy or whatever. Why are animals often reported to act strangely shortly before earthquakes? "Because" they have precognition. The behaviour is explained by a label, rather than carefully studied. A label can lead people to draw analogies which do not fit, and to misunderstand the phenomenon. The term "black hole" is used by astronomers and astrophysicists to describe an astronomical phenomenon which is predicted by the theory of relativity and which is now being sought after in the cosmos. Although there are still many unanswered questions about black holes, the phenomenon, if it is real, occurs when a star collapses onto itself and becomes so incredibly dense, and its gravity so great, that anything approaching it too closely will be sucked into and effectively disappear. Even light cannot escape—it too is subject to gravity—and thus the black hole cannot be seen. The term "black hole" has a certain appeal, but to many people the temptation to draw associations from the word "hole" is very strong. In consequence we hear and read all manner of wild speculations about where the matter goes when it "disappears down the hole"—perhaps it is draining out of this universe and into another dimension? Had the term "black spot" or "black point" been used, such wild analogical reasoning might not have occurred.

"Explanations", then, can serve as much to delude us as to enlighten us. Sometimes, it is better to categorize events as unexplained, and for the moment, inexplicable, without suggesting that these events are in some way unnatural or supernatural.

Sources of belief

Where do beliefs come from? Sarbin, Taft and Bailey (1960) described four sources of belief:

(a) *Authority*. A large proportion of the average person's beliefs are taught to him by someone in a position of authority. Children accept what they learn in school because of the authority of the teacher. The learning process lasts for years and covers many subjects, but throughout, children may accept that the teacher is unfailingly correct. Books are regarded as an authority by most people. They read of the existence of Henry VIII, that he was king of England, that he had six wives, and believe it although they have no proof of his existence.

(b) *Analogy*. Another source of beliefs is analogy. An individual forms a belief about something based on its similarity with something else he is more familiar with. (Imitative magical beliefs are of this sort.) Persinger (1976) provided a good example of this analogical process; for centuries, there has been a belief in the existence of a human "aura", a "radiation" which supposedly surrounds the body, projecting anywhere from several inches to up to 2 or 3 feet from it. Supposedly those with highly developed "psychic powers" are capable of seeing these auras, and can use the colour of the aura to assess the nature, character, and health of the individual (Day, 1975). In 1935 Semyon and Valentina Kirlian, two Russian researchers, discovered that when an object such as a leaf or a human hand was held against a photographic plate and weak current passed through the plate, the resulting "photograph" showed an "aura-like field" around the outline of the object. Rather than trying to ascertain the source of this "field" by carrying out systematic research to find out what factors might be responsible, the Kirlians assumed that what appeared on the photographic plate was an image of the hypothetical aura. While in this case the analogizing is quite obvious, in everyday life, we usually are not aware of the extent to which we derive new beliefs from old ones on the basis of analogy.

(c) *Inductive reasoning.* Inductive reasoning is a third source of beliefs. Based on limited experience with a certain person or object, people often come to believe that similar people or objects will behave in the same way. For example, someone who has had a bad experience with one or two long-haired "hippies" may come to believe that *all* long-haired males are to be distrusted. Induction is a process used by everyone. It is a matter of generalizing, of making predictions based on experience.

(d) *Theory.* Finally, beliefs may be derived from theories. Theories generate hypotheses (propositions) which serve as tentative explanations or descriptions of some aspect of reality.[2] As examples of theory-generated beliefs, scientists believed in the existence of certain elementary particles and certain planetary bodies long before empirical evidence to support these hypotheses was forthcoming. Not all hypotheses derive from theories. The hypothesis that paranormal phenomena exist is not drawn from a theory.

One of the important differences between scientific and non-scientific belief systems is the way in which hypotheses are evaluated. The hypothesis that the ingestion of Vitamin E will improve the ability to withstand stress may be "tested" by a layperson by taking Vitamin E for a few weeks and noting if his ability to withstand stress improves. He might conclude that the vitamin was effective. Such a verification procedure is open to many error-producing influences. It can lead to a "superstitious" belief in the efficacy of an action if "success" follows the action, but was not caused by the action. Scientific hypothesis-testing involves gathering empirical evidence in a way in which all extraneous variables that might affect the outcome of the test have been eliminated or "controlled". Even with the scientific method, there is still the possibility that some "hidden" variable is really responsible for the outcome of the test, since one can never be sure that all error-producing influences have been eliminated.

Confronted with conflicting sources of the belief and authorities which differ with one another, people must often choose between beliefs. An important influence in such a case is the opinion of their peers and those they respect. As Berger said,

> One of the fundamental propositions of the sociology of knowledge is that the plausibility, in the sense of what people actually find credible, of views of reality depends upon the social support they receive. (1970, p. 56.)

Any social group normally attempts, often quite unconsciously, to standardize the beliefs of its members. People who express deviant opinions are subjected to considerable pressure in the attempt to help them "see reason" and to return them to the common path. A member of an anti-communist group who believes that Castro has, despite his communism, been good for Cuba; a fundamentalist Christian who believes that premarital sex is not a sin; a parapsychologist who believes that the great sensitives of the past have all been frauds; a skeptic who is shaken by his own "paranormal" experience; all of these may be subjected to a certain amount of group pressure to return to the straight and narrow path of group-

---

[2] For the orthodox use of "hypothesis" in the advanced sciences and the contemporary philosophy of science, see Bunge (1967), chapter V.

sanctioned belief. There are, however, great differences in the extent to which individuals are influenced by group pressure.

Belief and disbelief

Rokeach (1960) proposed that people's beliefs are organized along a *belief–disbelief* dimension. For each belief, there are several disbeliefs, some of which are less subject to disbelief than others. For example, the devout Roman Catholic will have strong beliefs about the nature of God, as well as *dis*belief about the Judaic, Islamic, Hindu, and even Protestant views of the deity. However, while the Catholic view will be at the "belief" end of the dimension, and the Hindu view most likely at the "disbelief" end (because it is the most different), the other views will be somewhere in between. The Protestant conception of God would no doubt be closer to the Catholic conception than would be the Islamic notion of God. Belief–disbelief systems vary in the extent to which contradictory beliefs are held in isolation from each other, how much similarity or difference is perceived between disbelief systems, how many such systems there are, and so on. The ability to isolate beliefs from each other or to isolate beliefs from disbeliefs is an important factor in prejudice as well as other kinds of dogmatic thinking. If one "believes" that women are physically incapable of handling certain "masculine" jobs, and yet one is faced with the example of a woman who is successful in such a job, one can deny the contradiction simply by treating the example as an exception, and isolating it from the main belief. "The exception proves the rule" is an aphorism commonly used to deal with contradictions to our beliefs.[3] (In most non-scientific doctrines contradictions are explained away or ignored.)

As Budd (1973) observed, religious beliefs are usually isolated from secular beliefs, so that changes in secular beliefs brought about by experience may have no effect on religious beliefs. Similarly, beliefs about psychic forces might be quite isolated from most other beliefs, so that the physicist who believes in psychokinesis may totally ignore PK as a possible influence when he is carrying out his nuclear physics research. As shall be discussed later, it appears that most people have at least two entire *systems* of belief which are largely isolated from each other.

Another dimension in Rokeach's formulation is the *central–peripheral* dimension, which has three layers. First there is a collection of "primitive" beliefs, which are the equivalent of axioms. These are accepted without question either because they are shared by everyone in the society (e.g. "the world is round") or because they cannot be subjected to scrutiny by others (e.g. "I have experienced the presence of God"). These beliefs form the basis for the individual's entire belief–disbelief system, Rokeach argued. Incoming information is screened for compatability with them, and is either accepted, modified, or rejected as a result. Religious beliefs, such as "God exists", which are acquired as children and not submitted to rational analysis, are primitive beliefs.

If the notion of ESP violates one or more of a person's primitive beliefs, then he will be much more critical of claims for the paranormal than would a person whose primitive beliefs allow for a spiritual reality which is parallel to "normal" reality but not subject to normal scientific laws.

---

[3] It is curious to note that this expression originally meant just the opposite to what it is taken to mean today. The word "prove" was originally employed in its old-fashioned sense, meaning "to test". Hence, the presence of an exception *tests* the rule, and disproves it (Burnam, 1975).

The second layer in the central-peripheral dimension is beliefs about authority; that is, beliefs about which sources of information should be trusted and which should not. Relying on authority is not, in itself, an irrational behaviour; as Trueblood said,

> . . . when we rely on authority, we are not, *for that reason*, guilty of credulity. There *is a reason for our reliance*. We trust the men and institutions presenting the most reason for being trusted. We must use reason to determine *which* authority to follow. (1942, p. 72.)

For many people, the printed page is enough of an authority to establish some beliefs. Others require that writers possess "credentials"—academic degrees or whatever—before they are willing to accept them.

Imagine the reaction of two individuals to a report that a scientist has found conclusive evidence for the existence of ESP. If a skeptic has a set of primitive beliefs which make minimal the *a priori* likelihood of ESP in his mind, and if he also does not believe that all scientists are infallible, he will likely devalue the report. He may devalue the authority of the scientist *because* the scientist has reported favourably about ESP. If the second individual has a set of primitive beliefs which allow for ESP, he may be quite willing to accept the report as veridical. However, had the scientist found no evidence for ESP, he may have also devalued the importance of the scientist as an authority.

The third layer of Rokeach's conceptualization is the "peripheral" region where are found all non-primitive beliefs. Such beliefs are not axiomatic. New information, after having been screened for its compatability with primitive beliefs and assessed in terms of the authority of its source, passes to the peripheral region where it takes the form of a belief or a disbelief. Most beliefs are peripheral.

To summarize, primitive beliefs are generally difficult to change and require no logical support. Religious beliefs are generally of this sort, and for many people both belief and non-belief about psychic forces may also be of a "primitive" nature. To the extent that it is primitive, such belief would be relatively unaffected by evidence. In the final analysis, basic beliefs rest on fundamental premises that are for the believer not open to question and which cannot be proven or disproven by experience, but are articles of faith (Frank, 1977). If a person believes that the world is governed by the Olympian gods, that belief will surely influence his other beliefs, as does a fundamental belief in any other divinity, or a disbelief in the existence of divinities. But one can no more prove the existence of divinities, or their non-existence, than one can "prove" the solipsistic hypothesis that everything we experience is simply a manifestation of our own thinking processes.

Frank (1977) argued that people are taught in childhood to accept two opposing belief systems with radically different perspectives about how one can learn about reality.[4] The first of these, which he called the "scientific–humanist" belief system, assumes there is only one reality, and it is perceived and comprehended in the ordinary waking state and is subject to deterministic laws. The second system, the "transcendental" belief system, is based on the assumption that there exist one or more realities which are *not* directly perceivable in the normal waking state of consciousness. Man cannot directly perceive God or Allah or Lord Krishna, although some people claim to have done so through meditation.

The criteria used for assessing the reality of phenomena in the two systems is very different. The scientific–humanistic system requires an objective demonstration of the phenomenon

---

[4] This discussion is based on Frank's (1977) presentation to a psychological audience. It has been brought to my attention that his view of transcendental and scientific–humanist belief systems is considerably more complex than that presentation suggested.

which satisfies certain "rules of evidence", while the transcendental system is based on the supposedly inherent validity of personal subjective experiences and intuitions. Belief in God, or Allah, or Lord Krishna is not part of a scientific–humanist system because no objective evidence for their existence is available. Such belief can be accepted in a transcendental system, since it is the believer's personal experience or intuition that is important.

It is easy to see how the two belief systems might develop side by side. Most people in our society have been given considerable religious training while at a young and impressionable age (when magical thinking is almost automatic to them). At the same time, they spent 5 days a week in school being taught about subjects which do not easily admit religious interpretation. The child who asks a parent or cleric how, if Adam and Eve, Cain and Abel were the first four people on earth, Cain after slaying Abel could leave his family and find someone to marry, may be told that such questions cannot be answered, or that one should not ask such questions, but should accept the Biblical account on faith. Yet, if the child began with four, subtracted one, and ended up with more than three in an arithmetic class, he would be firmly corrected. People are taught *not* to question certain kinds of beliefs at the same time that they are taught to be logically consistent with respect to others.

The conflict between these two belief systems is perhaps most apparent in the case of some scientists. While demanding satisfactory evidence before accepting any proposition having to do with his field of expertise, a scientist may, when considering questions outside this domain of expertise, act with no more logic than an individual unschooled in methods of evidence evaluation. As social psychologist Gordon Allport remarked,

> No paradox is more striking than that of the scientist who as citizen makes one set of psychological assumptions and in his laboratory and writings makes opposite assumptions respecting the nature of man. (Allport, 1955, p. 100.)

Another person may believe in a deterministic, materialistic world when he is acting in the role of scientist, and yet, when outside that role, believe in religious miracles and the power of prayer. As William James so eloquently phrased it,

> At one hour scientists, at another they are Christians or common men, with the will to live burning hot in their breasts; and holding thus the two ends of the chain, they are careless of the intermediate connection.[5] (1896/1956, p. 11.)

Many prominent scientists have been deeply religious. Bunge (1980) suggested that the profound religious faith of both Faraday and Maxwell may have helped them to overcome the restrictiveness of the world-view of Comte and Mill, since their religion may have led them to think about fields, invisible energies, and so on.

People do seem capable of switching back and forth between belief systems quite readily. Thus, a scientist who has very high standards for the evaluation of evidence in the laboratory may accept the reality of Uri Geller's powers on the basis of watching him perform on television because he has switched, for this class of data, from the scientific–humanist system to a transcendental one.

---

[5] James, in that quotation, touched upon a crucial point addressed earlier: it is a typical reaction of human beings to desire immortality. This desire, perhaps more than any other, makes it difficult for large numbers of people to apply the belief system they use as scientists to their ordinary lives. In the laboratory, unless one is a parapsychologist, researchers never worry about excluding the effects of ghosts or other discarnate beings. Yet, if in our everyday lives we accept the notion that we have a soul that survives death, we may be quite emotionally moved by the appearance of what seems to be a ghost.

Sometimes, people find scientific explanations emotionally unsatisfying. The suggestion that "coincidence" explains why someone's dream of an airplane accident actually came to pass a day or two later is too prosaic to fit the emotional experience that person has had. A paranormal explanation may be more satisfying, since it gives the dream the importance that it was felt to have by the dreamer. Primitive societies show a similar preference for explanations which conform with transcendental belief. As an example of this, Marwick (1974) described how the Cewa people of Eastern Zambia used magical concepts to explain the death of a headman in a car accident. The official explanation was that the driver of the car was intoxicated. The Cewa, however, were not content to know how he was killed, they wanted to know "Why" as well. Why the headman? Why wasn't it someone else? "Coincidence" was not an acceptable explanation. Finally, it was through the magical explanation that some individual had put a hex on the headman that "understanding" was achieved.

Personality and belief

There have been many attempts to isolate personality factors which might be related to the readiness to accept or reject new information. Some factors which have been studied are discussed below.[6]

(a) *Dogmatism.* According to Rokeach (1960), an important characteristic of a belief–disbelief system is the degree to which it is "open" or "closed". If the individual can take in, evaluate and act upon relevant information from the environment on its own intrinsic merits without being influenced by irrelevant internal factors (e.g. habits, primitive beliefs) or external factors (social pressure, etc.), the system is open.

All forms of communication, Rokeach argued, have a dual character, giving not only substantive content but also information about the communicator. The reader of a scientific paper not only gains insight into the writer's beliefs, but will perhaps be able to judge the writer's competence as well. This will affect his reaction to the information. The more closed, or "dogmatic", the belief system, the more difficult it is for the individual to react to the substance of a communication independently of the judgement he makes about the communicator. A dogmatic believer in parapsychology might pay little attention to the argument made by someone who is recognized by his words as being a skeptic, while in the same way an individual who gives serious consideration to evidence for the paranormal may, by that very fact, lose credibility in the eyes of a skeptic who is close-minded. (This does not *always* reflect a closed belief system. It would be a waste of time and energy to consider seriously the views of someone who has repeatedly demonstrated a penchant for rhetoric at the expense of objectivity, regardless of whether he is believer or skeptic.)

In a closed belief system there is both a high rejection of all disbeliefs with little differentiation between various disbeliefs, and an isolation of beliefs so as to eliminate contradictions, Rokeach said. Peripheral beliefs are related to each other, not through intrinsic

---

[6] Although there have been various attempts to identify personality correlates of belief in ESP, the evidence presented has been weak and inconsistent. For example, believers in psi supposedly have been found to be neurotic (Jawanda, 1968), politically rightwing, ethnocentric and anti-hedonistic (Wilson and Patterson, 1970), and to have a tendency towards schizoid thought (Windholz and Diamant, 1974). Moreover, they have also been found to be politically liberal, *anti*-authoritarian, and flexible in their thinking (Cotgrove, 1973; Wuthnow and Glock, 1974). I can think of no good reason to suspect that there is any particular aspect of personality that is associated with such belief, given that the reasons for such belief are likely to be so varied.

connectedness, but through common origin in authority. Rokeach viewed this dogmatism as a personality characteristic arising in childhood, and he suggested that it develops as a consequence of being forbidden to express ambivalence towards the parents. He argued that such an aspect of mental functioning is attributable to personality (i.e. an enduring predisposition to react in a particular way) rather than to intellectual ability, and his research involving problem-solving lends empirical support to this conclusion.

Virtually everyone operates with belief systems that are neither completely "open" nor completely "closed". Rokeach attempted to devise a measuring instrument to measure the degree to which people tend towards dogmatism. A number of studies have found a relationship between dogmatism, as measured by Rokeach's scale, and difficulty in dealing with new information or novel situations (Kaufman, 1973). Highly dogmatic individuals have been found to forget more information that was inconsistent with their belief system than did individuals low in dogmatism (Kleck and Wheaton, 1967), and the source of information has been found to have a greater influence on the acceptance of information in high-dogmatic than in low-dogmatic subjects (Vidulich and Kaiman, 1961).

Rokeach (1960) also associated intolerance of ambiguity with dogmatism. People intolerant of ambiguity want immediate "answers" and tend to see issues in terms of black and white: For example, either build more nuclear power stations or, if they are sometimes dangerous, shut down all such power stations; there is no middle ground. While the person who can tolerate ambiguity might be willing to accept that a strange light in the sky was simply a strange light (i.e. there is no explanation available for it, although it might have been one of a number of things), a person intolerant of ambiguity may prefer to believe that the light was an alien spacecraft rather than remain in ignorance of what it was.

While both believers and skeptics vis-à-vis the paranormal sometimes accuse each other of dogmatism, there is some evidence that, at least among college students, believers in the paranormal are somewhat more dogmatic than are skeptics (Alcock and Otis, 1980).

(b) *Credulity.*
   "Credulity" (definition): "over-readiness to believe; disposition to believe on weak or insufficient grounds" (*Oxford English Dictionary*)

While it is not always easy to assess the "rationality" of the process by which a given individual arrives at a specific belief, there are people who are quite simply "credulous"— they readily accept what would seem to be very unlikely propositions, and they do so on the flimsiest of evidence, or on the authority of someone whose reputation for rigorous thinking is doubtful.

Although fairy-tale beliefs are often encouraged in children (e.g. the belief in Santa Claus, the Tooth Fairy, the Easter Bunny, the Bogey Man), it is considered a mark of maturity when they toss aside these "childish" beliefs (Jastrow, 1962). In our society, individuals are expected to act in a critical manner when evaluating evidence for a claim. Even the strongest proponents of paranormal claims often preface their remarks by reference to their initial skepticism about the reality of the phenomena, skepticism which supposedly was overcome by the weight of confirming empirical evidence.

Credulity, or over-readiness to believe, is something from which everyone suffers occasionally. The success that "con artists" enjoy is based on the credulity of their victims. (The victim's greed is often a catalyst to separation from his money.) Fourtune-tellers "succeed" in part because of their clients' readiness to believe. The readings given by some fortune-tellers are so general that they would apply to anyone.[7] Sun-sign horoscopes in the daily newspaper are another example of this. (Any individual who pays any attention to his daily horoscope would be well advised to pretend for a week that he was born under some other sun sign, and observe how well those horoscopes also apply.)

In demonstration of the effect that very general, widely applicable personality descriptions can have on people, Forer (1949) administered a "Diagnostic Interest Blank" (DIB) to his introductory psychology students. A week later, each student was given a typed personality analysis with his name on it. Students were asked to evaluate the accuracy of the analysis before discussing it with other students. All were given the *same* analysis, consisting of thirteen items such as "You have a great need for other people to like and admire you", "Your sexual adjustment has presented problems for you", "You have a tendency to be critical of yourself", and "You pride yourself as an independent thinker and do not accept others' statements without satisfactory proof". The mean number of items accepted as true by the students was 10.2 out of 13. All the students accepted the DIB as a good or perfect instrument for personality measurement, and all but five of the thirty-nine students rated the assessment of their own personality as good or perfect. Of the remaining five, only one felt that the analysis was poor.

I have repeated this demonstration in introductory psychology classes, always with results similar to those of Forer. The results have been the same whether a personality scale or "handwriting analysis" was employed. Ulrich, Stachnik and Stainton (1966) showed that it is not the prestige of the administrator that is crucial. In their study, which used a personality description based on that of Forer's, subjects in one group were students who were given "personality tests" by the instructor (a professional psychologist), while subjects in a second group were friends and neighbours of students, who were tested ostensibly by the students themselves. The interpretations attributed to the inexperienced students were accepted just as readily as those attributed to the professional psychologist.

In an unpublished study, Deutsch (1979) gave half his subjects a Forer-type personality analysis (e.g. "Your sexual adjustment has presented problems for you") and the other half a "mirror image" of that analysis (e.g. "Your sexual adjustment has not presented problems for you"). He found that in both cases, students rated the analyses as equally and highly accurate.

Forer (1949) added that the clients of fortune-tellers and other "pseudo-diagnosticians" not only accept as accurate a description which could apply to anyone, but they go further and increase their confidence in both the diagnostician and his method, be it crystal-gazing, astrology, graphology, or whatever.

Indeed, a vague description can be made to appear more accurate if the subject is led to believe it is based on specific information about him. When Snyder and Shenkel (1975) had students posing as astrologers give the same handwritten horoscope to each of a number of subjects, they found that the subjects' ratings of the accuracy of the horoscope depended directly upon the extent to which the subject believed the horoscope was specific to him. Subjects in one group were not asked for any information about themselves and were told that the horoscope was "generally true of people". Those in a second group were required to give the year and month of birth, while those in a third group were required to

---

[7] Skilled fortune-tellers are also able to glean considerable information from the client by keen observation of his non-verbal responses (e.g. gestures, hesitations) to what they say. This information, specific to the client, is then fed back as part of the reading. This is called a "cold reading". The interested reader is referred to Hyman (1977a).

give the year, month, and day of birth. Those in these latter two groups were led to believe that the horoscope was based on the information they gave. All subjects rated the accuracy of the horoscope on a five-point scale, with "5" indicating high accuracy. Those who gave no information produced an average rating of 3.2; those who gave month and day of birth, 3.8; and those who gave month, year, and day of birth, 4.4. This and other studies led Snyder *et al.* to conclude that after people receive a general assessment that they think pertains only to them, their faith in the procedure and the diagnostician increases.

Thus, the fortune-teller, the graphologist, and the phrenologist, in addition to anything they can learn *from* the client about himself, begin with the considerable advantage due to the common readiness of people to accept vague but non-threatening general descriptions as precise and personal.

Yet, as MacDougall said, a certain amount of credulity is probably essential to the functioning of social groups, since universal skepticism would mean universal distrust. MacDougall further argued that

> . . . knowledge [could never] have arrived at its present amazing height, had every intermediate step on the ladder of science, from profound ignorance and slavery of intellect, been disputed with bigoted incredulity. (1940, p. 10.)

The modern individual, surrounded by amazing products of science and technology which are incomprehensible to those without specialized knowledge, may find it extremely difficult to know when to be skeptical. Those lay people of the 1950s who scoffed at the idea of earth satellites were themselves objects of ridicule when the first Sputnik was put successfully into orbit. Those who laughed at the idea of three-dimensional television (apart from the rose-and-green-coloured glasses kind used in 3-D movies) are laughing a little less now, as holographic demonstrations become more common. The layperson must depend on the expert to judge what is possible and what is not. The "experts" line up to both promote and deny even the wildest claims. It is difficult for the layperson to decide which "experts" are correct. If Doctor X and Professor Y attest to the reality of thought transmission, a concept which might be appealing to the layperson since it serves to explain some of his own experiences, why should he be expected to reject their evidence, or even to be skeptical about it? Lewinsohn said:

> While the revolution that has been changing the Newtonian world picture ever since 1900 has made some people more skeptical, it has simply made others more credulous. . . . Because of these developments, laymen have begun to feel that it is impossible to distinguish truth from hypothesis. Now, laymen have always been sticklers for certainty, and where truth is uncertain, they will accept anything that is presented as being simple and sure. (1961, pp. 93–94.)

Even some readers of publications devoted to science, who might be expected to be less credulous than other members of the public, demonstrate the same overreadiness to believe that characterizes the victims of con artists. In the April 1975 issue of *Scientific American*, Martin Gardner's "Mathematical Games" section featured "six sensational discoveries that somehow or another have escaped public attention", such as "long-lost" drawings by Leonardo da Vinci showing that he had invented among other things the valve flush toilet. Other "discoveries" included (a) a super chess-playing computer (called MacHic because it so often plays as if it were intoxicated), that had demonstrated, after seven months of continual chess-playing with itself, that a "pawn to king's rook 4" opening is a win for White; (b) the discovery of a logical flaw in the special theory of relativity; (c) the discovery of a psychic motor that runs on psychic energy (constructed originally by "Robert Ripoff", the "noted Prague parapsychologist and founder of the International Institute for the

Investigation of Mammalian Auras" whose ideas were brought back to the United States by "Heinseitter Birdbrain"). The "motor" was very simple and could be built out of paper. Instructions for its construction were given and readers were invited to build one to "see for themselves".

As an April Fool's presentation, these "discoveries" were very amusing. The tongue-in-cheek aspect seemed so obvious that even if one were not scientifically or technically inclined (an unlikely situation, presumably, in the case of the majority of readers of *Scientific American*), the farcical nature of the article would be readily apparent.

Not so, however. In a later issue of *Scientific American* (July 1975) Gardner reported with some surprise that he had received more than 1000 letters from readers who "failed to see the joke in spite of the outlandish names and preposterous ideas" (p. 115). This is not to say that all writers *accepted* the claims made in the original column, although they thought they had been made seriously. For example, in reference to the section of the original article that discussed the "flaw" in the special theory of relativity, Gardner wrote, "having at one time written a book on relativity, I was abashed to receive more than 100 letters from physicists pointing out the stupid blunder I had made" (p. 116). These people were credulous enough to believe that Gardner was being serious. They overlooked the obvious signs of satire.

In April 1978 Gérald Messadié (1978a) published an article entitled "Le Mystère du triangle des Bouches-du-Rhône" in the French popular science magazine *Science et vie*. The article was a spoof on the so-called Bermuda Triangle mystery, and was headed by the title "Avrilogie" to draw attention to it being an April Fool's story. Messadié reported that an examination of the statistics concerning road accidents published by the Ministry of the Interior showed an anomaly for the department of the Bouches-du-Rhône. While the accident rate in Paris was 1.5 accidents per habitant per square kilometer, in the Bouche-du-Rhône, it was an astonishing 36. There was also a strange character to the accidents in the latter area; it was stated that between 3.10 and 3.20 p.m. on July 15, 1975, thirty-four vehicles collided. Over a 10 year period there had been a peculiarly high death rate in accidents. Cars had caught fire spontaneously. Over a 30-year period, *only* two UFO sightings had ever been made in this area, a much lower incidence than elsewhere. Messadié also cited evidence from the *Journal of Irreproducible Results* which indicated that there are surprisingly few "menhirs" (tall, upright monumental stones found in various parts of Europe) in that region. These menhirs, the author reported, had been used by the ancients to indicate, among other things, areas of magnetic stability—areas where one could wander without being bothered by the instability of magnetic fields. Compasses go wild in the Bouches–du–Rhône area, it was claimed, and homing pigeons let loose in the area never returned. He suggested that magnetic faults were responsible for these anomalies and for the avoidance of the region by UFOs. He concluded by suggesting that these facts were being withheld from the public to prevent panic, and wondered why geologists in the area, supposedly engaged in the search for oil, were all equipped with "gravity meters". What were they *really* investigating?

In a later issue, Messadié (1978b) discussed how his spoof had been intended to show that if exact facts (accident rates) are treated in a certain manner and mixed with unverifiable affirmations, one can find "mysterious triangles" everywhere. Yet, the article generated an exceptional amount of mail, the majority of which indicated that readers who bothered to write had ignored the heading which suggested it was an April Fool's Day piece, and took the story seriously.

Messadié concluded that to have such a story believed by large numbers of readers, one should follow certain rules of thumb:

1. Begin with an unverifiable fact, but one which fits in with some existing schema (e.g. levitation of objects).
2. Put it along side an indisputable scientific fact (e.g. the moon's gravitational effect on the earth).
3. Add a recently established scientific fact for good measure (e.g. the moon's gravitational effect can be demonstrated to affect not only water, but land as well).
4. Mix these all together in a serious manner, mentioning for good measure Professor 'X' at University 'Y' and so on.

Who are the people who fall for tall tales? Are they poorly endowed with a sense of humour, or are they uncritical about things they read, accepting them at face value? The kind of credulity Forer studied is understandable because the subjects match the personality analysis to themselves without thinking to compare its applicability to other people. However, Gardner and Messadié seem to have been dealing with a different sort of credulity. In this case, many people simply missed what were for others obvious indications that the writer was writing with tongue in cheek. Perhaps they simply lack a sense of humour, or perhaps they are overly influenced by the "authority" of the source, and are thus predisposed to take it seriously at all times. Whatever the explanation, a good many people came to accept some rather improbable "facts" on the basis of one article.

My own curiosity about credulity was aroused by the spontaneous reactions of students, colleagues, and others, to a postcard sent to me by Professor Robert Deutsch which bore a photograph of a fish covered with thick white fur. While most people chuckled at seeing the card, at least one-third of the people who saw the card responded with a puzzled expression and questions such as "Is this for real?", "Is this serious?", and so forth. These people obviously were aware of the mutual exclusivity of the categories of "fish" and "fur-bearing animals", but yet where reluctant to simply brand the picture as a hoax. It was natural to wonder whether such people are more credulous than others, or whether their overreadiness to believe, or to not disbelieve, was an exceptional occurrence. Since some aspects of the paranormal domain that are accepted by many people (e.g. the claim made by the Transcendental Meditation people that some of their members can levitate themselves, or the reputed ability of some psychics to bend spoons by psychokinetic power) are even more difficult to take seriously than the fur-bearing fish, to what extent is credulity a factor in belief in the paranormal?

In a study of professors in the natural and social sciences who either believed in or rejected the realm of the paranormal (Alcock, 1975), fifty-six professors were asked to rate the likelihood that each of six "unlikely" statements was true. All statements referred to events that were novel to the respondents. Three of them carried no suggestion of any transcendental forces (e.g. "Henry Curson became rector of the Church of Saxling, England, when he was only twelve years old") while the other three could have transcendental forces read into them (e.g. "The casket of Queen Elizabeth I, while on view in Whitehall Palace, London, on the eve of her interment, mysteriously exploded. The casket was shattered yet the Queen's body was unharmed.") The respondents were asked to rate the likelihood that each statement was true or false on a scale ranging from 0 to 100. The data indicated that both believers and skeptics *vis-à-vis* the paranormal assigned the same average subjective likelihood to the "non-transcendental" items, but the believers rated the "transcendental" items as *more* likely to be true than the non-transcendental ones. The non-believers rated the transcendental items as *less* likely to be true than the non-transcendental items. In addition, there was a significant but moderate correlation ($r = .39$) between the degree of belief in parapsychology and the likelihoods assigned to the "transcendental" items, but no correlation between belief in parapsychology and the likelihood assigned to the "non-transcendental" items.

The statements which seemed to involve transcendental forces seemed to appear more likely to believers. This could reflect a switch to a transcendental belief system when considering these items. Skeptics probably devalued these items because the suggestion of transcendental forces violated their primitive beliefs. These conclusions are only speculative, of course.

In a subsequent study of skepticism and belief among students, subjects were asked to evaluate the likelihood of various novel and "extravagant" claims (Alcock, 1977). For example, they were shown the realistic photograph of a fur-bearing fish described earlier, and they were given the description of a strongman so powerful that when he leaned against a railway locomotive, the locomotive wheels spun when the engine was put in motion, but the locomotive was unable to move. None of the statements involved transcendental forces. No difference in credulity between skeptics and believers was evident. This suggests that a (possible) overreadiness to believe in events which seem to involve transcendental forces does not necessarily extend to other domains.

Obviously, more research is required before the factors which elicit and influence credulity can be understood. But it does seem that people may react with credulity towards some kinds of beliefs and not towards others.

(c) *Critical thinking ability.* People differ in their mastery of skills needed to critically evaluate arguments and evidence. Researchers have studied the relationship between such ability and the acceptance of various transcendental beliefs. For example, "anti-religious" students have been found to possess significantly greater critical thinking skill than "pro-religious" subjects (Feather, 1964). In a study of student believers and skeptics with regard to the paranormal, Alcock and Otis (1980) administered Watson and Glaser's (1964) *Critical Thinking Appraisal Inventory.* This scale was designed to measure the ability to define and analyze a problem, to judge the validity of the inferences made, and to draw conclusions while recognizing stated and unstated assumptions. The skeptics demonstrated significantly better critical thinking ability than did the believers.

In summary, it would seem, then, that believers in the paranormal, at least in the student population, tend to be more dogmatic in their beliefs and less skilled at critical thinking than are skeptics. In addition, the believer in the paranormal appears to be more open towards novel and unsubstantiated evidence which may involve transcendental forces than he is towards novel but non-transcendental material, suggesting the use of rules of evidence from two different belief systems.

Belief change and resistance to change

Large sections of most introductory social psychology textbooks are devoted to the discussion of factors which lead to *change* in beliefs and attitudes. It would be inappropriate to discuss all such relevant factors here, but it is important to note that people's beliefs sometimes change when new information which is inconsistent with their beliefs is presented to them, and at other times, people will maintain their beliefs despite repeated evidence which contradicts them. The explanation for this inconsistent response lies with social factors—the beliefs held by others often have a powerful effect on the individual who must live and work with them, and with the importance, the centrality, of the belief in the individual's belief system. A peripheral belief often can be changed without much difficulty, but the central or primitive beliefs are more important to the individual; thus, they tend to be resistant to change.

Beliefs rarely exist in isolation from other beliefs, and a given belief may be very resistant to change because of the implications of such change for related beliefs. A Roman Catholic will have strong beliefs about secular matters which are tied to his religious beliefs. To change the orthodox belief that artificial birth control is sinful, the Catholic has to question the infallibility of the Pope. If he makes the change and thus accepts that the Pope is fallible, he must question many of the major tenets of his religion which are based on Papal infallibility, including the celibacy of the priesthood and the special relationship between priest and parishioner which celibacy supposedly ensures. If all these beliefs must be reevaluated, it may be less stressful to simply forget about birth control.

The degree to which people are influenced by evidence contradictory to their beliefs depends, among other things, on cultural factors. In Western society since Aristotle, logical contradiction is something that we are taught, even as children, to avoid. We are embarrassed if we find that we have contradicted ourselves. This is not so in all societies. Professor William Carment and I, while in India on a field-trip in 1970, were intrigued by numerous anecdotal reports, from Indians and from Westerners, of the Indians' lack of concern about self-contradiction. We were told by one Indian professor that it is the Westerners who have a real problem about contradiction. Just because two things are contradictory does not mean they are not both true, he said. We conducted a small pilot study in which respondents from a university setting were asked to state their degree of agreement or disagreement with each of a number of items. Several of the items directly contradicted other items. We found numerous examples of strong agreement with mutually contradictory items. We speculated that the much greater indulgence shown by Indian parents to their children, compared with typical Western parents, including a disinclination to correct them when they make incorrect or contradictory statements, is responsible for the greater tolerance of contradiction shown by adults. However, it could also be explained simply in terms of a different philosophical tradition. The Indians we talked to were as critical of Western intolerance of contradiction as Westerners typically are of contradiction itself.

Our discomfort with contradiction is likely the basis for what is known as "cognitive dissonance". Introduced initially by Leon Festinger, this notion attracted a great deal of attention from social psychologists during the 1960s. It suggests that the human being is a rationalizing animal who actively defends himself, by means of distortion and denial, against information which contradicts deeply held beliefs (Batson, 1975). Cognitive dissonance theory uses the concepts of "consonance" and "dissonance" to describe relations among "cognitions"—that is, opinions, beliefs, and knowledge, including knowledge about the environment and knowledge about one's actions and feelings. If two cognitions are inconsistent with one another, they are said to be "dissonant". A person who believes that it is dangerous to drive while not wearing a seatbelt, and yet who finds himself doing just that has two dissonant cognitions. Dissonance is uncomfortable, and there will be a psychological impetus to reduce it, to try to make the cognitions "consonant", or consistent with one another. The person could fasten the seat-belt, or else think of reasons why wearing a seatbelt may be dangerous—e.g. the possibility of being trapped should the car catch fire.

Incidents which seemingly violate "primitive" beliefs can be very disconcerting and dissonance-producing. If an individual were to witness someone flying through the air like Superman, he would be likely to experience an emotional reaction. Rokeach (1968) argued that violation of primitive beliefs brings about anxiety reactions which are relieved when suitable "acceptable" explanations are forthcoming. The once-popular television programme *Candid Camera* was based largely on incidents where primitive beliefs were violated. People often demonstrated visible relief when eventually told that they were on *Candid Camera*.

Strong convictions are often held *despite* the evidence. The highly committed individual faced with undeniable evidence that the belief is in error may react to a confrontation with the evidence by becoming more committed to his belief than he was initially. Festinger, Riecken, and Schacter (1956) described five conditions under which they would expect to find increased commitment resulting from disconfirmatory evidence:

1. The belief must be held with deep conviction, and must have some influence on the believer's behaviour (thus making it observable in part).
2. The person must have, as a result of his belief, taken some nearly irrevocable action (e.g. public commitment).
3. The belief must be such that real events can clearly refute the belief.
4. The disconfirming event must be recognized by the believer.
5. The individual believer must have social support subsequent to the disconfirmation.

Festinger *et al.* suggested that, without social support, few individuals would sustain a belief in the face of strong disconfirmatory evidence. However, it is not only when beliefs are questioned that social support is essential to belief maintenance. Social support may determine *which* beliefs are considered plausible by an individual:

> . . . we obtain our notions about the world originally from other human beings and these notions continue to be plausible to us in very large measure because others continue to confirm them. (Berger, 1970, p. 50.)

Festinger *et al.* (1956) observed that millenialistic and messianic movements centred around the idea of some highly important future event such as the end of the world, or the coming of Christ, may set a specific date for the predicted event, thus putting their believers in the position outlined by the five conditions above. People in such movements often take irrevocable actions based on their belief, such as selling all their possessions and quitting their jobs. This, plus the derision they must endure from those who do not share their belief, brings about a heavy commitment; it is difficult to undo their actions and to admit their error. Festinger *et al.* cited examples of millenial and messianic groups who, when the predicted day came and went without incident, became even stronger in their belief and actively proselytized, often with considerable success.

Festinger's cognitive dissonance interpretation can explain how disconfirming evidence can in some cases strengthen rather than weaken belief. Disconfirmation of a deeply-held belief produces a great deal of dissonance—dissonance between the knowledge that the predicted event did not occur and the actions based on the certainty that it would, and dissonance with other beliefs connected to and leading to these actions. To reduce the dissonance, several paths are open. The believer could abandon his belief, but if he has taken irrevocable actions and suffered considerable derision, this may be even more painful than the dissonance. He might attempt to deny that the prediction was not fulfilled, but he could only accomplish this by insulating himself from reality and surrounding himself with other people who think in the same manner. If they can convince others to share their belief, even after its disconfirmation, they feel more certain that the belief is correct.

Festinger *et al.* had the opportunity to observe such a situation. The event was heralded by a two-column story on the back page of an American newspaper which was headlined,

"PROPHECY FROM PLANET CLARION CALL TO CITY: FLEE THAT FLOOD. IT'LL SWAMP US ON DEC. 21, OUTER SPACE TELLS SUBURBANITE"

The prophecy had been made by a Mrs. Marion Keech, a suburban housewife. It was not her *own* prophecy, she said, but had been revealed to her through automatic writing, having been sent by superior beings on a planet called "Clarion".

Festinger, his two colleagues, and some hired observers joined Mrs. Keech's group of supporters to observe and gather data about the commitment, conviction and proselyting activity of the group.

A number of the believers gave up their jobs and gave away their possessions, since neither would be needed after December 21, 1955. Mrs. Keech claimed that those who accepted the truth of the prophecy and gathered at her home on the fateful evening would be whisked away by a flying saucer from Clarion before the cataclysm occurred.

A few days before the 21st, people began to prepare. Eleven people, plus the three infiltrating social psychologists and their two assistants, gathered at Mrs. Keech's home, while eleven others who could not get to Mrs. Keech's city were told to continue as usual in their daily routines; they would be picked up by the flying saucer wherever they might be.

The final two days saw increasingly frenzied activity; the group was instructed to remove all metal from their clothing, since contact with metal while riding in a flying saucer could cause severe burns. Zippers, eyelets in shoes and shoes with nails in them were removed. One of Festinger's observers was told to remove her brassière because of the metal clasps.

Mrs. Keech periodically received communications from the beings that were going to save them. At the stroke of the appointed hour, nothing happened. Mrs. Keech received a message indicating that there would be a slight delay. As the minutes and hours dragged by, anxiety mounted. One of the most committed of the group, a Doctor Armstrong from a nearby university, was heard to comment,

> I've had to go a long way. I've given up just about everything. I've cut every tie; I've burned every bridge. I've turned my back on the world. I can't afford to doubt . . . I've taken an awful beating in the last few months, just an awful beating . . . I don't care what happens tonight. I can't afford to doubt. I won't doubt even if we have to make an announcement to the press tomorrow and admit we were wrong. (Festinger *et al.*, 1956, p. 158.)

At 4.45 a.m. Mrs. Keech announced that she had just received another message. The strength of the group's conviction had been so impressive to the higher powers that the whole earth had been spared. This was met with great rejoicing.

The most interesting aspect of what happened following the "disconfirmation", now turned into a "confirmation", was that those who had met the moment of truth as a group appeared to strengthen their belief. Having avoided publicity and turned away people in the days prior to that moment, they now sought out the news media and actively proselytized. After all, the cataclysm had been called off because of them. On the other hand, those eleven believers who had been alone at the fateful moment, without social support, left the group and silently endured the discomfort brought about by the disconfirmation.

Festinger *et al.* (1956) interpreted this as confirmation of their predictions. By accepting the rationalization provided by Mrs. Keech's last message, those who had the social support of a group were able to reduce the dissonance created by the disconfirmation, and thus regain confidence in their original beliefs.

The cognitive dissonance hypothesis can perhaps explain how researchers who have publicly committed themselves to a belief which invites derision from their colleagues continue to cling to their belief in the absence of empirical confirmation. The researcher would have to face his own credulity if he abandoned the belief. He would have to admit that he was wrong and others right. Thus, when a scholar such as John Taylor, the British mathematician who was persuaded of the reality of psychic powers by the feats of Uri Geller, and who wrote a book about it, *Superminds*, has the strength of character to publicly change his views and express strong skepticism,[8] he deserves credit. It would be easier to rationalize one's way out by saying that psi phenomena are "mysterious", "elusive", "unpredictable", and so on, so that failure to produce evidence would not be at variance with the "known characteristics" of the phenomenon.

Festinger has also suggested that because cognitive dissonance results when people are faced with contradictory evidence, people tend to select information (newspaper stories, books, magazines, etc.) that is consistent with their views, and ignore other information. However, studies of this selective exposure hypothesis have yielded both supportive and contradictory evidence, so Festinger's analysis is not confirmed. Studies of belief in the paranormal have demonstrated the relevance of the selective exposure hypothesis, however: Believers and skeptics in one study (Jones, Russell, and Nickel, 1976) were exposed to either a "successful" demonstration of ESP or an "unsuccessful" one. The results indicated that only those believers who saw the successful demonstration accurately recalled it. Believers who saw the unsuccessful demonstration distorted their memory of it, and stated that ESP had occurred. Skeptics, on the other hand, accurately recalled the demonstration regardless of whether they had witnessed the successful or the unsuccessful one. This supports the selective information hypothesis only in the case of believers.

In a subsequent study (Russell and Jones, 1980), believers and skeptics received reports of a series of tests of ESP. Subjects in one condition were told that the results were significant and that they demonstrated that ESP exists. Subjects in the second condition were told that no ESP effects were found and that the studies suggested that ESP does not exist. These subjects also were administered a psychological test which is supposed to measure anxiety, hostility, and depression. Dissonance theory would predict more emotional arousal when the subject's initial belief is inconsistent with the information he receives.

The results for the "ESP disproven" condition showed an inverse correlation between accuracy of recall and belief in the paranormal; the greater the belief, the poorer the recall. This supports the selective learning hypothesis. In addition, arousal, as measured by the psychological test, was directly correlated with paranormal belief; skeptics showed lower arousal than believers. However, believers who had reversed in their memories the conclusions of the studies showed less arousal than those who did not, suggesting successful reduction of dissonance. In the "ESP proven" condition, there was no correlation between recall and belief, and skeptics and believers did not differ in terms of accuracy of recall, but skeptics showed greater arousal than believers.

---

[8] Balanovski and Taylor, 1978; Taylor and Balanovski, 1979.

The authors concluded that:

1. There was strong support for the cognitive dissonance interpretation—greater arousal was found for both believers and skeptics when their own belief was disconfirmed.
2. Selective learning appeared to occur only in the case of believers. It was successful in that it reduced the arousal that the dissonance would have otherwise created.

Russell and Jones added that paranormal beliefs seem to be of greater consequence to believers than to skeptics, and that, " . . . the persistence of paranormal beliefs is not a function of ignorance on the part of believers, but perhaps due to the high levels of dissonance aroused by challenges to important beliefs for the individual" (1980, p. 87). Contradictory evidence, they argued, may create enough dissonance to prevent the serious consideration of such information.

In a somewhat similar vein, Ross (1977) found that not only are errors in beliefs and judgements extremely resistant to new information, they may also survive total negation of the original evidence upon which they are based. Ross found that the weight assigned to new information seems to depend on its consistency with the initial impression. Although the original reason for the impression is shown to be without basis, the impression may continue because it is now supported by evidence that seems to be (but is not) independent of that which has been discredited. The secondary evidence assumes autonomy. Thus, if an individual has accepted that a given performer has psychic powers on the basis of a specific demonstration, and in consequence later uncritically accepts as psychic other accomplishments of the performer, the demonstration that the original event was accomplished by conjuring rather than by psychic means may have little effect on the person's evaluation of psychic phenomena. The observer believes he has witnessed a whole series of other "psychic events". He forgets that he was not critical about these latter demonstrations because he was convinced that the first was genuinely psychic.

In the face of conflicting evidence, Ross suggested, the intuitive observer views data that fit his hypothesis as reliable, valid and free from error, while data which contradict it are dismissed as unrepresentative, unreliable or erroneous. Perseverent belief in ESP despite disconfirming experimental evidence may reflect this process. Ross cited Martin Gardner's description of a project to teach ESP by machine (Gardner, 1975). When the experiment was well "controlled" no ESP effect was found. Rather than accept this outcome, the researchers dropped the control condition from their analysis. They believed that they were eliciting ESP; the disconfirming evidence was explained away or ignored. (One can always argue that experimental controls inhibit the subjects' psychic abilities. This is a common view among parapsychologists.)

Thus, people with strong opinions on a complex issue tend to accept confirming information uncritically, while critically evaluating evidence which contradicts their view. Both sides in a dispute may draw support for their position from the same body of mixed empirical findings, leading to greater polarization rather than reduction of disagreement (Lord, Ross and Lepper, 1979).

The saga of the Fox sisters provides a real-life example of the lack of impact of disconfirming information. In the middle 1800s, two girls, Margaret and Kate Fox, became known across the United States for their abilities to contact the spirit world. The spirits would answer questions through them by mysterious raps—one rap for no, three raps for yes. Their demonstrations marked the beginning of modern spiritualism. Forty years later, one of the sisters confessed that they had produced the raps by cracking their toe and ankle joints in a manner similar to that of cracking knuckles. As Sagan (1979) pointed out,

> The most instructive aspect of the Fox case is not that so many people were bamboozled; but rather that after the hoax was confessed, after Margaret Fox made a public demonstration . . . of her "preternatural big toe", many who had been taken in still refused to acknowledge the fraud. They pretended that Margaret had been coerced into the confession by some rationalist inquisitor. (pp. 48–49.)

Thus was dissonance avoided.

I witnessed another example of how two dissonant "cognitions" can push a person to eliminate the dissonance. The Amazing Randi was giving a performance in which he did all the well-known Geller feats explaining that what the audience saw was done by trickery but that Geller, when doing the same things, tells his audience that paranormal powers are at work. In the midst of Randi's extremely skilful presentation, a spectator (who as it turns out was a university professor) jumped angrily to his feet and loudly denounced Randi as a fraud. To this attack, Randi replied that he was indeed a fraud, that everything he had done, as he had several times stated, was done by trickery. But his accuser was not easily quieted; he proclaimed that Randi was a fraud because he really was using psychic powers, but was keeping this fact from the audience!

As Batson concluded, that the effect of disconfirming evidence creates a very difficult situation:

> In attempting to force a firmly committed believer to "face up to the facts", one may be damned if he does and damned if he doesn't. . . . If, on the one hand, the believer does not accept the facts as facts, then clearly one's arguments are without impact. But, on the other hand, if the believer accepts them as true, this may actually drive him into even more fervent adherence to his initial position. (1975, p. 184.)

Jean-Pierre Deconchy (e.g. Deconchy, 1971), a French social psychologist, has carried out a fascinating series of studies of orthodoxy and belief. He focused on Roman Catholicism, with particular attention to the ways in which orthodox believers maintain beliefs in the face of demonstrations of the logical weakness of the beliefs. Deconchy found that the more aware a believer was of the rational frailty of a religious proposition in which he believed, the greater his certainty that the proposition was a part of church dogma, and thus shared by others, and the greater his underestimation of the validity of the contradictory arguments. Conversely, if the orthodox believer became aware that the belief was not part of church dogma, then he was much more capable of perceiving the rational frailty of the proposition.

Deconchy's studies are unique in that they demonstrate the effects of regulation of opinion where rationality is not the final arbiter. From a cognitive dissonance perspective, the individual must attempt to reduce dissonance between the cognition that he accepts the interpretation of the Bible and the interpretation of God's will provided by the Church, and the cognition that some of the tenets of church dogma cannot be rationally defended.

In summary, then, important or central beliefs often prove highly resistant to the effects of disconfirming information. It is often easy to observe this resistance in others. *It is extremely difficult for us to be aware of it in ourselves.*

Scientists: The Guardians of Rationality?

One of the norms of science is the distrust of belief based only on authority. Yet the layperson having been educated in a school system which makes scientists appear to be hyper-rational, logical, and dispassionate seekers of truth is often persuaded of the correctness of one claim or another because it is backed by a scientist. Linus Pauling's recommendations about the virtues of vitamin C no doubt influenced many people simply because he was Linus Pauling, Nobel Prizewinner, and whether or not judgements about the efficacy of vitamin C *vis-à-vis* the common cold were within his field of competence was probably not considered.

Yet, of course, scientists are people, and despite the intellectual discipline that they may acquire in their own area of expertise, they are often as capable as anyone else of acting less than rationally when they step outside their domain.

Before turning to the matter of most interest, the belief systems of scientists, it is an interesting diversion to briefly consider some of the studies that have searched for differences in personality traits between scientists and non-scientists.

In a series of studies, Roe (1951a, 1951b, 1953) examined the personalities of eminent natural and social scientists, and reported that, as a group, natural scientists, and in particular physicists, tended to be shy, lonely, indifferent to close affective relationships with others, disinterested in group activities and politics, and in general, slow in social development. Most of them described themselves as being happiest when at work, and as having a feeling of "apartness from others", sometimes brought on originally by the death of a parent while they were children. Among theoretical physicists she found a very high incidence of severe childhood illnesses which contributed to feelings of isolation. Unlike natural scientists, social scientists did not show this pattern of general avoidance of intimate personal contacts, preference for a very limited social life, or postponed development of heterosexual interests.

However, this picture of natural scientists as being cool, timid, and aloof contrasts somewhat with the findings of one researcher. The single most prominent result of Mitroff's (1974) study of the Apollo mission scientists[9] was the discovery of their intense masculinity; masculinity as defined in the most traditional and narrow sense: " . . . it is the intense, raw, and even brutal *aggressiveness* of scientists that stands out. It is an aggressiveness that not only deeply influences their perceptions of one another but even their abstract concept of science itself" (p. 56).

Roe (1953) found that the religious background of most of the sixty-four social and natural scientists she studied was similar; most had gone to Sunday School, but few as adults had any church connections. While a few were strongly agnostic, most were simply not interested. Leuba (1934) found a difference between natural and social scientists with regard to religion. A greater proportion of scientists concerned with inanimate objects (e.g. physicists) believed in God and immortality than did those who studied human behaviour (e.g. psychologists).

Terman (1955) reported on a longitudinal study begun in 1921 which followed the progress of 1400 students who were in the top 1 percent of the school population in intelligence as measured by standard tests. Terman examined the histories of those who had

---

[9] Professor Mario Bunge has suggested that applied scientists and space engineers engaged in aerospace research are "an unusually rough and aggressive crowd quite different in psychological makeup from basic scientists" (Personal communication, 1980).

become physical and biological scientists, lawyers, engineers, or worked in the humanities or in business. As did Roe, he found that the scientists scored lower than non-scientists in terms of social relations. He concluded that the bulk of scientific research is carried on by people who consider research their life and view social relations as relatively unimportant.

Mahoney's (1976a, b) research led to the following conclusions about scientists, based on the samples of scientists that he studied:

1. Many scientists have surprisingly poor problem-solving skills, and tend to form their beliefs rapidly and based on only meagre data. (Somewhat surprisingly, Rokeach (1960) had found that scientists are sometimes less tolerant of ambiguity than non-scientists. This may make sense to the extent that scientists are not usually content to leave some link in a causal chain unexplained. Yet scientists, when confronted by an unusual event in their daily lives, might be expected to be more prepared to believe that there is a rational, but at the moment unknown, explanation for it.)

2. Once they have developed a hypothesis, some scientists are very tenacious and will not abandon it even in the face of accumulating evidence to the contrary. Research by Mitroff (1976, 1974) is instructive in this regard, since he obtained the opinions of some leading scientists about just this point. Mitroff studied forty-two of the scientists involved in the lunar soil analyses during the moon exploration programme. He interviewed them individually several times, both before and after the arrival of the moon rocks. While the notion of "disinterested observer" seems basic to the idea of science, he found that not only did all of them consider the view that scientists are purely objective, disinterested observers to be very naïve, but they also rejected it as an ideal. Mitroff summarized their views in this way: The real process of science is much more complicated, and contains many more subjective and even irrational elements than has ever been acknowledged. Commitment and bias, even if these go beyond logical inference from known "facts", is one of the strongest sustaining forces for the creation of scientific ideas and for their subsequent testing, they said. These scientists were able to identify three "types" of scientists. One is the theoretician, who is perceived as extremely biased, brilliant, creative, aggressive, vague, rigid, and speculative in his thinking. Another type is the extreme empiricist, virtually obsessed with data, disdainful of theorists, and viewed by the former as impartial, dull, precise, unimaginative, and analytical. The third type is midway between these two. While the empiricists modified their views when faced with new information from the lunar soil analyses, the theoreticians tended to cling to their prior beliefs even when faced with contradictory evidence.

Indeed some of the greatest innovators in science have shown such conviction about the strength of their theories that they apparently went so far as to "fudge" their data somewhat so as to persuade others.[10] The data presented by Gregor Mendel to support his theory of genetic transmission of traits were so perfect as to be almost impossible, according to calculations made by statistician Ronald Fisher in 1936 (Brush, 1974; Koestler, 1971). (Some people shift the blame for this from Mendel to his assistants.) Nor did Isaac Newton hesitate to tamper with his data to convince others of the soundness of his theory[11] (Westfall, 1973).

---

[10] The greatest astronomer of antiquity, Claudius Ptolemy, has been accused of being the "most successful fraud in the history of science" (Newton, 1977). Yet this view has been strongly challenged. See Wade (1977) and Goldstein (1978).

[11] In the earlier days of science, glorification of data was not as pronounced as it is today, partly because of the lack of precision inherent in measuring instruments. Nonetheless Newton's "fudging" was not simply a matter of rounding off numbers and dropping outliers in his data. His fudging was of a much more substantial and blatant nature.

He displayed even less of the image of the unemotional seeker of truth when he took advantage of his position as President of the Royal Society to appoint a committee of his supporters to decide whether he himself or Leibniz deserved the credit for the invention of the calculus. Newton was awarded the honour (Mahoney, 1976a). Newton again took advantage of his position of President of the Royal Society to suppress the work of a highly competent scientist and astronomer, Stephen Gray, simply because the latter was a colleague of John Flamsteed, the Astronomer Royal, for whom Newton had a particular animosity:

> The unavoidable conclusion to be drawn is that Newton was probably responsible for suppressing the scientific output of Stephen Gray during a period of twenty-five years. . . . Whatever the reason, it appears that Newton may have held back the advancement of electrical knowledge by a full two decades, and been responsible for one of the outstanding astronomers of the era not being given recognition until almost two and one-half centuries after his death. (Clarke and Murdin, 1979, p. 655.)

3. Like non-scientists, many scientists tend to selectively seek out data that are in line with, rather than in opposition to, their beliefs. One way in which this may be reflected is in the review phase of the publication process. Mahoney (1976b) asked seventy-five behavioural scientists[12] to review a manuscript concerning a controversial subject in psychology. The introduction and experimental procedure were always the same, but one group of subjects received results and discussion which supported their known viewpoint on the matter, while for another group the results and discussion were contrary to their viewpoint, and a third group saw only the introduction and methodology. These scientists tended to recommend the article only when it presented evidence which supported their prior position. When the data went against their own position, they criticized the method and interpretation, and urged that the article not be published.

Similarly, Goodstein and Brazis (1970) asked psychologists to evaluate a research report dealing with astrology. Half the subjects received an abstract reporting positive results; the other half received abstracts reporting negative results. Five hundred of each sort were sent out, and a little over one-quarter of the people in each group responded (posing a problem of selective response). At any rate, those who were sent the negative abstract rated the study as having more validity and better design than those who had received the positive abstract.

Mahoney's findings, and those of the related studies described above, require replication before one can be confident in the generalizations Mahoney drew. Nonetheless, this research does suggest that the belief systems of scientists, like those of other human beings, are subject to "irrational influences", and scientists would no doubt be the first to argue that we should never accept something as being true simply on the basis of a scientist's testimony. This point should be kept in mind when the problem of non-replicability in parapsychology is discussed in Chapter 6.

One additional point—some expert scientists, like experts in other areas, sometimes come to believe that they are incapable of being duped. This can be a particular problem when phenomena on the fringes of science are being investigated. For example, the scientists who investigated (and proclaimed to be real) the powers of the nineteenth-century spiritualists assumed that they could not be fooled. It took Houdini to expose their credulity, just as today the Amazing Randi has demonstrated to those scientists who were taken in by the conjuring of Uri Geller and Jean-Pierre Girard how little expertise they really have when it comes to detecting fraud. Randi has even gone so far as to argue that scientists, because of

---

[12] Note that in this instance Mahoney examined only behavioural scientists, and not natural scientists.

their faith or confidence in their "logical" approach to things, are in some ways even easier for a magician to deceive than other people less certain of their skills at evaluating evidence.

Human foibles and the propensity for self-delusion are as much a part of a scientist's make-up as any one else's. These foibles and irrationalities may be most visible when a scientist leaves his own area of special competence and makes pronouncements on matters not directly within his expertise. Here, he runs the risk of being partially blinded by his confidence in his own intellect. We should not accept or reject an idea or theory merely on the basis of a scientist's pronouncement.

Concluding Comments

While we may like to think ourselves masters of our beliefs, it is more correct to say that our beliefs, shaped as they are by circumstances and by our own psychological needs, are in many ways our masters. We do not freely choose them; we do not always like them. Many a person intellectually dedicated to a liberal and egalitarian view of other human beings is bothered by nagging, half-suppressed "beliefs" redolent of the prejudice of the society in which he has grown up. Sometimes we may recognize the usefulness of certain beliefs, without being able to adopt them. We may better our chances at survival in a concentration camp if we have an enduring belief in a God who in his wisdom is forcing us to suffer such horrible circumstances. Without a belief in immortality, when things are temporarily very difficult for us, we may choose to die. The belief that we might be punished if we commit suicide, or the belief that someone is watching over us, may better enable us to get over the rough spots so that we can live to enjoy the smooth. Nonetheless, we cannot simply adopt a transcendental belief because it might be good for us. Nor, as we sit trembling with fear in the midst of some disaster, unable to react effectively because of our emotional upset, can we "decide" to believe "for the time being" in magic or the power of prayer, so as to calm ourselves to the point where we can take effective action.

Obstinacy about one's beliefs is not always to be discouraged either. Many great innovators have had to endure considerable ridicule before they have seen their ideas confirmed and accepted. In Sargant's words,

> The whole process of civilization depends almost entirely on a number of people being born in each new generation who have important new beliefs and ideas, and hold on to them with obsessional tenacity. . . . This means that the originators of new ideas and the founders of new systems are rarely themselves "normal" people; if they were they would drop their new notions comparatively quickly in the face of the hostility of their fellows. (1973, p. 197.)

Yet, obviously many people who are tenacious in their beliefs do prove to be mistaken: "We need faith, but must suspect it. We need to be suggestible but our suggestibility is dangerous" (Sargant, 1973, p. 199).

CHAPTER 4

The Psychology of Experience

Belief, ritual, and spiritual experience: these are the cornerstones of religion, and the greatest of them is the last.

I. M. Lewis[1]

. . . all the perceptions both of the senses and the mind bear reference to man and not to the universe, and the human mind resembles those uneven mirrors which impart their own properties to different objects, from which rays are emitted and distort and disfigure them. . . .

Francis Bacon[2]

As was indicated in the last chapter, paranormal experience is the reason that most people give for belief in the paranormal; very few cite laboratory evidence as their basis for belief. "True believers" in the paranormal almost always report having had a "confirmatory" incident at some point in their lives (Ayeroff and Abelson, 1976).

Yet, as Francis Bacon said, experience is often an unreliable guide to reality. If we do not understand the many ways that our perceptions and memories can deceive us, if we are not aware that *because* of the way our brains are structured we should *expect* to have moving and seemingly inexplicable experiences from time to time, then we may fall prey to our transcendental expectations and conclude that we have had a paranormal experience whenever rational explanation seems to fail. It is foolhardy to study the putatively paranormal unless we have educated ourselves about normal experience in all its diverse forms.

Regardless of whether we accept or reject the view that we have a mental or spiritual existence which is distinct from our physical bodies, all of us act in everyday life as though we believe that we are somehow in control of our thought processes. We pass a delicatessen and "decide" to go inside and order a sandwich. We return home and "choose" to mow the lawn because it seems in need of cutting. It is natural for us to think that we are consciously making the decisions. Yet, in all likelihood, we are unaware of our actual thought processes. In the words of a leading cognitive psychologist, "It is the *result* of thinking, not the process of thinking, that appears spontaneously in consciousness" (Miller, 1962, p. 56). Miller offered this demonstration of how our information-processing system works without our conscious awareness—think of ("remember") your mother's maiden name. For most people this leads to the immediate appearance of the name in consciousness. But how was it found, how did it "pop into mind"? It is the result of unconscious cerebral activity that underlies all conscious thought. We have no idea how we find names. We want them and usually they appear, as if by magic.

There are times, however, when a word we want, a word that we "know" we know, does not appear in consciousness, although we say that it is on the "tip-of-the-tongue" (TOT).

---

[1] Lewis (1971), p. 11.
[2] Bacon (1620/1902).

This produces, as Brown and McNeill (1966) have described, a kind of mild torment, something like being on the brink of a sneeze, and the individual experiences considerable relief if and when the word finally appears in consciousness. Although the person cannot produce the word during the TOT experience, he has some knowledge about it, even though he has no idea from where that knowledge comes. In a study of the tip-of-the-tongue phenomenon, Brown and McNeill (1966) induced TOT experiences by presenting definitions of infrequently used words (e.g. nepotism, ambergis) to college students, and asking them to state the words being defined. Sometimes the word was identified, sometimes the definition provoked no response, and sometimes it elicited a TOT experience. When a subject had a TOT experience, he was asked to guess the first letter of the word, the number of syllables in it, and any words that sound like it or that have similar meanings. The subjects were impressively accurate. In 57 percent of their guesses they could accurately name the first letter; in 57 percent they guessed the number of syllables correctly. In guessing "sounds-like" words, 47 percent named words with the same number of syllables and 49 percent named words beginning with the same letter. Thus, although the word itself remained unavailable, information about it did become available in consciousness, even though this information had no explicit basis. It was expressed as though it were a "feeling" or a guess by the subject.

One common strategy for finding the word in such a case is to deliberately turn one's attention to something else altogether, which usually results in the sought-after word spontaneously appearing in consciousness. Distracting oneself seems to allow unconscious processes to do their work without interference from whatever conscious processes one can command.

Sometimes people express their inability to logically defend a point of view by referring to an emotion they have about it, as in "My gut reaction is that Harry just can't handle the job", or, "I have a feeling that . . . ". Sometimes, they decide to act in accordance with these feelings, or "intuitions", rather than to take the path that common sense dictates. (If the intuition proves to be correct they are reinforced for relying on it, and consequently more likely use intuition the next time.) But what is "intuition"? It is possible that this term is used to describe a reaction which the individual "knows" must have a basis, but cannot justify verbally. Again, unconscious processing is involved. For example, a physician remembers tacitly that several years ago, he saw a patient with a given symptom, and this patient developed disease X. If he explicitly or tacitly observes this symptom in a new patient, it may lead him to suspect, "intuit", "guess", that the patient is developing disease X. He has no *rational* basis available for this "hunch", because it is not based on explicit information.

A related kind of experience is unconscious problem-solving. Frederick Banting, the co-discoverer of insulin, reported that the solution to one of the most perplexing problems of his research came to him while he was asleep. He awoke suddenly, jotted down what had occurred to him and went back to sleep. In the morning, his written note proved to provide the solution to the problem. Similarly, the great mathematician Poincaré, described his experience of sudden insight:

> . . . the changes of travel made me forget my mathematical work. Having reached Coutances, we entered an omnibus to go some place or other. At the moment when I put my foot on the step the idea came to me, without anything in my former thoughts seeming to have paved the way for it, that the transformations I had used to define the Fuchsian functions were identical with those of non-Euclidean geometry.[3]

---

[3] Cited by Nisbett and Wilson, 1977, p. 240.

This kind of anecdote is not rare, particularly among highly creative people;

> . . . creative workers describe themselves almost universally as bystanders, differing from other observers only in that they are the first to witness the fruits of a problem-solving process that is almost completely hidden from conscious view. (Nisbett and Wilson, 1977, p. 240.)

More evidence of the individual's lack of awareness of his own thought processes was provided by a study of problem-solving and insight by Maier (1931). Maier hung two cords from the ceiling of a laboratory. Various objects lay around the room. Each subject was told that his task was to tie the two ends of the string together, but the cords were far enough apart that the subject could not, while holding one cord, reach the other.

After the subject was stumped for several minutes, Maier casually set one of the ropes swinging. He found that, typically within 15 seconds, the subject would tie a weight to one string, swing it like a pendulum so that he could grab it while holding the other string, and tie the two together. Maier then asked each subject how he discovered the solution. Despite persistent probing less than one-third of the subjects reported having been affected by his hint. However, Maier found reason to doubt that even these subjects really "remembered" having used his hint. In another experimental condition, instead of setting a rope swinging, he tied a weight to it and twirled it. This would seem to provide a direct cue, yet *none* of the subjects were helped by it. He then presented the useless cue (twirling) prior to the helpful one (swinging). All the subjects reported that the *useless* cue had been helpful, while denying any role to the one that obviously had helped them. They evidently were *choosing* an explanation, *post hoc.*

Maier's study, and many others, suggest that people, at least in some circumstances, explain their behaviour by generating or applying causal theories that make logical sense given the available stimuli and the responses that they produced:

> . . . when people are asked to report how a particular stimulus influenced a particular response, they do not do so by consulting a memory of the mediating process, but by applying or generating causal theories about the effects of that type of stimulus or that type of response. (Nisbett and Wilson, 1977, p. 248.)

In other words, the individual may explain his own behaviour in the same manner that he would evaluate that behaviour if it were performed by somebody else.

These examples illustrate that a great deal of information processing lies outside of consciousness; we do not know how we arrive at decisions; we do not know why we act as we do; and we often possess information of which we are not conscious. This is what Polanyi (1958, 1967) referred to as the "tacit" dimension of knowledge, as opposed to the "explicit" dimension of which we are conscious.

This tacit dimension, this unconscious knowledge and unconscious information processing, is likely to be highly relevant to an understanding of paranormal experience. By definition, paranormal experience is that which defies normal explanation. For instance, people may have a strong feeling of anxiety about some forthcoming event, and if this fear turns out to be justified, they are unlikely to consider the possibility that "normal" information which was available in the tacit dimension made the worry quite appropriate. They may conclude that they had experienced precognition.

The difference between tacit and explicit knowledge, between unconscious and conscious mind, was startlingly demonstrated in a study of patients who had undergone "split-brain" operations. In the normal brain, the cerebral cortex, that part of the brain which is the seat of "consciousness", is divided into two hemispheres which are connected by a large bundle of nerve fibers, the "corpus callosum". These two parts of the cortex, while sharing many responsibilities, also have separate dominions. The left side of the body is controlled mainly by the right hemisphere, while the right side of the body is controlled by the left. The right side of each retina, which receives information from the left visual field, feeds only to the right hemisphere, while the left side of each retina is connected to the left cerebral hemisphere. Language is primarily a left-hemispheric function; damage to the left hemisphere can destroy or seriously impair language ability, but damage to the right hemisphere does not affect language. The right hemisphere appears to be more important in non-verbal skills such as artistic ability, the capacity to recognize "familiar" people and objects, and the ability to work with spatial concepts.

In the normal individual, the two sides of the brain communicate constantly and immediately. If something is perceived only in the left visual field, thus involving directly only the right hemisphere, the individual has no difficulty in verbally describing it since the information is passed immediately to the left hemisphere where verbal ability resides.

What happens when the interconnecting fibers of the corpus callosum are destroyed? There have been a number of cases of people who have undergone surgical cutting of these fibers in the attempt to control severe epilepsy. At first, such individuals seemed almost completely normal. However, more careful psychological testing revealed some fascinating consequences of the operation. If a "split-brain" individual held an object in his left hand, out of sight, he could not describe it, although he could later select that object from among several, using his left hand. The information from the left hand went to the right hemisphere, but the linguistic centre in the brain's left hemisphere had no knowledge of the object. Holding the object in the right hand allowed normal verbal responding.

When people are led to perform some action, such as opening a window, as a result of post-hypnotic suggestion, they typically rationalize their action for which they do not "know" the cause by saying something like "It's hot in here". Similarly, the verbal left hemisphere of a split-brain subject rationalizes actions which were initiated by the independent right hemisphere. For example, when the command "rub" was flashed to the right hemisphere of one subject, he rubbed the back of his head. When asked what the command had been, he (the left hemisphere) replied "itch". He was guessing, but guessing in a manner consistent with the action he had observed. Such rationalization occurred quickly and without any signs of doubt, although the left hemisphere was totally ignorant of the reasons for the right hemisphere's actions. (LeDoux, Wilson, and Gazzaniga, 1979)

It also has been found that *emotional* information can pass from one hemisphere to the other following the cutting of the corpus callosum, provided that other nerve bundles are left untouched. During a study of responses to commands (LeDoux *et al.*, 1979), the command "kiss" was flashed to the right hemisphere of an adolescent boy. He (his left hemisphere) immediately said, "Hey, no way, no way, you've got to be kidding," although he was unable to indicate what it was that he was not going to do. When the same word was flashed to the left hemisphere, he said, "No way, I'm not going to kiss you guys"—virtually the same reaction, except now the left hemisphere knew what it was refusing to do.

This demonstration that the verbal system is capable of reading the tone of an emotional reaction elicited by an external stimulus of which it has no awareness led Le Doux *et al.* to suggest that the normal individual may also be unaware of the source of his moods or his actions, yet capable of noticing and rationalizing both. This could underlie sudden feelings of contentment, joy or depression. An individual who is experiencing joy at a given instance will have his attention focused on only one part of the situation, and will be unaware that the other sights, sounds, and smells are being processed by non-verbal parts of the brain. The subsequent reoccurrence of these stimuli may elicit an emotional reaction such as "I feel just terrific today, I wonder why?" without the original experience being recalled. The verbal system is likely to quickly invent an explanation for the emotional reaction.

Although it has always proven difficult to satisfactorily define "mind", the split-brain patient seems in many ways to possess two of them. Only the left hemisphere, the one with linguistic ability, seems to possess what is normally thought of as consciousness; in fact, the experience of consciousness may be directly dependent on linguistic ability. Le Doux *et al.* (1979) speculated that the infant's brain contains a collection of separate mental systems, each capable of producing behaviour and each with its own impulses to action, and each initially without communication with the other. The behaviours produced by these separate systems gradually come to be monitored by one system, the verbal language system, which learns to regulate and coordinate the behavioural impulses of the various systems. It is the verbal language system which seems to be the essence of consciousness. Yet it is not "aware" of what is going on in the other systems; it is only aware of their outputs. Thus, LeDoux *et al.* concluded that,

> . . . the environment has ways of planting hooks in our mind, and while the verbal system may not know the why or what of it all, part of its job is to make sense out of the emotional and other mental systems and in so doing allow man, with his mental complexity, the illusion of a unified self. (1979, p. 553.)

The brain as information processor

Dodd and White (1980) presented an information-processing model of the brain and central nervous system in which a Central Processor, which can be loosely identified with "consciousness" or LeDoux *et al.*'s "verbal system", coordinates the flow of information through the total system, which includes a sensory system, a memory system, and a response system. The Central Processor in this model is primarily concerned with planning the steps necessary to achieve goals. It is assumed, along with its goals and plans, to be of a completely deterministic nature. Because people are goal-directed, Dodd and White (1980) stressed the goal-directed nature of the Central Processor. Sequences of behaviour are guided by desired end-states. Whether it is the series of sub-goals leading to the goal of eating dinner in a downtown restaurant, or the sequence which leads to foraging behaviour in the refrigerator, the Central Processor has to monitor behaviour so that sub-goals are tackled in an appropriate order, while allowing other goals which suddenly assume higher priority to take precedence.

The Central Processor directs the flow of information through the sensory and memory systems, yet is "unaware" of the processes in those systems that produce information for it. "Consciousness" is in many ways like a busy executive who determines what is going on in the commercial world by reading summaries prepared by others. Lower parts of the brain, like lower echelons of a corporation, respond to demands for information and analysis, and select and organize information to be passed to the top. It is possible that management is being given only what lower levels assume it would like to see. Consciousness may indeed be surrounded by sub-cortical "yes-men". Information that upsets the system is never as welcome as information that is consistent with one's beliefs, needs and desires.

The ways in which perceptual and memory processes can mislead the Central Processor about what is really happening and what has happened in the past is crucial to the understanding of experiences that might seem to be paranormal. These processes shall be considered one at a time.

Perception

"Seeing is believing" is an old truism. "I heard it with my own ears" is an expression of confidence about the reality of what was experienced. People learn to trust their sensory experiences, and usually that is a practical approach. Their interpretation of the world, based on analysis of incoming sensory information, is accurate enough for most purposes. But how can anyone *know* that what he sees or hears is "reality"?

The objects an individual sees are clearly outside his body; they certainly *look* as though they are. However, a moment's reflection raises an age-old philosophical puzzle—how does the brain *know* that they are outside? The brain receives its information from within the body. It has no direct access to walls or trees or earth or sky. Light reflected from such things strikes the retina and causes an impulse or a train of impulses to be sent along the optic nerve and into the brain. Moreover, the brain does not receive a photographic image of the world outside, but something quite different, for the visual system reports only a part of the information-bearing stimulation which strikes the retina:

> The fact is that one does not see the retinal image; one sees with the aid of the retinal image. The incoming pattern of light provides information that the nervous system is well-adapted to pick up. This information is used by the perceiver to guide his movements, to anticipate events, and to construct the internal representations of objects and of space called "conscious experiences". These internal representations are not, however, at all like the corresponding images on the back of the eye. The retinal images of specific objects are at the mercy of every irrelevant change of position; their size, shape and location are hardly constant for a moment. Nevertheless, perception is usually accurate; real objects appear rigid and stable and appropriately located in three-dimensional space (Neisser, 1968, p. 204.)

Adults do not realize that they had to *learn* to form a coherent and stable image of the world outside. They cannot recall most of their own experiences as an infant probably because the very structures used to organize memories, to classify perceptions, were not fully developed until later in childhood. The infant is like the congenitally blind person who following an operation in adulthood has vision for the first time. He must learn to make sense out of the swirling sea of sensory information bombarding his nervous system. Especially during the first few months of life, the infant lives in a world where objects, people, and sequential events do not exist, and the contents of his universe exist only as long as they are perceived (Monte, 1975). He has to construct a reality for himself. He must acquire through interaction with the environment the ability to see forms as entities; to recognize that the brown pattern on the blue wall really indicates one object (a picture-frame) superimposed upon another (the wall).

As Fischer and Landon wrote,

> In the beginning, the newborn's only "reality" is his central nervous system (CNS) activity, but the child soon learns—by bumping into things—to erect a model "out there" which corresponds to his CNS activity. This model that we learn to project is the representation of a world ordered and stabilized by constancies . . . including [the conceptual constancy] of the self. (1972, p. 159.)

The child must learn to categorize and label objects and experiences. Piaget described this process as one of "assimilation" and "accommodation". As the child develops a small number of categories, or "schemata", for organizing his experiences, novel experiences will be forced into existing categories, and the perception and memory of them will be modified ("assimilated") somewhat to fit the category. If the experience recurs, the inadequacy of the category will eventually become apparent and the category itself will be enlarged, modified, or divided into new categories to "accommodate" the distinctive features of this new experience. Thus, the child who is familiar with the concept of birds but has never seen a flying squirrel will at first treat it as a bird, and will probably remember it as having wings. Upon repeated exposure to the flying squirrel, the child will become more impressed with the details, such as the obvious absence of wings, and enlarge the category "birds" to include non-winged flying creatures. Eventually, he will create a new separate category for flying squirrels. We learn to categorize and label even though we usually cannot verbalize the rules by which we assign an object to a category. Try to verbally describe the rules for inclusion of an object in the category "table". It is virtually impossible to define the rules so as to allow the inclusion of dining tables, telephone tables, folding tables, and so on while excluding non-tables such as stools, benches, and the like. Yet we never seem to have any difficulty in immediately making the correct categorization when we encounter a table or a bench or a chair.

The processes of assimilation and accommodation do not end with the onset of cognitive "maturity". We continue to put novel objects and experiences into existing categories, and to expand and eventually sub-divide the categories. This is an important consideration for the study of unusual experiences, since the person's perception and recall is likely to be greatly affected by the category and associated verbal label that was used at the time of the experience.

Our perception of the world is highly dependent on our past experience. We *learn* to perceive things in certain ways which allow us to function appropriately in the physical world around us. As a person walks away from us, the size of the retinal image shrinks, yet we do not see the person diminish in size. We have come to automatically compensate for distance between the observer and the observed when we perceive size. However, learned aspects of our perception can lead to anomalies of perception. Consider the "moon illusion": When the moon is rising over the horizon it appears to be much larger than when it is directly overhead. It has been suggested that the image of the moon at the horizon is magnified by atmospheric refraction, but that is not the case, for if we view the moon when it is at the horizon through a small hole in a piece of cardboard, it no longer seems any larger than when it is overhead. Some people have speculated that comparison with objects of known size near the horizon (buildings, etc.) leads to the illusion. That explanation is incorrect, since the illusion is also seen over large bodies of water. Kaufman and Rock (1962) demonstrated in a series of experiments that the effect is caused by the apparent distance of the moon from us. When it is directly overhead, we have no way of estimating its distance. But when it is at the horizon, our perceptual system "knows" that it is far away. For an object to create so large an image on the retina from such a distance, it must be very large indeed. Thus the automatic adjustment in our interpretation of size as a result of perceived distance leads to "error" in this particular case.

Another interesting illusion, tied more directly to our physical apparatus, is the "Pulfrich illusion" brought about by the fact that the nerve impulses triggered at the retina by dim light take longer to reach the brain than the impulses triggered by light of higher intensity. The illusion can take various forms; one is the common observation made by motorists that when the streetlights come on at dusk, those closest to the driver seem to light up first, followed in quick succession by those further and further away. Our perception is incorrect. The light reaching our retinas from more distant lamps takes longer to create an awareness in the brain, and hence it appears that they were illuminated later. Menzel and Taves (1977) reported that Edwin Land, the inventor of the Polaroid camera, startled an audience at Johns Hopkins University when he had each spectator cover one eye with a piece of dark glass, and then showed them a suspended bright ball which swung back and forth in a plane orthogonal to their lines of sight. The observer in such a situation sees two images, since the image created in the covered eye lags behind that in the other eye. The spectators having been shown the pendulum in advance, automatically and without awareness merged the two images, resulting in the perception of a pendulum swinging in an elliptical orbit. The illusion was so vivid that some of the spectators lifted their arms to shield themselves from the moving ball.

The important point is that we do not perceive reality directly. What we perceive is subject not only to distortion by the physical construction of the perceptual system (e.g. the Pulfrich illusion), but also vulnerable to errors based on the way we *learn* to perceive the world.

The tacit dimension of perception

A considerable degree of perceptual activity occurs in the "tacit dimension". The sensory system acts as a highly selective filter, allowing only some of the stimulation reaching the sensory receptors to reach consciousness. It is unlikely that the reader is now conscious of the pressure of the chair upon which he is sitting, but now that the pressure of the chair has been mentioned, attention is directed to it. What about the sound of the air-conditioning or heating system? Or the noise of traffic in the street? What about the sound of one's own breathing? We may not be aware that a streetlight outside the window is illuminated until it suddenly goes out. We notice changes in stimulus intensity; our nervous systems habituate to unchanging stimuli. Were it not for this ability to focus on only a limited range of stimuli, we would be swamped with information and unable to sort it out. (There is some evidence that it is just such a situation that the schizophrenic experiences (Reed, 1972).) Yet, while we focus our attention on one set of incoming data, we are "unconsciously" monitoring other information so that if sudden changes occur, our attention can be switched to the stimulus dimension involved.

We do not switch our attention to every change in stimulus intensity. Imagine what would happen if we did this while driving down a street — our attention would be switching so fast that we could not focus on anything. That does not mean that we are unaffected by sensory input that never reaches consciousness.

The presentation of a visual stimulus can under certain conditions prevent an *earlier* visual stimulus from entering consciousness. If a brief (25 milliseconds) image of a black disk on a white background is presented to a subject, the subject will perceive it. If a black ring whose inside area is such that the disk just fits inside is then presented with an interval greater than $\frac{1}{2}$ second between the two presentations, the viewer will see the ring as separate from the disk. If the interval is about $\frac{1}{4}$ second, *only* the ring will be perceived, and the person will not be conscious of the earlier presentation of the disk (Werner, 1935). This occurs even when the ring is presented to one eye and the disk to the other. This implies that, relative to the rate at which nerve impulses are conducted, it takes a long time (more than $\frac{1}{4}$ second) for a conscious event to be built up following a stimulus presentation. Despite the lack of conscious awareness of the initial stimulus, the individual can physically react (e.g. press a button) in less time than it takes him to consciously perceive the stimulus (Fehrer and Raab, 1962). Thus, although our conscious perception of the world lags behind reality, *we can respond to a stimulus even before we are conscious of it.*

To what extent can we be influenced by stimuli of which we are not consciously aware? The subject of subliminal perception (the unconscious perception of stimuli that are too brief or too weak to produce a conscious awareness) has produced a great deal of controversy. It has been linked with concern that unscrupulous advertisers might persuade us to buy their products without us knowing about their deliberate influence attempts. In 1957 an advertising firm in New Jersey ran an experiment in which the words "Eat popcorn" and "Drink Coca-Cola" were alternately flashed on a moviescreen every 5 seconds during the presentation of a regular film. The messages were exposed for 1/3000th of a second, and the viewers were unable to consciously perceive them. The firm claimed this led to a 57.5% increase in popcorn sales and an 18.1% increase in the sale of Coca-Cola (Anastasi, 1964). People were naturally alarmed when these results were made public. However, since the commercial group that ran this demonstration refused to allow others to examine either their procedures or their data, claims about the "success" of that demonstration cannot be evaluated. It is likely that other, uncontrolled, variables played a critical role. It is even unclear from the reports whether the increase in popcorn and cola sales occurred only *after* the exposure to subliminal advertising.

Psychologists are skeptical about claims of the effects of subliminal advertising since the threshold of perception is variable both within and among individuals. A stimulus so brief or weak that people cannot pick it up unconsciously would be ineffective. Moreover, weak stimulations also risk misperception, should perception occur. Finally, why should people be influenced to buy a product even if such stimulation was unconsciously perceived? Since people do not respond immediately to overt advertisement, why should it be assumed that they are more likely to follow "unconscious" instructions (Moore, 1980)?

While we should be very skeptical about the power and effectiveness of subliminal advertising, there is no question that we are often unconscious even of superliminal stimuli, and these stimuli may certainly influence us without our conscious knowledge. Animals, as well as humans, can respond to subtle cues which are not noticed by the people around them. Clever Hans, a horse famous at the turn of the century for its ability to solve mathematical problems, to read, and to spell, answered the questions put to it with taps of its hoof. The German psychologist Pfungst studied Clever Hans' ability and by systematically varying aspects of the question–answer procedure discovered that the horse was responding to visual and auditory cues given unconsciously by the questioners. The horse had a go or no-go response governed by the cues from the questioners. It continued tapping until an appropriate cue caused it to stop. Sebeok and Umiker-Sebeok (1979) argued that recent demonstrations apparently showing that chimpanzees can master language if they are taught a system of signs are of the Clever Hans variety. Their conclusions are based on studies of films of the human-ape communications. The researchers and observers involved in the ape language studies are, Sebeok *et al.* (1979) suggested, deceiving themselves in the same way that many who study psychics allow themselves to be deceived. They are unaware of subtle cues that they or others about them are providing.

If animals can learn to respond to non-verbal cues, humans with their vastly superior intellect can do even better. Consider "contact thought reading", where the "reader" holds the subject lightly by the wrist. If the goal were to write on a blackboard a word that the subject is thinking about, the reader would begin by making slightly exaggerated motions with his hand holding the chalk a fraction of an inch away from the board. By making motions which could correspond to one group of letters but not to another, and by monitoring the subject's unconscious reactions as indicated by changes in muscle tension, the reader can be guided directly to the word in question. Some highly skilled readers have been capable of "non-contact" thought reading, responding to slight changes in breathing or tenseness without actually touching the subject directly (Christopher, 1970).

The influence of mental set

The perceptual system not only selects information, it organizes it into a coherent whole. An observer's expectancies or set (i.e. the predisposition to interpret certain patterns of information in a given way) about an event can greatly influence the way in which this organization proceeds. The creaking of the heating ducts may be perceived as footsteps by a timid person alone in an old house late at night. Experimental studies have demonstrated that subjects given one "set" about what to expect in a film observe something quite different from those given another set (e.g. Massad, Hubbard, and Newtson, 1979).

Past experience often establishes a set. In consequence, our perception of events will go beyond the information given. The conjurer's magic depends on this. Without consciously thinking about it, we "see" a downturned palm as "empty" because downturned palms have always been empty in past experience. A magician covers a bird cage with a cloth, murmurs an incantation, and whisks the cloth away to reveal that the cage has vanished. Spectators are startled because they "expected" to see the cage again if the cloth were lifted, since they had perceived no way for it to disappear. They assumed that what appeared to be an ordinary birdcage possessed the properties of ordinary birdcages they had seen in the past.

Mental set has most influence in situations where the stimulus being perceived is ambiguous. A barely discernible shadowy form that we see as we walk along a lonely road at night may take on the appearance of a person waiting to pounce. This would not occur if the stimulus was well enough defined that we could recognize it as a fence-post.

The late Donald Menzel, an astrophysicist who was an authority on aerial phenomena and a staunch critic of "flying-saucer" interpretations of unidentified objects in the sky, reported that an ambiguous stimulus almost gave him a flying-saucer experience (Menzel & Taves, 1977). While a passenger aboard an aircraft flying into Amsterdam, he was staring out the window at the green countryside when he noticed that the airplane was overtaking three shiny aircraft flying in formation. He was surprised by the lack of detail on these aircraft; however, their silvery, swept-back wings were clearly defined. Just as they reached the left side of his field of vision as restricted by the window, they vanished into thin air. He leaned forward, but could not see them. Then he spotted another group of aircraft drifting backwards, relative to his airplane. This made him think of the report of the pilot who in 1947 sighted the first "modern" unidentified flying object (UFO) while flying over a mountain range. Menzel, with some difficulty, refocused his gaze on the window's surface and was surprised to see the brilliant UFOs shrink into tiny raindrops drifting slowly across the outer surface of the window. The airplane's slipstream gave each droplet the form of a tiny horseshoe and, reflecting the light of the sky, they looked just like swept-wing aircraft flying in formation. Had he not made this realization, it is unlikely that the hypothesis of out-of-focus raindrops would have occurred to him later. He would have been left with a mysterious experience which might have altered his beliefs about UFOs.

The selective and organizational aspects of perception can provide us with experiences that are substantially different from reality. There is an interplay between perceptual and inferential systems, particularly when the perceiver evaluates hypotheses about an unusual occurrence:

> Perception can do the work of inference, by searching for and obtaining information that directly verifies a causal interpretation that might be achieved by more elaborate inferential analysis, and inference can do the work of perception by "filling in" information when perception is inefficient or inadequate. (Massad, Hubbard, and Newtson 1979, p. 531.)

In summary, once it is recognized that our perceptual experiences are constructions based not only on sensory input but on the context of the experience, on past experiences and on beliefs derived from such experiences, the cautious seeker of truth will never take for granted that experience is isomorphic with reality. Seeing should not always be believing.

Memory

We do not have access to everything in memory; part of memory is tacit, as was discussed earlier. We do not even know how much we know. A person may be unable to recall explicitly the route from his home to that of a friend he visits occasionally, yet he can drive to the friend's house without difficulty. Cues along the way trigger decisions about which way to turn next.

Memory is not simply the replay of a cerebral tape-recorder, contrary to our personal impressions. Like perception, the memory process involves active *construction* of the memory at the time that we are remembering. An example, based on one given by D.O. Hebb, is the following: Remember sitting down to breakfast this morning. Imagine the scene. You probably "see" yourself as part of it, as though you were at a vantage-point outside, perhaps slightly above the scene. This is not memory in the sense of an accurate recall of experience, because you have never perceived yourself from such a perspective, nor did you see yourself as part of the scene this morning. Your brain constructed that image. You remembered the context of the situation, several important features of it, and you constructed the rest.

The categorization made when we perceive an object or event has a great influence on its recall. If we categorized a light in the sky as a UFO, later recall of the object will be more "UFO-like", and less airplane-like (if that is a competing explanation for what we saw). It is almost pointless to argue with a person's memory of an event, because that memory is real to him. He cannot tell, and is unlikely to believe, that it is not an accurate image of what was perceived. As a result of "assimilation" into a category, details of the stimulus object inconsistent with the category will tend to be forgotten, while details which are consistent with the category may be added. People who have mistaken the planet Venus for a UFO (this is the *leading* source of UFO reports, according to Klass (1974, 1978)) may recall the "object" having windows, as they might expect to see in a spaceship.

When we watch a magician, we perceive what he wants us to perceive, and when we remember his actions later, we probably do not recall what appeared to be trifling, "unimportant" movements which were in fact critical for the conjurer's miracle. We cannot conceive how the trick was effected because we cannot remember the details, although we think we remember everything of importance. Novel events usually have this effect on memory. If a skeptic attempts to suggest a rational explanation for someone's paranormal experience, the reconstruction of that experience in memory will in all probability be lacking in the details necessary to provide a rational explanation.

In the past, psychologists treated errors of memory as though they were *defects* of memory. They believed that if memory always worked as it should, there should be no errors. They asked themselves why memory does not always work perfectly. As long as memory was considered to be a literal record of what had been experienced, errors of memory did not make sense. The modern view, however, is that errors of memory are not defects, but illustrations of general characteristics of the memory system. What is represented in memory seems to be a non-literal representation of what was experienced. Memory is *by its nature* inexact. If a person memorizes a list of emotionally neutral words and later is asked to recall them, he may recall, instead of a given word, a word similar to it, just as though that word had itself been presented. This is a manifestation of the thematic, rather than literal, character of memory.

The non-literal nature of memory is very important in understanding the propensity for inaccuracy in any testimony based on memory of events. Numerous studies have demonstrated that the eyewitness is often in error in his recall because he reaches conclusions based on a reconstruction of the events from fragments of information stored in memory (Buckhout, 1974). The fragments recalled can be poorly representative of what occurred. Often stimuli in the original situation which later turn out to be of crucial importance are ignored. If the original situation was stressful for the observer, his emotional response may also have interfered with his ability to pay attention to details.

Language influences memory in that we may remember the verbal label better than we remember the actual event. The choice of words used to recall an event can also alter its reconstruction in memory. A striking demonstration of this was provided by a study (Loftus and Palmer, 1974) in which subjects were shown a film of a traffic accident. Following the film, they were questioned about what they had seen. Some of the subjects were asked this question: "About how fast were the cars going when they smashed into each other?", while other subjects were asked the same question with the word "smashed" replaced by "hit". The subjects who had been asked the first question responded with higher estimates of the speeds of the cars than did those who were asked the second question, demonstrating that the form of a question can actually influence the memory of the event. A more striking finding was that when asked one week later whether they had seen broken glass in the film (there was none) more than twice as many of those who had been asked the first question reported having seen broken glass than of those who had been asked the second question. Broken glass is consistent with high-speed accidents. The words in the *initial* question following the presentation of the film influenced the memory of the film itself.

These findings raise many questions about the reliability of eyewitness testimony of the paranormal. Consider, for example, reports of near-death experiences. Raymond Moody (1975, 1977) has written about the great similarities among the reports of people who were resuscitated after having been judged clinically dead, or who, through illness or injury, had come very close to death. Features such as the feeling of floating out of the body, seeing the resuscitation team working, being drawn rapidly down a long dark tunnel and encountering various spirits, including a "being of light", recurred in the reports. Moody's data base is dependent on the memories of those who came to him with their reports, often years after the experience. Moody had originally gathered anecdotal evidence in an informal way, but,

Eventually a friend of mine talked me into giving a report to a medical society, and other public talks followed. Again, I found that after every talk someone would come up to me and tell me about an experience of his own.

As I became more widely known for this interest, doctors began to refer to me persons whom they had resuscitated and who reported unusual experiences. Still others have written to me after newspaper articles about my studies appeared. (1975, pp. 16–17.)

Since there was such great similarity in the reports, Moody argued that these reports must reflect reality. (There are physiological reasons for expecting such similarities which shall be discussed later.) Considering how memory can be shaped after the event, it is not unlikely that one's memory of a near-death experience will conform to the pattern described in the lecture or reading one has just experienced. Moreover, Moody's questions to his subjects certainly would not have been without influence.

People tend to reconstruct memories in line with what they want to believe. We sometimes "remember" predictions we made in the past as though they had been confirmed by the subsequent occurrence, even when this is not the case. This occurs even if we know that our remembrances can be checked against objective records about the predictions we made (Fischhoff and Beyth, 1975). Because of the non-literal nature of memory, such bias in reconstruction is relatively easy to accommodate. In addition, any embellishments added to one's report of past events, whether they are added to make the report more consistent with the point one wants to make, or to save face if the person's interpretation of past events is challenged, can quickly become part of the "memory" of the incident.

In summary, the recall of an event depends on much more than the event that was originally perceived. Subsequent information, the effects of attitudes and values, the reactions of other people to the account, and even the individual's level of arousal can alter the recall and the representation in memory. This has been referred to as "retrospective falsification", and it causes even first-hand anecdotes to be unreliable. Important details often do not seem important when an event occurs and are not noted at all.

Transcendental Experience

If the perception of external reality is subject to serious distortion, what about experiences that seem to go beyond "ordinary" reality? Mystical, or "transcendental" experience has always played a part in religious life. Throughout history, sudden and dramatic religious conversions have followed "illuminations", visions of God, or related experiences. Mystical experience is more common than is generally presumed, even though the interpretation of such experience varies from individual to individual. This interpretation will be consistent with the person's belief system and possibly with his needs. Some may interpret the experience as the presence of God, others may view it is "astral projection". Cultural factors are also important in determining how such an experience will be viewed, and whether it will be considered of divine origin (Lewis, 1971). An indication of the frequency of mystical experiences is Greeley's (1974) report that, based on his surveys, half of the American population claims to have had experiences of union with "a powerful spiritual force that draws me out of myself" (p. 11).

In the past, only one kind of consciousness was usually spoken of—a person was either conscious or not. It now seems that consciousness can take forms different from normal, waking consciousness. The kind of hypnotic state one sometimes experiences while driving for a long time down an unchanging stretch of highway, or dreaming, or hypnosis, all represent some kind of alteration of consciousness. The term "altered states of consciousness" (ASCs) has come into common usage. Ludwig (1966) provided a hazy definition of an altered state of consciousness, describing it as any mental state that can be recognized by an individual (or sometimes by an observer) as a sufficient deviation in subjective experience or psychological functioning from what is normal for that individual during alert waking consciousness (e.g. greater than usual preoccupation with internal sensations, or thoughts, or impairment of reality testing).

Mystical experience has come to be viewed as an altered state of consciousness. William James (1902) listed ineffability, noetic quality (profound feelings of insight), transiency, and passivity as the key characteristics of the mystical experience. Ludwig (1966) listed feelings of losing touch with reality, a disturbed sense of time, a greater likelihood of experiencing emotional extremes, perceptual distortions, a sense of the ineffable, feelings of rejuvenation, and hypersuggestibility as key features. If he is hypersuggestible, the individual is more likely to accept statements or suggestions uncritically, and to misinterpret the situation in line with his own wishes and fears.

Abraham Maslow (e.g. 1959) devoted a great deal of time to the study of such experiences, which he referred to as "peak experiences". He discussed them as being typified by an emotional reaction flavoured with wonder, awe, and humility, and by a characteristic disorientation of time and space. Such experiences are so beautiful that they are often described as an eager, happy dying, a "sweet death"; they are seen as being "good" and never painful or undesirable, he said;

> The peak experience is felt as a self-validating, self-justifying moment which carries its own intrinsic value with it. . . . It is felt to be so valuable an experience, so great a revelation, that even an attempt to justify it takes away from its dignity and worth. (Maslow, 1959, p. 49.)

According to Greeley (1974), the individual often comes away from a transcendental experience with a feeling of immortality, and records often contain statements such as "I felt that I could willingly die" or "No one can ever tell me again that death is bad". The person now "knows" that life continues after physical death. (See Greeley, 1975, for a summary of the results of a survey of mystical experiences.)

Ludwig (1966) classified altered states in terms of the conditions bringing them about. There are, he said,

1. altered states brought about by *increased* exteroceptive stimulation and/or motor activity, or emotion, e.g. ecstatic trances, religious conversions during revival meetings, fugues, and amnesias;
2. altered states brought about by *reduced* exteroceptive stimulation and/or motor activity, e.g. dreaming, somnambulism, hypnagogic and hypnopompic sleep (to be discussed later) and states brought about sensory deprivation;
3. altered states brought about by increased alertness or mental involvement, e.g. prolonged observance of a radar screen, fervent praying;
4. altered states brought about by decreased alertness, relaxation, e.g. daydreaming, meditation states, mediumistic trances, deep relaxation;
5. altered states brought about by physical factors, e.g. hypoglycemia (spontaneous or as a result of fasting), dehydration, hyperventilation, temporal lobe seizures, drug effects, and drug-withdrawal effects.

But how can decreased alertness or increased motor activity bring about an altered state? There appear to be several ways that this can occur:

(a) Deautomatization

Deikman (1966) hypothesized that mystical experiences are a consequence of a breakdown in the automatic selection/organization process brought about by focusing attention away from incoming sensory information. This stream of incoming information normally prevents the perceptual system from attending to ongoing neurological activity which might otherwise be experienced as a series of images, a "stream of consciousness" (cf. Fischer and Landon, 1972). The "deautomatized" brain allows into consciousness stimuli which might otherwise have been excluded because they were not salient. Deikman noted that two techniques practiced to produce mystic experiences—contemplation and re-nunciation—seem to produce such a deautomatization. In contemplation, the individual attempts to free the mind of all thoughts, focusing on a single percept in an effort to exclude normal outer and inner stimuli and to provide an opportunity to experience stimuli which would in normal waking life be excluded. A word or "mantra" repeated rhythmically begins to become unrecognizable as a word after a short time, and focuses the mind away from the external world. Renunciation of sensual pleasures such as eating and sleeping is also an attempt to free the mind of distractions, Deikman suggested. However, lack of food and sleep may produce direct changes in the functioning of the central nervous system, as will be discussed below.

Ornstein (1976) expressed a view similar to that of Deikman. If awareness is a construction and not a "registration" of the external world, and if the nature of the construction process is altered, he said, then one would expect that the awareness resulting from it would also be changed. Methods of meditation that involve focusing attention on an unchanging stimulus, either visually, or through thought, or through behaviour such as chanting, or through methods that involve restriction of sensory input, apparently affect the nervous system so that a "turning off" of consciousness of the external world follows.

(b) Biochemical changes

Some altered states may be brought about indirectly through changes in body chemistry which affect brain function. This is clearly the case when psychoactive drugs are involved. But non-drug experiences can also involve biochemical changes. For example, fasting produces hypoglycemia which may lead to hallucinations. Hyperventilation and medi-tational breathing exercises can alter the carbon dioxide level in the blood and bring about the experience of an altered state (Deikman, 1966). Aldous Huxley (1959), having experienced an altered state after breathing a mixture of seven parts oxygen and three parts carbon dioxide, suggested that the endless psalm-singing of Christian and Buddhist monks, the chanting of medicine-men and shamans, and the shouting and screaming of revivalists for hours on end serve to increase the carbon dioxide level and bring about an altered state. Unless singers are highly trained, they exhale a larger volume of oxygen than they inhale, he said. Self-flagellation, Huxley suggested, brings about altered states via increased adrenalin and histamine secretion.

Huxley argued that those seeking mystical experience have, throughout history, worked to change their body chemistry. This is in line with the historical evidence that many of the great mystics of Christianity and other religions experienced their first great mystical experience, or illumination, when enduring extreme adversity or affliction or deprivation and penury (Lewis, 1971).

(c) Cognitive labelling (attribution)

Yet, people do not always need to meditate, to fast, to hyperventilate, to chant, to ingest drugs, or otherwise manipulate their bodies to have a mystical experience. It is the spontaneous experiences, often triggered by experiences of pleasure or beauty (Greeley, 1974), that are most likely to be misinterpreted since they seem to arrive without cause. The mental set of the individual, his expectations based on personal and cultural beliefs and values and the context of the situation, determine whether the experience will be pleasant or unpleasant, and whether it will be interpreted as metaphysical in nature.

Kleinke wrote with regard to meditation that " . . . it is not the *state of mind* that causes a person to have a favourable experience. Favourable experience in meditation comes from the positive labelling of behaviour that results from the *practice* of relaxation, imagination, and attention to one's body" (1978, p. 5).

This presumably explains why subjects who believed that being in an "alpha" state (characterized by higher than normal alpha wave activity in the brain) can lead to ecstatic experience reported highly moving and "meaningful" experiences when they believed (erroneously) that they were in such a state (Lynch, 1973). One researcher (Doxey, 1976) personally experienced the power of this kind of set: When testing his equipment with himself as subject, he saw the equipment signal that he was in an alpha state and experienced what he described as "near ecstasy". Later analysis of brain-wave recordings of the experience showed that he had not been in an "alpha state" at all. There had been an equipment malfunction, and the signal he had received was erroneous.

Thus, while the interpretation an individual gives to such an experience may involve metaphysical processes (since the experience seems far different from anything in the "normal" realm of experience), there need be nothing metaphysical involved.

In the attempt to demonstrate the effects of such labelling, Pahnke and Richards (1969) examined experimentally induced "mysticism" in what has come to be called the "miracle of Marsh Chapel" study. Students at a seminary were given either the psychedelic drug psilocybin, or nicotinic acid, a vitamin that produces feelings of warmth and tingling and which was chosen to maximize the placebo effect. Subjects, not knowing which drug they had received, then sat in a chapel to listen to organ music and readings and engaged in prayers and personal meditation. This was on Good Friday. Analysis of a post-drug questionnaire, a follow-up questionnaire administered 6 months later, and the content of the subjects' written accounts of their experiences indicated that the experiences of the subjects who had received the psychoactive drug were indistinguishable from a typology of mystical consciousness derived from descriptions given by mystics. The mysticism scores of the drugged subjects were significantly higher than those of the controls who took the vitamin.

Pahnke and Richards concluded from these results that the altered state brought about by the psychoactive drug was, in the context in which it was experienced, the same as a religious "peak state",[4] and they argued (as did Huxley) that all altered states probably involve underlying biological changes of one kind or another.

(d) The relaxation response

Benson (1975) studied practitioners of transcendental meditation and found that, while meditating, they demonstrated a marked decrease in rate of metabolism as measured by

---

[4] See Dittes (1973) for a dissenting viewpoint.

oxygen consumption. While during sleep, oxygen consumption decreases slowly over a period of 4 to 5 hours to a rate about 8 percent lower than during the waking state, the meditators were experiencing between 10 and 20 percent reductions, and these occurred within the first 3 minutes of meditation. In addition, brain-wave activity showed an increase in alpha waves, which usually occur when people feel relaxed, while heart rate and respiration and blood lactate level (which seems to be linked with feelings of anxiety) all decreased significantly shortly after meditation began. Yet, Benson found, meditation is neither a form of sleep nor a substitute for it.

Benson began to experiment, and discovered that these changes were in no way unique to transcendental meditation; rather, they were part of an integrated response opposite to the "fight-or-flight response". Whereas in the fight or flight response, autonomic nervous system activity prepares the body for danger—adrenalin flows into the blood stream, heart rate and respiration increase, surface blood vessels contract—this other response, this "relaxation response", leads to opposite reactions. It can be considered to produce an altered state of consciousness, a state that is not commonly experienced because it does not occur without being deliberately invoked. Mystical experiences and feelings of transcendence can accompany the relaxation response, and Benson suggested that the relaxation response has been experienced throughout history, and that the methods used by mystics and monks to achieve feelings of transcendence are precisely those which should elicit a relaxation response. There are four necessary components to bringing about the response; (a) a quiet environment, so that there will be no distractions; (b) a comfortable position, so as to eliminate muscular tension; (c) a mental device—by repeating a constant stimulus, word, or phrase over and over, or by staring at an object, or by focusing on one's breathing, one can avoid or interfere with the train of distracting thoughts; (d) a passive attitude—one should not worry about distractions should they occur. The relaxation response must be allowed to happen; it cannot be actively pursued.

Benson emphasized that there are many different methods, all incorporating in some way the above components, of bringing about the relaxation response. Subjectively, most people feel very relaxed and have a sense of tranquillity during this response; some immediately experience feelings of ecstasy.

As Benson said,

> The Relaxation Response is a universal human capacity, and even though it has been evoked in the religion of both East and West for most of recorded history, you don't have to engage in any esoteric practices to bring it forth. (1975, p. 175.)

The importance of Benson's work in the present context is that we seem to have a natural propensity to bring about an altered state which for some people is accompanied by feelings of ecstasy. This ecstasy will be interpreted in terms of the circumstances which brought it about. Because our social learning history does not prepare us for what appears to be quite a natural experience, it is not surprising that it is often imbued with profound metaphysical importance.

Ornstein pointed out the great similarities in techniques used in various societies for bringing about altered states:

> It may be that men in different places at different times have noticed that by repeating an action or a phrase over and over again, or continuously focusing on breathing, the awareness of the external world can be shut out. Since we, the Bushmen, the Eskimos, the monks of Tibet, the Zen masters, the Yoga adepts, and the dervishes all share a common nervous system, it is not so surprising that similarities in techniques should have evolved. (1976, p. 163.)

In the final analysis, it would appear that peak-state, ecstatic experiences are part of the normal range of human emotional experiences, even though they are rarely experienced because people do not know how to elicit them. The stresses of modern society wreak havoc with whatever propensity we have towards relaxation. Nonetheless, such experiences do occur, and if the individual either is not expecting such an experience, or has the experience in the context of some metaphysical endeavour (religious contemplation, Transcendental Meditation, etc.) the experience may be interpreted as something beyond the realm of normal reality, as something of a transcendent nature.

Ultimately, it may prove to be the case that most mystical experiences can be accounted for in terms of a common physiological state accompanied by whatever labelling is pertinent to the situation. This was Sargant's conclusion, based on his study of mysticism and religious conversion in a number of different cultures:

> . . . the same, physiological processes underlie experiences of 'possession' by gods or spirits or demons, the mystical experience of union with God, the gift of tongues and other phenomena of 'enthusiastic' religious experience, the inspired utterances of oracles and mediums, faith-healing, and some aspects of witch-doctoring, and the behaviour of people under hypnosis, under certain drugs, or in states of sexual excitement. (1973, p. 194.)

Experience of the Paranormal

As was indicated at the beginning of this chapter, most people who believe in the paranormal cite personal experience as their primary reason for doing so. Whether this is actually the case or whether personal experience is used to justify in their minds a pre-existing belief is difficult to ascertain. However, every one of us, whatever our beliefs about the paranormal, do have odd experiences from time to time that could be taken to be instances of the paranormal. Someone is daydreaming about another person that he has not seen for some time, and suddenly to his great surprise that person walks into his office. Someone else has a vivid dream of an aircrash and the next day learns that an airplane did indeed crash during the night. Another person is talking to his wife and just as he is about to bring up some incident that occurred long ago, she mentions it first, almost as though she had read his thoughts. Another individual visits an old house that he has never been in before, but once inside he suddenly is overcome with the certain feeling that he has been there before.

All of these incidents are very common ones. All of them, once the nature of the human information-processing system is understood, are events which we should *expect* to experience from time to time. Because no one teaches us to expect them, and because they often seem so jarring, most likely because they violate the primitive beliefs of the individual's rational, scientific–humanist belief system, it is not surprising that people often fall back on a transcendental belief system to explain them. The concepts of precognition and telepathy allow people to "make sense" out of these experiences.

Dreams, perhaps because of the importance accorded to them in literature, psychiatry, and folk myth in Western society, can be particularly striking. A very vivid dream which involves some emotionally charged event (e.g. death of a relative) can bring anxiety to even the hardiest skeptic. An anecdotal example of this was provided by a fellow psychologist. He does not believe that precognition occurs, or that premonitions arrive via dreams. Yet, he once had a dream about the death of a favourite uncle that was so vivid, so compelling, that each time the telephone rang during the following day he "half expected" to receive news of his uncle's death, even though he continually reminded himself that he did not believe in precognition. The uncle did not die, but imagine how difficult it would have been for his rationality to prevail had the emotionally striking dream been fulfilled. The individual who becomes extremely ill several hours after having eaten may develop a great dislike for some one small part of the meal, perhaps some small but salient taste such as Roquefort dressing, even though he "knows" that there is no reason to believe that it was the dressing that made him ill. The saliency of that taste, coupled with the fact that he has rarely eaten it in the past, are enough for his nervous system to make a connection between the taste and the illness, leading to an avoidance response in the future (Seligman and Hager, 1972). Analogously, logic is not enough to prevent the development of an "emotion-based" belief that premonitions occur from time to time, if one by chance has had such an experience.

The role of emotion in the experience of the paranormal cannot be underestimated. Not only do paranormal experiences often generate emotional reactions, it is also very often the case that the opposite is true: traumatic, emotion-laden experiences may give rise to the paranormal interpretation. Perhaps, as Persinger suggested, this is because of a temporary weakening of critical thinking ability during emotionally charged circumstances:

> When considering psi phenomena, one must be especially sensitive to the possibility that much of the phenomena may be associated with distortions or irregularities not in the environment but within the measurement system: "thought". The fact that the majority of psi experiences occur contiguously in time with aversive (traumatic) events, known disorganizers of other response systems, is important in this context. (1976, pp. 78–79.)

Such disorganization may make perception and memory even more prone than usual to distortion.

Anyone who has ever spoken critically on the subject of the paranormal has undoubtedly been faced with questions of the form "But how do you explain the fact that my aunt dreamed of her husband's death the very night he died at sea?" Such questions are of course unanswerable. The experience was a personal one. However, given what is known about the ways in which memories can deceive, how embellishments are added to increase consistency, how critical details may have been ignored or forgotten, it is unwise to attempt an explanation. Parapsychologists themselves long ago learned not to be impressed by anecdotal evidence. In the early days of parapsychology, considerable effort was put into the investigation of such anecdotes, but time after time, whenever details of the story could be checked against objective records, such glaring discrepancies were found as to cast serious doubt upon the accuracy of any part of the report (Rawcliffe, 1959). Even the reports of individuals whose integrity and intelligence were beyond questions were found to have fallen victim to the distortions of memory.

The fact that several people have witnessed some paranormal event and gave similar reports should not *a priori* increase confidence in the accuracy of the reports. First of all, people with similar backgrounds are predisposed to interpret novel events in similar ways, and secondly, there is a strong tendency for people who are interacting with one another to converge on a single judgement when faced with ambiguous stimuli (Sherif, 1935).

Sources of paranormal experience

If seemingly paranormal experiences have rational explanations, what might they be? In the pages that follow, some factors which can generate such experiences are discussed. Before proceeding, however, it is of the utmost importance to point out that we should not automatically expect to be able to explain every such event. Many will be due simply to coincidence (e.g. dreams of a car crash the same night that some friend is killed in a car accident), in which case no link between the two events exists. The exploration of that subject must await the next chapter.

It must be emphasized that the following discussion of how common "paranormal" experiences could come about is not meant to imply that they all come about in those ways. There may be other possibilities. One cannot demonstrate, of course, especially after the fact, that they were not due to paranormal processes. However, since there is, as shall be discussed later, little reason to believe in the reality of such processes, and considerable reason to doubt their existence, it would seem reasonable that such experiences should first be considered in the light of processes known to be capable of generating them. Whether the paranormal exists or not, we should have such experiences from time to time, given the way our experiential apparatus is organized.

(a) *Ghostly phenomena.* Some reports of apparitions are no doubt simply the result of a mental set imposed on an ambiguous stimulus situation: A person spending a night in a haunted castle is more likely to interpret strange sounds as being ghost-like than were he to hear the same sounds in his own home. However, some experiences are more compelling than that; Reed (1972) pointed to hypnagogic sleep and hypnopompic sleep as sources of such experience. Both are common enough "altered states" of consciousness, the former occurring as a person is drifting off to sleep, and the latter as the person is awakening. In such a state, dream-type imagery may be mixed with stimulation from the environment, resulting in a kind of hallucinatory experience which seems vividly real. (People who wake up thinking that the telephone is ringing and then suddenly realize that it has not been may be experiencing such imagery.) The imagery is often vivid, realistic, and sometimes bizarre; the most common image is that of a "face in the dark". These experiences seem *real*. While they occur to any one person infrequently, they are not uncommon. Reed (1972) cited a study of 182 students by McKellar in 1957. Almost two-thirds reported having experienced hypnagogic sleep, and one-fifth reported hypnopompic sleep.

That such realistic imagery, mixed in as it might be with stimuli from the environment, can have a powerful emotional effect, and that it might be interpreted by certain people in certain contexts as ghostly, is hardly surprising.

It must be remembered that visual imagery can be indistinguishable from visual perception (Segal, 1970). As Finke said:

> . . . mental images can stimulate visual processing mechanisms directly . . . resulting in the sensation that an image can be "seen" as if it were an actual object or event. Further, the more vivid the image the more strongly these mechanisms would respond, and the more similar to actual objects or events the mental image would appear. (1980, p. 130.)

Reed (1972) also referred to another type of experience which can be interpreted as evidence of ghosts: The "sense of presence" sometimes felt by people. It is as though another person, although not visible, is in one's presence. Such a feeling, Reed said, is frequently reported by psychologically normal people, particularly in certain contexts (e.g. when one is alone in a graveyard late at night). Natural stimuli such as a draught or an echo may lend itself to unconscious misinterpretation, Reed suggested, and the fact that no visual illusion has been observed only adds to the sense of unease. Fatigue, Reed added, can increase the likelihood of such experience by increasing suggestibility and reducing the capacity for critical thinking.

(b) *Near-death experiences*. In the last few years, several books have been published which purport to demonstrate that experiences reported by persons near death reflect the reality of a world beyond death (e.g. Osis and Haraldsson, 1977; Moody, 1975, 1977). While it is commonplace for skeptics to simply ignore such reports, considering them to be based on misinterpretations of experience or to be due to emotional "overload", it is important to consider what such experiences may tell us about the nature of the nervous system itself. For example, we are told by Raymond Moody (1975, 1977) that the reports of (some) patients who survived cardiac arrest (or "death", as he would have it) provide very strong evidence for the survival of the "soul" beyond death. As mentioned earlier, some people report that after having heard themselves pronounced dead they felt themselves being drawn rapidly through a long tunnel. They may even have seen their body on the hospital bed with the resuscitation team gathered around it. They caught sight of dead friends and relatives, and encountered a "being" of very intense light, a spirit which helped them to review panoramically the events of the life just ended. The individual was overwhelmed by feelings of joy, feelings of having obtained the wisdom of the ages. When unexpectedly forced to return to the physical body, the individual, following resuscitation, was no longer afraid of death.

While Moody's work suffers from numerous methodological and interpretative flaws (Alcock, 1979), such as the dependence on people's recall of emotional events which often occurred years before, the most serious criticism is that such writers have ignored or downplayed the extent to which these experiences might be direct consequences of nervous system organization. For example, hallucinations, rather than being totally unconstrained in content, appear to be constructed around a small number of "form-constants": grating/lattice, cobwebs, tunnel/funnel, and spirals (Kluver, 1926). These forms involve intense brightness and vivid colours. Siegel (1977), in a study of drug-induced hallucinations, reported that such imagery seems to have two stages, the first being characterized by these form-constants, and the second involving more complex imagery, with religious images being very common. In fact, in cannabis-induced hallucinations, Siegel found that the typical subject reported a very bright light in the centre of the field of vision which created a tunnel-like perspective. An aerial view of oneself was also very common, along with the vivid memory of childhood experiences. What is more, the subjects reported that they believed these experiences to be veridical at the time. Moody's description of near-death experiences is very similar to the experiences reported by Siegel's subjects. Siegel concluded that, " . . . the experiments point to underlying mechanisms in the central nervous system as the source of a universal phenomenology of hallucinations" (1977, p. 132). Moody (1977), on the other hand, suggested that such hallucinations themselves are indicative of premature release of the soul!

It is hardly surprising that a patient recovering from cardiac arrest, being told (erroneously)[5] that he had been clinically dead, and having no schema in which to place such an hallucinatory experience (if that is what it was), treats it as an "after-life" experience. Assigning that label then makes it even more wondrous to the individual.

(c) *Déjà vu*. The experience of *déjà vu*, something which occurs to virtually everyone at one time or another, involves a strong feeling of familiarity or recognition in a situation which one "knows" one has never seen before. The feeling is compelling enough to demand

---

[5] Contemporary definition of clinical death is tied to cessation of neural rather than cardiac activity. This is a relatively recent development.

explanation, and it has been explained in terms of such paranormal constructs as precognition (the person is familiar with the scene because it was viewed earlier precognitively) and reincarnation (the persons viewed the scene or experienced the event in an earlier life). However, to ask how we can have a memory of something that we are apparently experiencing for the first time is to ask the wrong question (Reed, 1972). Rather than assuming a memory of a hypothetical earlier experience, it would be more to the point to ask why it is that a novel experience elicits a feeling which we label as "recognition" or "familiarity".

In order to decide that something is "familiar", the brain has to take into account a great many different stimuli. We readily recognize a friend, despite changes in hairstyle, clothing, and so on. Recognition must be based on a decision process in which some stimulus dimensions are given more weight than others. An army friend whose face was painted black as part of his camouflage for army manoeuvres might not be recognizable at first glance, but the moment he spoke he would likely be recognized. Another friend whose face is not disguised but who is speaking in a squeaky voice because of laryngitis will also be quickly recognized. Thus, recognition is based on a weighing of a variety of cues, some visual, some auditory. But suppose we saw someone who was clearly not our friend, but who had the same characteristic way of walking. It is quite possible that even if this similarity is not noticed explicitly it might register tacitly, and it may give rise to a feeling of recognition, based on the manner of walking, which conflicts with conscious, explicit knowledge that it is not our friend. Such a situation might well create the feeling that "I know that person from somewhere but I don't know where". *Déjà vu* experience in general could be based on a similar process. Some important cue which might normally be weighted strongly is at variance with a host of other cues, yet "erroneously" leads unconscious processes to generate a feeling of recognition. Thus, as Reed (1972) suggested, *déjà vu* may represent a failure to notice those features of the current situation which are very similar to stimuli which were present in past situations. It could be that even if none of the stimuli in the present situation correspond to those of past ones, the present situation may lead to perceptual organizing activity sufficiently similar to such activity in the past that a feeling of familiarity is generated.

(d) *Precognition.* Most people at some time or other experience a strong feeling that they have foreseen the future, often through a dream. Precognitive experiences can come about in two different ways:

1. The precognition is strongly felt as such, and the foreseen event subsequently occurs. (When the foreseen event does not occur, the feeling of precognition is usually readily forgotten. This selective remembering will be discussed in the following chapter.) There are several ways that normal processes could generate such a feeling.

The individual can be tacitly, but not explicitly, aware of information which can quite accurately predict the forthcoming event. Consider this example, suggested by Segal (1970): A man walking down the street looks casually over a crowd of people crossing at an intersection two blocks away. He unconsciously picks up some sensory input, a face or a particular gait, which remind him of a friend he knows to be in Europe. His automatic and unconscious evaluation of the stimulus information, combined with an analysis of the contextual probabilities (in other words, his expectations, or "mental set"), lead to the conclusion that it is not a recognition situation; it is not his friend. But the sensory input does elicit some memories and causes him to think about this friend. As he comes closer to the person in question, still unaware of the unconscious processes that were triggered off by the person's face or gait, he receives stronger and stronger input which overweighs the knowledge that the friend is out of town, and he makes a proper identification and says, "Is this ever amazing, I was just thinking about you". Since he is unaware of the information which prompted his thoughts, he has no way of seeing the causal link between the person's presence and the thoughts about him.

Another example of "precognition" is more straightforward. This one is a personal one. I was standing in a cinema waiting to buy some popcorn, and was idly recalling a conversation I had once had with the brother of a colleague. I had only met the brother once or twice and had not seen him in months. A few moments later, I turned around, and there about 30 feet away was the man himself. I recall the momentary sense of shock I felt. But then, instead of attributing it to ESP, I turned away and thought about it for a moment. I realized that I could clearly hear his rather distinctive voice. Obviously, I had been hearing it *without* awareness, and it was that stimulus which brought forth the otherwise unmemorable conversation of several months earlier.

Precognitive dreams can be expected to occur in a similar way. Consider an example: Someone visits a friend who is in some way a bit "different" that day—paler or quieter than usual, or perhaps breathing with slight difficulty. The individual does not consciously detect any difference in his friend's appearance or behaviour, but may carry away this information as part of the tacit dimension of memory. He may even be a bit anxious consciously, without being able to "put his finger on" why he feels that way. That night, he has an anxiety dream where the cues from the tacit dimension elicit imagery involving his friend's death. Should he wake up to find that his friend did indeed die, he will naturally believe that he had had a precognitive experience.

Sometimes, if one is sleeping, one's dreams can be influenced by cues from a radio or television set playing in the background. The sleeper "hears" fragments of a news report about two passenger trains colliding and this becomes woven into a dream. The person awakes to find that his dream that two trains have collided corresponds to what really occurred during the night.

Dreams believed to be precognitive may bring about their own fulfilment in some cases. If one dreams that he will be in a car accident, he could conceivably become so disturbed that he actually brings on the fulfilment of the dream because of his tenseness and anxiety while driving.

Hypnopompic sleep may be another source of precognitive dreams. Much of the imagery of hypnopompic sleep seems to bear reference to the individual's anticipations about the day to come (Reed, 1972). It should not be surprising that occasionally the fiction of dreams mixed with anticipation of reality should provide an unexpected combination of events which do indeed occur.

2. The second way in which precognitive experiences can come about is of a *post hoc* nature—something occurs which leads to the sudden realization that the event had already "taken place" in an earlier dream. In such a case, information from tacit memory may again be responsible for the correspondence between dreams and the subsequent reality. Often the dream is all but forgotten until the "confirmatory" event occurs, which suddenly gives great importance to the dream (Vetter, 1973). Naturally, by this time the recall of the dream is usually quite hazy and it is easy for the circumstances of the dream to *seem* to correspond to those of the incident which has occurred.

A few years ago, psychologist Carson Bock, was treating an accident victim for a post-traumatic phobic fear of closed spaces. In the treatment of such phobias, he often uses a tunnel which connects two wings of the hospital where he works, telling the patient to relax as he moves further and further into the tunnel. This particular patient, at the moment he saw the tunnel, expressed great shock because he had seen this very tunnel in a dream the night before! The dream had not seemed to be particularly significant until this time. The apparent mystery was cleared up when the patient was shown an article which had appeared several years ago in a magazine supplement in many newspapers. The article carried a picture of the tunnel; the patient indeed remembered reading the article but had not remembered the picture. Presumably, having just arrived at the hospital described in the article, relevant material from his "tacit" memory was manifested in his dreams.

Occasionally, a person may dream twice about another person. The order of the two dreams is later mixed up in memory so that the "significant" dream, which followed the significant event, is recalled as having *preceded* it, whereas in reality the first dream was insignificant in nature.

I have on several occasions invited people who have reported having frequent precognitive dreams to write down the details of all dreams as soon as they awake in order to have a record against which to assess subsequent events. In every case, the precognitive dreams stopped, presumably because errors of recall which made the dream fit subsequent events were eliminated. It is all too easy to be struck by some small correspondence between the vague memory of a dream and some subsequent event, and then come to believe that significant features of the event were also part of the dream. Sometimes, too, non-specific anxiety dreams laden with all sorts of unrelated imagery, or involving some traumatic event such as an explosion, may subsequently be taken to have heralded almost any salient traumatic event (an air crash, the death of a relative, etc.) which follows it.

(e) *Telepathy*. The same cue, received without awareness by two people, may very well start off the same process of association. This is much more likely to be the case when two people with a long common history are involved, since they are more likely to make the same kinds of associations. A personal example: A few years ago while driving down the street with a close friend of mine that I had not seen in a while, I was about to mention the name of a fellow student, W. S. H., with whom we had both gone to school 10 years earlier, when suddenly he said "I wonder whatever happened to W. S. H.?" I felt that natural sense of astonishment one usually feels in such circumstances. However, instead of immediately saying "I was about to say that!" I asked him to recall his previous thoughts, going back a few minutes in time, and I attempted to do the same thing. It became quite clear that a large pendulum clock in a store window that we had passed had led both of us to think of W. S. H.—he was noteworthy in that he invariably walked around with a pendulum-style podometer (used to measure distance walked) swinging from his belt.

Any two people who have shared considerable common history should expect that from time to time some stimulus, perhaps only tacitly observed, will set off a similar chain of thoughts leading some moments later to the common thought of some event or person remote from the stimulus that began the thought sequence. This *should* happen from time to time. It would be surprising if it did not. Even strangers might experience a similar effect, for most people in a given society have some experiences in common. Suppose that two people are waiting in a physician's office. A radio is playing softly. An announcer talks briefly about the fact that a farewell dinner is being planned for the outgoing mayor. Both begin thinking about the traffic congestion they experienced on the way to the physician's office, congestion caused by people trying to find parking places in order to go into a nearby polling office and vote in the mayoral elections which are just now being held to replace the retiring incumbent.

In the midst of the traffic melee, two cars had run into each other and the drivers had become involved in fisticuffs. One of the patients turns to the other and to strike up a conversation says, "Did you see those two guys fighting down at the corner?" The other is startled because he was just thinking about that very incident.

This rather obviously contrived example is simply meant to illustrate that an initial stimulus can lead two different people to arrive at identical points in their thinking, and the realization that they are thinking about the same thing may be quite surprising to them both, and may be interpreted as possibly having been the result of telepathy.

(f) *Psychokinesis*. Ouija boards and the water-witcher's dowsing rods (Y-shaped willow sticks or similar devices made of metal, used to search for water, and sometimes for minerals) "work", it seems, because of unconscious motor responses on the part of the practitioner. If a person suspends a pendulum from his fingers and is told that the pendulum will answer questions by moving in a straight line for "yes" and in a circular path for "no", then despite conscious efforts to hold the hand as still as possible, most people will find that when questions are put to them (to which they explicitly or perhaps even tacitly know the answer) the pendulum will "respond".[6]

Michael Faraday (1853) conducted a series of studies of the then popular psychic feat of table-levitation. A psychic would press his fingertips onto a table, and as he concentrated, the table would begin to move. Faraday constructed an apparatus by which he could tell whether or not the hands moved before the table did. When the pointer which indicated whether the table or the hands moved first was hidden from his subjects, the movements of the table were observed to always lag behind the movements of the hands. When the subjects could see the pointer, none of them were able to get the table to move. Faraday concluded that the table moved because it was pushed, yet he stated that, "The parties with whom I have worked were very honourable. It is with me a clear point that [they] do not intend, and do not believe that they move [the table] by ordinary mechanical power."[7]

In 1977 the American Society for Psychical Research announced in the *Parapsychology Review* (September–October, p. 9) that it was prepared to lend equipment for studying table levitation to any serious group wishing to use it. The equipment consists of a table large enough for four people and a polygraph which attaches to it so that any levitation is automatically recorded along with readings of pressure on the sides or surface of the table. Thus, table levitation has not entirely disappeared as a matter of parapsychological interest, despite Faraday's work.

Other "psychic" phenomena can also be explained in terms of processes similar to those already discussed. This does not mean that the explanation is necessarily correct. It only means that until such possible normal explanations can be eliminated, there is little reason to fall back on paranormal ones.

Concluding Comments

Our conscious experience is often based on information of which we are not aware. There is a strong temptation to assume that we know whether or not we have been exposed to

---

[6] These are the same kinds of muscular responses exploited by conjurers to do "contact readings". This was discussed earlier on page 73. Further information about dowsing is available in Christopher (1970), Randi (1979b), and Vogt and Hyman (1959).

[7] This account, and the quotation, were reported in "Science and the citizen", *Scientific American*, 1975, **232**(1), p. 53. See also Faraday's (1853) own account.

information about some event or other; that our memories are accurate; that our experiences are veridical. The very fact that all three of these assumptions are not correct, at least not all the time, must give the cautious observer pause when he draws conclusions about his experience. Before one makes a leap of faith to paranormal explanations, one should be careful to become familiar with the sometimes seemingly bizarre products of normal cognition. I cannot resist ending this chapter with colleague Graham Reed's remarks in which he makes the same point, but so much more eloquently:

> For if cognitive processes are constructive, interpretative, and problem-solving in nature, then there can be no question of objectively 'correct' . . . perceptions and memories. It is no longer mystifying that our recollections of a place or person may turn out to be sadly amiss. We need not invoke reincarnation to explain why we "recognize" something we have not previously encountered. We need not rely upon spiritualism to explain why we occasionally "see" somebody who is not there or "hear" our name called when no living person has called it. Our cognitions are dynamic, and each of us is continually constructing his own models and arriving at decisions according to his experiential history and his personal schemata. It is to be expected that discrepancies will occur—both between and within individuals. (1972, p. 162.)

CHAPTER 5

The Fallibility of Human Judgement

The empiricist thinks he believes only what he sees—but he is much better at believing than at seeing.

G. Santayana[1]

All men are applied scientists: Very few are philosophers or ideologists of science.

R. A. Shweder[2]

A VISITOR to a beautiful old wooden church thinks to himself how sad it would be if the church were to catch fire. Three months later the church burns to the ground, and the former visitor is struck by the possibility that he had experienced precognition. A "receiver" in an ESP study experiences success greater than one would expect "by chance", and a parapsychologist concludes that ESP is operating. A newspaper reader notices that his horoscope predicts he will receive an unexpected sum of money and later that day he wins the sweepstakes. He increases his faith in astrology.

Humans continually, and almost automatically, seek to find explanations for events around them. While we may often be curious about everyday phenomena which seem mysterious, we are most likely to be motivated to find causal explanations when events defy our primitive beliefs. A door that opens by itself is upsetting if no one else is around; if no breeze is detectable, and if no mechanical contrivances are attached to the door, the average person might experience considerable fear. Most people, particularly those who have difficulty tolerating ambiguity, will want to find an explanation for the event. In mysterious circumstances, when reason seems to fail, recourse may be made to a transcendental belief system, which may be able to furnish a paranormal explanation for the event (e.g. the activity of ghosts). Mental set will affect the eventual conclusion. Transcendental explanations are more likely to arise if the door is in a centuries-old castle in Europe and the individual is alone at night than if the door is to someone's apartment in a modern apartment building and the event occurs in the middle of the day. In the first case, the timid may resort to prayer, in the second, they will probably call the building superintendent.

In the last chapter the ways in which our senses and memories can mislead us and how this can lead to paranormal interpretations of experience were discussed. This chapter will show how our reasoning processes themselves are subject to error and bias. These failings undoubtedly contribute to the imputing of paranormal explanations to normal events.

Probabilistic reasoning is necessary whenever we are faced with decision-making under conditions of uncertainty, uncertainty about the weather, uncertainty about the course a disease will take, uncertainty about an enemy's intentions, or uncertainty about what we saw flash across the sky. Before drawing conclusions, we have to consider the relative likelihoods of various outcomes or explanations.

---

[1] Scheibe (1970), p. 32.
[2] Shweder (1977), p. 618.

Humans are not good at judging likelihood. We often overestimate the rarity of events and then imbue them with wonder because of their rarity. Few people would intuitively realize that for a group of twenty-three randomly chosen people the odds are better than 50–50 that at least two people share the same birthdate. In a group of thirty-five, the probability rises to .85 (Gardner, 1972). A group of bridge players are astonished to see that one of them has been dealt all hearts, another all diamonds, a third all spades, and the fourth all clubs. This is certainly a rare event. But it is remarkable only because it is highly visible. It is no more and no less rare than any other distribution of cards dealt at bridge. (The "perfect" bridge hand just described can in fact be expected to occur *more* frequently than would be predicted by a probability model based on dealing from randomly shuffled deck. This point will be elucidated in a later chapter.)

As Gardner cautioned, estimating the probability that a hidden cause is at work behind a series of apparent coincidences is a difficult task, but, "the number of astonishing coincidences that continually occur as the result of ordinary statistical laws is far greater than even occultists realize" (1972, p. 110).

Bertrand Russell once said that we experience a kind of miracle every time we see a car license plate while driving down the highway. The *a priori* probability of seeing that *particular* license number is very small indeed. Similarly, the probability of winning a lottery is miniscule, but someone always wins it.

Psychologists have conducted considerable research into the human ability to estimate and evaluate probabilities. The overall conclusion drawn from these studies is that people systematically depart from statistical principles when they deal with probabilistic tasks.

The Monte Carlo (or "gambler's") fallacy is one which grips all of us from time to time, even though we may be trained in statistics and "know better". If we play roulette and black comes up twenty times in a row, we get a strong feeling that red is "overdue", that it should come up soon. Yet the wheel has no memory. It does not "know" that the last twenty outcomes were black. Each spin of the wheel, like each toss of a coin, is independent of whatever happened before. Many non-gambling situations reflect this same fallacy: parents of three girls may decide to have a fourth child because they are "due" to have a boy (Offir, 1975).

The statistical principle of "regression towards the mean" is relevant to many everyday situations and can lead the layperson (and even the careless professional researcher) to draw spurious inferences. Consider a somewhat overly-simplified example. Suppose one has ten marbles of equal size, but of different weights. The first weighs 1 gram, the second 2 grams, the third 3 grams, and so on, up to the tenth which weighs 10 grams. The mean weight is of course the sum of these weights divided by 10, or $5\frac{1}{2}$ grams. Suppose all the marbles are put in a hat and one is drawn at random. It happens to weigh 3 grams. It is replaced. If we draw another at random, we know in advance that seven of the marbles weigh more than 3 grams while three (including the one just drawn and replaced) weigh 3 grams or less. There is a greater likelihood of choosing a marble which weighs more than 3 grams; in other words, the weight of the second marble is more likely to deviate from that of the first marble in the same direction that the mean lies.

If the ten marbles were replaced by ten people, and it so happened that the person chosen at random had the third lowest IQ of the ten, then if the whole group were given some kind of training believed to affect IQ positively, the next sample of one is likely to have a higher IQ than the first person, even if the treatment had *no* effect. This effect is very pertinent to various research problems; larger samples are normally used, but the principle is the same.

A related problem occurs if one is dealing with some trait that follows a cyclic variation, such as from a low value to high value and back to a low value. If some treatment is applied when the value of the trait is at its peak, then the next time the trait is measured, it is likely to be lower again, even if the treatment had no effect. The arthritic who, during a bout of particularly severe pain, decides to try wearing a copper bracelet because of its reputedly beneficial power is almost certain to experience improvement simply due to the cyclic nature of the pain and quite apart from whatever effect the copper might have. Yet such a person is likely to attribute the relief to the bracelet and may even invent an explanation; e.g. the copper "absorbs" some of the energy causing the pain.

Consider a real-life example recounted by Kahneman and Tversky (1973). In an Air Force study of pilot-training methods, the goal was to find whether praise for good performance or punishment for bad performance was the more effective method of encouraging improvement in performance. To study the effects of reward and punishment as motivating factors, the researchers looked at performance in the flight following a particularly good flight for which the student pilot had been praised, as well as at flights following poor ones which had been met with verbal punishments. However, any trainee's performance will vary from day to day due to various factors, not all of which are under his control. The flight following a particularly good one is likely to be poorer, and a flight following a poor one is likely to be better (i.e. regression towards the mean). Thus, poor flights, followed by punishment, are likely to be followed by a better flight the next time, while good flights, followed by praise, are likely to be followed by a poorer flight the next time. This would be likely to happen in the absence of praise or punishment, but without knowledge of regression towards the mean the obvious conclusion would be (and was, in the incident cited) that praise produces a deterioration in performance while punishment improves performance. In everyday life, Kahneman and Tversky noted,

> We normally reinforce others when their behaviour is good and punish them when their behaviour is bad. By regression alone, therefore, they are likely to improve most after being punished and most likely to deteriorate after being rewarded. Consequently we are exposed to a lifetime schedule in which we are most often rewarded for punishing others and punished for rewarding. (1973, p. 251.)

The Monte Carlo fallacy and regression towards the mean are but two examples of how events in everyday life can be misinterpreted because of a lack of statistical acumen. Other errors of statistical reasoning which are potentially even more serious are often involved when inferences are made about causality.

The Inference of Causality

The human being is quick to see causal relationships in events around him, and usually he is correct. A hammer is struck against a pane of glass and the glass shatters. The hammer blow is seen to have caused the distruction of the glass. A musician raises a trumpet to his lips and a characteristic note is heard; it is assumed that the musician blew into the horn, causing the sound. A child whistles, and his dog runs to him. One might immediately conclude that the dog came because it had been trained to do so at the sound of a whistle. The first of these examples provides more compelling evidence of causality than the other two, for in that case, one sees the hammer penetrate the window. In the second case, it would be possible that the trumpeter only pretended to play, while the sound was produced by a tape-recorder. In the final example, the assumption that the dog came because of the whistle is still more difficult to justify. Perhaps the whistle, rather than serving as a command, simply drew the dog's attention to the boy's presence, and the dog approached him "of its own volition". The imputation of causality is often based on assumptions that may or may not be true, assumptions that are products of one's learning history.[3]

The child must learn causality. He must learn that there is a cause and effect relationship in the movement of objects, in the production of sound and so on. To the baby, objects have only a transient existence. They exist only as long as they are perceived. By the time the child becomes an adult, he will be capable of creating in his mind novel images and events using mental imagery. As was described in Chapter 2, before concepts of permanence and causality are mastered, the child uses a "magical" basis for interpreting reality. His universe is centred on himself, and he believes that his actions can control or influence objects without need of physical contact. Monte (1975) observed that an infant playing with a dangling crib toy does not understand the relationship between his action of pulling on the string and the movement of the objects above him. Monte suggested that to demonstrate this, one only needs to approach the crib and make some sound that the child likes and he will employ the same "pulling scheme" that worked to make the objects move to try to elicit the sound again.

The newborn child is even without awareness of being separate from the rest of the environment; only when he can distinguish between what is "himself" and what is outside himself can the concept of causality take root. Then, based on his early experience with the environment, the child behaves as if external events occur because of his personal activity. If he observes the moon from two different windows in the house, he assumes that the moon is following him. Yet, this model of the environment quickly proves to be inadequate for dealing with the world, and he has to develop a more accurate one.

Piaget (1954) described six phases in the development of the concept of causality:[4]

Stage 1 (age 0–4 months approximately). *Global causality*. The child has no sense of object permanence. Objects which move out of sight (e.g. a ball which rolls behind a chair) are treated as though they no longer exist.

Stage 2 (age 5–7 months approximately). *Feelings of efficacy*. The child gradually learns to associate certain stimuli (e.g. images and sounds) with one another, but is still unable to distinguish between what happens to him and what happens because of him. His concept of causality is no more than a vague feeling of efficacy when some action of his happens by accident to bring about some desired outcome.

Stage 3 (age 8 months approximately). *Magico-phenomenalistic causality*. From this stage on, the infant begins to realize, without understanding how, that he can control certain things in the environment. By accident he moves a string and hears the sound of the chimes attached to it. Wanting to hear the chimes a second time, he pulls the string again. Like the pigeon that happened to be standing on one foot when food was presented, the child's learning at this point is superstitious in nature:

> Piaget calls this type of causality *magico-phenomenalistic*: "magico" because it is based on the actions of the subject (infant) without regard for external physical connection between cause and desired effect, and "phenomenalistic" because phenomenally (subjectively) observed coincidence in time of two events is sufficient to make them appear causally related . . . this is precisely the same variety of semicognitive operation that Frazer termed sympathetic magic. Power and efficacy lies in your ritual, not in the external environment. And so, the magician believes, does causality. (Monte, 1975, pp. 24–25.)

---

[3] See Bunge (1959b) for a detailed discussion of the concept of causality.
[4] I am borrowing here from Monte's (1975) excellent summary of Piaget's work in this area.

It is this magical thinking that we all experience that provides us with an unconscious which, as Gilmore (1980) put it, "remains confidently magical to this day". It is this same stage of intellectual development into which we regress in periods of severe stress which lead to a breakdown of organized response patterns, and may make reason and logic seem inadequate for the problems at hand (Greenfield and Bruner, 1969).

Stage 4 (age 9–11 months approximately). *Elementary externalization and objectification of causality*. The child learns to view objects outside himself as independent and as causal agents. He is not the sole source of causality; other people can also cause events; he learns he must push a hand away to prevent it from removing an object he desires.

Stage 5 (age 12–15 months approximately). *Real objectification and spatialization of causality*. The child now is able to perceive the causes of events correctly, but is not yet capable of controlling objects at will. A child may touch a toy with a stick to move it (correct spatialization), but does not understand the need to apply directional pressure to the stick to move the toy in the way he wants. Causality has been externalized, but the child has not yet abandoned his attempts to magically control events.

Stage 6 (age 18 months–2 years approximately). *The child in this stage becomes capable of logical thought*. He adopts a kind of "scientific attitude": He can foresee the effect of a potential source of action, and can observe an effect and infer a cause. The development of language allows him to recall past experiences in a systematic manner. In Monte's words:

> It is this capacity to transcend the immediate and the tangible, to search beyond the present to what *might be*, that characterizes the efforts of scientists and children. (1975, pp. 27–28.)

The child develops the concept of causality through trial and error. Certain actions are "reinforced" because they lead to desired consequences. Pushing certain buttons on the radio produces music. Sliding objects over the edge of the table produces sounds. The young child appears to be motivated to find novelty. He is an explorer and novel stimulation that is not so intense to be painful or frightening is his quest.

While causality is a complex concept in modern science (cf. Bunge, 1959b), our everyday conception of causality is so simple that we can easily be misled in our application of it to events around us. To understand how people make inferences of causality, it is necessary to consider the way the nervous system functions in the process of learning.

Two aspects of the way the nervous system "learns" play a direct role in the inference of causality. The first is the special importance of temporal contiguity of two events in learning, and the second has to do with the asymmetry in the effects of "reinforcement" and "non-reinforcement" in a learning situation. Each of these is very important, and each will be discussed some length below.

(a) Temporal contiguity and inferences of causality

The nervous system, human or animal, is constructed so that events occurring in quick succession become associated with each other; this is the essence of learning. There are two basic kinds of learning. One of these, operant learning, has already been discussed in some detail; when an individual produces an action which is followed closely in time by some reinforcer (which might be food, attention from others, reduction of anxiety, etc., depending on the current state of the individual), the action is more likely to recur when a similar need is again salient to the individual. Repeated pairings of the action and the reinforcement produce "learning". The second kind of learning, respondent learning, occurs when the person's body automatically responds to some prepotent stimulus (i.e. a stimulus which produces a particular physical reaction without learning having been necessary, such as a puff of air against the eye, which causes blinking) which has been preceded by a previously neutral stimulus. The neutral stimulus, after repeated pairings of this kind, will come to have the power to elicit the response when it is presented by itself. If a specific sound always occurs immediately before a puff of air is delivered against the eye, the individual will soon begin to blink at the sound alone, even if no puff of air is forthcoming.

Both types of learning are based on temporal contiguity, on the repeated co-occurrence of two events. Reason is not necessary; even the simplest members of the animal kingdom learn in this way. But temporal contiguity is also the basis that people learn to use for making the attribution of causality; it is a necessary condition that two events co-occur, one before the other, before they will be perceived in terms of one causing the other.

When the time lapse between two events is short, "learning" occurs automatically, and in situations when we "know" that no causal connection exists, we have to make a conscious effort to overcome this. Our perception is similarly influenced. If a person bangs on the desk and an instant later the radio comes on, it is natural to "feel" that the former "caused" the latter, although we "know" it did not. More dramatic evidence about the power of temporal contiguity was provided by Michotte (e.g. 1946), who studied the velocities and time delays necessary for the perception of causality when two or more coloured spots in a cartoon film approach each other, touch, and then move away. He found that with certain combinations of velocity and delay (i.e. delay between touching and changing direction), subjects reported an overwhelming impression that one spot struck the other and forced it away, as though the spots were billiard balls in collision. People in this case "know" that their feeling of causality is in error once they stop to think about it.

What happens in real life when, by coincidence, events occur in temporal contiguity? Our knowledge is such that we limit our interpretation of causes between events. We "know" that a strange light in the sky cannot *cause* a war. But if the light is distinctive enough and if it precedes the war closely enough, it may be seen as a portent, a sign of war. I recall as a young child growing up on the Canadian prairies seeing the sky blanketed with an incredible display of Northern Lights one evening. A display of Northern Lights was common enough, but *these* Northern Lights had a distinctive reddish hue. Such an occurrence was rare. It was so rare that one adult said that the last time she had seen red Northern Lights, World War Two broke out a day later. I recall feeling a chill of fear at those words. If the woman's memory was correct and such an awe-inspiring display of aurora borealis occurred just before the outbreak of the war, one can understand how a strong association between the two could be established in her mind. The aurora could not have *caused* the war, but it could be seen as a portent of war. This is the power of coincidence. As G. K. Chesterton wrote, "Life is full of a ceaseless shower of small coincidences. . . . It is this that lends a frightful plausibility to all false doctrines and evil fads."[5]

As was discussed in Chapter 2, magico-religious belief does not embody the concept of coincidence: If a runaway bull gores one person instead of another, the magico-religious attitude demands a reason other than it was a "coincidence" that the person was standing in the bull's path. Even people who presume themselves above magical thinking can find "coincidence" a difficult "explanation" to accept. Was it "coincidence" that a man visiting

---

[5] Cited by Gardner (1972), p. 110.

his mother in another city gave in to her pleading to stay one more day and by so doing avoided dying in an airplane crash? Was it "coincidence" that a woman dreamed about a storm at sea the night before her husband was drowned in the sinking of his fishing boat? "Coincidence" is an unappealing explanation for anyone who has experienced such striking co-occurrences.

Temporal contiguity resulting from the "chance" co-occurrence of two non-related events is probably responsible for more belief in paranormal powers than is any other single thing. We think of someone and a moment later they telephone. We "feel" that someone is looking at us and look around to see that they are. If we are unhappy with "coincidence" as an explanation, the concept of telepathy might readily be invoked.

Consider dreams—millions of people are dreaming at any given moment. Over a lifetime one would expect that by chance alone some dreams of some people would correspond with something that actually occurs the next day. One can easily imagine that each night there are people who have dreams involving the death of friends. There may even be more specific content if the dreamer has been anxious because a relative or friend is ill. If by chance the friend or relative dies that night or soon after, it is difficult for most people having such a dream to attribute it to simple coincidence, just as it is difficult, were we to have 1,000,000 people tossing a coin 20 times each, for the person who makes ten or twenty correct predictions to attribute it to "coincidence", although statistically we could predict that a certain number of people should have that experience.

Similarly, we see something special in "near misses". A person whose lottery ticket is one digit away from the winning number feels that he came very close to winning. Almost being hit by a car also takes on special significance. Venn (1876) put this in perspective;

> Another fallacy arises from the practice of taking only some of the characteristics of such an event . . . I toss up twelve pennies, and find that eleven of them give heads. Many persons on witnessing such an occurrence would experience a feeling which they would express by the remark, How near that was to getting all heads! . . . But in what sense were we near to twelve? The number eleven, of course, is nearer to twelve than nine or ten are, but there is surely something more than this in the person's mind at the moment. . . . The eleven are mentally set aside, looked upon as certain (for they have already happened) and then we introduce the notion of chance merely for the twelfth. (Cited by Cohen, 1960, p. 125.)

There is a story, perhaps apochryphal, about a group of confidence men who persuaded a number of investors to part with a large amount of money. They contacted a lot of people (for purposes of example, say 1,000,000), told them that they had developed a new economic model that accurately predicts stock-market fluctuations, and mentioned one or two stocks which would shortly go up, adding that no one else was making such a prediction. In fact, they had divided up the 1,000,000 people and made about fifty different predictions to fifty groups of 20,000. In some cases, the stock mentioned did go up. Only those people received a second mailing and a second prediction. After three or four series of predictions a few thousand people had had outstanding financial advice and many were lured to sign up and pay handsomely for future advice.

Events which occur independently (e.g. thinking of a person and receiving a phone call from him) will occasionally occur together. The probability of co-occurrence may be enhanced by other factors. A woman reported that she was convinced that ESP exists because once, just as she was about to telephone a friend living in a distant city to whom she had not spoken in some time, the friend called her. Yet, they had agreed the last time they had spoken to get in touch before the friend left for Europe on a certain date. The call occurred at supper time on the evening preceding the latter's departure. Both women worked; thus, the likelihood of calling during the early evening was quite high. The "coincidence", viewed with this information in mind, is hardly surprising.

Apart from the common lack of appreciation of the frequency of coincidences, and apart from the role that our automatic learning apparatus plays in imbuing coincidences with emotional impact, there are two notable "traps" that people fall into when thinking about a coincidence or series of coincidences that they have experienced.

First there is the logical fallacy of *post hoc ergo propter hoc*: "After the fact, therefore because of the fact." Romm (1977) illustrated this problem with the example of the telephone ringing while one is in the shower. The statement "When I am in the shower, the phone always rings" cannot, most people agree, be rewritten as "*Because* I am in the shower, the phone always rings". (Romm referred to, but did not name, a prominent parapsychologist who argues that when people step into the shower, they can unconsciously by means of psychic energy cause other people to phone them!) Yet people often will commit such an error when other events are involved. "I was thinking of her just before she telephoned" becomes "*Because* I was thinking of her, she telephoned" or "*Because* she was in the process of telephoning me, I thought of her".

Secondly, there are coincidences which may recur often for a given individual, but never occur for others. Graphology postulates that people who slant their handwriting to the left have certain personality traits, among them a tendency towards introversion. Although there may be no connection between handwriting and personality, there are likely to be introverted people among those whose handwriting slants to the left. If a person with such handwriting who happens to be introverted and knows it has his writing analysed by a graphologist and is told that he is introverted, he may be impressed by graphology. If he subsequently has his writing studied by other graphologists and they also tell him he is introverted, he is likely to believe graphology gives a reliable analysis. He would have no knowledge of all the others who write as he does and do not consider themselves to be introverted. Goldberg (1979) referred to this same point in the case of astrology. Some people who are "Virgos" *do* have the characteristics attributed to Virgos, and they will continually encounter amazing accuracy in character assessment whenever they are analysed by anyone versed in astrology. They may be told their sun sign on the basis of obvious aspects of their personality or vice versa.

(b) Asymmetry in the effects of positive and negative outcomes and inferences of causality

Why should coincidence have the effect it has if the coincidence is not often repeated? Many wars break out without brilliant displays of reddish aurora. The occasion that I first saw such a display, war did not break out. Yet I know that whenever I shall see the sight again, the woman's words will come back to me, and I may automatically shudder at the (unconscious) prospect of war. Why was this reaction not "extinguished"? True, I have not had a lot of subsequent pairings of red aurora and no war. But it would take more than one or two occurrences of red aurora without war before I would forget the emotion engendered by that first incident. There is the crux of the matter. In general, associations which are built up on the basis of a single emotionally-charged pairing are not undone by a single or even several non-pairings.

If a person is once attacked by a dog and develops a fear reaction (phobia) in consequence, a single instance of putting the person in proximity with the dog without the dog attacking him will not "undo" the association which was so rapidly built between dogs and fear or pain. A non-pairing does not have the same (but opposite) effect of a pairing. A positive instance (A followed by B) creates some kind of representation in the nervous system which is clearly not eliminated by a single, or even several, negative instances. This simple fact accounts not only for the durability of partially-reinforced behaviour (i.e., when reinforcement follows only some, not all instances of the behaviour), but in all likelihood accounts for the inherent lack of appreciation for negative occurrences (i.e. non-pairings) that typifies human thought as well.

We tend to remember only those times when an emotionally salient event A was followed by another appropriate emotionally salient event B and forget the times that A occurred without B. We may dream ten times a year about the death of an elderly parent and if one of these dreams occurs shortly before the person dies, we may become convinced that the dream was a portent of the person's death and remember the conjunction of these two events. We forget the dreams which were not reinforced. In the same manner, popular psychics like Jeanne Dixon are assured of success.[6] They make many predictions, most of which are vague, and some are bound to "come true". People forget the much larger number that are not confirmed by events.

Over three and a half centuries ago, Francis Bacon drew attention to this same tendency:

> The human understanding, when any proposition has been once laid down . . . forces everything else to add fresh support and confirmation. . . . It is the peculiar and perpetual error of the human understanding to be more moved and excited by affirmatives than by negatives. (1620/1902, pp. 23–24.)

If one event is always quickly followed by another (we press on the light switch and the light comes on) we can easily and usually correctly identify the cause. When the joint occurrence of two events stands out against a background in which neither event has occurred alone, a single joint occurrence may lead us to accept that there is a causal relationship between them (Jenkins and Ward, 1965). However, if each of the events are also observed to occur independently, their joint occurrence could be simply adventitious. How can one judge whether there is a causal link in such a case? One has to judge whether the frequency of joint occurrence is greater than one would expect by chance if the events are independent. One must try to judge the degree of covariation, or *correlation*, between the two events. There is the inherent possibility that although the degree of correlation is substantial, it may be due to the presence of a third variable. If, as was once claimed, the incidence of poliomyelitis is correlated highly (and negatively) with the viscosity of asphalt, it is not likely that there is some *causal* relationship involved. Polio is more likely in hot weather, and asphalt is less viscous in such weather. The correlation is caused by each variable having a relationship with a third variable.

There is reason to be pessimistic about the ability of people to detect and judge correlations. Smedslund (1963) examined correlational ability by presenting subjects with 100 cards. On the upper half of each was written + A or − A, and on the lower half, + F or − F. The subjects were nurses, and they were asked to judge whether the presence (+) or

---

[6] In one famous case, Dixon is credited for a prediction she did not make, the prediction of President Kennedy's assassination. In 1956 her prediction was this:

> "As for the 1960 election . . . it will be dominated by labour and won by a Democrat. But he will be assassinated or die in office, although not necessarily in his first term."

In 1960 she contradicted her 1956 prediction stating that John Kennedy would fail to win the presidency, and suggested that Richard Nixon would win (Tyler, 1977).

absence (−) of a symptom (A) had any relationship to the presence or absence of a disease state (F) on the basis of the cards. Thirty-seven cards bore + A + F, thirty-three bore − A + F, seventeen bore + A − F, and the remaining thirteen bore − A − F. The subjects were allowed to see the cards as often as they wanted, to arrange them as they wished, and to make tabulations using the pencil and paper provided. About 85 percent concluded that A and F were related. Only two correctly concluded that there was no relationship, and two others gave up altogether. The majority of those who judged that a relationship existed gave as their reason the fact that the number of + A + F's was the largest or was large. They did not make a comparison between the proportion of times + A occurred with + F and the proportion of times − A occurred with + F. As Smedslund concluded, the data indicate a general absence of correlational reasoning on the part of the subjects. Their approach was non-statistical in nature, and they were too greatly influenced by the number of + + cases. As we shall see, the exclusion of "failures" (i.e. in this situation, − A + F and + A − F cases) is very typical of the human observer.

Were Smedslund's study an isolated example, one would hesitate to draw generalizations from it, but it does not stand alone in its conclusions. Other studies using different tasks have had similar results. In one such study (Ward and Jenkins, 1965), the events to be judged strongly suggested only the operation of chance. Subjects were required to judge the amount of control exerted by cloud seeding on rainfall. One group of subjects was given a serial presentation of the events (seeding or no seeding followed by rain or no rain), while subjects in a second group saw only a tabulated summary, and subjects in a third group were given the serial presentation followed by the summary. Only when the subjects saw the summary alone did a majority make judgements which were in line with the actual probabilities instead of with the frequency of positive confirming events. The authors concluded that the presentation of summary information, to be effective, has to be provided when the subjects first begin to assimilate the information. It has little influence after the trial by trial presentation (which is typical of the occurrence of events in the real world) has taken place.

Such "illusory correlations" (to use Chapman's (1967) term) are also facilitated by taking "resemblance" to be an index of co-occurrence probability: things which *seem* to "go together" are *seen* to go together (Shweder, 1977; Tversky and Kahneman, 1974). People make attributions about the character and motivations of other people as a means of "explaining" their behaviour. We see a man lurching down the street with an empty whiskey bottle in his hand, and we readily judge that inebriation is responsible for his incoordination; we perhaps also judge the person to be an alcoholic, and may go further in our character assessment. Our attributions in such a case are a function of our beliefs about "what goes with what". The man's behaviour "goes with" drunkenness and alcoholism. Both professional researchers and laypeople have been found to be misled by resemblance. In one study involving clinical materials (Chapman and Chapman, 1969) subjects were presented a series of paired stimuli. Each pair consisted of a statement of a patient's emotional problem and a response ostensibly made by the patient to a psychological test instrument (the Rorschach test). The subject was required to estimate at the conclusion of the series which kind of test response was most closely associated with each emotional problem. Their answers did not reflect the co-occurrence of a given problem and a given response; they instead reported that the response which had the highest "associative" connection with the patient's stated problem also had the highest frequency of co-occurrence. For example, although patients who were described as non-violent had given more "aggressive" responses than patients described as violent, subjects concluded that there was a high correlation between aggressive responses and violent personalities. Items which "went together" conceptually were seen to co-occur, quite contrary to the evidence to which the subjects were exposed. When these subjects were shown a "valid" but not "obvious" sign of homosexuality paired in 100 percent of cases with homosexuality, and an "invalid" sign popularly associated with homosexuality paired only randomly with homosexuality, the subjects saw a correlation between the invalid sign and homosexuality disproportionately often. The conclusion is straightforward: People "lack an abstract concept of contingency that is isomorphic with the statistical concept" (Ward and Jenkins, 1965, p. 240), and the failure to adequately assess the degree of relationship between events when information is presented on a trial-by-trial basis, as it generalizes to real life, persists even when the events are such that it must be clear that "favourable" outcomes could occur by chance.

In situations where people are not exposed to actual data which would allow them the opportunity to correctly estimate co-occurrence probability, they rely on their memories and on what Tversky and Kahneman (1974) have called the "availability heuristic". Using this heuristic, or "method of discovery", one judges the probability of an event by the ease with which one can imagine or recall similar occurrences. If asked whether skin cancer is more or less frequent than stomach cancer, the individual may, using this heuristic, base his response on the number of instances of each with which he is familiar. Sometimes the availability heuristic will generate correct results, since instances of frequent events are usually easier to recall than infrequent ones. However, the degree to which one can recall instances is influenced by factors which have no relation to their likelihood, and when such influences occur, the judgement will be in error. Such influences include:

(a) *Biases related to retrievability of instances.* Recent instances are more likely to be recalled than those that occurred some time ago. The risk of having a car accident may seem greater after one has just witnessed an accident, reflecting both the proximity of the event, and its salience for the observer. Some instances are easier to retrieve than others. Tversky and Kahneman (1973) demonstrated this by presenting subjects with lists of well-known personalities and then asking them whether a given list contained the names of more men or more women. When the list included the names of men who were relatively more famous than the women, or vice versa, subjects concluded, erroneously, that the sex that had more famous names was more frequent. Thus the salience of instances can influence availability. We can more readily recall instances when our dreams were "prophetic" than instances when the dream seemed prophetic but did not prove to be. In consequence, it may seem to us that the class of "confirmed" prophetic dreams is larger than the class of "non-confirmed" prophetic dreams. (This of course relates back to the difficulty of learning from non-confirming instances.)

(b) *Biases of imaginability.* When one has no instances of a class of events in memory, one typically generates several instances and judges the probability by the ease with which the generation occurred. The social psychologist who can imagine a lot of possible errors in an ESP experiment is more likely to consider that there is a high probability of error in the conclusions drawn from an ESP experiment than a person who is not familiar with such possibilities.

Yet, why do we not learn through our experience that our judgement is sometimes flawed and that we do not regularly take into account disconfirming evidence? Why do we continue to rely on heuristics such as that of availability? Tversky and Kahneman (1974) argued that these errors are the result of a learned process which is *generally* but not always accurate. Instances of large classes are more readily recalled than instances of small classes; associative connections between events are reinforced when they frequently co-occur and likely events are more easily imagined than unlikely ones. As for correlation, it is not an intuitive concept. It involves a comparison between two relationships (Is the probability of observing B when A is present greater than the probability of observing B when A is absent? The relationship between A and B must be compared with the relationship between not-A and B). Shweder (1977) argued that people have the capacity to think correlationally, but neither the training nor the inclination to do so. (Indeed, even subjects who are pretrained against making the error of illusory correlation have been found no less likely than untrained groups to make such errors (Kurtz and Garfield, 1978).)

The most important reason that correlational thinking is so difficult is that the relevant information is processed and stored in terms of frequencies rather than as probabilities (Estes, 1976; Inhelder and Piaget, 1958). People have great difficulty in using disconfirming information gained from the non-occurrence of an event given that the "predictor event" has occurred, yet this information is essential for the calculation of probabilities. In real life, information is usually presented to us in a serial fashion; we would have to keep a running tally of positive and negative instances in order to establish probabilities. Furthermore, we would have to be exposed to and attend to the occurrence of all alternative events. However, we do not live in a world characterized by conditionally independent data; that is, we are not exposed to a series of outcomes which were preceded by event A, and a series of events not preceded by A (Einhorn and Hogarth, 1978). If a person experiences ten instances where someone threatens suicide, the person's reaction to those threats may affect the outcomes. People do not tabulate a contingency table saying that six of the ten times that people threatened suicide, they did not carry it out. The person making the judgement most likely responds to the threat in a way which makes the suicide less likely; he helped the potential suicide victim deal with his problems. In addition, the person will have little information to judge how many times suicide occurs without a prior threat, since the victims in such cases may have threatened suicide to someone else.

The Illusion of Control

Another source of error in our interpretations of causes of events is what has been referred to as the *illusion of control*. Langer (1975) cited evidence that the more similar a chance situation is to a skill situation, the greater the likelihood that the individual will see himself as having control over what are, objectively, chance-determined events: Participants in a lottery who were allowed to choose their ticket were less likely to take the opportunity to resell their tickets than those who were not allowed this choice. Moreover, while the tickets each cost the participants one dollar, the subjects who had chosen their tickets demanded on the average $8.67 in the event of resale, compared with the $1.96 demanded by subjects in the no-choice condition. Thus, those in the choice condition presumably evaluated their likelihood of winning as being much greater than did the other subjects. Subjects in another study were found to place more daring bets before dice were rolled than after the dice were rolled but before the outcome was known (Strickland, Lewicki, and Katz, 1966). Perhaps they believed that through wishing or mental effort they could influence the way the dice were thrown. In another study, Langer and Roth (1975) found that by having subjects predict the outcome of a coin toss and then giving them false feedback about the outcome, beginning with ostensible success which declined in frequency over time, subjects were more likely to perceive the situation in skill-oriented terms. They perceived themselves as better at the task than did subjects who were given either random feedback or an ascending sequence of successes, and they remembered more successes on the experimental trials, and predicted significantly more successes on future trials. The "ascending success" group was consistently more likely to view the task as depending on chance than was the "descending success" group. (This finding should be kept in mind when discussing "chronological decline" of ESP ability—the highly reliable observation that good ESP subjects decline in ability over time. Their belief that they were using paranormal powers may come about because of the initial success and then be resistant to the effects of declining success.) Langer and Roth concluded,

> It appears that the motivation to see events as controllable is so strong that the introduction of just one cue, a fairly consistent sequence of wins . . . is enough to induce an illusion of control over the task of coin flipping even in sophisticated subjects. (1975, p. 955.)

Note that in this case it was the experimenter, not the subjects, who actually tossed the coins. The more similar the chance situation is to a skill situation, the more likely it is that the task will be misperceived as involving skill. Thus, if the subject were to do the tossing presumably he would have even more confidence that he could influence the coin, even if steps were taken to ensure that he could not do so by means of systematically tossing it in a certain way (e.g. beginning with the coin heads up on his thumb, and flipping it one foot into the air. Such procedures actually do influence the proportions of heads and tails observed.)

Ayeroff and Abelson (1976) extended Langer's analysis to the examination of factors which might increase the tendency to believe in ESP. Sender—receiver pairs tried to mentally transmit one of five possible symbols from one to the other on each of 100 trials. After each trial, each subject indicated whether or not he believed a "hit" had been made. It was found that those subjects randomly assigned to the role of sender had higher belief in their success than did receivers. The pairs showed higher belief in success if they themselves chose the set of symbols to be used and the sender shuffled and dealt the deck of symbol cards for the trial. Subjects who had been in communication with each other during a warm-up also had higher belief in their own success than did subjects without this experience. While actual success rate was at the chance level, the objectively irrelevant situational variables had great power in producing strong feelings of skill at ESP. In almost 60 percent of trials in the involvement/communication experience groups, one or both felt a "success".

Other studies (Benassi, Sweeney and Drevno, 1979; Jones, Russell, and Nickel, 1976) have found the degree of general belief in the paranormal to be related to subjects' estimates of their own success in a psychokinesis experiment, even though actual success was at the chance level. The more the subject believed in the paranormal, the more likely he was to conclude that he was being successful in the PK task.

In evaluating their rate of success, subjects undoubtedly develop illusory correlations, focusing more on positive 'hits' than on 'misses'. Jenkins and Ward (1965) in the context of a study of correlational influence concluded that subjects do not discriminate between the ability to predict outcomes and the ability to influence them. Illusory correlations between prediction and success are taken to indicate that their influence attempts are having some effect.

The Illusion of Validity

The amount of confidence people have in their predictions typically depends on the extent to which the predicted outcome is representative of the inputs. Tversky and Kahneman

(1974) referred to this as the *illusion of validity*. They found, for example, that people are more confident about predicting the final grade point average of a student whose first-year marks are all Bs than of a student with many As and Cs. Yet, high consistency of input information usually reflects highly correlated or redundant input, which in fact leads to lower accuracy than if the inputs are independent. Redundancy in inputs decreases accuracy but increases confidence. This is a serious problem in the domain of clinical judgement. A clinician may often be more certain of his diagnosis when two or more test results are very similar although this might be expected since the two tests may be redundant in what they are measuring. Of course, independent confirmation of the results of a test should add to one's confidence in the interpretation of the first. The problem is that we often forget to even consider the extent to which two results do not give us independent evidence in many situations.

Slovic Fischhoff and Lichtenstein (1977) concluded that there is one generalization that can be made: People tend to be overconfident in their judgements. This overconfidence continues because feedback is often impossible to obtain or because feedback is distorted to make it fit the predictions. As an example of the latter, people asked to recall their predictions about past events remember a higher proportion of their predictions as correct than is really the case (Fischhoff and Beyth, 1975).

Summary and Concluding Comments

People sometimes make erroneous judgements about events because of a lack of understanding of certain statistical principles such as regression towards the mean. However, once such principles are understood, most of us continue to make the same errors in our everyday analysis of events because we usually do not approach our experiences in an analytical way; we fail to see that many common situations involve the statistical principles learned about and used in the classroom and the laboratory. The same applies to inferences about correlation and causality. Regardless of the degree of statistical acumen we possess, the "feeling" that one event has caused another, because of their close temporal contiguity, and the difficulty we have in processing data in terms of probabilities rather than frequencies, often lead us into error. In general, we will not learn about our errors. Our correlational deficiencies do not interfere greatly with adaptive everyday life because in general, events which are highly contingent in a statistical sense on some antecedent also tend to follow that antecedent closely in time (Jenkins and Ward, 1965). In other words, we do not normally need to rely on correlational reasoning; temporal contiguity normally is enough to correctly inform us about which events are related to each other.

This leaves us vulnerable to error, however. If a physician or nurse notices on two or three occasions that during the full moon period the delivery room was unusually busy, it is easy to come to believe that the birth rate is somehow affected by the lunar cycle.[7] It is easy to read precognition into dreams when we are not influenced in our judgements by the many such dreams that are not "confirmed" by later events. We may think we can make people turn around by staring at their backs; we fail to take into account the many times that this does not succeed. Horoscopes whose predictions were confirmed establish the efficacy of astrology in our minds, regardless of how many astrological failures we have experienced.

Anyone who seriously wishes to evaluate his own "paranormal" experiences *must* be

---

[7] See Abell and Greenspan (1979), "The moon and the maternity ward".

aware of all this. Yet, awareness is not enough. As in the case of other judgemental and perceptual errors we often persist in drawing illusory correlations and in falling victim to the illusion of validity even when the illusory character is recognized. Good researchers have learned not to trust their own judgements; experiments are run using control groups in order to provide an objective basis for judging the effects of experimental treatment relative to non-treatment.[8]

The inability or disinclination to make correct correlational inferences from experience accompanied by the universal inclination to look for symbolic and meaningful relationships among objects and events is the basis of magical thinking, a form of thinking which is as characteristic of our everyday mental activities as it is of "primitive" peoples (Shweder, 1977). People have considerable difficulty in organizing information into a format that is amenable to correlational inference, and, Shweder argued, because of this difficulty most people rely on likeness to estimate co-occurrence likelihood:

> Magical thinking does not distinguish one culture from another. Resemblance, not co-occurrence likelihood, is a fundamental conceptual tool of the everyday mind. (1977, p. 638.)

We are all prone to see relationships among events where none exist, and such is the basis of much erroneous belief. The cautious student of nature must not fall too quickly for the causal attributions that come so readily to him. A crucial question remains (Einhorn and Hogarth, 1978, p. 414): "If we believe that we can learn from experience, is it possible to learn that we cannot?"

---

[8] The idea of using a control group to provide information about non-occurrences developed relatively recently in our history (Boring, 1954), and the notion of equating experimental and control groups through randomization prior to applying the independent variable came about only in the twentieth century, through the work of R. A. Fisher (Einhorn and Hogarth, 1978).

CHAPTER 6

Science or Pseudo-science:
The Case of Parapsychology

"No amount of experimentation can ever prove me right; a single experiment can prove me wrong."

Albert Einstein[1]

"It is . . . a good rule not to put over much confidence in the observational results until they are confirmed by theory."

Sir Arthur Eddington[2]

SCIENCE may be the only form of human endeavour about which we can say with confidence that we have made real progress. Politics, religion, and ethics have not changed a great deal in substance over the centuries, and it is difficult to judge whether the change that has occurred in these fields represents real advancement (Harris, 1970). But science, both pure and applied, *has* advanced. We understand much more about life, and so, for instance, smallpox has been almost eliminated from the planet. Thanks to science we can have light in our homes 24 hours a day. We have achieved flight, we have harnessed the energy of the atom. The list seems almost endless. Applied science has given us powers to control the environment barely dreamed of by the priests and magicians of the past.

Why is science so successful? Because it demands logical consistency and empirical validation rather than simple opinion and oracular pronouncement. Modern science began around 1500, according to Boulding (1980), when a small sub-culture developed in Europe, distinguished by the high value it placed on curiosity and upon testing expectation against experience. In addition,

> . . . a high value [was] placed on a curiously uneasy combination of logic and imagination in forming theories . . . with testing as the selective factor. Without fantasy, science would have nothing to test; without testing, fantasy would be unchallenged. Testing comes both by logic and by organized input of information from outside the person, from the senses directly, and from the trustworthy records of others. (Boulding, 1980, p. 832.)

Karl Popper, in *The logic of scientific discovery* (1935/1959), emphasized the importance of testing in science:

> Our method of research is not to defend [our theories], in order to prove how right we were. On the contrary, we try to overthrow them. Using all the weapons of our logical, mathematical, and technical armoury we try to prove that our anticipations were false. . . . (p. 279.)

> Bold ideas, unjustified anticipations, and speculative thought are our only means for interpreting nature. . . . And we must hazard them to win our prize. Those among us who are unwilling to expose their ideas to the hazard of refutation do not take part in the scientific game. (p. 280.)

---

[1] Cited by Truzzi (1979, p. 26).
[2] Cited by Flew (1980).

Theories, Popper said, are not verifiable, but they can be corroborated to a greater or lesser degree. A theory is corroborated if it stands up to tests which could well have shown it to be false, and the more precise the theory, the better it can be corroborated because it is easier to detect its falseness if it is false.

Popper added,

> One of the reasons we do not accord a positive degree of corroboration to the typical prophecies of palmists and soothsayers is that their predictions are so cautious and so imprecise that the . . . probability of them being correct is extremely high. (1959, pp. 269–270.)

However, more recent analyses suggest that the strict falsificationist view is probably inadequate as a description of the prime method of science. It is too simplistic. Were such falsificationism to have been strictly followed, some very general scientific theories of great merit would have been ruled out. (Even Popper himself now insists that he never espoused strict falsificationism, and that this usual interpretation of his arguments in *The logic of scientific discovery* was misleading (Brown, 1977).)

Science is not easily defined. It is not just a body of knowledge, of "truth", since what is considered to be "knowledge" at one point in time may well be considered to be "error" at a subsequent time. It is not just the application of logic. Nor is it unstructured research and observation; as Rothman (1970) noted, since the beginning of our species people have observed apples falling and the moon moving across the skies, yet it took a Newton to develop a theory which could account for both events with a common mechanism.

Philosophers of science, having discarded the overly simplistic positivist philosophy of science of the 1930s and early 1940s, have yet to reach consensus on a new philosophy which provides a satisfactory treatment of such crucial concepts as rationality, explanation, objectivity, and so on. Yet, one need not await the development of a new philosophy of science in order to evaluate parapsychology. Its shortcomings will undoubtedly still be shortcomings whatever the revised philosophy of science turns out to be, for its weaknesses are not tied to those parts of the philosophy of science that are undergoing revision.

As was discussed in Chapter 2, the formal pursuit of parapsychology was linked at the beginning to the search for survival of the soul. It is no less the case today that most parapsychologists express the feeling that materialistic views of the universe are too limited, that there is another metaphysical reality which has been too long held separate from science, and that the scientific pursuit of evidence of this spiritual reality, through parapsychological research, will ultimately lead to an integration of materialistic and spiritual beliefs.

The metaphysical beliefs of parapsychologists are not at issue here. After all, many a good scientist who believes that parapsychology is bad science maintains strong metaphysical (religious) beliefs which do not interfere with his work. Yet, such people typically compartmentalize their religious beliefs from those of their science. Parapsychologists find themselves in a somewhat more difficult situation. Rather than compartmentalizing physical and metaphysical beliefs from one another, they are attempting to show that such compartmentalization is not necessary. This creates a certain ambivalence about science for many parapsychologists. On the one hand, the prestige of science, or at least the prestige of the scientific method, is often invoked in their presentation of claims about the paranormal. Yet, they are not unaware of the suspicion of scientists which is aroused whenever metaphysics creeps into supposedly scientific endeavour. Recognizing their tenuous position in the scientific community, parapsychologists often seek to explain the lack of broad acceptance of their ideas by scientists by arguing that their ideas are *premature*, and that eventually, perhaps after another scientific revolution (or "paradigm shift", in Kuhn's

(1970) terms), paranormal phenomena will take their rightful place in the scientific scheme of things.

Since the arguments about parapsychology's ideas being premature are often very forcefully put, it is essential to devote some discussion to the concepts of prematurity and paradigm shifts.

Scientific Revolutions and Premature Ideas

Science is based on presuppositions. The accepted presuppositions will determine what observations are to be made, how these observations are to be interpreted, what phenomena are problematic, and how these problems are to be handled (Brown, 1977). Presuppositions greatly influence whether discrepancies between theory and data will lead to a rejection of a theory. The laws of conservation of energy and of momentum were not rejected because of the discovery that beta particle emission during radioactive decay apparently violates these laws. Such rejection would have acquired a total reformulation of physics. Instead, as Brown (1977) pointed out, this observed counter-instance was treated only as an *apparent* counter-instance, and a hypothetical new and massless particle,[3] the "neutrino", was postulated and endowed with the amounts of energy and momentum needed to balance the conservation equations. It was another 20 years before empirical evidence for the neutrino's existence was forthcoming. Brown (1977) concluded that,

> The decision as to how a discrepancy between theory and observation is to be handled requires a judgement by scientists. The decision cannot be made for them by the simple application of an algorithm, and, as the history of science adequately shows, the decision procedure is fallible. (p. 147.)

This "relativistic" view of science is not accepted by everyone, and yet the history of science seems to justify it. Presuppositions direct us to search for certain kinds of information, while at the same time, the accumulation of evidence which gainsays the presuppositions will eventually lead to their modification. A belief which is scientifically justifiable at one point in time can turn out to have been a false belief at a later time.

Despite what most textbooks and storybooks say, this dialectical interplay between presuppositions and observation has hardly been one of a continual straightline quest after "truth" with deviations from the straight and narrow caused only by error or foolishness (Harvey, 1978). Rather, the evolution of science has been marked by a number of rather sharp discontinuities, or "revolutions", which have markedly altered the set of presuppositions upon which research is based (Kuhn, 1970). Prior to such a discontinuity (or "paradigm shift") discrepancies between theory and data are treated as problems to be resolved empirically and by adjustments of theory, not as falsifications of the theory. However, accumulating discrepancies, coupled with a new theory which can better encompass these discrepant findings, eventually lead to a rejection or reinterpretation of the old theory. The progression from Newtonian to Einsteinian mechanics is one notable example of a drastic change in world-view which radically transformed both theorizing and

---

[3] Originally considered to be massless, there is now some evidence that the neutrino has mass of approximately one-thirteen-thousandth of that of an electron. There is, however, some controversy over the claim. See Robinson (1980).

methodology. The Newtonian formulation was reduced to the status of a sub-set of Einsteinian mechanics.[4]

Kuhn (1970) referred to a structured world-view as a "paradigm". The scientific community becomes attached to a paradigm that has proven very useful in explaining and predicting the environment. Thus, it is not likely to be discarded just because it leaves unexplained a few curious observations. Only when the number and the importance of such anomalies reaches a certain level will it become necessary to consider new paradigms:

> By ensuring that the paradigm will not be too easily surrendered, resistance guarantees that scientists will not be lightly distracted and that the anomalies that lead to paradigm change will penetrate existing knowledge to the core. The very fact that a significant scientific novelty so often emerges simultaneously from several laboratories is an index both to the strongly traditional nature of normal science and to the completeness with which that traditional pursuit prepares the way for its own change. (Kuhn, 1970, p. 65.)

Before one can effectively challenge a current scientific theory, it is necessary to master the relevant tools (e.g. mathematics) required to understand it. When criticism of a particular theory by an "outsider" show gross ignorance and/or gross misunderstanding of the theory, then, of course, the criticisms lose their force. This in itself contributes to a kind of conservatism, since in mastering a theory, one often comes to think in terms of the conceptual framework provided by the theory.

Because ideas at great variance with the existing paradigm are generally ignored or dismissed, from time to time a discovery or theory is rejected which years later, following either an evolution of theory, or an accumulation of corroborative evidence, or advances in measurement capabilities, or perhaps even a paradigm shift, is then embraced as fundamental to our understanding. Stent (1972) referred to such an event as an example of "prematurity" in science. A discovery or theory is premature, he said, if its implications cannot be connected to generally accepted knowledge by a series of simple logical steps. For example, Alfred Wegener, a German meteorologist, argued in 1912 that continents are actually in movement, and the theory he presented to account for this supposed activity anticipated a great deal of what has become basic to the present-day understanding of our planet (Hallam, 1975). Yet, his view did not replace the older conception until the 1960s when new geophysical and oceanographical data made it essential to do so. Until that time, Wegener's continental drift theory had suffered not only neglect, but even the outright scorn reserved for cranks and crackpots. Wegener's theory was obviously "premature". In fact, prior to the 1960s, if an American geologist expressed sympathy for the continental-drift hypothesis he was risking his career, for, as a geologist at the 1928 symposium of the American Association of Petroleum Geologists said,

> If we are to believe Wegener's hypothesis, we must forget everything that has been learned in the past seventy years and start all over again. (Cited by Hallam, 1975, p. 97.)

Wegener was not a geologist or geophysicist. He appeared to geologists as an amateur and was dismissed as such. Yet, as Hallam concluded,

> . . . his position was an advantage because he has no stake in preserving the conventional viewpoint. Moreover, we can see that he was not an amateur after all, but an interdisciplinary

---

[4] Strictly speaking, however, it is not. While it is "correct" for all practical purposes when velocities which are small relative to the speed of light are concerned, even at this level the Einsteinian equations give different results than do the Newtonian equations, but the differences are so minute as to be meaningless from a practical point of view.

investigator of talent and vision who surely qualifies for a niche in the pantheon of great scientists. (p. 97.)

Wegener's case is only one of many. The German physicist Julius Mayer degenerated into madness when his law of conservation of energy was rejected by the scientific world of the 1840s, and Ludwig Boltzman finally committed suicide when his work on the kinetic theory of gases was not accepted. Yet, today the work of Mayer and Boltzman is not only accepted, but eulogized. And everyone knows what happened to Galileo because of the prematurity (more ecclesiastical than scientific) of his theory.

However, in evaluating the way in which the scientific establishment has reacted to radical new ideas, one must be careful not to fall into the trap (described in Chapter 5) of ignoring negative instances. True, the great French chemist Lavoisier erred in refusing to believe that meteorites fall from the sky, despite the claims of many witnesses. True, scientists erred in rejecting the theories of Wegener, Boltzman, Mayer, and others. But how many times was science *correct* when it rejected what appeared to be a crackpot idea? Its record is very much better than it appears when one only considers the times that it was, by its own account, wrong.

Michael Polanyi is one contemporary scientist who has personally suffered the consequences of prematurity. In the second decade of this century, his theory on the adsorption of gases by a solid was "consigned so authoritatively to the ashcan of crackpot ideas that it was rediscovered only in the 1950s" (Stent, 1972). Polanyi himself later argued that such a miscarriage of scientific justice was unavoidable:

> There must be at all times a predominantly accepted scientific view of the nature of things, in the light of which research is jointly conducted by members of the community of scientists. A strong presumption that any evidence which contradicts this view is invalid must prevail. Such evidence has to be disregarded, even if it cannot be accounted for, in the hope that it will eventually turn out to be false or irrelevant. (1963, p. 1012.)

Polanyi's view is not universally shared, but it is an important reminder that science as an endeavour *needs* structure. Scientists cannot seriously investigate every far-fetched new claim on the chance that a small minority of them may prove to be correct. Consequently, the scientist with a novel view is forced to gather considerable evidence before his theory is given serious consideration.

It should be noted as well that the importance accorded to cases of prematurity today reflects the fact that science eventually did come to accept theories which had been viewed as ridiculous in the first instance. Science is conservative but it is not close-minded. It must also be remembered that premature ideas have *not* first been accepted by the public and then later accepted by scientists as is often claimed by proponents of popular beliefs and theories which have not won scientific acceptance. Asimov (1979) has suggested that it has *not* been a case of the "knowing" public versus the skeptical scientific community which has characterized the "errors" of science. With few exceptions, the public, to the extent that it was involved at all in the debate, has sided with the scientific establishment. The public did *not* support Darwin in his fight in defence of his theory of evolution; it was squarely against him, just as there was no public support of Galileo when he was being persecuted. Asimov warned that although there are cases when the public did support the scientific "deviant" and proved to be right (for example, Jenner's claim that his vaccination technique offered protection against small-pox was accepted by the public, which *wanted* Jenner to be right), these cases are few and far between. If we are to learn from history, Asimov added, perhaps a good rule of thumb for deciding what to believe and what to dismiss should be this:

If scientific heresy is ignored or denounced by the general public, there is a chance it may be right. If a scientific heresy is emotionally supported by the general public, it is almost certainly wrong. (1979, p. 66.)

Parapsychology and Prematurity

A common theme running throughout the literature of parapsychology is that parapsychology, like Galileo's heliocentric theory[5] and Wegener's theory of continental drift, is simply premature. The putative anomalies to the current scientific paradigm which have been presented over the years by parapsychologists may well contradict the basic principles of contemporary science, but the day is coming, according to this view, when a new paradigm will replace the current one, and then psi phenomena will readily "fit in". This is, of course, a possibility. Perhaps the theory of extrasensory perception *is* a case of prematurity. But the problem is that one can say the same thing about *any* idea that is not accepted by scientists. We now do believe in meteorites falling from the sky, but we do not believe in vampires. We do believe in anti-matter, but we do not believe in unicorns. And we do believe in continental drift, while we do not believe in perpetual-motion machines, even though many an inventor has darkened the physicist's door over the years with claims of a working perpetual-motion apparatus. Some ideas which run afoul of current scientific belief may in the future be viewed as having been premature; the vast majority will not. However, many parapsychologists are given hope by the idea that another paradigm shift is coming which will vindicate their beliefs. Yet experimental parapsychology was around before the shift to Einsteinian mechanics, and that did not help parapsychology at all (although, as we shall discuss later, some parapsychologists believe that it did). Robert Thouless, former President of the Society for Psychical Research and currently Reader Emeritus in Educational Psychology at Cambridge University, not only espoused the view that parapsychology will be accepted after another paradigm shift has occurred, but he even explained why parapsychologists are made to suffer the slings and arrows of outrageous criticism:

> Kuhn's theory of scientific revolutions contains many illuminations of the problems of parapsychology; amongst others it suggests why we should expect to have critics who deny the reality of the phenomena reported in our experiments and why they will not be convinced merely by increased weight of experimental evidence. . . . We are, in parapsychology, far from the situation of being able to formulate a new paradigm. So we must expect incredulity to persist among our critics, and not expect that this incredulity will be overcome by mere increase of experimental evidence obtained under new conditions of stringency. (1972, p. 101.)

Whatever the applicability of Kuhn's paradigm model, it is safe to say that one cannot take for granted that the so-called anomalies reported by parapsychologists are either real or compelling enough to lead to a significant change in the scientific world view. But for the mission-minded in parapsychology, Kuhn's analysis offers hope:

---

[5] Parapsychologist Lawrence LeShan (1978) commented that parapsychologists find themselves in Galileo's position, when his colleagues refused to look through his telescope. One can understand the reasoning and confusion of Galileo's colleagues, he said. He added that,

> "It is, however, harder to see when the modern scientist, not looking at the facts of parapsychology, simply dismisses them as necessarily false and therefore unnecessary to examine as—for him—they contradict a known fact. He is as confused as were Galileo's contemporaries . . ." (1978, p. 13).

What is required from us is flexibility of mind and readiness to accept paradigm change. When the time is right, the work of Kuhn suggests that the individual who introduces the new paradigm will be young or new to the field. Many of us are neither, so we should not be tempted to see ourselves as the Einsteins of parapsychology, but rather as having the task of preparing his way by increasing knowledge of the field. (Thouless, 1972, p. 102.)

Indeed, Thouless takes over the surface of Kuhn's discussion of paradigm shifts while ignoring the core of Kuhn's treatment. The pressure toward a paradigm shift from a current theory to a brand new theory lies within the current theory itself. When the current theory fails to accommodate data which are increasingly recognized to be important by the proponents of the theory themselves, then a paradigm shift may occur. However, no such discomfort is being displayed by physicists at the present time. As one physicist observed,

> The major difficulty with the notion that parapsychology is going to produce a paradigm revolution in physics is the fact that most physicists are *not* unhappy with basic laws such as conservation of energy. The parapsychologists may be dissatisfied, but that does not produce a revolution in physics. (Rothman, 1978, p. 45.)

It would seem, then, that there is a basic difference between the "anomalies" which have, according to Kuhn, brought about paradigm shifts in the past, and the anomalous data of parapsychology. Parapsychological anomalies for some reason do not get in anybody's way. Particle physicists are not confronted with phenomena that are produced only when a certain physicist is around, or only when someone wants them to be produced. They do not have to keep people who are skeptical about quantum mechanics out of the laboratory. If they did not read the parapsychological literature, physicists would be unaware of any "psi" anomalies that supposedly require explanation.

Parapsychology and Modern Physics

It is only to be expected that any parapsychologist who is attempting to find scientific evidence of the paranormal (as contrasted to those students of the paranormal who view it as something which is not amenable to scientific research because it belongs to a realm of reality where scientific laws do not apply) should look forward to the day when the scientific community accepts psi phenomena as being real. While some, as we have seen, speak of the need for a paradigm shift, others argue that the paranormal phenomena are comprehensible in terms of *current* physical theory.[6] They suggest that the shift to a relativistic, quantum mechanical world-view has brought physics to a position where it shares a common basis with not only parapsychology but also the mysticism of the East.[7]

Since the "quantum mechanical attack" seems to be gaining in intensity, it is worth considering what some parapsychologists are saying in this regard:

> Both physicist and (para) psychologist find themselves on common ground. . . . Indeed, the two pictures of the world as they have emerged from the physicist's and the (para) psychologist's

---

[6] There have even been attempts to explain psi in terms of "everyday" physics. Mathematical physicist John Taylor, having been overwhelmed by Uri Geller's feats, attempted to demonstrate the reality of psi and to explain its basis by looking for evidence of electromagnetic radiation from the brains of people involved in various psi experiments. When he demonstrated that no such radiation was involved, he reversed his position with respect to psi, and declared that it is very doubtful that the psychic phenomena he had attempted to study really exist (see Taylor, 1975; Balanovski and Taylor, 1978; Taylor and Balanovski, 1979).

[7] See, for example, Fritjof Capra's *The tao of physics* (1975).

labours could have been created by one and the same artist. They are companion pieces, conforming to the same style; they suggest the same basic ideas, the identical overall design. . . . (Ehrenwald, 1974, p. 5, parentheses in original.)

. . . the often-held view that [parapsychological] observations . . . are incompatible with known laws is not only out-dated but false, being based on the naïve realism prevalent before the development of modern physics. (Targ and Puthoff, 1977, p. 169.)

The theories about reality . . . that the physicist finds necessary to use are so different that what is impossible and paranormal in one [theory] frequently is perfectly possible and normal in another. (LeShan, 1978, p. 14.)

. . . they have failed to adequately appreciate the substantial shift that has occurred in modern physics from Newtonian to Quantum Mechanics. As Arthur Koestler puts it, they are still entranced by the greatest superstition of our age—the materialistic, clockwise universe of nineteenth-century physics. (Eisenberg, 1977, p. 24.)

Modern physics has reached the stage where the clear outline of a new world-view and methodology are visible, and these provide an "integral understanding" of the world and its psychological and mystical background. With the wider acceptance of such a world-view, new fields of research may be expected to open up and parapsychology may be considered to have become an established science. . . . Opposition arises, however, not only from ignorance of modern physics, but also . . . from adherence to the simple one-level locational view of reality which nature offers . . . for ordinary practical purposes and for minds not yet capable of deeper insights. (Whiteman, 1977, pp. 751–752.)

Ideas emanating from modern physics are often pushed to great lengths to support a belief in parapsychology, and such ideas may appear convincing to the individual totally unfamiliar with relativity and quantum mechanics. Several examples of the attempts to use modern physical theory in the defense of parapsychology merit discussion:

(a) *The theory of relativity and the concept of of simultaneity.* Various parapsychologists suggest that relativity theory, and some of its surprising implications, provide a "normal" basis for psi phenomena. To take one such example, Lawrence LeShan, a psychologist turned parapsychologist, has written extensively about quantum mechanical interpretations of paranormal and mystical phenomena. Consider what he has said about precognition and relativity theory:

. . . we have the normal phenomena of event A occurring before event B from the viewpoint of one observer, the two occurring at the same time from the point of view of a second observer, and event A occurring after event B from the viewpoint of a third observer. It is literally impossible with many events to say whether they occurred simultaneously or in sequence. From the "commonsense" everyday theory about reality, this would lead to precognition and retro-cognition—paranormal phenomena. (LeShan, 1978, p. 14.)

LeShan's comments are misleading. It is true that if two observers, one moving at high speed relative to the other (i.e. two different "frames of reference"), observe two spatially separated events, one may conclude that event A occurred before event B, and the other may conclude that B preceded A. As Gardner explained,

. . . the greater the distance between two events, the greater the difficulty in deciding about simultaneity. It is important to understand that this is not just a question of being unable to learn the truth of the matter. *There is no actual truth of the matter.* There is no absolute time throughout the universe by which absolute simultaneity can be measured. Absolute simultaneity of distant events is a meaningless concept. (1976a, p. 45, italics in original.)

However, when two events occur at the same time at the same location, it can be said definitively that they occurred simultaneously for *all* observers, regardless of how fast they may be moving relative to one another.

What implications does this hold for the possibility of precognition then? *None at all.* LeShan's argument would suggest that somehow an event A which causes (and therefore necessarily precedes) event B in one system, may be seen to *follow* event B in another frame of reference, allowing an observer in the latter frame of reference to perceive the effect before the cause. But that is an incorrect interpretation of relativity theory. Such is *not* the case. Causality is not violated, for relativity theory does *not* suggest that A could *"cause"* B and still appear to have occurred after B.[8] Moreover, it is hard to imagine how relativity theory could be involved in typical precognition experiments. Where are the two frames of reference or the two distant events when one is dealing with a subject making predictions about which card will be turned up next, or which of a series of lights will next be illuminated by a random number generator?

(b) *The EPR paradox.* More complex than LeShan's relativity argument is the suggestion that the famous Einstein–Podolsky–Rosen (EPR) paradox of quantum mechanics may provide an explanation for putative psi processes. This paradox concerns a pair of particles moving in opposite directions and which must always have opposite values of certain properties. Yet it is impossible in principle to determine the value of one of these properties until it is measured, for it seems that only at that instant[9] does "nature" decide what the value is. Then, instantaneously, the other particle, regardless of how far away it now is, must assume the opposite value (Gardner, 1979b).

Some proponents of psi (particularly those who are "paraphysicists", physicists who have become involved in paranormal research) argue that this paradox implies that quantum information can be transmitted virtually instantaneously from any part of the universe to any other (Gardner, 1979b). Thus, information could travel faster than light. While energy, according to relativity theory, cannot move faster than light, *information* could be received at some point, it is argued, before the physical effect upon which the information is based reaches that point.

While paraphysicists take the EPR paradox to support their arguments for the paranormal, other physicists do not share their views. In fact, the possibility of effect preceding cause, which makes no sense logically, is typically seen as something which renders such interpretations of quantum theory very unlikely indeed: d'Espagnat, discussing the enigma of the EPR paradox, commented,

> Must the principle of the finite propagation of signals therefore be abandoned? To that question no rash answer should be given. The principle was introduced as a premise of the theory of relativity, which cannot be made consistent without it. Moreover, signals that outrace light give rise to bizarre paradoxes of causality in which observers in one frame of reference find that one event is "caused" by another that has not yet happened. It turns out, however, that the instantaneous influences that seem to be at work in the distant-correlation experiments do not require such a drastic revision of accepted ideas. (1979, p. 150.)

---

[8] This reversal of order of occurrence of A and B, from the perspectives of two different frames of reference, does not apply to all events. It only applies to events which are distant enough from each other that a causal relationship between them could not exist, i.e. no communication between them could occur unless a signal exceeded the speed of light which, under relativity theory, is impossible (Hawking and Ellis, 1973).

[9] It is important to note that, while the measurement appears to bring about the determination of the value of the property in question, it is never the case that the observer's knowledge alters the outcome of a real measurement. There is no hint of mind over matter (cf. *Scientific American*, July 1978, p. 78).

John Archibald Wheeler, a theoretical physicist whose views have been widely cited, to his dismay, as *supporting* the claims of parapsychologists[10] has spoken very bluntly about the EPR paradox,

> And let no one use the Einstein–Podolsky–Rosen experiment to claim that information can be transmitted faster than light, or to postulate any "quantum interconnectedness" between separate consciousnesses. Both are baseless. Both are mysticism. Both are moonshine. (Cited by Gardner, 1979b, p. 40.)

What is important is not that one can line up experts who take a very dim view of the paraphysicists' attempts to provide a quantum mechanical basis for psi, but rather that there exist many genuine enigmas in quantum mechanics, and that the paraphysicists are engaging in wild speculation in their assumptions that the eventual explanation for these enigmas will support the notion of paranormal processes. No one knows how the EPR paradox will be resolved. There is no justification for arguing that the paradox itself suggests that information can be transferred in a way which makes precognition possible. There is even less justification for such speculation given that, as shall be discussed later in this chapter, a *prima facie* case for the simple *existence* of precognition has not been established.

(c) *Time reversal.* Another argument sometimes put forth to defend the notion that psi forces can be understood in terms of contemporary physical theory is based on the concept of time reversal.

Since it has been assumed by physicists the laws of physics would be just as valid if we imagined time flowing backwards instead of forwards (an assumption which appears to have been violated by recent evidence, see Sachs, 1972), parapsychologist Charles Panati concluded:

> The fact that all fundamental laws of nature give no intimation as to a preferred direction of time should make us realize that precognition—and retrocognition—are not impossibilities. In fact, seeing into the past or the future with equal ease is attributing to nature perfectly symmetrical behaviour. (Panati, 1975a, p. 3.)

Panati's conclusion is based on a complete misunderstanding of the concept of time reversal. The concept of time reversal does *not* lead to the conclusion that effect precedes cause, or that we flit around in "time" going in one "direction" at one moment and in another at another moment.

(d) *The Heisenberg uncertainty principle.* Another quantum mechanical argument used by some parapsychologists involves Heisenberg's uncertainty principle. This principle is based on the fact that every physical measurement involves an exchange of energy between the measuring apparatus and the object that is being measured. Such an exchange of energy will change the state of the object. At the atomic level, a photon of light being employed to "see" a particle will exert a relatively strong force on the particle. It is possible to arrange conditions such that one can measure either the position or the momentum of a particle with precision, but not both. Therefore, one cannot, in principle, predict the path of the particle, since the measurement needed to make that prediction alters its path (Popper, 1959).

Casual, almost flippant, references to this principle are often used to suggest that at the subatomic level determinacy breaks down, that the mind of the observer interacts in some way with the matter being observed, and that physics and metaphysics merge into one. Most parapsychologists who refer to the uncertainty principle appear to have little more than a

---

[10] See, for example, the reference made to Wheeler's work by Lee and Petrocelli (1977), pp. 4–5.

superficial comprehension of physics to begin with, and appear to "latch on" to Heisenberg as a way of demonstrating the "scientific" basis for their position. The reader should realize that the Heisenberg principle is more complex than popular translations of it suggest. It has been much misused among the partially informed.

Popper, who took serious issue with the validity of Heisenberg's discussion of measurement which led to the uncertainty principle, concluded that,

> The immense influence of Heisenberg's imaginary experiments is, I am convinced, due to the fact that he managed to convey through it a new metaphysical picture of the physical world, whilst at the same time disclaiming metaphysics. (1959, p. 452.)

Bunge, too, warned against metaphysical interpretations of Heisenberg's principle:

> Whatever the interpretation that will finally prevail, one thing seems beyond dispute, namely that the present state of quantum theory offers no secure basis to the doctrines asserting that Heisenberg's relations show the haziness of reality, or the ultimate indeterminacy of being and becoming, or the material basis of free will—nor the free will of the material basis. (1959b, p. 240.)

(e) *Tachyons*. There is speculation among theoretical physicists that exist particles which move faster than light. These hypothetical particles, called tachyons, would have to move "backwards" in time to be consistent with relativity theory. This suggests to some proponents of the paranormal that tachyons could provide a basis for precognition, since the tachyons that exist at the present time have come to us from the future. Martin Gardner (1974) pointed out that quite apart from the fact that such particles remain hypothetical at the moment, such particles clearly cannot provide a means of communication, although some physicists looking for tachyons have overlooked this point.[11]

While the EPR paradox, time reversal, the uncertainty principle, and so on have been used in the attempt to explain putative psi forces, there are people within parapsychology itself who are critical of those who make these quantum mechanical arguments. Phillips, a physicist/parapsychologist, wrote in the pages of *Parapsychology Review,*

> Modern physics, to be sure, is concerned with phenomena which can be as bizarre at first as psi, and the two can sometimes resemble each other on a superficial level. But on close inspection, the physics problems turn out to be comprehensible within a powerful and coherent set of ideas which have brilliantly withstood years of testing. (1979a, p. 8.)

Phillips further said that arguments based on some of the more bizarre implications of quantum mechanical theory and relativity are not very appropriate:

> Psychic phenomena take place in situations where . . . physical theory is ordinarily thought to be perfectly adequate. Certainly there are strange effects to be noticed around black holes, and if living beings could exist there it would be interesting to know what kinds of psi they displayed. But what we are primarily concerned with, as parapsychologists, is understanding the levitation of an ordinary table in an ordinary room on this earth. Here even the microscopic non-locality of the wave functions of the atoms (which every physicist accepts) will not help us much so long as the interactions are local. (1979b, p. 25.)

Even Arthur Koestler, also a proponent of parapsychology, admitted that the only *rapprochement* between quantum mechanics and the concept of ESP is a negative one, in that

---

[11] Gardner (1974) pointed to the work of Benford, Book, and Newcomb (1970), who have chastised such physicists for this oversight.

... the surrealistic concepts of the former make it easier to suspend disbelief in the latter; if the former is permitted to violate the "laws of nature" as they were understood by classical physics a century ago, the latter may claim the same right. (1974, p. 281.)

As an example of Koestler's point, consider what Firsoff (1974) had to say in response to arguments that psi phenomena are *a priori* unlikely: Quasars, neutrinos, and wave-particle duality were all *a priori* extremely unlikely, but are now accepted concepts in modern physical theory, so why might this not be the case for psi phenomena as well? However, why not point out that the duck-billed platypus is also *a priori* extremely unlikely? Just because a few things from the immense set of "extremely unlikely" concepts are now accepted gives no support to something else labelled "extremely unlikely". It is extremely unlikely that we shall be struck down by lightning tonight, but should we fear that that event probably will take place?

In summary, despite criticism from some people within parapsychology itself, the quantum mechanical arguments continue unabated, and they tend to give a sort of "respectability" to parapsychology at the same time that they remove the focus of argument between proponent and critic from the mundane world of statistical analysis and experimental design to a plane where it is very difficult for the non-physicist to debate. The fundamental problems remain: Where is the evidence that there is any paranormal process which needs to be explained? Where is the replicable experiment or the reliable "gifted" subject? Where is the theory which specifies when psi must *not* occur, so that differential predictions may be tested?

Is Parapsychology a Science?

Because parapsychologists themselves quickly learned about the inherent unreliability of people's reports about their psychic experiences, they turned to laboratory studies in the hope of *demonstrating* phenomena that they *a priori* believed to exist. Then, using almost endless runs of dice rolls and card predictions, they adduced statistical evidence which they claimed demonstrated the existence of the various psi forces. Just as people who believed in vampires interpreted all sorts of mundane events (the death of a cow, footprints, etc.) as evidence of the vampire's existence, most parapsychologists take non-chance statistical evidence as verification of the operation of something which has, at best, many compelling alternative explanations which compete with it.

But is parapsychology a "science"? Is its methodology scientific? If so, one should have no qualms in accepting parapsychological research. If there really is "something there" to be studied, such research would be very valuable. On the other hand, if there is "nothing there", one would presume that scientific investigation would soon lead researchers to lose interest simply because of the lack of empirical support for their speculation.

Most parapsychological researchers do claim to use scientific methodology. In addition, most of them claim to have strong empirical evidence for the existence of the paranormal. How should such evidence be treated? Is the evidence "scientific"? Or is it merely "pseudo-scientific"?

It is not easy to distinguish science from pseudo-science, partly because science itself is so difficult to define. Philosopher Mario Bunge (1980) has proposed a description of pseudo-science based not just on its methods but also on its accomplishments. Bunge emphasized that it is unrealistic to divide the domain of the quest for knowledge into non-overlapping regions of science and non-science. It is slightly more realistic to view this domain as consisting of a region of an established science, a region of emerging science (proto-sciences) and a region of non-science. In addition, pockets of science exist in the other two segments, and pockets of pseudo-science exist in both the regions of science and emerging science. As Truzzi (1977a) cautioned, it is important not to denigrate those who assiduously abide by the rules of scientific inquiry just because at this point in time we do not accept the data they present as being strong enough to justify acceptance of their claims. At the same time, we should strive to avoid being taken in by those who dress themselves in the cloak of science without either knowledge of or interest in the methodologies and rules of evidence which have come to be accepted as "scientific". It is also important to keep in mind that even within a single discipline, there are great differences among researchers in the degree to which they are devoted to science.

Bunge (1980) has listed these factors as characterizing a pseudo-science: (a) its theory of knowledge is subjectivistic, containing aspects accessible only to the initiated; (b) its formal background is modest, with only rare involvement of mathematics or logic; (c) its fund of knowledge contains untestable or even false hypotheses which are in conflict with a larger body of knowledge; (d) its methods are neither checkable by alternative methods nor justifiable in terms of well-confirmed theories; (e) it borrows nothing from neighbouring fields, there is no overlap with another field of research; (f) it has no specific background of relatively confirmed theories; (g) it has an unchanging body of belief, whereas scientific inquiry teems with novelty; and (h) it has a world-view admitting elusive immaterial entities, such as disembodied minds, whereas science countenances only changing concrete things.

In Bunge's view, parapsychology is a pseudo-science, but unlike most pseudo-sciences, it is a research field, although its research is characterized by weak methods, and it has been unable to establish any "laws". At the end of this chapter, we shall return to consider parapsychology *vis-à-vis* these criteria of Bunge's. In order to do so, however, it is first necessary to examine the workings of parapsychology: its theories, methods, and quirks. Consideration of experimental design problems and statistical analysis will for the most part be left until the next chapter.

A Theory in Parapsychology

1. The body of knowledge

What constitutes a paranormal event? Broad (1962) provided a basis for definition of the paranormal in terms of a set of nine "basic limiting principles" which he said represent the "bottom line" in scientific axioms about the physical world. Among these were:

(i) We take for granted that a person cannot foresee (as distinct from inferring, or being led, without explicit inference, to expect on the basis of regularities in his past experience) any event which has not yet happened.

(ii) We take for granted . . . that a person cannot *directly* initiate or modify by his own volition the movement of anything but certain parts of his own body. (1962, p. 4.)

When an event which is in conflict with one or more of these basic limiting principles can be demonstrated to have really occurred, then, Broad said, one has an example of a genuine paranormal phenomenon. It is the business of psychic researchers, he added, to investigate allegedly paranormal phenomena to try to discover whether they are genuinely paranormal.

Parapsychologists and skeptics alike define the paranormal in terms of events which violate basic scientific axioms such as those referred to by Broad. However, this leaves one with a rather unusual negative definition. As Beloff said in his 1963 presidential address to the Society for Psychical Research (London),

> the field . . . must be unique in one respect at least: no other discipline, so far as I know, has its subject matter demarcated by exclusively negative criteria. A phenomenon is, by definition, paranormal if and only if it contravenes some fundamental and well-founded assumption of science. (Cited by Flew, 1980.)

Boring (1966) also discussed the negativeness of the definitions of the paranormal. He pointed out that it was believed at one time that bats could dodge wires in the dark because they possessed clairvoyance. When a sensory explanation ("sonar") was found, the clairvoyance hypothesis evaporated. This was a success for science, a failure for parascience. Boring continued,

> To prove that ESP exists requires confirmation that communication can and does occur by no known sensory channel. It is easy to establish one's own ignorance of the channel, but not of a universal necessity for the ignorance, which may suddenly evaporate as it did in the case of bats. A universal negative of this sort cannot be proven. Ignorance is too plentiful. (1966, pp. xiv–xv.)

Thus, the first and fundamental problem with parapsychology is the definition of what is *extra* sensory. If extrasensory simply means that information can be received by processes not yet *known* to us, then, as Tinbergen wrote in 1965,

> . . . extrasensory perception among living creatures may well occur widely. In fact . . . the echo-location of bats . . . and the way electric fishes find their prey are all based on processes which we did not know about—only twenty-five years ago. (Cited by Mundle, 1976, p. 159.)

Most parapsychologists would not accept this view of "extrasensory". ESP is currently defined by the *Journal of Parapsychology* as "experience of, or response to, a target object, state, event, or influence *without sensory contact*" (italics added). However, we can never prove that there are not sensory channels of which we are not aware.

Leaving the question of what "extrasensory" means, when one considers the major constructs in parapsychology, it is very difficult to imagine how they might be operationalized and measured. Thakur, while sympathetic to parapsychology, drew attention to the fuzziness of the definition of "telepathy",

> Telepathy is not "communication" in any recognized sense of the term. Since the subject is not aware of being in communication with the agent whose thoughts he is trying to guess; he simply ticks certain numbers on a piece of paper which turn out (by a margin of a percentage point over mean chance expectation), to be the numbers symbolically representing certain pictures that the agent was supposedly concentrating on at a specified time. This coincidence, it might be argued, is what we call telepathy. (1976, p. 106.)

Flew (1980) also recognized the importance of this problem, and underlined the fact that subjects who come up with "extrasensory" information are unable to recognize that they are at that moment receiving information via their ESP "channel", and cannot distinguish it from ordinary guesses or hunches. The laboratory evidence of ESP is limited to extra-chance scoring; it is impossible to tell *which* of the various hits are the "extra-chance" ones (i.e. due to ESP) and which are just "chance".

As mentioned earlier, even Rhine (1974a) was troubled by problems of operationalizing constructs. He despaired of ever being able to demonstrate the existence of telepathy as a distinct process, since clairvoyance, he said, could never be ruled out as an alternative explanation.

Given these problems at the conceptual level, one should not be surprised that parapsychology is devoid of anything approaching a coherent theoretical base, and this after a hundred years of sustained effort. Nor is there a clearly established corpus of empirical evidence in need of theory to organize and interpret. Many a student of the paranormal has been uneasy about this virtually unique lack of progress. In 1909 the eminent psychologist William James, who had devoted considerable attention to psychical research, lamented,

> For twenty-five years I have been in touch with the literature of psychical research, and I have had acquaintance with numerous "researchers". I have spent a good many hours . . . in witnessing (or trying to witness) phenomena. Yet theoretically I am no "further" than I was at the beginning. . . . (Cited by Boring, 1961, p. 150.)

James concluded that parapsychologists must be patient, that progress in this domain would be slow.

Philosopher Antony Flew did not always speak with the profound skepticism that he does today. In 1953 he published his first book, *A new approach to psychical research*, in which he argued that although there was not a repeatable experiment, and though there was a lot of nonsense perpetrated by charlatans, nonetheless one could not dismiss the case as closed. Too many sophisticated and distinguished persons had contributed to the research, and it seemed that at least some of the phenomena just might be real. Yet 25 years later, Flew found himself disillusioned by the lack of progress;

> . . . the research has indeed gone on. In all probability, its sum in the years between is as great or greater than the total for all the years before. Yet it is hard to point to any respect in which the general situation is better now than it was then. Certainly there is still no repeatable experiment[12] to demonstrate the reality of any putative psi-phenomena. (Flew, 1979, p. 3.)

Even Scott Rogo (1972), usually a staunch apologist for parapsychological research, expressed his chagrin at the failure of the laboratory approach to make progress in parapsychology. He appeared to be distressed to the point of advising that parapsychologists should leave the laboratory and return to the observation of psychic phenomena in everyday life.

Beloff, too, is disturbed by the lack of progress, and he has expressed the view that the laboratory evidence is so unimpressive that,

> To me . . . the records of the great sensitives of the past still offer the best assurance we have that psi is not just a mirage or an artifact, even if, in every case, the authenticity of such evidence is less than absolute. (1973, p. 292.)

However, with regard to Beloff's sensitives, it should be noted that not a single person has ever been found who could demonstrate psychic powers to the satisfaction of independent investigators (Hansel, 1980).

In summary, the "body of knowledge" in parapsychology is all but non-existent. There is no general agreement on what constitutes core knowledge, or even on how to define basic constructs. There are no articulated theories,[13] and, after a century of research, no clearly demonstrable phenomena.

---

[12] The problem of replicability is discussed in greater detail later in this chapter.

[13] A new family of theories, called "observational theories" (e.g. Schmidt 1975, 1978; Walker, 1975), have been heralded as providing the foundations of a theoretical framework for parapsychology. The interested reader is referred to the works by Schmidt and by Walker cited above, and as well to a critique of these theories by Braude (1979), who wrote bluntly that

> " . . . the conceptual underpinnings of the [observational theories] are exceedingly weak at best, and . . . the theories themselves seem largely nonsensical and lacking in explanatory power." (p. 349.)

2. The lack of "competition"

Science is partly a cooperative enterprise in which various researchers pool their knowledge and their resources in the quest for the solution to mysteries and problems of mutual interest, but more importantly, science is also competitive (Flew, 1980). Scientists are motivated by both intrinsic and extrinsic factors to try to reach the solution to a problem before anyone else does. This friendly (and sometimes not-so-friendly) competition leads to careful criticism of opposing theories. As each person involved in a search for a particular "solution" examines the claims of progress made by others, it is natural to look for the weaknesses as well as the strengths, and it is this that, on the one hand, ensures that a given individual will try to anticipate all possible criticisms in doing his research, and, on the other, often leads to the quick death of poorly thought out theories, or of conclusions based on data gathered by poorly controlled techniques. Before one risks one's reputation by taking one's theory or set of observations and "running it up the flagpole to see who salutes", one wants to be as careful as possible to make sure that, instead of saluting, people do not simply laugh or turn away.

Unfortunately, parapsychology lacks anything at all that resembles a serious theory and thus lacks *competing* theories (Flew, 1980). There is little or no "competition" among parapsychologists, and thus there is little sorting out of wilder speculation from more conservative notions. In consequence, there is little motivation towards criticism within the field, little effort to demonstrate that a given experiment must have been poorly controlled because its results go against someone's pet theory. Such intra-discipline competition and the critical attitude it spawns is essential to progress; otherwise little distinction is made between the results of carefully designed and well-executed experiments and the results of careless and unsophisticated studies.

One should not be led by these comments to believe that there is *no* critical commentary within parapsychology itself. Indeed, there is a wide diversity of belief about what constitutes "real" psychic phenomena. Leading parapsychologists disagree among themselves. Some, such as Adrian Parker and John Beloff, are almost as critical as the most critical skeptics. Others accept some phenomena and scoff at others. Charles Tart, for instance, who espouses a belief in astral projection, totally rejects dowsing (water-witching) as a paranormal phenomenon (Tart, 1980).

The problem is that such criticism generally tends to be subject oriented. Some parapsychologists uncritically accept the results of research into one particular area of parapsychology, yet reject other studies because they reject the phenomenon upon which those studies are based. The writings of parapsychologist-author Scott Rogo, while not representing the best of what is available in parapsychological literature, nonetheless furnish an all too typical example of how many proponents of parapsychology (a) choose for themselves what is basic in the subject and what is nonsense, and (b) present two opposing viewpoints depending on their audience. Rogo, who believes in most aspects of parapsychology, rejects out-of-hand psychic surgery ("to my mind, there is not one sliver of evidence that psychic surgery is anything more than a shrewd trick, detectable to the trained eye, but clever enough to delude the uncritical" (1976, p. 130)) and the Kirlian process (which is supposed to allow one to photograph aspects of the "human aura"). With respect to the latter, he commented that even respected parapsychologists such as Dr. Thelma Moss and Douglas Dean became involved in research in this area, and that

... the results of these "researches" have been published in journals and have had wide media exposure. My argument, however, is not with Kirlian photography per se, but with many of those engaged in research on the subject. It would seem that there is an antipathy toward correct experimental procedures coupled with a lack of background in either physical science or photography. No wonder incredible results are forthcoming. (1976, p. 139.)

Rogo then discussed a "tightly controlled" study by Dr. William Joiner which was carried out at Duke University, and the results of which were presented at the 1974 convention of the Parapsychological Association. Joiner conclusively demonstrated, said Rogo, that the Kirlian effort is nothing but simple corona discharge. Rogo added,

... despite his findings I am sure Joiner will merely be labelled an iconoclast and that those parapsychologists engaged in Kirlian work will ignore any finding contrary to their own. They will go on taking photographs and revering their bogus auras in awe. . . . People who are involved in psychical research often do not *want* to know the truth. (1976, p. 140.)

However, Rogo sometimes dances a curious dance.[14] In 1977 he wrote in the pages of *Parapsychology Review* that parapsychologists have a tendency to be *too* skeptical (Rogo, 1977a). They have, he says, a culturally conditioned "will to disbelieve". Yet that same year writing for a more skeptical audience, he said,

The notion that parapsychologists are deaf to the voices of their critics is an unfounded myth. . . . No one, I can assure you, is more aware of the controversial and disputable nature of ESP and PK than the parapsychologist himself. (1977b, p. 44.)

and,

As a science, parapsychology has nothing to apologize for. In fact, it represents the Western scientific ethic at its best. (1977b, p. 44.)

3. Response to critical views and negative evidence

Discussions of a particular aspect of parapsychology by its proponents (apart from those of a few "critical" parapsychologists) rarely even mention the existence of negative evidence or give any serious consideration to critical views. The parapsychological literature abounds with examples of major articles and books which seem to treat some area of parapsychology exhaustively, without even making simple reference to alternative normal explanations or to criticisms of methodology made by others.

As an example, and this is only one of a great many similar instances, in the July 1958 issue of the *Journal of the American Society for Psychical Research* was reprinted an article by a chemist, M. R. Coe, which had originally appeared in a psychology journal. The editors of the psychology journal had witnessed Coe's own mastery of fire-walking, of plunging of his fingers into molten lead, of popping red-hot coals into his mouth, and many related activities. Coe described how he had mastered these things and provided a "scientific explanation" for them. He concluded that neither trance states nor paranormal abilities are involved:

No paranormal explanation is necessary for fire-walking and related behaviours. With incandescent objects, protection is afforded by the spheroidal condition assumed by liquids. With glowing coals, a combination of spheroidal condition, cutting off of oxygen, liquid absorption, and skin thickness operate to prevent a person from being burned. (p. 97.)

---

[14] See also pp. 119, 123, 126, 141.

It is to that journal's credit that it reprinted the article. Many other people have also provided demystification of firewalking, showing that it requires pluck, care, and confidence, but nothing else. In fact, as Rawcliffe (1959) pointed out, the University of London Council for Psychical Investigation carried out studies in 1935 and 1937, and the results were published both in *Nature* and the medical journal *The Lancet*. These studies, too, yielded a prosaic explanation of the firewalking feat. Milbourne Christopher (1970), a critic of parapsychology, publicized this information, as did Rogo (1976), a parapsychologist.

Why, then, it would seem appropriate to ask, would the eminent parapsychologist, Robert Van de Castle, in the prestigious *Handbook of parapsychology* (1977), a book described in its introduction as a compendium of "much of the most important work and thought achieved in the field of parapsychology", sum up his brief treatment of fire-walking, in a section entitled "Anecdotes involving possible psychokinesis", with these words?

> A frequent explanation offered for firewalking is that the individual is in a trance state, but we still know very little about what constitutes a trance state. (1977, p. 675.)

He offered not a word about the normal, non-trance explanations which were the result of various careful experiments. Were none of the people who must have reviewed this article before it was included in the book, and were not the editors themselves, knowledgeable enough to notice this serious lapse? And why is it that in various and sundry other parapsychological books, there are still questions raised about whether or not fire-walking involves "paranormal" abilities?

Firewalking is just one example of a *general* tendency in the parapsychological literature to ignore or misrepresent prosaic explanations that have been offered for putative psi phenomena, often as the result of careful, systematic research. Again using the *Handbook of parapsychology* as an example, when William Roll (1977), Project Director at the Psychical Research Foundation, Durham, North Carolina, concluded his chapter on poltergeists, he wrote,

> . . . physical and mental space become complementary or synonymous. The things in a poltergeist house are at the same time the thoughts of the people who live there. When an investigator enters the space surrounding [a poltergeist], in a literal sense he enters that person's mind. . . . (1977, p. 410.)

Why, we must wonder, given that he provided a lengthy bibliography, did he not see fit to even *mention* the account given by magician Milbourne Christopher in his book *ESP, seers, and psychics* (1970) of his critical analysis of poltergeist incidents that he had investigated. Christopher offered prosaic explanations for poltergeist activity, and while Roll may not accept this interpretation, if he was interested in truth should he not have attempted to bring a critical viewpoint to the attention of his audience?

Consider another example. In 1972 Bruce Layton and Bill Turnbull submitted a manuscript to the *Journal of Experimental Social Psychology* describing a study in which they had found that subjects exposed to a positive evaluation of ESP scored higher on ESP tasks than did subjects exposed to a negative evaluation. This journal had not in the past reported research dealing with parapsychology, so the editor entered into an agreement with the authors; the authors agreed to conduct an exact replication, and the results of it would be reported, whatever the outcome. The two studies were published together (Layton and Turnbull, 1975) and the second study revealed no such effect. Since the editor's note appeared on the first page of the article, and since even the abstract clearly indicated a failure to replicate by the same authors using the same conditions, one would expect that anyone referring to this article would take this into account. Yet, in the pages of *Parapsychology Review*, O'Brien, referring directly to that article, reported simply that, "Layton and Turnbull found that subjects exposed to a positive evaluation of ESP scored higher than those exposed to a negative evaluation" (1976, p. 26).

Again, Gardner (1957) described how Rhine was once taken in by the feats of Lady, the "wonder horse", to the point of concluding that the horse had psychic ability (Rhine and Rhine, 1929). Magician, Milbourne Christopher, later showed the horse's trainer controlled its responses by means of subtle cues. Yet Randall (1974) asserted that Lady, unlike wonder horse Clever Hans,[15] was *not* reacting to visual cues, and as a basis for this referred to Rhine's own original assessment, making no mention of the negative evidence at all.

The point is that while in regular psychology students are taught to review the literature in a comprehensive way, discussing both the evidence that supports their ideas and the evidence that goes against it, and while in regular scientific literature reviewers attempt to ensure that important and pertinent works are discussed before articles are published, it seems that in parapsychology critical viewpoints are almost never given serious treatment. If mentioned at all, they are set up as straw men to be quickly dispelled. Parapsychologists seem critical only when discussing some putative paranormal phenomenon that *they* do not happen to believe in.

Failures to replicate are generally ignored in parapsychology (although this is not a problem restricted to parapsychology). For example, Cleve Backster's (1968) demonstration of the psychic ability of plants (and of their emotional reaction to the killing of shrimp in the next room) has not been replicated. Various careful studies by skeptics and believers alike have generally failed to support Backster's "findings" (see, for example, Panati's (1975b) report in *Parapsychology Review* of the proceedings of a parapsychology seminar held at the 1975 annual meeting of the American Association for the Advancement of Science). In a chapter in the *Handbook of parapsychology* Robert Morris reviewed the evidence and concluded that the replication studies, which were better controlled than Backster's (although they were unfortunately not exact replications, in that the environmental and methodological set-ups were somewhat different), cast doubt on Backster's findings. So far so good. Might one not expect the careful scientist to stop at that point? Morris did not. After casting his doubt, he completed his discussion with these words, which in effect make Backster's claims non-falsifiable by positing an "experimenter effect":

> Although the experimenters [who made the replication attempts] made every effort to avoid physical involvement with the experiment while it was running, we still cannot rule out the possibility that, assuming the results of these [replication attempts] are valid, the plants in Backster's study were activated by his own intent or that the natural activities of the plants in [the replication attempts] were suppressed by the intent of the experimenters involved. (1977, p. 705.)

In summary, parapsychologists usually fail to report negative outcomes and skeptical criticism in their discussions of the paranormal. Moreover, since there is no core material that everyone involved with parapsychology accepts with a high degree of certainty, different writers give opposing views on the reality of some aspects of the paranormal, *not* because these aspects do not "fit in" with some theoretical overview, but because, for some reason, they have chosen to be critical of the research in those particular areas, while they relax their criteria when other areas are considered.

---

[15] Rogo (1980) argued that the explanation skeptics found for Clever Hans' ability is misleading, that Clever Hans and other animals have been taught to answer questions even when it was impossible for them to receive sensory cues.

4. Testability

Not only is there no established theory in parapsychology, its basic hypotheses (concerning the existence of various psi processes) are ultimately untestable, except, it seems, by those who already are predisposed to believe that these hypotheses are true. Widely accepted "effects" such as the experimenter effect, the sheep–goat effect, the decline effect, psi-missing, displacement, and even the "shyness effect", if they were real, would mean on the one hand that the agnostic is unlikely to ever witness, experience, or be able to demonstrate psi processes, while on the other hand, researchers less concerned about the exigencies of careful experimentation could read "psi" into events which to more cautious observers would appear to be failures to demonstrate psi. These effects are so important to an understanding of parapsychology that they bear discussion in some detail.

(i) The experimenter effect. The experimenter effect is the most important "catch-22" in all parapsychology. It is said to occur when one experimenter is unable to replicate another's findings, or when two co-experimenters using the same procedures obtain different results.

In normal psychology, when different experimenters using the same methodology and employing subjects from the same population obtain different results, it is cause for serious concern about the extent to which one or more experimenters introduced unconscious bias or other sources of artifact into the experiments. The psychologist's reaction to experimenter effects is quite straightforward: ". . . to the extent that such [experimenter] bias operates, it undermines the validity of conclusions drawn from psychological experiments" (John Jung, 1971, p. 41). Parapsychologists have long been inconvenienced by such problems. Skeptical experimenters are unable to replicate successful experiments, and even some believers, such as Beloff, have had little or no success in their parapsychological research despite a deep commitment to it. Rather than giving careful consideration to the possibility that those who obtain positive results do so because of flaws in the carrying out of the experiments, parapsychologists have come to view the experimenter effect as a manifestation of the psi-ability of the experimenter, and thus, in a sense, vice becomes virtue. Indeed, it has even been argued that the experimenter effect may be the *single* clearly demonstrable effect coming out of laboratory parapsychology (Parker, 1978).

Not only may the experimenter influence the outcome of the experiment using his own psychic ability; it has also been suggested that it is possible that he might unconsciously use his psi to choose subjects whose scores will support his experimental hypothesis (Weiner and Morrison, 1979).

Presumably, the same phenomenon accounts for the regularly observed effect of skeptics; psi phenomena do not manifest themselves in their presence. Either the skeptic by his mere presence inhibits the psi powers of others, or possibly he unconsciously counteracts their psi by his own psychic energy.

Unfortunately, it seems, one will never know whether a demonstration of, say, psychokinesis in a laboratory setting was the work of the subject or the experimenter himself, for there is no way of blocking the experimenter's psi. This problem has been identified as posing a crisis for parapsychology by none other than Rhine (1977) himself, for he pointed out that all the relevant research of the past demonstrates that it is impossible to screen out psi (either in terms of space or time). It is therefore impossible to isolate an experiment from the experimenter's psi.

A related aspect of parapsychological belief that adds to its non-falsifiability is the view that strict scientific procedures inhibit psi, that controls must be somewhat loose in order to allow its manifestation. In fact, Fritjof Capra, a physicist-parapsychologist and author of *The tao of physics*, has argued that

> Psychic phenomena may manifest themselves in full strength only outside the framework of analytic thought and may diminish progressively as their observation and analysis becomes more and more scientific. (n. d., p. 7.)

Rhine, too, made a similar argument, noting that experimental controls seem to make the manifestation of psi very unlikely. Rhine's position moved B. F. Skinner to write,

> . . . the impartial investigator faces only two possibilities: he may prove the existence of psi or be judged guilty of suppressing it through the use of scientific method. (1948b, p. 459.)

Thus, all failures to obtain results can be explained away, and taken to be the manifestation of the influence of the experimenter's own psi. If there is no such thing as psi, parapsychologists are left no way to learn that.

(ii) *The sheep–goat effect.* In 1952 Gertrude Schmeidler (1952) published the results of an experiment in which subjects attempted to match the order of target symbols which were sealed in opaque envelopes. Schmeidler reported that the subjects who had a prior belief in ESP (the "sheep") scored above chance while skeptics (the "goats") scored below chance and that these differences were statistically significant. This study was criticized by Burdock (1954) who argued that Schmeidler's statistical analysis was inappropriate and that proper analysis of her data led to the conclusion that there were no significant differences. Schmeidler continued to collect data, and in 1958 published a book (Schmeidler and McConnell, 1958) which presented new data which she argued supported the interpretation she had given to the results of her earlier study.

Since that time there have been various studies which have found the sheep–goat effect, and others which have failed to find it (e.g. Wilson, 1964). (It is important to remember that the sheep–goat effect is not normally accompanied by any departure from chance by the group as a whole, and does not always involve a below-chance score on the part of skeptics.) The acceptance of this effect as veridical by parapsychologists means of course that the skeptic is expected to be closed off from experiencing the paranormal directly. From the skeptic's point of view, it may simply be that, to the extent that subtle non-paranormal cues exist (cf. the study of Marks and Kammann discussed on pp. 163–164), those who believe in parapsychological processes are likely to be more highly motivated to use those cues, even if they are not fully conscious of them.

(iii) *The decline effect.* A decrease in scoring in a psi experiment across a series of trials is so common that it has been named the "decline effect". Similarly, "gifted" subjects seem to "dry up" as the study of their abilities continues over time. To the skeptic, this might be taken to be the result of normal statistical fluctuation (regression towards the mean), or as evidence that the subjects experienced more difficulty in using deception or in exploiting subtle cues as the researchers focused more closely on his behaviour and as controls were tightened up. West has written,

> A much more important reason for skepticism is that, as soon as anyone tries to investigate with persistence and determination, the alleged phenomena become strangely fleeting and uncertain. (1971, p. 23.)

Gulliksen sarcastically commented on Rhine's book *New frontiers of the mind:*

> We have, when we consider all the facts in the case, very marked limitations. This marvellous ESP ability is found primarily with a special deck of cards. It does not even seem to extend successfully

to ordinary playing cards, which would give some people a new leverage on bridge and poker. It is a "weak and delicate" ability that "fades" when subjected to hostility or doubt; and even when carefully nurtured at [Rhine's] Duke Laboratory and not subjected to observation of doubting outsiders, it fades anyhow. (1938, p. 630.)

Yet, the decline effect strikes few parapsychologists in this way. Quite typical (e.g. see Rhine, (1953)) is the reaction of Rogo:

. . . there is one aspect of ESP and PK research that I find even more convincing than the evidence that has been obtained from so-called conclusive experiments. This is the fact that many researchers, working totally independently and in different laboratories, and even in different countries, have often observed the same trends and patterns in their data. (1977b, p. 42.)

For Rogo, the decline effect is one such trend. It is taken as evidence for psi. (Recall the discussion of Langer and Roth's study, pp. 101–102.)

(iv) *Psi-missing and displacement.* If a subject in a psi experiment does more *poorly* than one would expect by chance, this too is taken as evidence of psi ("psi-missing"). Or if on the average a subject's "displaced" responses (i.e. responses in a series which are one, two, or three trials behind or ahead of the target series) have a "significant" association with the target series, even though the responses with zero displacement do not, then this too is evidence of psi. Since researchers do not and apparently cannot predict *in advance* what degree of displacement is to be expected, or whether psi-missing will occur, there are a number of possibilities that one can examine after the experiment to see if any of them have come to pass. (This is what is referred to in conjuring as "exploiting multiple end points". If the audience does not know what the final goal is, the magician can successfully produce any of a number of effects depending on the circumstances. Similarly, if one does not know in advance what form a successful outcome of a psi experiment will take, and if any of several possible outcomes could be considered a success, it is quite likely that at least one such outcome can be found.)

(v) *The "shyness" effect.* When John Taylor (1975) studied children who were supposed to be able to accomplish some of Geller's feats, he found that their powers worked only if no one was watching them, and he dubbed this the "shyness effect".

While the psi-missing effect makes it possible to interpret a subject's failures as successes, the other effects described above would, if real, make it impossible for the skeptical investigator to ever put parapsychological claims to the test. If he does not find evidence of psi, this can be interpreted as being due to his own skepticism[16] and/or that of his subjects. Even if one is not a skeptic, one may still be unable to detect the paranormal because of some odd personal quirk which inhibits psi. If the experimenter should find evidence suggestive of psi in an informal situation, only to find that the evidence evaporates when controls are made formal, this can be explained either in terms of the decline effect, or the "known" inhibitory effects brought about by rigorous controls. There is no escape, no way to know that psi did not occur.

A major problem with respect to testability in parapsychology concerns what Giere (1979) has described as the two conditions which are necessary and sufficient if a test of a hypothesis is to be a *good* test. The first condition is that there must be a conditional relationship between the hypothesis (along with the initial conditions and auxiliary assumptions) and the

---

[16] Given that psi seems unaffected by time, space, and shielding, one might expect that the existence of a single skeptic might be enough to inhibit paranormal processes throughout the universe. As far as I know there are no data to suggest that the effects of a skeptic's inhibitory psi can be overcome by the positive effects of the psi of a large number of believers.

prediction such that it is impossible for the premises to be true and the prediction false. This condition is readily satisfied in most cases since the prediction is a logical deduction from the hypothesis. Only if the hypothesis is very vague, making disputable what it implies, is there a problem.

Thus, if the hypothesis is that a given individual has ESP ability which allows him to score at an above-chance level in an ESP experiment, the prediction of above-chance scoring follows directly from the hypothesis and Giere's first condition for a good test is satisfied.

Giere's second condition for a good test is that the prediction must be such that it is unlikely that anyone should correctly arrive at such a prediction unless they used the hypothesis in question. If the hypothesis is false, then, even if the initial conditions and the auxiliary assumptions are correct, it is very unlikely that the prediction will be confirmed.

It is this second condition that is virtually *never* satisfied by tests of paranormal hypotheses. There are always other possible hypotheses that would lead to the same prediction. In the case of the subject reputed to possess ESP powers, to satisfy this second condition the situation would have to be such that if he did not have ESP ability he would be very unlikely to score at an above-chance rate. This condition is difficult to satisfy since any unsuspected normal sensory transfer could lead to extrachance scoring, and, in addition, by chance alone some subjects will score at an "above-chance" level.

Whenever parapsychological studies appear to support the hypothesis that paranormal processes produced the predicted results, one must always keep in mind Giere's second condition: What other hypotheses (e.g. fraud, normal sensory transfer of information, etc.) could have led to the same prediction?

5. Relationship with other areas of research and theory

✗A major source of skepticism about parapsychology is that its claims, if true, run counter to well-established theories in other areas of research, theories which have over the years successfully withstood many a challenge.✗

Parapsychologists often appear to show little interest in such things as the law of conservation of energy or causality. For example McConnell (1977b) offhandedly suggested that if one were worried about where the energy for psi processes comes from, one could invent a new energy to account for it. In general, there seems to be a disinterest in the theories and "facts" of other research areas, except when these may be loosely translated into terms that might seem to support parapsychology, as was mentioned earlier with regard to quantum mechanics. Moreover, the extent to which the vast majority of parapsychologists are ignorant of or disinterested in "normal" science is striking. For example, little or no attention is paid, it appears, to "normal" perceptual processes. Yet, from the point of view of normal perception, the question of ESP raises some important questions. Hansel (1971) pointed out that ESP experiments have typically treated ESP as though it were like visual perception in the absence of a visual stimulus, or auditory perception in the absence of an auditory stimulus, yet they have used materials usually associated with some kind of coding system. Is ESP a thought, a feeling, Hansel asked? How does the receiver differentiate it from other sensory input? We have to learn to communicate with each other via language, and two people who do not speak the same language have considerable difficulty in communicating. How do ESP communicators learn to "decode" messages? The information transmitted must be quite precisely encoded and decoded. If one person concentrates on a king of diamonds and the receiver receives the image of a bejewelled nobleman, how does he recognize it either as a bejewelled nobleman or as the king of diamonds? In regular perception, one must learn the meaning of various stimulus patterns which themselves, as we have seen, are only an arbitrary representation on the environment.

There are no answers for these questions, and they are only rarely even asked by parapsychologists. While it is true that some parapsychologists have attempted to study the effects of various psychological "states" on psi, or tried to correlate psi performance with known psychological variables, this does not in itself represent an overlap with psychology anymore than would the use in a parapsychology experiment of coins made from various metallic substances represent an overlap with metallurgy or chemistry. Psychologists and parapsychologists, and physicists and paraphysicists do not overlap in their research. Physicists do not find it necessary to turn to the parapsychological literature to gain insight into problems that they are working on, nor do psychologists. Moreover, parapsychologists are quite able, it seems, to carry out their research without knowledge of physics or psychology being essential or even important.

The lack of overlap between parapsychology and normal science is a major strike against the former. In the words of the eminent psychologist Donald Hebb,

> The external reasons for doubting ESP lie in the fact that it would mean a revolution of natural science, and the evidence is not that good. If it doesn't matter how far apart the two heads are when one brain radiates to another (in telepathy), then there is something fundamentally wrong with physics; and if the second brain can sort out and make sense of such broadcast waves, there is something equally wrong with neurophysiology. Mistakes have been made in those fields before, maybe they're wrong again. But their practical successes make that unlikely, and the question is, what experimental data are there that are solid enough, and reliable and repeatable enough, to justify the conclusion that physics and neurophysiology are fundamentally in error? There are no such data, and actually there is good reason to doubt the reliability and the validity of the parapsychological data. . . . The existing evidence is so little able to withstand such scrutiny that I am obliged to conclude that the parapsychologist acts the part of a mystagogue, not that of a scientist; for science is one body of knowledge, and one can't play little games off in one part of the field without regard to their meaning for other parts. If the parapsychologist believes that he has conclusive evidence of ESP, he should be asking how the brain does it and what independent evidence can be found for that physical influence of one brain on another—not to mention what the source is of those waves that must be given off by Rhine cards, to make clairvoyance possible. (Personal communication, 1978.)

In a similar vein, when an apparently sincere effort to replicate Cleve Backster's work dealing with the emotional life of plants failed, Galston and Slayman commented,

> It is the lack of any plausible anatomical substratum rather than any simple experimental fact or flaw which . . . drives the final nail into the coffin for the Backster, Tompkins and Bird view of plant "sensory perception." (1979, pp. 343–344.)

Parapsychologists deal with such criticisms in an almost cavalier way. For example, if we are concerned by the fact that ESP seems unaffected by distance or by shielding, parapsychologists respond that it may not be necessary for transmission to occur at all (Palmer, 1978). Making reference to Jung's notion of synchronicity (which is supposed to explain the common occurrence of "meaningful" coincidences by means of "acausal" processes), Palmer commented,

> My intent here is not to suggest that we perfunctorily abandon the transmission models, but only that we keep our options open and our construct systems flexible. Indeed, synchronistic theories of psi are showing signs that they may be coming of age. (1978, p. 209.)

And in a highly partial review of psychokinesis research for the recent *Handbook of Parapsychology*, Rex Stanford concluded that,

> . . . PK success does not depend on knowing the PK target, upon knowing the nature or the existence of the REG [random event generator], upon knowing that one is in a PK study, upon the complexity or the design of the REG, or upon the subjects knowing anything about the mechanics of the REG . . . [these findings] suggest that PK somehow occurs such that the favourable outcome (or goal event) is directly accomplished without mediation through sensory guidance *and probably without any form of computation or information processing by the organism*. (1977, p. 341 italics in original.)

Such thinking, of course, is indistinguishable from magical thought. Wish it and it will occur. This lack of any solid conceptual framework to guide research and interpretation, as Kurtz (1978) said, allows parapsychologists to slip from one *ad hoc* explanation to another whenever objections are voiced.

In conclusion, parapsychology has, after a century of research, failed to develop any coherent theory, failed to come up with testable hypotheses, and failed to develop any norms which might help to distinguish creative speculation from magical thought.

B. Methodology in Parapsychology

The research methods used in normal science have gradually evolved to help protect the researcher from his own biases and his propensity for magical thought, and to maximize the likelihood of discovering causal relationships between variables. Research using animate subjects is open to a great many sources of artifact which do not plague the physical scientist. Social psychologists, for example, have learned a great deal over the years about the subtle problems involved in studying human subjects. This has led to a weakening of belief in the conclusions drawn in many of the classic social psychological studies, as well as to considerable soul-searching about the ability of social scientists to ever produce "laws" of social behaviour, as opposed to simply *describing* relationships between variables, relationships which may not hold some years hence as society and culture change.

In the section that follows, some of the major methodological weaknesses in parapsychological research will be examined.

1. Experimental controls

Research in parapsychology varies from almost uncontrolled observation to what is, according to the reports at least, very tightly controlled experimentation. The problems of doing research in parapsychology and the difficulties associated with careful control of all extraneous variables will be addressed in Chapter 7. For the present, we are concerned with the way in which poorly controlled experimentation is often presented as having been very carefully controlled. Thus the layperson is told that painstakingly careful scientific research demonstrated such and such a paranormal phenomenon. In many cases, such reports belie the extent to which controls were either inadequate or lacking.

Consider simply one example, an "experiment" which has been given a great deal of importance by many parapsychologists, Charles Tart's (1968) study of the out-of-body experiences ("OOBEs") of a woman who was supposedly able, while sleeping, to leave her body, float up and "read" a five-digit random number which had been placed on a shelf above her bed. We shall not concern ourselves here with the obvious question of how a person can receive and interpret patterns of light without benefit of retina or brain, nor does this kind of question concern parapsychologists. Nor shall we wonder why natural evolution should have led to the development of a highly complex visual system if an individual can "see" without the need of his fleshy body. Rather, our interest here is in the fact that a conclusion was drawn on the basis of weak methodology, and that the conclusion appeared stronger in successive reports as reference to the weaknesses was dropped.

Tart's (1968) original 25-page article reveals that the "experiment" was so loosely controlled that even its author had to admit that the subject's "reading of the target number cannot be considered as providing conclusive evidence for a parapsychological effect" (p. 18). It is indeed surprising that anyone would be even the *slightest* bit impressed with what was reported to have occurred. The subject, who had reported having experienced frequent OOBEs during sleep, spent four nights sleeping in a bed in a laboratory, her head attached to polygraph electrodes which led to a box on the head of the bed and from there to the experimenter's equipment room next door. The two rooms were connected by a window "covered with a venetian blind in order that the subject's room could be reasonably dark for sleeping", and by an intercom which allowed the experimenter to hear anything the subject said. About $5\frac{1}{2}$ feet above the subject's head was a small shelf, and above that, a wall-mounted clock. The experimenter would place a small piece of paper in the shelf at the beginning of the session without the subject seeing it. Written on it, in 2-inch high black figures which would only be visible to someone whose eye level was about $6\frac{1}{2}$ feet above the floor, was a five-digit number chosen from a random number table. The subject was to try to float up via an OOBE experience and "read" the number. The electrode wires strung between her and the box at the head of the bed were only 2 feet long, so that she could not get up without disconnecting them, an action which we are told would be obvious from the polygraph recordings of EEG, galvanic skin response, and basal skin response. (We are not told whether or not it was possible to lift the box from the head of the bed.)

The experimenter monitored her activity from his own room:

> I monitored the recording equipment throughout the night while the subject slept and kept notes of anything she said or did. Occasionally I dozed during the night, beside the equipment, so possible instances of sleep talking might have been missed. (1968, p. 7.)

If he was interested in sleep talk, why not use a tape recorder? Why did he not *visually* monitor her, perhaps by a video camera? After all, if she really could read that number without leaving the bed, one would like to have that on videotape.

Although by the end of the first three nights, the subject reported having experienced leaving her body and even at one point calling out the time (ostensibly from having seen the clock via an OOBE), nothing really important occurred until the fourth night, when at 6.04 she awoke, and reported correctly that the number was 25132 (the probability for a correct guess being $p < 10^{-5}$).

Now pay particular attention to what Tart, a man of considerable experimental savvy so far as "normal" psychological research is concerned, did next, not *before* the experiment, but following it:

> . . . I inspected the laboratory carefully the next day to see if there was any way in which this number could have been read by non-parapsychological means. (1968, pp. 17–18.)

He discovered two possibilities, both of which he thought unlikely. The number was reflected by the base of the clock above it, but the reflection was so faint that neither he nor a colleague could read it in the semi-darkened room unless they shone a flashlight onto the slip of paper so as to make its reflection brighter. Secondly, however,

> She might have concealed mirrors and reaching rods in her pajamas and used these during the period when the EEG was difficult to classify (due to movement artifacts) to read the number. While this is possible, I personally doubt that it occurred. (1968, p. 18.)

Apparently, the editors of the *Journal of the American Society for Psychical Research* shared this doubt, or they would have demanded more stringent controls before accepting the paper, but Tart himself seemed to have felt some need for more controls, for he said in a footnote,

> The set-up of the room was changed slightly in preparation for a fifth laboratory night, and the shelf was extended so that no reflection could be seen off the clock from the subject's position in bed. However, personal difficulties forced [the subject] to return to her family's home in Southern California before a fifth laboratory night could be scheduled. (1968, p. 18.)

One might wonder about the probability of such personal difficulties occurring just as changes were being made to decrease the possibility of cheating. (One must also wonder why Tart, with his belief in paranormal processes, would consider the alleged feat to be an OOBE and not clairvoyance.)

While Tart paid lip service to conservative interpretation in his journal article, noting that the evidence was not "conclusive", this report has been used many times by various people as an example of psi under highly controlled circumstances. What did Tart himself say about it in his book, *PSI: Scientific studies of the psychic realm?*

> On the one occasion Miss Z reported that she had floated high enough to see the target number, she correctly reported that it was 25132. The odds against correctly guessing a five-digit random number, making only one guess at it, are 100,000 to 1, so this argued strongly for a psi component to Miss Z's OOBE's. . . . It was very disappointing when she moved to a distant city, and we could not continue the laboratory research. (1977, p. 185.)

No mention of possible mirrors and reaching rods. No mention of changes in the physical set-up just before she had to return to her family's home. No mention of the lack of conclusiveness of the interpretation.

This study, as *originally* reported, made clear the lack of controls. However, it would appear that many times the reports of studies which are described as having been very carefully controlled are, from the beginning, very misleading, and as Diaconis has observed,

> Indeed, ESP investigators often insist on nonnegative observers and surroundings. Because of this, skeptics have a difficult time gaining direct access to experimental evidence and must rely on published reports. Such reports are often wholly inadequate . . . it is not easy to notice crucial details during ESP experiments. (1978, p. 133.)

The reader's reaction to this discussion might simply be, "But this kind of thing happens in regular science all the time. Why should one be particularly concerned with a particular instance such as this just because it occurs in parapsychology?" The answer to this is straightforward. Tart reported what would be considered from the point of view of normal science to be a miracle. That particular miracle is used as evidence time and again by parapsychological writers who wish to convince their audience of the reality of out-of-body experiences. It is not something that independent researchers can demonstrate for themselves. (Quite apart from the supposedly inhibitory effects of any skepticism they might have, they do not have access to that special individual who was the subject in Tart's experiment. Even if they had, and were unable to find any evidence of psi, that would not indicate that she had not had an OOBE in Tart's laboratory.) When one finds that the initial sloppiness of the laboratory conditions is forgotten in subsequent accounts of the event, even by Tart himself, this should serve as a warning about accepting such a report at face value. As West observed

> Scientists in ordinary fields of endeavour can afford to be more relaxed. The occasional false lead, deriving from careless or disingenuous research, is relatively harmless. As more valid observations accumulate, all pointing in another direction, the false lead is soon left behind and forgotten, being overtaken by the inexorable advance of knowledge. In parapsychology, unfortunately, there is hardly any recognizable advance and the phenomena remain as mysterious, and as uncontrollable, as they were before the effort to investigate them began. Because the observations of parapsychologists do not, as yet, form a coherent pattern, the findings of any particular investigation cannot be evaluated against a background of already assured knowledge. Each observation stands on its own as a separate miracle, which the critic must accept or reject according to the strength of the evidence presented on a particular occasion. In fact, parapsychology consists of a series of historic demonstrations of miracles rather than a body of scientific knowledge. (1971, p. 23.)

Time and again, careful analysis of the original conditions under which widely cited studies were run uncovers evidence of lack of good experimental control. Targ and Puthoff (1974) reported in their *Nature* article that Uri Geller's most sensational feat was to correctly identify eight times in succession the number on a die that was inside a metal box which had been shaken by one of the experimenters. It was later learned that Geller had been allowed to handle the box, and that many trials had been made:

> Because the experimenter always shook the box before Geller was permitted to touch it, Geller's handling of it seemed irrelevant, so it was not mentioned in the *Nature* report. This seemingly trivial detail gave Geller a splendid chance to obtain information by a technique known to conjurers. (Gardner, 1976b, p. 43.)

Nor do Targ and Puthoff's research reports of their tests of Geller point out that, as those authors were later forced to admit, Geller's best friend Shipi Stang was present at every test. This is the very person who, according to both Geller's sister and Geller's former manager, often acted as Geller's accomplice in trickery in his demonstrations (Gardner, 1979a).

Recently, parapsychologists have been encouraged by results coming from studies using the "Ganzfeld". The Ganzfeld procedure, used originally by psychologists in the study of visual perception, involves presenting a subject with a completely undifferentiated visual field. One way of doing this is to cut ping-pong balls in half and place one half over each of the subject's eyes. Parapsychologists have employed this technique with the idea that reduced visual input might increase the likelihood of detecting psi. (Why simply putting a subject into a darkened room would not be just as useful is not clear.) Honorton and Harper (1974) reported the landmark research in this area, yet, once again, closer scrutiny of the conditions under which the research was carried out revealed considerable sloppiness in their experimental conditions, including the use of a crude randomization procedure (shuffling and cutting a set of numbered cards). Hyman (1977b) concluded that the deliberate or inadvertent transfer of information via normal sensory cues between sender and receiver had not been ruled out in this study.

Crumbaugh (1966) wrote about his own disillusionment. A parapsychologist himself, he had been unable to obtain evidence of psi in his own experiments, but was virtually convinced about the existence of paranormal phenomena on the basis of some of the studies reported in the literature. Two such studies in particular seemed to him to be very well done and just about foolproof judging from the written reports. However, when he himself was on the staff of Rhine's laboratory at Duke University in 1954, he discussed these two studies, which had been done at Duke, with other members of the staff, and he discovered that neither study enjoyed a good reputation there. In one of them, rumour suggested that the scoring had not been carried out by the student scorers in the way that the researchers believed and reported, and in the other, a case of "phenomenally high" ESP scores in a distance experiment, the subject was known to suffer from serious psychopathology, and, moreover, she had had access to the home of the experimenter where the ESP target cards were kept. It was commonly believed that she had seen them before making her calls. Crumbaugh stated that,

> The reports deeply jolted my confidence in the ability of any experimenter to report with absolute accuracy exactly what he has done. Both of the aforementioned experimenters were probably completely honest and believed they reported exactly what happened. But in both cases there were those close to the experiment who believed the true events occurred—unknown to the experimenters—somewhat differently. (1976, p. 528.)

Persi Diaconis, who is both a statistician and an accomplished magician, has been an observer in many parapsychological studies. In discussing a series of studies which purported to demonstrate paranormal ability on the part of various psychics, but in which skeptical observers had detected cheating by the subjects he commented,

> Even if there had not been subject cheating, [these experiments] would be useless because they were out of control. The confusing and erratic experimental conditions I have described are typical of *every* test of paranormal phenomena I have witnessed. (1978, p. 133.)

The clear lesson here is that we should not be seduced into belief that there is good evidence for the existence of psi on the basis of written research reports. To treat such reports as one would the reports of regular science, one must implicitly assume that if the research was poorly controlled, or if the reports are misleading, we shall soon hear about it from others who try but fail to replicate the study. But such is not the case, for replication in any meaningful sense has never been achieved by parapsychologists.

2. *Replication—the elusive goal*

The late S. S. Stevens (1967) argued that even if ESP is real, the signal-to-noise ratio is just too low at the moment to be interesting. When ESP effects could be demonstrated reliably under highly controlled conditions, he said, he would believe in them just as he believed in the migration of holes in a semiconductor, which is a mysterious but readily demonstrable phenomenon. If there is a single problem that is the bane of parapsychologists, it is that of the remarkable *lack* of replicability of experiments and demonstrations. All experimental sciences have long viewed replicability as a foundation stone in the edifice of their methodology. It is not enough for a researcher to report his observations with regard to a phenomenon; he could be mistaken, or even dishonest. But if other people, using his methodology, can independently produce the same results, it is much more likely that error and dishonesty are not responsible for them.

There are at least three kinds of replication (Lykken, 1968). First of all, a "literal replication" is one in which the experimenter carefully duplicates the sampling procedures, the measuring techniques, the experimental conditions and the methods of data analysis of the original experiment. Such a replication, while providing a check on the accuracy and the veracity of the original reports, does not assure that the results of the original experiment and the results of the replication, should they be the same, are not both due to some artifact inherent in the original experiment or study. For example, if a researcher runs a study of the clairvoyant powers of an alleged psychic and fails to control for all possible sources of normal sensory information (suppose that, for example, as occurred in some of the earlier studies of ESP using Zener cards, the cards were so heavily embossed with the symbols that one could detect the symbol from the back of the card), then a literal replication using the same situation would be likely to produce the same results.

A second kind of replication is what Lykken (1968) called "operational replication". In this case, one attempts to duplicate exactly only the sampling and the experimental procedure, and not the measuring technique and method of data analysis. Lykken uses as an example of such a replication the attempts to replicate the demonstration of the wonder horse *Clever Hans'* ability to add numbers. The necessity of having the horse's trainer in the field of view had not been specified as a crucial part of the method, and was left out of the replication, which for that reason was unsuccessful. The trainer had used almost imperceptible signals to indicate to the horse when it should stop "counting" as it stamped its foot counting out the answer.

Operational replication is difficult whenever, as is often the case, write-ups of experiments do not contain all the essential details of the experimental set-up. If, as in the Clever Hans case, critical but unrecognized elements of the experimental situation are not reported, replication is unlikely to succeed, and this in itself is a protective device in the decision-making process about the validity of experimental results. If, however, replication is not attempted, or if failure to replicate is not reported, then the same scarcity of detail in experimental reports can render impossible any methodological critique of the original study. If the researcher says that all possible transfer of information by normal sensory channels was eliminated, how can the reader confirm that this was in fact the case? How can the reader evaluate whether the experimenter was not fooled by some subtle ruse known perhaps only to magicians?

The third type of replication discussed by Lykken (1968) is "constructive replication". In this case, the researcher deliberately avoids directly imitating the methods of the original research. One begins with only a clear statement of the empirical "fact" which was supposedly demonstrated by the first researcher, and then devises ways of putting that fact to the test. If a psychic is "clairvoyant", then one would presume that he could "read" the contents of a sealed opaque plastic envelope just as well as he can those of a sealed paper envelope. The envelope should not be important, unless, for example, he is surreptitiously applying alcohol to the paper envelope with this thumb in order to render it momentarily transparent. By not imitating the original experimental set-up one reduces to some extent the likelihood that artifact was responsible for the results.

Constructive validation is vital since,

> Just as a reliable but invalid test can be said to measure something, but not what it claimed to measure, so an experiment which replicates operationally but not constructively could be said to have demonstrated something, but not the relationship between meaningful constructs which the author originally claimed to have established. (Lykken, 1968, p. 156.)

However, even a successful replication of this type does not assure that experimental artifacts were not responsible for the results in the replication as well as in the original experiment.

Skeptics have long argued that the onus is on the parapsychologists to produce an effect which can be replicated by, or at least in the presence of, skeptics. Parapsychologists often respond by arguing that since the fact that various "effects" have been demonstrated many times in different laboratories, replicability has already been achieved. For example, as was discussed earlier, Rogo (1977b) has argued that the commonness of the decline effect in parapsychology experiments constitutes replicability. This, of course, is incorrect, since the decline effect itself may be indicative of methodological or statistical artifact.

Moreover, as Broughton (1979) has said, despite the efforts made to show the *diversity* of replications in parapsychology, one cannot avoid the fact that most of the successful experiments are associated with only a few names. (Indeed, McConnell (1977a) pointed out that over one-half the research articles published in the *Journal of the American Society for Psychical Research* are produced by only five people!)

To underline the absolute and critical importance of the replication problem, I have cited below from the writings of some of the more serious and careful parapsychologists themselves. It is only a pity that these words are not given more importance by other parapsychologists.

D. J. West in discussing the "best" experiments on ESP:

> . . . they fall short of the requirements for usual scientific conviction for several reasons, the chief one being that they are more in the nature of demonstrations than repeatable experiments . . . no demonstration, however well done, can take the place of an experiment that can be repeated by anyone who cares to make the effort. (1966, p. 17.)

F. C. Dommeyer:

> The reader inexperienced in parapsychology is likely to believe . . . that psi phenomena are relatively commonplace. The scientific investigator knows that this is not so and that such phenomena, as J. B. Rhine so often asserts, are very "elusive". The present reviewer, after spending the greater part of two summers in the 1960's at the Parapsychology Laboratory at Duke University, was unable to observe over those months a single identifiable instance of ESP or PK. (1975, p. 11.)

John Beloff:

> The Rhine revolution, in short, proved abortive. Rhine succeeded in giving parapsychology everything it needed to become an accredited experimental science except the one essential: the know-how to produce positive results when and where required. Without that the rest could never amount to more than trappings of a science. (1973, p. 291.)

Gardner Murphy:

> . . . if it has no clear rationality its only chance of demanding scientific attention is replication. (1971, p. 4.)

Adrian Parker:

> . . . Rhine's view is that we have repeatability in a more general sense, and that specific repeatability will come when we accumulate enough knowledge about the phenomenon so as, so to speak, fit the pieces of a jigsaw together. Even if we discount the inconsistency in the argument, there is unfortunately no sign that this piecing together of findings is actually happening. A high degree of replicability, in this writer's opinion, is essential to both the progress and the recogniton of parapsychology. (1978, p. 2.)

Parker went on to paint a gloomy picture of the progress made in the laboratory so far:

> The present crisis in parapsychology is that there appear to be few if any findings which are independent of the experimenter. Indeed, it can be claimed that the experimenter effect is

parapsychology's one and only finding. This is the impasse that parapsychology has reached today. (1978, p. 2.)

Child, a psychologist very sympathetic to parapsychology:

> On the question of the reality of psi phenomena, no demonstration has been devised that is dependably repeatable whenever and wherever one wishes. (1978, p. 12.)

Crumbaugh, who began to pursue parapsychology in 1938 leading to a Master's thesis dealing with ESP:

> At the time of performing the experiments involved I fully expected that they would yield easily all the final answers. I did not imagine that after 28 years I would still be in as much doubt as when I had begun. I repeated a number of the then current Duke techniques, but the results of 3,024 runs [1 run = 25 guesses] of the ESP cards—as much work as Rhine reported in his first book—were all negative. In 1940 I utilized further methods with high school students, again with negative results. (1966, p. 524.)

Beloff commented on these remarks of Crumbaugh's:

> My own story is very similar. I recently completed a seven-year programme of parapsychological research with the help of one full-time research assistant. No one would have been more delighted to obtain positive results than we, but for all the success we achieved ESP might just as well not have existed . . . I have not found on comparing notes with other parapsychologists . . . that my experience is in any way out of the ordinary. (1973, p. 312.)

However, Hyman (1977b) has argued that what is at issue is not really repeatability, but *respectability*. We will be no more convinced that people can at will become invisible if we read ten reports of "highly controlled" demonstrations than if we read only one. What is needed is to be able to specify in advance what conditions are required in order for a given effect to be produced. But, as Hyman noted, for certain effects such as the "Ganzfeld" effect and the sheep–goat effect, there have been as many successful replications as non-successful ones, all made by researchers who *believe*. What is lacking, as always, is the capability of skeptical researchers to produce the effect. As Kurtz cautioned,

> It is not enough for parapsychologists to tell the skeptic that *he*, the parapsychologist, on occasion has replicated the results. This would be like the American Tobacco Institute insisting that, based on its experiments, cigarette-smoking does not cause cancer. The neutral scientist needs to be able to replicate results in his own laboratory. Esoteric private road-to-truth claims need to be rejected in science, and there needs to be an intersubjective basis for validation. (1978, p. 23.)

Collins (1976) has argued that there is a kind of negotiation between believers and skeptics that takes place over what constitutes a replication in a given instance. As an example of this, he reported the reactions of certain skeptics and believers to Schmidt's (1969b) precognition studies involving random sequences generated by radioactive decay. Parapsychologists Beloff and Bate (1971) were unable to replicate the Schmidt results, which they had considered to be one of the most rigorous demonstrations ever of a psi effect, but yet they concluded that their failure to obtain results "in no way detracts from Dr. Schmidt's success". As Collins notes, Beloff and Bate were prepared to extend the boundaries of legitimate subsidiary explanation to include the effects of the experimenters' personalities (the experimenter effect) in order to save the phenomenon.

Yet Hansel, a well-known critic of parapsychology, was interviewed by Collins, and was unwilling to accept Schmidt's conclusions because not everyone who repeated the study obtained the same results. According to Collins, Hansel was disposed to view the competence of the experimenter as the important variable in such a case. Collins summarized his interview with Hansel, and the conclusion drawn by Beloff and Bate in this way:

. . . for Hansel, . . . if half the people get the same result as Schmidt they are likely to be incompetent—insufficiently rigorous. For Beloff and Bate (and most other parapsychologists) *consistent failure to get results* is taken as demonstrating some imponderable personality defect which renders the experimenter incompetent. (1976, pp. 23–24. italics in original).

If parapsychologists, when they choose experiments to constitute a set of successful replications, treat some experiments as competently done and others as incompetently done then, Collins said,

. . . in negotiating the acceptance of this set—in which project they may well succeed if they are sufficiently persuasive—they have not only negotiated the existence of the phenomenon, but have also negotiated its character—i.e. it is of such a nature as to be affected by certain subtle psychic influences, and not such a nature that the mere scientist, trained in a scientific orthodoxy could hope to discover it. In this way can a new phenomenon come into existence, and then can its characteristics be socially determined. (1976, p. 27.)

By arguing that psi's existence has already been demonstrated, parapsychologists have already constructed some of its attributes, since they "know" it is a very reticent phenomenon. The fact that certain people never seem to be able to witness it at all means that even more is "known" about it.

Some parapsychologists downplay the importance of replicability altogether, either arguing that there are so many variables that affect psi that not enough is known about what factors are crucial for its production, or that parapsychology's record of replicability is just as good as that of psychology. This hardly impresses the many competent researchers who have tried and failed, sometimes over and over again, to replicate a given finding. Moreover, few if any parapsychologists would really credit whatever degree of repeatability they believe to have been established as having any *predictive* value for future replications (Broughton, 1979). As for the comparison with psychology, there is a wealth of readily replicable effects in psychology, and one should not be distracted from this fact just because in some areas of psychology replicability is more elusive. It is hardly a defence to compare one's own record to that of the weakest areas of another discipline.

Is it fair to continually berate the parapsychologists for their lack of replicability? When Price (1955) did so, suggesting that without independent replication the possibility of fraud was quite strong, he was taken to task by Meehl and Scriven (1956) who argued that had Price taken the same line in evaluating the critical Michelson–Morley experiment (which led to the downfall of the ether theory of light transmission), he would have had to brand them as liars simply because the results of their single experiment contradicted an accepted theory, and their honesty as researchers was equally not sure. However, Flew (1980) listed three reasons why Meehl and Scriven's analogy is false,

1. The Michelson–Morley experiment was not part of a lengthy series of experiments which included many "impressively disillusioning" instances of fraud and self-deception.
2. There was and is no reason to suspect that the experiment would not be repeatable, as well as being subject to indirect confirmation by other repeatable and repeated experiments.
3. Even if no one could immediately provide a theory to encompass the Michelson–Morley findings, there was no good reason to fear that such a theory could not be produced. In parapsychology, on the other hand, investigators have had almost a century for theorizing without making any progress.

Thus, replicability is even *more* important in parapsychology than it is in normal science and this brief review should make it clear to the reader that the onus still rests with the parapsychologists to deliver what the skeptic has demanded for so long—an experiment that is replicable by anyone who makes a careful effort to replicate it. Anything short of this puts the parapsychological corpus of knowledge outside the realm of science, for, as Flew said,

> If scientific-minded people view the evidence of psychical research with suspicion because it is not repeatable, then they are quite right. The whole object of the scientific exercise is to discover true laws, and theories that explain the truth of these laws. If the alleged phenomena are not repeatable at all, then they clearly cannot be subsumed under any natural laws, even if they do occur. (1976, p. 30.)

Without it being possible for any competent researcher to replicate a given set of findings, one is left with no way of checking either on the methodological propriety of the original researcher, or on his honesty. Dishonesty crops up in research from time to time, just as it crops up in other areas of human endeavour. In regular science, the dishonest researcher will eventually be found out, when others are unable to reproduce his results. Since replication by independent, impartial researchers seems not to be possible in parapsychology, the possibility of fraud poses a particularly serious danger.

3. The spectre of fraud

The history of mediums has from its very beginnings been riddled with fraud and on many occasions scientists of high reputation were deceived into declaring the paranormal powers of a medium to be genuine. Harry Houdini spent much of his life exposing phony mediums, and in fact he never found one whom he was not able to unmask as a fraud. Believers, however, typically respond with the remark that while the medium may have resorted to cheating on occasion, most of the time he used real paranormal powers.

One parapsychologist of considerable repute declared,

> The investigator who is rigidly skeptical when he is told stories of the marvellous, must not be foolishly credulous of stories merely because they claim to undermine the marvellous. (Thouless, 1963, p. 25.)

and then he asked,

> Does the fact that the Creery sisters sometimes cheated when they had the opportunity reduce the evidential value of those experiments in which they had no chance of cheating?

The answer is, of course, "Yes, it does!"

Margaret Mead (1977) also argued that, since the occurrence of psychic powers cannot always be predicted, mediums and psychics sometimes resort to cheating, but that should not be held to weaken the case for their psychic abilities.

The rise and fall of Uri Geller is a recent case that should give people pause the next time a miracle worker comes along. Geller, an Israeli psychic brought to the United States by Dr. Andrija Puharich, became the star attraction of many television talk shows. His powers were bestowed on him by extraterrestrials come to save the planet Earth, he claimed. These powers allowed him, not to cure the halt and lame as one might expect of a miracle worker, but to bend forks and keys.

Geller became more than a show business magician turned psychic. He succeeded to a remarkable extent to convince many scientists of his paranormal powers. Much of this conviction on the part of such scientists was based on the results of "carefully controlled" research done at the Stanford Research Institute (*not* part of Stanford University as is commonly believed) by two physicists, Russel Targ and Harold E. Puthoff. Some of their research into Geller's psychic abilities was published under the title "Information transmission under conditions of sensory shielding" in the prestigious British science journal, *Nature*. The editors of *Nature* took the unusual action, however, of editorializing about the paper, pointing out that it was weak in design and vague in detail. The report was being published, the editors stated, as a "high risk" type of paper. Publication was not to be taken as a seal of approval by the editors, but as a way of bringing to the attention of the scientific community the kind of evidence that is becoming available from psychic researchers, which might merit their attention. The editors commented that, ". . . the unusual must now and then be allowed a toe-hold in the literature, sometimes to flourish, more often to be forgotten in a year or two" (*Nature*, 1974, **251**, p. 560). A summary of the objections raised by the reviewers of the article was included. One reviewer was against publication, one did not feel strongly either way, and the third was guardedly in favour of publication. In addition the editors drew attention to the simultaneous publication in *New Scientist* of an article by Dr. Joseph Hanlon which was highly critical of the tests of Uri Geller's psychic powers.

Predictably, however, the publication of the Targ and Puthoff paper, despite the editor's caveats, was taken by many parapsychology enthusiasts as a breakthrough. At last, reputable scientific journals were opening their pages to paranormal research!

It was through the diligent efforts of conjurer James ("The Amazing") Randi that Geller was finally, at least in most people's eyes, exposed. Randi demonstrated that he could by ordinary conjuring means duplicate Geller's feats. His perseverance in investigating and unveiling the circumstances of many of Geller's more spectacular performances (including the discovery of confederates who aided Geller when necessary) made it very difficult for anyone with any degree of critical thought to continue to accept Geller's claims. Randi's motivation?

> . . . I *am* a conjurer, "one who gives the impression of performing acts of magic by using deception". And I am proud of my profession. I am even jealous of it and resent any prostitution of the art. In my view, Geller brings disgrace to the craft I practice. Worse than that, he warps the thinking of a young generation, and this is unforgiveable. (Randi, 1975, pp. 4–5.)

One cannot easily dismiss the Geller phenomenon, and here I mean the near-success he had in fooling the world, scientist, and layperson alike. We must wonder, had it not been for Randi's determination and perseverance in showing the world the other side of Geller, where Geller would be today. Would the Geller demonstrations have continued to persuade some scientists of the reality of the paranormal?

It is not just the flashy show-business psychics who have been guilty of fraud. Time and time again, from the earliest beginnings of scientific parapsychology, fraud on the part of subjects from every walk of life has plagued experimental research. Great efforts have been made to eliminate subject cheating, but even if such cheating *is* eliminated, there is always the possibility of fraud on the part of the experimenter as was mentioned in Chapter 1. Hansel (1966) examined the "conclusive experiments" upon which the case for ESP seemed to be most solidly based, and in each case found that cheating and trickery were at least *possible* given the experimental set-up.

There have been numerous cases of demonstrated fraud in parapsychology, perhaps none more celebrated in recent times than that of Walter Levy. Levy spent his summer vacations from medical school working in Rhine's laboratory, and when he graduated he went on to become Director of this same laboratory. He had great success in repeating what was considered to be a very important study (that of Duval and Montredon, 1971), and this led McConnell (1977b) to comment that such near-perfect repeatability had never before occurred in parapsychology. Sometime later, one of Levy's co-workers became suspicious of the continual and unnecessary attention Levy paid to his recording apparatus. After discussing this with other co-workers, he secretly hooked up independent recording equipment which established beyond any doubt that Levy was altering his data. Quite properly and promptly, Rhine relieved Levy of his position, and wrote publicly at some length about the event (Rhine, 1974b), describing its serious implication for his laboratory and for parapsychology in general. Rhine himself at this point emphasized the need for repeatability or a safeguard against experimenter dishonesty: one must rely on objective and independently verifiable evidence, and not on mere personal testimony, he said.

It is because the claims of parapsychologists would be of such extreme importance, if true, that extraordinary precautions are needed. It is because replicability has not been achieved by parapsychologists that, when fraud is a possible explanation in a given experiment, we cannot dismiss it as an important alternative explanation. The famous Soal–Goldney experiments carried out between 1941 and 1943 were designed with elaborate safeguards against fraud; independent witnesses were called in, copies of the records were made at each sitting and independently checked, and so forth:

> Above-chance scoring was achieved, in general, on the card one ahead of that being looked at, suggesting precognition. When the rate of queries was speeded up, success shifted to the card two ahead. The series has long been quoted as a model of meticulous technique in experimental parapsychology, and, for some people at least, has stood as a mainstay of the evidence for extrasensory perception. (Scott and Haskell, 1973, p. 52.)

Yet, troubling suggestions of possible fraud were heard here and there. Hansel (1966) and Price (1955) suggested possible ways that Soal could have cheated with the assistance of several confederates, but it remained for Scott and Haskell (1973) to provide persuasive evidence of outright fraud perpetrated by Soal. They described the events leading to this conclusion in this way: Soal responded to a skeptic's request in 1956 to see the original data by stating that they had been lost in 1945, although hand-made copies of the originals were available. In 1960 Soal and Goldney reported that one "agent" in some of the sittings, "Mrs. G. A.", had told Goldney that she had seen Soal "altering the figures" during the sittings, changing "1's" into "4's" and "5's". This public report by Soal and Goldney came only after Scott had interviewed "Mrs. G. A." and had threatened to publish an account of the matter himself. Scott and Haskell (1973) then carefully examined the copies of the Soal–Goldney data for the "G. A." sittings. In all three, Soal had recorded the targets, which were numbers chosen by a random process, at or before the sittings. The set-up was such that the experimenter would sit on one side of a table separated by a screen from the sending "agent" who sat on the other side. The experimenter would hold up a card with the target digit, n (between 1 and 5), to a window in the screen, the agent would choose the nth of five animal picture cards (giraffe, elephant, etc.) and briefly look at it, while in the next room the receiver would write down one of five letters corresponding to the animal names. It had previously been discovered by Medhurst (1971) that either Soal's description of the choice of the sequence of numbers was in error or there had been considerable tampering, for the generated numbers could not have come from the process Soal described. Scott and Haskell found that in the three sittings they examined, the target sequence was consistent with the notion that Soal had begun with an excess of 1s and with a deficit of 4s and 5s, and that he later changed 1s into 4s and 5s when so doing would increase the receiver's "success". They concluded that the evidence for manipulation in the three sittings was "overwhelming". Since it is unlikely that anyone would bother to cheat if genuine ESP results had been coming in in the earlier sittings, they argued, the targets in the earlier sessions were most likely manipulated as well. These authors absolved Mrs. Goldney since she was away for one of the sittings and since she had been clearly desirous of publishing the G. A. allegations.

Yet Beloff defended Soal, and commented that:

> It is ironic that one of the most highly regarded investigations in the whole of the experimental literature which was deliberately designed to safeguard the experimenters from subsequent suspicion of duplicity, by having outside observers present at every session, failed miserably at this objective. . . . Eventually Soal became the victim not merely of insinuation but even of outright accusation of fraud. (1973, p. 259.)

Also in defence of the Soal–Goldney experiments, Mundle questioned G. A.'s reliability as a witness, and questioned the credibility of Scott and Haskell's interpretation. Independent observers were present at some of the sessions which would have made any such cheating highly risky, he said. In addition,

> Is it credible that Soal would have [cheated] at sitting 17, having received from Goldney what if guilty he would have recognized as a danger signal? He could not rely upon Goldney not to watch him during the decoding or to inspect the target list before decoding and notice an unusual shortness of the "1's" (which would have been necessary for later conversion to 4's and 5's). The fact that the statistical anomalies found in sitting 16 recur in sitting 17 seems to count rather strongly against the Scott and Haskell interpretation. (1973, p. 54.)

Are we to accept that paranormal processes exist because it is unlikely that Soal would have taken such a risk? And how else apart from fraud would one explain the very real statistical anomalies in the *target* sequences?

Consider another set of studies (Kanthamani and Kelly, 1974; Kelly and Kanthamani, 1972; Kelly *et al.*, 1975) which are regarded by Beloff (1980) as "perhaps the most evidential in the entire parapsychological literature". The studies involved a Yale University law student, "B. D." (Bill Delmore), who had what seemed to be an uncanny ability for guessing playing cards. This task was the principal but not the only one used in the tests.

Yet statistician-magician Diaconis (1978) witnessed a presentation of B. D.'s powers at Harvard in 1972. Even though the conditions in this demonstration were not meant to be well-controlled, his observations at that time highlight the problems which make it very difficult to draw correct inferences even from apparently well-controlled experiments. Among other things, he saw B. D. occasionally using sleight of hand to help chance along. Diaconis concluded that his own curiosity about the possibility of B. D. having powers that upset the known physical laws was laid to rest. There was no evidence of anything other than deception.

Kelly (1979) argued with Diaconis' critique, claiming that B. D. was able to produce psychic effects under carefully controlled conditions. Diaconis (1979) responded that either Kelly was unaware that B. D. was skilled at using sleight of hand, or Kelly was aware but chose not to say anything about this in any of his research articles about B. D. "Neither possibility", Diaconis said, "makes me put much faith in Kelly's research with B. D."[17]

It is not only skeptics who are concerned about the problem of fraud. Scott Rogo, a frequent contributor to the parapsychology literature, wrote:

> One can indeed be amazed at the fact that while Rhine, Soal and others were stringent in trying to safeguard against both recording error and the criticism of experimenter fraud, modern experiments are many times run and evaluated by a single researcher with no supervision. (1972, p. 6.)

---

[17] See also Rao (1978) for another parapsychologist's attempts to rebut Diaconis.

In summary, because of the inability for skeptical scientists to replicate parapsychological findings, and because of the long history of fraud in parapsychology, one cannot avoid considering fraud as an important alternative hypothesis, one which must be ruled out before the contemporary laws of physics are called to account.

4. The lack of systematic research

A serious weakness in much of parapsychology, independently of whether or not psi exists, is the failure to pursue a putative demonstration of a paranormal phenomenon by doing further systematic research. Partly, this is because of such things as the decline effect—further study typically leads to a disappearance of the phenomenon. However, it is partly due as well to a kind of ambivalence which seems all too evident in much of parapsychology. Despite repeated claims that the existence of paranormal phenomena has been clearly demonstrated and that effort should now be directed towards understanding the mechanism by which such phenomena are produced, the bulk of the parapsychological literature continues to reflect an obsession with trying to demonstrate that psi occurs. (Skeptics, of course, are not surprised at this, since in their view, such evidence has not as yet been forthcoming.)

Unfortunately, as is the case in sections of the social sciences, the research then takes the form of a series of one-shot demonstrations. Helmut Schmidt (1970), a paraphysicist who received considerable acclaim from parapsychologists for the introduction into para-psychological research of a random-event generator based on radioactive decay, reported that a cat in a cold garden shed was able to keep a light (the only source of heat), which went on and off as a function of the random event generator, illuminated more than one would expect by chance. If one accepted that the slight but significant departure from chance expectation that he observed was an indication of psi, would not one want to repeat the study, using many different cats and varying the physical conditions in order to try to understand more about the mysterious ability? If the light in the garage did stay on longer than expected for five trials (but not, as it turned out, for the next five trials (Davis, 1979)) how could Schmidt conclude that psychokinesis had been demonstrated, treat that case as "closed", and go on next to study the ability of cockroaches to influence a random-number generator so as to avoid shock? Why not focus on the cat's "ability" and hypothesize various alternative explanations and then run studies to differentiate between them? Would the cat "keep" the lamp off if the shed was made too warm? Would it do so if it were anesthetized?

Schmidt reported in the same article that even cockroaches seem to have psi ability, but that they must be masochistic since they influenced a random generator to give them *more* shocks than chance would dictate (odds 143 to 1 and 8000 to 1 in two different experiments). Schmidt suggested that this finding might be due to his *own* psi abilities, yet he did not consider it worthwhile to empirically examine *this* hypothesis by using a variety of experimenters. In normal science when something "unusual" is observed, effort is focused on finding a causal explanation for the anomaly. Rawcliffe asked bluntly, ". . . Why not . . . actively *seek* the causal connection instead of passively falling back on a tradition of occultism to explain [their] experimental results?" (1959, p. 482).

Acupuncture, although excluded from the domain of parapsychology by most parapsychologists, provides a case in point. Acupuncture has been around for centuries. In the West, there has been continued interest in it in occult circles, but this interest never went beyond accepting the dogma. No one was interested in running evaluation studies. No one tried to integrate it with normal science. No progress was made in demonstrating its reality or its value. However, when Western scientists finally became interested in it, following the report of the personal experience of a respected American journalist who underwent an operation in China while under acupuncture analgesia, it was approached in a systematic way. Attempts were made to fit its mode of operation into theories of pain (e.g. Melzack's (1973) gate-control theory). Double-blind studies were run to assess its effects. The separate discovery of an internal source of morphine, "endorphin" (*endogenous morphine*), led to the finding that acupuncture seems to stimulate the release of endorphin. Research is continuing in this area. The point here is that even when scientists felt that the reports were strong enough to make the study of acupuncture worthwhile, they did not begin by accepting the occult assumptions which had long been associated with acupuncture "theory".

In summary, is it not justifiable to expect that parapsychological research should be systematic rather than being dominated by one-shot miracles? X-rays were once mysterious, bizarre. Yet within 2 months of his discovery of X-rays, Roentgen had identified seventeen of their major properties (Platt, 1964). Is it not reasonable to expect that a century of research into psi should have produced a demonstrable set of properties, other than negative descriptions such as that psi is not affected by time or space?

Conclusion

It would be unfair to treat all parapsychologists as though they shared a common approach to the study of the putatively paranormal. Some accept even the wildest claims in the absence of evidence, and some have no idea of what constitutes evidence and no inkling of the many problems involved in drawing inferences from experiments. But there are others who are much more sophisticated and *capable* of doing careful research, although they sometimes seem blinded to error and artifact by the intensity of their guiding beliefs.

The major weakness of parapsychology is, as it has been from the beginning, the absence of clearly definable and demonstrable phenomena. This leaves parapsychologists in a position somewhat like trying prove that a murder has taken place in the absence of a body. They argue that various people saw the corpse, but critics demand to see it for themselves. The latter cannot prove that a murder did not occur, while the former cannot demonstrate without the body that it did. In a court of law, of course, eyewitness accounts and circumstantial evidence may be enough to "establish" that someone was killed, if the evidence is both internally consistent and consistent with other facts. In the court of science, such testimony, too, will be accepted as establishing a *prima facie* case for a phenomenon, but only if it is both internally consistent and consistent with other well-established facts. Parapsychologists have not been able to establish consistency of either type, despite a century of effort. Some critical parapsychologists themselves admit this, but often are willing to overlook the weaknesses of individual studies and take the illogical position that although each of a number of studies is independently subject to deserved criticism, taken together they can be viewed as forming a strong case for the existence of psi. This argument is often referred to as a "bundle-of-sticks" argument — a bundle of sticks can be very strong even though each stick is by itself weak. John Beloff has done considerable research in the area without detecting any convincing manifestation of psi. In many ways, he is a good critic of the domain, and yet, despite the lack of evidence coming from any given study or set of studies, he lets his guard fall to the combined appeal of a collection of weak studies. After critically summarizing seven major experiments in parapsychology, and pointing to weaknesses in most of them, he wrote:

> It is not my contention that any of the aforegoing experiments were perfect . . . or beyond criticism. . . . Moreover, unless a much higher level of repeatability becomes possible, the skeptical option, that the results can be attributed to carelessness or to conscious or unconscious cheating on the part of one or more of the experimenters, remains open and valid. Nevertheless, it is my personal opinion that these seven different investigations represent an *overwhelming* case for accepting the reality of psi phenomena. (Beloff, 1980, p. 94, italics added.)

Parapsychologists cannot expect to win converts from the world of science with arguments such as that. What is required is a solid, reliable demonstration of a phenomenon to study. Once that is found, if it can be found, parapsychologists will be in danger of being pushed aside in the stampede of researchers from all domains of science who want to study what would surely be the most exciting discovery in the modern history of science.

In answer to the question posed earlier—Is parapsychology a proto-science or a pseudo-science?—the table below summarizes what has been said about parapsychology in this chapter.

Bunge's criteria for pseudo-science	Parapsychology
Theory of knowledge subjectivistic, with aspects accessible only to initiated	Experimenter effect and sheep–goat effect imply only believers will detect or experience psi
Formal background modest, little mathematics or logic	True of parapsychology (but also true of much of social science)
Untestable hypotheses in conflict with a larger body of knowledge	True of parapsychology
Methods neither checkable by alternative methods nor justifiable in terms of well-confirmed theories	True of parapsychology: There is no independent measure of psi, and no well-confirmed theory
No overlap with another field of research	True of parapsychology. Apparent overlap is illusory, and only represents parapsychologists trying to extend their findings to other domains
No specific background of well-confirmed theory	True of parapsychology
An unchanging body of belief	True of parapsychology
A world-view admitting elusive immaterial entities	True of parapsychology

The conclusion is inescapable. By these very reasonable criteria, parapsychology constitutes neither science nor proto-science. This does not mean, of course, that an individual who carries out an empirical investigation of putative psi phenomena is *necessarily* being pseudo-scientific. However, if he chooses to explain away failures to replicate by reference to such "principles" as the "experimenter effect", or if he ignores competing "normal" explanations for whatever he might observe, preferring instead to leap to a "paranormal" explanation, then he *is* being pseudo-scientific. It has taken a very long time to overcome the myriad metaphysical explanations for natural phenomena that grew out of the ignorance and magic of our ancestors; no thoughtful scientist is about to admit into the fold of science an approach or a belief system which argues for the existence of the miraculous while at the same time pleading the necessity for a special relaxation of the rules of evidence.

CHAPTER 7

Parapsychology and Statistics

> In the scientific process, each successive detail is provided for. In the magic process, there are just
> the wish and the result, and all intermediate steps are omitted.
>
> G. R. Price[1]

> . . . [parapsychology] with its statement of non-chance but with its utter failure to produce any
> regularities or to perform a single repeatable experiment is the only instance of which [I am] aware
> in which a serious claim has been made that non-chance should be capitalized just because it is
> non-chance.
>
> P. W. Bridgman[2]

ALMOST a half-century ago, psychologist Kurt Lewin (1931) wrote that the methodological
and theoretical approaches of psychology are more like those of Aristotelian physics, which
was preoccupied with the classification of events and objects, than like those of Galilean or
post-Galilean physics. Aristotelian physics sought laws governing classes of events, and it
was assumed that some classes of objects, such as rocks, might be subject to laws which are
different from the laws governing other classes of objects, such as feathers. Aristotelian
physics used as one of its criteria for establishing laws the frequency of the event, and events
that occurred regularly were considered "lawful" while unique events were considered to be
due to chance. The goal was to abstract from many instances a general tendency which *most
often* characterizes the behaviour of an object (Atkinson, 1964). Galilean physics, on the
other hand, rejected the idea of different laws for different categories, and sought universal
laws applicable to all events and objects. Galileo did not, Lewin noted, enumerate the law of
falling bodies after calculating an average based on many trials. Rather, he transcended
observation and conceived of a common factor underlying the fall of all objects. Had he
based his "law" on mere observation, he would have observed that rocks and feathers do fall
at different rates (because of air resistance).[3]

Psychology too is concerned with classification, in terms of "biological–environmental",
"normal–abnormal", "sensory" or "perceptual", etc., Lewin argued. Its researchers seek
laws of behaviour by calculating the "average" characteristics for each of the categories.
They typically work with group data and means, treating individual variation as "noise" to
be overcome through the process of statistical analysis, which is intended to maximize the
"signal" and minimize the "noise". Signorelli summarized Lewin's argument:

> The physicist thus uses experimentation to demonstrate the validity of a law, to show its
> application under various conditions, or to demonstrate an exception to a law. The psychologist,

---

[1] Price (1955), p. 361.
[2] Bridgman (1956), pp. 16–17.
[3] Professor H. W. Proppe has brought to my attention a "thought experiment" which makes clear, without the
need for observation, that objects of different masses must fall at the same rate: If it were the case that rate of
fall *did* depend on mass, what would happen if a rock broke into two separate pieces as it was falling—do the
pieces instantly slow down to the appropriate rate of fall? What if two falling rocks coalesce? Does the
ensemble suddenly speed up?

on the other hand, performs much of his experimentation or records numerous observations in the hope of discovering or detecting in the data lawful relationships. In general, such laws, which are thus apparently discovered, apply only to a limited class of events rather than to the totality of behaviour. (1974, pp. 776–777.)

Experimental parapsychology, like much of psychology, is an Aristotelian[4] endeavour; the researcher gathers data over a great number of trials and then attempts to show that the data, on average, are different from what one would expect "by chance". Any such difference is "explained" in terms of paranormal processes. Rather than make specific predictions, the researcher merely looks for departures from the chance model. It is not possible to specify in advance what form that departure will take—a greater than expected success rate, a smaller than expected success rate ("psi-missing") or one or the other of these that is manifested only when one compares responses with targets one away, two away or three away from the supposed target in the series ("displacement").

Parapsychologists often argue that their critics seem unwilling to give serious consideration to the data parapsychological research has produced. Stanley Krippner, a parapsychologist, wrote:

> . . . it can be seen that psychical research poses many challenges. The data challenge parapsychologists to construct theories as to the mechanisms of psi as well as to find possible applications for the constructive use of ESP and PK. *And the data challenge non-parapsychologists to accept them or to find logical reasons for not doing so.* (1977, p. 12, italics added.)

It is curious that Krippner five pages earlier in the same work seemed to have provided such logical reasons himself:

> Since Charles Richet (1884) first applied statistics to psychical research data nearly 100 years ago, no experimental procedure has emerged which would invariably produce the same results no matter who followed it. Furthermore, no mechanism underlying psi has been discovered. . . . Finally, no practical use of ESP or PK has been validated by laboratory research. If any of these possibilities should develop . . . parapsychology could leave its place at the fringes and be swept into the mainstream of scientific inquiry (1977, p. 7).

Krippner himself thus acknowledged that these are logical reasons for not accepting parapsychological data. It can even be argued that there is not even a *prima facie* case for the existence of psi, as will be further discussed in this chapter.

Only the statistical evidence for parapsychology generates any degree of interest among scientists. The fork-benders and table-tilters, the automatic writers and the psychic healers may dazzle psychical (and other) researchers for a while, but their appeal is short-lived. Invariably, they are unmasked as tricksters and only the most loyal of their supporters continue to have faith in them.

But *statistical* evidence is another thing. Many an otherwise skeptical individual is puzzled, or intrigued, or sometimes even swayed by highly significant statistical results which are adduced to support a paranormal hypothesis. "How can you explain these findings?" the critic is often asked. "Maybe there really is something there?" Weaver demonstrated the kind of conflict that statistical evidence can create in the mind of someone who believes psi phenomena to have low *a priori* probability of existence. He said that,

---

[4] Indeed, as Professor Bunge has pointed out to me, it would be more accurate to say that experimental parapsychology is a *Baconian* endeavour. Aristotle, although he gave too much weight to experience, was also a theorist, while Bacon, although he spoke of theories, proposed none. Bacon is the source of modern empiricism, according to which scientific research consists of data collection (Personal communication, 1980).

On the one hand, we are asked to accept an interpretation that destroys the most fundamental ideas and principles on which modern science has been based; we are asked to give up the irreversibility of time, to accept an effect that shows no decay with distance and hence involves communication without energy being involved; asked to believe in an "effect" that depends on no known quantities and for which no explanation has been offered, to credit phenomena which are subject to decline or disappearance for unexplained and unexplainable reasons. On the other hand, we are asked not to believe that a highly improbable chance result has occurred. All I can say is, I find this a very tough pair of alternatives. (1963, p. 360.)

In this chapter, I shall attempt to persuade the reader that the second horn of Weaver's dilemma, the highly improbable chance result, may be little more than an illusion produced by experimental "contamination" (i.e. uncontrolled variables which influence experimental results) and/or the vicissitudes of statistical analysis. The automatic leap from extra-chance results to extrasensory explanations is, it will be argued, a leap of faith.

Statistical Inference

While the importance of logical deduction in decision-making has been recognized since the days of the ancient Greeks, *induction* became a systematic tool of formal reasoning only late in the eighteenth century (Weaver, 1963). It was Francis Bacon (1561–1626) who first urged the use of inductive procedures. He not only emphasized the importance of experiments, but also argued that theory and experiment, used together so that one checks the other, provide the most efficacious way to advance our knowledge of the natural world (Platt, 1964). Induction becomes necessary when it is impossible or impractical to observe or measure all instances in a set of events that one wishes to study, either because there are so many, or because of their inaccessibility. Induction, unlike deduction, is a method of uncertain inference, leading to judgements about the *likelihood* of a general conclusion.

Suppose someone tries to guess in advance how a coin will land on each of a series of tosses. Sometimes, the individual will be "lucky" and guess correctly a large number of times running. This is balanced, in the long run, by incorrect guesses. By the use of inferential statistics, one can make decisions about how likely it is that the number of successful predictions observed would have occurred if the tossing of the coin was totally "fair", and if no one was influencing the coin in its fall. Although the correct prediction of twenty successive coin tosses is an occurrence which would be expected to happen rarely if there are no biases operating in the situation, it should be expected to happen *sometimes*.

Parapsychologists interpret extra-chance results in their experiments as manifestations of psi. However, the non-chance results are also the evidence used to argue that psi *exists*, leading to circular reasoning (i.e. the "nominal fallacy") again:

"How do you know the subject used ESP?"
—"He obtained non-chance results."
"How did he obtain non-chance results?"
—"He used ESP."

Until parapsychologists can demonstrate the existence of psi independently of these non-chance results, the vicious circle will remain.

Another way of looking at this is in terms of the logical fallacy known as "affirming the consequent". Consider these two demonstrations of this faulty logic:

1. All birds have two feet.
   Beavers have two feet.
   Therefore beavers are birds.

2. Subjects using ESP will score above (or below) chance in an ESP experiment.
   These subjects scored above (or below) chance.
   Therefore, these subjects used ESP.

The point is that statistical evidence is never, of itself, "proof" of anything. All statistical analysis can do is to indicate how likely it is that the data collected would be randomly drawn from a specific *population* of data (i.e. How likely is it that the sample of data gathered in an ESP task would have been observed had no extra-chance factor been involved?) If a coin is tossed one hundred times and lands heads up seventy-five of those times, statistical analysis will help us decide how likely it is that the coin was a "fair" coin; that is, that the observed outcomes came from a hypothetical distribution of outcomes corresponding to those which would be generated by a fair coin. Even if we decide, on the basis of the analysis, that the sample of outcomes is unlikely to have come from such a distribution, we cannot *necessarily* draw conclusions about the intrinsic fairness of the coin. It could be, for instance, that the person tossing the coin always began with his hand the same distance from the table, and with the coin head up on his thumbnail. Such regularity in the starting position could quite easily bias the sequence of outcomes in one direction or another. There are other possible factors too, both obvious and subtle, which might lead to a misleading statistical decision quite independently of the fairness of the coin. But if all possible biases are eliminated (and one can never be sure that one has discovered all possible biases, let alone controlled or eliminated them), it is possible, though highly unlikely, that a perfectly fair coin will come up heads one hundred times in a row. On the other hand, if one hundred researchers became interested in the effects of wishful thinking on coin-outcome, and each sat down with twenty different subjects, and after "controlling" all recognized sources of bias, perhaps by having a machine whose "fairness" had been demonstrated do the tossing, it should not be too surprising if some of them had subjects who were able to "produce" heads, say, ten times in succession. One would *expect* it to happen sometime. To the individual who produces a series of ten heads, however, the outcome may seem to be more than mere "coincidence". As was said in an earlier chapter, coincidences are often so emotionally striking that one cannot easily accept "coincidence" as an explanation.

It is necessary to briefly discuss how one goes about making a statistical test before further discussing the use of statistics in parapsychology. One begins with a "null" hypothesis, "H_0" (e.g. men and women have the same average resting pulse rate), and an alternate hypothesis, "H_1" (e.g. men and women differ in their average resting pulse rates). Since it is impractical to examine *all* men and *all* women, one is obliged to work with samples of each (typically drawn *at random* from the collections of men and women of interest). On the basis of these samples, inferences are made about men and women in general. Sometimes, one will obtain by chance a sample of men whose average pulse rate is lower than that of the sample of women, even if H_0 is true. Since one knows that such chance occurrences are possible, it is necessary to judge whether a specific difference between the two samples is great enough to lead one to justify the inference that the average pulse rate of all men in the population of interest differs from the average for all women. Statistical inference methods allow one to choose in advance a certain likelihood of error. (The smaller the error that one is willing to risk, the more strict is the test, and the less likely it is that a true difference will be detected.) For example, one might say in advance that he wants to test the hypothesis that men and women differ in pulse rate, with the proviso that if they do *not* (i.e. H_0 is true) then one would be likely to erroneously reject H_0 (i.e. decide that there *is* a difference), less than five times in one hundred hypothetical tests. This is written as $p < .05$, (which means that if the null hypothesis is true, the data from the samples is likely to "fool us" into thinking that there is a difference, when none exists, less than five times in one hundred), and is usually verbalized as "there is a significant difference at the .05 level".

It is important to stress that every p value is based on the prior *assumption* that H_0 *is* true (with probability $= 1$). The p for the data one has collected is the probability of seeing these data *if* H_0 is true.

While one can arrive at a statistical decision that men and women differ in resting pulse rate, this by itself does not explain why that difference, if it is real, exists. Had the experimenter speculated that "men are less loving than women; loving is associated with the heart; men's hearts must therefore be smaller than women's, leading them to beat at a different rate", the statistical evidence would in no way lend any support to his hypothesis (nor does it argue against it). Many other factors, apart from size of heart, could be responsible. Further testing of size of heart and capacity for love would be necessary to evaluate the hypothesis.

The purpose of an experiment (with a control group which is treated identically to the experimental group in every way except that it does not receive the experimental "treatment") is to eliminate extraneous variables which could conceivably influence the results and perhaps by themselves produce an extra-chance effect.

Consider another example. An experimenter believes that giving people doses of vitamin A will improve their "night vision" and compares people given vitamin A and those not given it in terms of night visual capability. *If* differences are found between the two groups, the *statistical* result itself does not prove or disprove the *theory*. The experimenter may *infer* that the difference is due to vitamin A, but the statistical test does not demonstrate that. If the experimenter is certain that the two groups of subjects did not differ in any important way and if there was no difference in experimental treatment other than vitamin A administration (i.e. both groups were administered something in the same way; both had the same experiences, expectations, etc.), then he might infer with some confidence that vitamin A is the crucial ingredient. But if his hypothesis were more detailed (e.g. vitamin A improves the ability of the visual system to respond to night-time stimulation) he *could* be wrong. *Perhaps* vitamin A makes people more calm, allowing them to better concentrate on the visual task. Perhaps a tranquillizer would have the same effect. Thus, the experimenter must try, in subsequent studies, to eliminate these alternate explanations by coming to understand the mechanism by which vitamin A exercises its effect. The reasonable researcher would not be content with the demonstration of a difference alone. He would run a series of studies to identify the causal chain.

Parapsychological researchers rarely use control groups, and instead usually compare the outcomes of a psi experiment with what one would expect if chance alone were operating. The null hypothesis in such experiments is that if psi is not operating no extra-chance relationship between responses and targets will be observed. For example, in a chapter on statistical methods in the recent *Handbook of Parapsychology*, Burdick and Kelly (1977) stated that in a forced-choice experiment in which the subject chooses from a fixed number of responses in a series of trials,

A significant overall association between targets and responses is evidence of psi and reflects in general the presence of either or both of two main kinds of effects: systematic excess [of associations between targets and responses] (direct hitting) . . . [or] consistent but erroneous associations of targets and responses (consistent missing). (1977, p. 86.)

Both above-chance hitting and above-chance missing are treated as evidence of psi.

Theory is important, not only to generate hypotheses that can be tested, but to provide continuity from what is "known" to what is being hypothesized. The Gauquelins in their *Laboratoire d'etude des relations entre rythmes cosmiques et psychophysiologiques* in Paris have collected considerable data which they have used to argue that sports champions, but not less successful athletes, are more likely to be born when the planet Mars is rising or culminating during its diurnal movement (e.g. see Gauquelin and Gauquelin, 1976). This research has created considerable criticism based on the argument that the Gauquelin work contains errors in methodology and/or statistical analysis. The Gauquelins answer each criticism with a reasoned response. The debate continues.[5]

Whether there are statistical or methodological errors in Gauquelin's work on this so-called "Mars effect" is irrelevant to arguments about astrological influences. Even if the "Mars effect" may actually be shown to exist, it would remain, or *should* remain, a statistical curiosity until there is some theory which could connect the position of Mars to an influence at birth. Given current knowledge of physics and physiology, it is unreasonable to assume that the position of Mars in the sky at the moment of a baby's birth will produce any effect, let alone an influence which will endure throughout the life of the individual.

When two groups of subjects are compared, there is usually no reason to believe that the null hypothesis of no difference with respect to some variable of interest is true to begin with. Why should we expect that even if no important variable is operating differentially on, say, city dwellers and farm dwellers, they would have *exactly* the same IQ or height or whatever on average? If we were able to measure every member of the two populations of subjects, or of any two arbitrary halves of the same population, it is unlikely that the two averages would be identical.[6]

Thus, if we begin with two samples from two populations, and if the size (N) of the samples is large enough, we should expect to find "significant differences". As Nunnally has pointed out,

> If the null hypothesis is not rejected, it is usually because the N is too small. If enough data are gathered, the hypothesis will usually be rejected. If the rejection of the null hypothesis were the real intention of psychological experiments, there would usually be no need to gather data. (1960, p. 4.)

Some researchers might respond to this by arguing that they do not just predict a difference, but a *directional* difference. The "experimental" group, it is predicted, will have scores on the average either higher or lower than those of the "control" group. This in itself is not much of a defense, however, since it merely leads to the conclusion that half the time rather than all the time, the alternate hypothesis is true.

When one talks about *significance*, what one should really be concerned with is not just the probability that the results did or did not come from a distribution specified by H_0, but also the magnitude of the effect (of the independent variable, of the putative psi process, etc.). It is

---

[5] The interested reader is advised to study the debate between the Gauquelins and their opponents in the pages of the *Skeptical Inquirer*.

[6] Of course, if we have measured *everyone* in two groups, and then compare averages, the notion of statistical significance does not apply, since no inference is being made about a population on the basis of a sample. We have measured the whole population of interest in each case. We need simply look to see if the numerical averages are the same or not, in order to conclude that they are the same or not. And it is very unlikely that they would be identical. Why should they be?

not worth the bother to take a longevity pill which, in controlled tests, leads to "significantly longer life spans" if the addition to the life span, statistically significant or not, is only of the order of 5 minutes. Yet, most parapsychological (and psychological) research focuses on the existence of a difference, and not on the size of the difference. When large numbers of trials are run (as is typical in parapsychology), slight influences will be detected with high reliability. It is this high reliability that is reflected by a vanishingly low p value. Thus, if the "chance rate" in a card-guessing experiment were 5.0, a subject could obtain very highly "significant" results with an average score of 5.1 if enough trials were run. Schmidt's (1973) studies of psychokinesis produced "highly significant" results even though the individual scoring rate was seldom above 51 per cent compared to the chance level of 50 per cent.

Bakan (1966) listed three erroneous interpretations of the p-value that are common in psychological and parapsychological research, interpretations which are explicitly taught in some psychological statistics texts. These three erroneous beliefs, which shall be discussed below, are that the p-value is:

(a) the probability that the results are due to "chance";
(b) a measure of the power to predict the behaviour of the population;
(c) a measure of our confidence that the same results could be obtained if we attempted to replicate the experiment.

Parapsychologists often talk about their data in terms of the astronomical "odds" against them being "due to chance". This is an erroneous interpretation. We read in the usual psychological literature of effects significant at the "$p < .05$", "$p < .01$", or in the case of some parapsychological studies, "$p < 10^{-35}$ and $p < 10^{-70}$ (e.g. in one of Soal's studies (Hansel, 1980)). This p-value is taken, erroneously, to indicate the strength of the effect one has found.[7] In reality, it is tied in large part to the sizes of the samples used. If we have two populations of subjects, one of which has an average height $\frac{1}{2}$ inch greater than the other, and if we take larger and larger samples, we will have more and more confidence that any differences between samples reflects differences between populations. When we examine the entire populations, our certainty is 1.0 as to whether there is a difference or not (ignoring measurement problems), and we then have $p = 0.0000$ since we are now "certain" that the data have not come from a population where H_0 is true. (i.e. the probability of having observed such a difference, while there really is *no* difference, is zero. We *know* there is a difference.)

As Bakan concluded,

> There is little question but that sizable differences . . . in samples, especially samples of reasonable size, speak more strongly of sizable differences . . . in the population; and there is little question but that if there is a real and strong effect in the population, it will continue to manifest itself in further sampling. However, these are inferences which *we* may make. They are outside the

---

[7] Parapsychologists (and psychologists) are guilty not only of interpreting statistical significance as a measure of the strength of the effect, but also of violating the statistical inference model by setting their criteria for rejection of the null hypothesis *after* examining the data. While by convention, they are unlikely to reject the null hypothesis if $p > .05$, on the other hand, they typically calculate the test statistic and then look up the p-value, instead of setting the criterion level of the test statistic in advance (e.g. at the $p < .05$ level) and comparing the calculated test statistic against it. Consequently, one habitually sees research reports which contain varying p-values, and these are implicitly and erroneously taken to indicate the strength of the effect. There is a close parallel with horse racing: the bettor who has so much confidence in his hypothesis (Red Dog will *win*) is paid more handsomely if Red Dog indeed does win, than is another bettor who bets that Red Dog will place or show. The bettor who bets "show" wins whether Red Dog wins, places or shows, but he cannot, after the race is *won* by Red Dog, go to the window and argue that he was *really* betting that Red Dog would win. In a similar vein, the assignment of the p-value *after* the test is done violates the classical statistics model.

inference model associated with the test of significance. The *p* value within the inference model is only the value which we take to be as how improbable an event could be under the null hypotheses which we judge will not take place to "us" in this one experiment. It is not a *measure of the goodness of the other inferences which we might make*. It is an a priori condition that we set up whereby we decide whether or not we will reject the null hypothesis, not a measure of significance. (1966, pp. 153–154, italics in the original.)

Probability Models

If a person is surprised that a coin tossed 10 times in succession came up heads each of those times, it is because of an implicit model (or underlying probability distribution) of the two outcomes: He expects to see heads come up approximately one-half the time. Seven heads out of ten would not be surprising, but ten out of ten would seem very odd. Yet, if he were to find that the coin was a two-headed coin, he would no longer look for influences in the tossing procedure that produced unlikely deviations from his model. He would now apply a *different* model, one with a single outcome, and in this case he would be surprised (indeed, shocked!) if any outcome was other than a head.

Even if events appear to occur with a frequency far in excess of what a chance model would predict, and bias and fraud have been virtually eliminated as possible factors, there is yet another possibility to consider; there are times when the chance model against which comparisons are being made is itself inappropriate. As an example of how the wrong "model" can lead to correctly computed but totally misleading results, consider the mystery of the "perfect" bridge deal mentioned earlier in Chapter 5. In the "perfect" bridge deal, one player receives all the hearts, another all the clubs, another all the diamonds, and the remaining player, all the spades. Such a hand is no more rare than *any* other bridge hand, but because other distributions of cards are not so noteworthy, people do not notice their rarity. However, any given distribution of cards, including the perfect one, *is* exceedingly unlikely because of the astronomical number of possible combinations. Any given distribution of cards is so unlikely (since there are 2.23×10^{27} different possible distributions) that;

> Such an event having once occurred, it should not logically recur, even if the entire world population made up in fours and played 120 hands of bridge a day, for another 2,000,000,000,000 years. (McWhirter and McWhirter, 1969, p. 492.)

Yet, every year, cases of four players each being dealt complete suits are reported. There have been suggestions that this "incredible" departure from chance indicates some kind of paranormal process at work, but most people knowledgeable in statistics are likely to concur with the conclusion of McWhirter and McWhirter (1969) that such a bridge deal, " . . . is so unlikely, not merely to strain credulity, but to be virtually certain evidence of rigged shuffling or hoaxing." Some people, then, are prepared *a priori* to reject as fraudulent any claims about perfect bridge hands because they are so improbable.

However, perhaps it is not the observations that are in error but the model against which they are being compared. It is implicitly assumed that the distribution of cards observed is chosen "at random" from all possible distributions. Yet, how does the deck get organized in the first place? Almost all new decks of cards are organized in ascending order by suit and as Epstein (1967) has observed, two "perfect" shuffles (in which the deck is divided exactly into two halves, and perfect interleaving of the two halves is accomplished) followed by any number of simple cuts (which have no effect on the cyclic order of the cards, merely changing the starting point) will invariably generate a "perfect" bridge deal. Thus, the likelihood of obtaining a perfect bridge deal, if one begins with a fresh deck, depends directly on the likelihood of doing two perfect shuffles. Epstein observed expert card dealers in Las Vegas and found that they

> create sequences with single-card interlacings approximately eight times as frequent as two-card interlacings; a group of three cards appears less than once per shuffle. (1967, p. 185.)

It is not unlikely that during the millions of bridge games played annually around the world, many commencing with fresh decks, someone will make two perfect shuffles.

This illustration is important because it emphasizes how erroneous conclusions can be drawn about events (e.g. the reported perfect bridge hand *must* be the result of fraud, since it is so "unlikely") because the probability model used to reach this decision is inappropriate as a description of the situation. If the "chance" model is inappropriate, the statistical decisions based on it will be in error, and as Diaconis observed, "in complex, badly controlled experiments simple chance models cannot be seriously considered as tenable explanations" (1978, p. 133).

Thus, any statistical decision one reaches in a parapsychology experiment is based on two important assumptions: (1) that the appropriate "chance" model was employed in the analysis and (2) that no extraneous variables have been in operation which would vitiate a comparison of the observed data with that model. The problem, as was said earlier, is that one is never *certain* that all extraneous variables have been eliminated. Further more, just as people were convinced that reports of perfect bridge deals must be fraudulent because they could not conceive of the way in which the assumptions of their probability model could be violated, so the experimenter may be unable to specify the important factors which may make his model inappropriate.

J. B. Rhine has insisted that the existence of ESP has been demonstrated beyond all reasonable doubt by several million tests with *Zener* cards, a twenty-five-card deck which includes five cards carrying a cross symbol, five a square, five a circle, five a star, and five some wavy lines. The paradigm is simple; the deck is shuffled, one person (the "sender") looks at one card at a time, and the other (the receiver), usually in another room, attempts to identify it. It is assumed that if the receiver is guessing, he should be expected to have an average of five correct guesses in each pass of the cards.[8]

One might expect that demonstration "beyond all reasonable doubt" would involve dramatic success rates, but this is not the case. If a large number of trials is run, only a slight effect is required to have statistically significant results. In a classic and important series of studies from the parapsychological literature known as the Pratt–Woodruff series[9], it was concluded that the odds were 1,700,000 to 1 that the results were not "due to chance". (Note that this is an erroneous interpretation of a *p*-value.) Yet Dommeyer (1966) has indicated that the average success rate in this study was only 5.204 (as opposed to the expected 5 if only chance were operating) over a large number of trials. He cited R. T. Birge (1958), who said that, although this study is considered to be one of the most convincing on record, in fact there was on average only one more hit than expected by chance in each 123 trials.

Whenever a large number of subjects and/or trials is used, very *small* effects can be highly statistically significant. The problem in these cases is that minor biases, which normally

---

[8] For example, if a subject responded with "star" on each of the twenty-five trials, he would be correct five times.
[9] This was a series of studies carried out in 1939 in Rhine's Parapsychology Laboratory at Duke University. See Pratt and Woodruff (1939).

might not have any effect, can in a long series of trials produce minor effects which are highly significant statistically.

The chance model used in the analysis of card experiments, particularly the earlier ones, may have been an incorrect one. Just as the calculations of the extreme improbability of a perfect bridge hand were absolutely correct *for a randomized deck*, the statistics used by parapsychologists could be absolutely valid, but for a model the underlying assumptions of which may not in fact apply to the data. Using as an example the twenty-five-card Zener deck, the expected score from guessing can be considerably higher than it might at first seem. If the subject guesses the same card on each of twenty-five trials, without replacement, he will be correct five times out of twenty-five, since there are five of each kind of card. This was the traditional manner of calculating the effects of guessing. However, the subject has an important if not consciously recognized advantage because he usually is aware of the constitution of the deck. Epstein (1967) argued that, rather than guessing one or a few cards throughout, the subject will likely choose responses corresponding to the composition of the deck, that is, five of each kind of card. Epstein showed that, if the composition of the Zener deck is known (i.e. there are five of each kind of card), an error of 2 percent in the test statistic, which would favour the ESP hypothesis, can occur.[10]

If the subject is given feedback (i.e. is told what the card was after he makes his choice, as is done in some studies), the best strategy is to choose for the next unexposed card the symbol which has so far come up the least often, since there are more of that symbol left in the unexposed part of the deck. In this case, the chance expectation is not five cards correct out of twenty-five, but 8.647 (Epstein, 1967).

Another problem cited by Epstein is the incorrect treatment of forward or backward displacement of the guesses. Displacement is common in parapsychological research, the argument being that the receiver may not be "synchronized" with the sender, and may in fact be "seeing" one or two cards ahead or behind. It was displacement that convinced S. G. Soal of the reality of ESP. During the first 4 years (1935–1939) of his research he ran 160 subjects and recorded 128,000 responses, but found only "chance" results. However, when Whately Carrington, also a parapsychologist, persuaded him to recheck his data for displacement, Soal was apparently surprised to find a significant indication of precognitive responding (Epstein, 1967). Yet again, if in a test involving a series of twenty-five Zener cards, one decides after the fact to search for forward or backward displacement, the expected success rate when a displacement of only one card is involved is 6.740 out of 25, and this figure is even higher when two or more card displacements are considered. (However, if the length of the series is quite long, this particular problem disappears.)

Most modern parapsychologists are now aware of these problems, and take them into account, although there are exceptions even today. Yet, some of the classic studies, the studies often referred to as providing the best case for ESP, were run without taking account of such problems.

Since parapsychological research typically compares subjects' success rate with what

---

[10] If the composition of the deck is unknown (i.e. all twenty-five cards could be identical) the standard deviation of the binomial probability distribution would be 2.0, while if the composition of the deck is known, and the subject distributes his guesses in line with this distribution, the standard deviation is 2.041. Since the significance of the result is evaluated in terms of standard deviations away from the expected value, the assumption that the probability of guessing a given card correctly is 1/5 introduces an error of 2 per cent in the value of the standard deviation which favours the ESP hypothesis.

would be expected if their responses were purely random, it is necessary to treat the subject of randomness itself in some detail.

Randomness, chance and parapsychology

Randomness and chance are fundamental concepts in any discussion of probability. Researchers often talk about "chance" as though it were of a causal nature. "These results were *due* to chance." Yet chance is not a non-determinate process that generates an observed outcome. The result of a coin toss is fully determined; the coin is exactly obedient to the laws of physics. However, because in ordinary circumstances we are unable to predict the outcome with certainty due to our lack of knowledge about how much pressure the tosser will apply to the coin, about how far it will drop and so forth, the outcome is *indeterminable*, although it is not *indeterminate*. People are prone to think that somehow the outcome of the coin toss *is* indeterminate, as though some sort of "randomizing homunculus" gives the coin a kick in one direction while it is in mid-flight. When we say that the outcome of a coin toss is due to chance, we mean that it is governed by variables that we are not able to measure. "Chance" in this case means that we are ignorant of the information needed to predict the outcome with certainty.

Gilmore (1974), in discussing chance and randomness, said that the concept "random" is used to mean several different things. For example, the digits 12345 could be truly random in certain respects (i.e. if they were the product of a random number generator) but non-random in other respects (i.e. given the first digit, and the rule that $digit_{n+1} = digit_n + 1$, each succeeding digit can be calculated). Randomness is sometimes defined, as in the first instance, as any sequence produced by a randomizer, and sometimes as any sequence not having a pattern. These two definitions are different.

Randomization is widely used in normal psychological research. We choose a sample *at random* (i.e. in a way such that each element in the population has an equal likelihood of being chosen) and we assign subjects to conditions at random. As Gilmore (1974) indicated, randomization is used in experimental settings to try to prevent contamination of our data by various error variables. If a sample of a population is composed of the first fifty people who walk through the door, it is quite possible that these fifty people are not typical of the population of interest. They may, for example, all be university students, and whatever conclusions we might draw using these people as subjects may not apply to the general population. If intelligence has an effect on outcome, and if these students are of higher than average intelligence, then results obtained with them may not be relevant to less intelligent persons. Random sampling does not always help, since we can occasionally choose samples "at random" in which most or all the subjects in one group are clearly different in some important way from those in another group. If a researcher chooses two samples at "random", and one turns out to be predominantly male and the other predominantly female, he might resample with the proviso that he wants equal representation of the sexes. But what about dimensions that cannot be so readily seen? As Gilmore pointed out, randomization is less effective than strictly controlling each error variable by identifying it, measuring its effects and then deliberately equalizing its effects at all points in the experimental sample space:

> Randomization has the claimed advantage that it can eliminate the effects of error variables the existence of which we do not suspect. But it must be remembered that *randomization is*

powerless to affect any error variable that is not markedly correlated with the randomized variables. (1974, p. 5, italics in original.)

If, for example, subjects after being chosen at random are randomly assigned to one of two groups, and a check is made to see that the two groups do not differ in terms of sex composition or age distribution, it does not mean that the groups do not differ in terms of variables (e.g. skin colour) not related to age or sex. If most of the subjects in one group happened to be white and most of those in the other happened to be black, this would be noticeable. However, with regard to error variables whose presence is not suspected, unless they were related to age or sex, there would be no assurance that they are distributed in a similar manner within each group.

Randomness is an essential concept in most parapsychological research. A deck of cards is thoroughly shuffled ("randomized"), and as the "sender" in a telepathy experiment turns up each card, the "receiver" is required to name the card. It is accepted that, because the cards were subject to "randomization", the resulting sequence of cards is "unpredictable". One then calculates the probability associated with the subject's success rate if only chance is operating.

If the randomized sequence is random only in the first sense of the word (i.e. the outcome of a random number generator), it is not necessarily free of readily learnable generational rules which correctly predict succeeding targets, at least over a short range. A slight advantage is all that is needed to obtain "highly significant" success rates, since the number of trials is generally very large. Various critics have raised this point, along with the related point that traditional random-number generators can be shown to depart from pure "randomness" over a long series of digits.

Several demonstrations have been made of how "non-chance" results in an ESP experiment could be obtained simply by matching two "random" sequences. Pitkin and Mulholland (Mulholland, 1938) with the aid of IBM began with a set of 200,000 cards. Half were red, and half white. Twenty thousand cards of each colour were marked with the digit 1, another 20,000 of each colour with the digit 2, and so on up to digit 5. The red cards and the white cards were separately mechanically shuffled. Then the two sets of cards were run through a machine, and a tape record was produced of the sequence of digits in each set of cards. The red card and white card sequences were then compared; this could serve as a type of a "control group" against which the results of ESP card tests could be compared. While one would expect a "hit" between the two series to occur once every five trials (by "chance"), some sequences were as long as thirty-two pairs without a match. Runs of eight matching pairs occurred 780 per cent more than would be expected by chance. Runs of five matching pairs occurred well below the expected frequency, while runs of six were well above. Runs of seven matching pairs occurred 59 per cent more often than would be predicted. There were three times as many runs of five in the first 40,000 pairs than in the remaining 60,000 (a "decline effect").

Other similar studies have been carried out; Bugelski argued that while a truly controlled experiment eliminates all variables except the experimental one, "there is one crucial variable that Rhine has not controlled and that is the function of chance itself" (1962, pp. 57–58). It is not enough to show that an event occurs in the presence of a given phenomenon (in this case, presumed psi ability). One must also show that the event does not occur in its absence. In discussing Rhine's work, he argued that Rhine should have shown that it is impossible to get high scores by chance alone over a reasonable period. (This gets back, of course, to the absence of a control group in parapsychological experiments. However, parapsychologists could argue that control groups are useless, since, if *both* experimental and control groups score equally above "chance", it is possible that the controls also used ESP. How can one *eliminate* the independent variable?) Earlier, Leuba (1939) had tried to see if he would get high scores in ESP-like experiments even when ESP was not a factor. He simply used two Zener decks, shuffled each, and turned each up, one card at a time, recording hits and misses. He gave the decks human names, and if the score on a given run was greater than 5, he retained the "subject's" identity and made another run. Otherwise, he changed the identity of the subject and began again. In this way, after running eighty-seven "subjects", he found three that would satisfy Rhine's criterion as possible possessors of ESP. However, Rhine was not satisfied with the conditions under which Leuba's study was run, and Bugelski and Bugelski (1940) undertook to meet Rhine's own specifications in a similar experiment. They used a mechanical shuffler and predetermined numbers of runs for each "subject". They found five "subjects" out of 1000 who scored "good" or "very good" by Rhine's criterion.

In a similar vein, Spencer Brown (1957) argued that it is incorrect to define randomness in terms of the absence of patterns, on the ground that it is a mathematical contradiction to say that there is no pattern.[11] He believed that

> any attempt to randomize, *of which tables of random numbers and psychical research experiments are both typical examples,* will lead all too frequently to the curious results which have been thought in the past by psychical researchers to be evidence of telepathy . . . . (p. 116, italics in the original.)

He suggested (Spencer Brown, 1953) that if many of the psychical research scores were examples of the 'failures' likely to result from attempts to randomize, then similar examples should occur in, for example, published random number tables:

> . . . I have evidence, also to be published shortly,[12] that statistically significant results similar to those of psychical research are obtainable simply by making selections in published tables of random numbers as if tables were themselves the data of a psychical research experiment. (1953, p. 154.)[13]

Oram (1954), with the help of fifty-five members of the Society for Psychical Research, then took a published set of 100,000 random numbers and treated them as the data from a card-guessing experiment. The random digits were printed in two-digit columns and the first digit was treated as the "guess" and the second as the actual value of the card. They not only looked for hits, but for displacement (e.g. comparing the "guess" with the *next* "card" to come). Oram found no significant frequency of hits or of one card displacements.

However, Spencer Brown (1957) argued that Oram missed one essential feature of his own results, and that was that if the "data" from Oram's study were treated in the same way that PK data were being treated at the Duke Laboratory at that time, which was to divide the data sheet into quartiles and compare the first and last quartile for position effects, there was a very significant position effect, a "quartile decline" (QD) effect.

---

[11] Scott (1958) demolished much of Spencer Brown's arguments about randomness. However, he agreed that Brown did show that unexpected departures from randomness can be found in allegedly random sequences, and he urged that Brown's data on this point should be taken seriously.

[12] These results were never published.

[13] Koestler (1972) in *The roots of coincidence* suggested that Spencer Brown's results might be an example of "seriality", a concept based on the notion that coincidences, whether occurring alone or in series, are manifestations of a universal principle in nature which operates independently of physical causation (pp. 85; 102–103). Thus Spencer Brown's critique is turned into an argument for an acausal process.

The "position effect", the relationship between rate of success and the position in which the score is recorded on the scoring sheet, has been given considerable importance in parapsychological research. Consider what Rhine himself had to say on the subject:

> The mere location on the record sheet of the trials in a psi test has been found to influence the rate of success. These variations have been found to show significant patterning in many researches and are called position effects (PE's). The most common PE is a decline of scoring rate in the column on the record sheet representing a run. . . . In a sheet composed, let us say, of ten vertical columns, or runs, the run may show a decline or U-curve, but the pages may show a decline from left to right. With both a lateral and a vertical decline, a diagonal decline will result.
> . . . these PE hit patterns are now recognized as a result of the subject's reaction to the structure of the test as reflected in the record sheet. If the subject has no awareness of the position of a trial in the run or other series, position effects are not to be expected. (1971, Appendix A.)

The quartile-decline effect with performance in the first quarter typically being superior to performance in the last quarter of the page—a page usually corresponding to the results of an entire session—was considered important by parapsychologists because it was felt that it is entirely immune to non-psi processes such as, for example, the bias of dice in a psychokinesis study (Stanford, 1977). And yet it showed up in Oram's data which came only from matching sections of random number tables. Indeed, Nicol (1955) stated that Oram's results provided the most significant single QD in the annals of psychical research.

Position effects are still considered to be of considerable importance today. Burdick and Kelly had this to say on this subject in the recent *Handbook of Parapsychology*:

> One class of non-random occurrences in the distribution of scoring involves various possibilities of systematic correlation of the scoring with *location* of one or another type, for example, location in the run, in the series, or in the structure of the recording sheet. A substantial amount of work has been done in this area, and effects of this sort are widely regarded as one of the more dependable manifestations of psi processes. (1977, p. 104.)

As far as this writer has been able to determine, Brown's comments about the position effect in the Oram data has not had an adequate response from parapsychologists. Nonetheless, most parapsychologists and many critics (e.g. G. R. Price (1955)), perhaps unaware of the quartile decline "effect" found in Oram's data, believe that Spencer Brown's arguments were rendered untenable by Oram. However, parapsychologist Gertrude Schmeidler, writing in the *Handbook of Parapsychology*, made a somewhat different comment on the Spencer Brown work:

> He attempted to show that random number tables were non-random by the naïve method of selecting a short sample of digits from the table, then entering the table at arbitrarily selected points and matching his initial sequence with these new ones. He found significant correspondences, followed by declining correspondences. They supported his argument but alternatively *could be interpreted as showing his successful use of ESP (or PK) in his first choices of the "right" places to enter the table.* (1977, p. 148, italics added.)

Thus, again a critique of psi methodology is interpreted as being possible evidence for psi! Harvie[14] (Hardy, Harvie, and Koestler, 1973) selected 50,000 digits from various sources

---

[14] For Harvie, departures from chance in the absence of ESP agents were interpreted as evidence of "synchronicity", a supposedly acausal principle of nature which accounts for coincidences. As it turns out, although Harvie interpreted his data in terms of synchronicity, and others have viewed it as illustrating the problems involved in using a chance probability model, Harvie's statistical analysis was seriously flawed. See Marks and Kammann (1980).

of random numbers and used them to represent "target cards" in an ESP experiment. Instead of having subjects make guesses, a series of 50,000 random[15] numbers were produced by a computer. Harvie's results showed a successful hit rate that was significantly *less* than would be expected if only chance were operating (i.e. the probability that that number of matches would be produced by chance was 0.0017).[16]

Ward (1979) ran a similar study, and used a computer-generated (pseudo) random "guess" series, while the random digit target series was obtained from another parapsychology laboratory. Neither series of numbers was seen in their numerical form at any time. Hits were compared by a computer scan of the two series, and the results indicated neither a significant deviation from chance in the number of hits, nor a "decline effect". Ward concluded,

> Given that much of the evidence for ESP collected over the past two or three decades is in the form of statistical deviation from chance expectation over a large number of trials, many researchers will be relieved to know that under rigorous control conditions which minimized the possible of psi operating, deviations from chance over large sets of numbers did not occur. However, Harvie's results remain to be fully explained. Rather than casting doubt on the validity of . . . ESP, this author believes Harvie's results actually support the notion of ESP by giving evidence of a backward PK effect. (1979, pp. 111–112.)[17]

Once again, a critique of psi research is turned into evidence of psi!

These studies, with the exception of Harvie's and Ward's, were intended to assess the basic paradigm of most ESP experiments—a series of matches of guesses against target. All the studies except Ward's indicate that even when no subjects are involved, but when large numbers of trials are run, very significant departures from theoretically predicted frequencies can be observed. Rather than ignoring these results, or begging the question by interpreting them in terms of psi, one would expect the cautious researcher to seriously question whether or not the probability model being used in ESP research is an appropriate one. Given the lack of independent scientific evidence for ESP, it is difficult to understand how the results discussed above do not weaken in everyone's eyes the arguments for ESP that are based on extra-chance scoring. Whether the results of the simulations were caused by subtle errors of randomization, or by some error in the formulation of the theoretically expected probabilities, or were simply due to chance (since even extremely unlikely events do occur) it should be assumed, until *demonstrated otherwise*, that whatever the sources of those extra-chance effects, ESP studies are vulnerable to precisely the same problems as studies using only random generators. In a real sense, these studies provide a semblance of a "control group" against which ESP effects can be measured. Their immediate implication is that psi effects which have been observed might be no more than manifestations of the vagaries of chance.

Randomizing procedures are clearly of critical importance in ESP research. The reader of an ESP report usually has little opportunity to assess such procedures, and is forced to rely

---

[15] They were in fact "pseudo-random", since they were produced by an algorithm, and if the same initial value is used twice, the same sequence is produced (Ward, 1979).

[16] See Koestler (1972) and Hardy, Harvie, and Koestler (1973) for more details of what seems to this author to be a highly unlikely explanation of coincidences.

[17] Ward (1979) suggested that Harvie unconsciously made his initial selection from random number tables in such a way that a deviation from chance would occur. He referred to this as "retroactive psychokinesis": Harvie saw the computer-generated "guess" series only after he had selected the target series. At that time, Ward suggested, his psychokinetic influences operated backwards in time to somehow change the original selection process!

on the experimenter's word that the randomization process was adequate. Recall the Ganzfeld study (Honorton and Harper, 1974) which was mentioned in Chapter 6, it employed a very inadequate randomization procedure, hand-shuffling of cards (Hyman, 1977b). Hand shuffling is a precarious way to attempt randomization in any case, but there is a special problem with the Zener deck. Epstein (1967) showed that more shuffles are required to randomize odd-numbered decks than even-numbered decks. Thus, with the twenty-five-card Zener deck it is important to be especially careful about shuffling procedures. [For a fifty-two card deck, using an "amateur shuffle" (which divides the deck into two approximately equal groups of cards and interleaves them singly or in clusters of two, three, or four) *at least* five shuffle operations are required, and often as many as twenty or thirty. As for "perfect" shuffles, eight perfect shuffles return the deck to the original order.]

Epstein made this important observation:

> Although the mental feat of predicting cards by estimating the shifts in position due to shuffling is a prodigious one, it is not above the ability of some practiced individuals. Further, only a limited success is required to provide a significant improvement in the results. (1967, p. 423.)

It is *possible* that, when feedback is given, subjects establish chains of cards in their minds which tend to be reproduced the next time through.

Another procedural pitfall which has marred some psi research is allowing a series of trials to terminate at the option of the subject or the experimenter (e.g. when the subject gets "tired"). Epstein demonstrated that if "optimal stopping" is allowed, the usual statistical procedures are often inappropriate; if a series of guesses is normally distributed then there is always some number of trials for which, if the experiment is terminated at that point, the null hypothesis of chance outcome must be rejected, whether or not it is true, regardless of how rigid the criterion is. The laws of probability may not balance the early success of a psi subject if he is allowed to stop at any time.

These and related problems are generally known by leading parapsychological researchers and probably do not play a part in more recent research, much of which does not involve cards or dice. However, as pointed out earlier, many of the classic telepathy and precognition studies, studies which are still held up as providing some of the best evidence of psi, did involve cards, and were conducted at a time when the problems we have been discussing were not generally known, and thus one must be very cautious in the interpretation of these earlier studies. A similar caveat applies to the classic dice studies of psychokinesis.

As an example of newer methods of randomization, consider the following: In recent years, much acclamation has been given by parapsychologists to the work of paraphysicist Helmut Schmidt, who introduced into parapsychology a random event generator ("REG") which does not depend on random numbers, tables or computer algorithms, but is based on the unpredictable emission of beta particles by decaying strontium-90. A typical Schmidt set-up is as follows (Schmidt, 1969a): A high-frequency oscillator is used to drive a four-position switch rapidly through its four positions. When a gate is opened between the switch and a Geiger counter, which monitors beta emission from a strontium-90 source, the switch stops in the position in which it happens to be when the next electron registers. On the basis of the position of the switch, one of four lamps lights. Subjects are required to press a button corresponding to the lamp which they think will light next (precognition), although in some experiments they could supposedly use PK to affect the radioactive decay so as to cause a specific lamp to light.

Schmidt has conducted a great deal of research into psi using his "quantum mechanical random event generator", and he is careful, he says, to check the output of his machine before, between, and after trials to insure that the output is random. As we have seen, there are various criteria for randomness, and, given the importance of "chance expectation" in such studies, careful consideration of how Schmidt verifies the randomness of his machine would seem necessary. Exactly what he does is not clear from his writings. Schmidt's research will be discussed in more detail later in this chapter.

The problem of control in psi research

When inferences about the existence of a phenomenon are drawn from statistical evidence, as in the case of psi, it is never possible, as I have said repeatedly, to conclude that the putative phenomenon is responsible for the non-chance results because one can never be certain that one has eliminated all possible contaminating variables. Since "psi" appears to be synonymous with unexplained extra-chance results, the critic is concerned with the conditions under which the study producing the results was run. But the contaminating variables can be very subtle, and if one is to find them one must begin with the assumption that they might exist. As Hansel (1980) said, if a spectator watching a conjurer cut a woman in a box in half believed that she might *really* be cut in half, he would be unlikely to tumble on to the idea that there are *two* women in the box. If one assumes that ESP exists, then one may be unlikely to detect minor but crucial sources of contamination in one's studies. The same is true in any research depending on statistical decisions. In a drug test, mere participation by itself, (because of the self-esteem the subjects derive, or the attention given by the researcher), may be enough to produce observable "effects". Unless one can compare the results with those from a group of subjects who are similar ("matched") to the first group, and who are treated identically in every way except that they receive a placebo instead of the drug, one cannot ascertain how much of the "effect" was due to variables other than the drug.

The early research into telepathy and precognition depended, as I have said, on the use of the twenty-five-card Zener deck. Nowadays, "respectable" parapsychologists do not allow subjects to handle the cards, but that was not the case in the earlier days when the most successful demonstrations took place. As Gardner (1979a) observed, all a person would have to do to raise his score to a significant level would be to mark a few cards, either using magician's "daub" which leaves a faint smudge on the back of a card, indistinguishable to the uninitiated from the smudges which accrue from normal handling, or by nicking a card's edge with the finger nail, or by using the thumbnail to scrape a short ($\frac{1}{8}$ inch) whitish line along a card's border. Indeed, Gardner added, it is not always even necessary to mark the cards; normal handling produces small imperfections on individual cards which can quickly be memorized by the astute card handler. And some of the cards used in the earlier experiments were imprinted so heavily that one could detect the symbol from the back side of the card.

Gardner also said that, "It is not generally known, even by magicians, that the official ESP cards now in use (authorized by J. B. Rhine) have what magicians call 'one-way' backs" (1979a, p. 18). Close examination of the cards' backs reveals that they do not look the same if rotated 180 degrees—for example, the upper right-hand corner has a star or no star, depending on which way the card is turned. As Gardner said, there are many ways a psychic-cum-magician could take advantage of such a situation to enhance his "ESP" score.

There are many other kinds of influences that can contaminate a psi study. If subjects set out to cheat, the situation is even more difficult. Such is the case when so-called psychics are examined. Communication can be practiced by methods ranging from "silent" dog whistles[18] (which children can hear, but adults cannot) to temporal cueing, where senders and receivers silently count at a measured rate from some initial signal; seemingly unimportant sounds made by the sender can be translated into letters or numbers corresponding to the position in the counting sequence. There have been cases as well of hyperasthesia, in which one individual unconsciously verbalized the "target" while the receiver who happened to have hypersensitive hearing unconsciously picked up the verbal information.[19] The problem is that one can never be certain that all sources of "sensory leakage" and all sources of statistical artifact have been properly dealt with.

Much has been made of the "sheep–goat" effect, which refers to the oft-found (and sometimes not found) difference in performance between those sympathetic to the psi hypothesis ("sheep") and those who are skeptical of it ("goats"). The former, many but not all studies have found, do better at psi tasks. However, this could be because sheep, being motivated to "produce" good results, are more sensitive to whatever cues might be available in the situation, and use them to their advantage, consciously or unconsciously.

Psi experiments rarely use control groups, as I pointed out earlier. One reason for this is the lack of an independent variable. Since subjects, if psi exists, supposedly cannot turn it on and off at will, they cannot be asked to use psi on some trials and not use it on others. Similarly, since it is apparently impossible to know when psi will suddenly show up, it is not possible to use a group of "sensitives" and compare their performance with "non-sensitives", since these latter, if both groups score equally above- or below-chance expectations, could have suddenly acquired psi. Nor can psi be blocked.

Boring (1955) said that if one could turn ESP on for some trials and off for others, one could compare the two. While this is apparently not possible, Sprinthall and Lubetkin (1965) attempted to do something similar. They had noted that Rhine had underscored the importance of subject motivation, calling it *the* mental variable that seems most closely related to the amount of psi observed in the test results. This effect had been demonstrated, said Rhine, in various situations, which ranged from betting $100 that a subject could not correctly identify a card, to offering financial and other inducements for perfect scores. Rhine (1964) reported that this technique led to very high scores.

Sprinthall and Lubetkin assigned subjects at random to an experimental group and a control group. Subjects were individually tested for telepathy using a twenty-five-card Zener deck and those in the experimental group were offered $100 for twenty correct responses out of twenty-five, while those in the control group were given no such instructions. The results were clear: no one won $100, the highest number of hits was ten, and the average number of hits did not depart significantly from the chance level. Contrary to other findings reported in the parapsychological literature, the subjects' attitude towards the concept of ESP (i.e. sheep or goat) was unrelated to their success in this study.

One might wonder why both the results of this study, and even the technique itself, have been virtually ignored by parapsychologists. It has the advantage of a type of control, in that any conditions favourable to above-chance results, although they may be caused by the patterned output of the randomization procedure, are the same for both groups. Surely, if so many studies of psi ability have been done, some must have used "control groups". But one is hard-pressed to find them. The inherent "catch-22", as mentioned earlier, is that if both

---

[18] Two school boys from Wales provided convincing demonstrations of ESP ability until it was discovered that they may have communicated by a "silent" dog whistle (Scott and Goldney, 1960).
[19] See Bender (1938).

groups should do better than chance, but do differ from each other, the skeptic would count this as non-significant, but the believer could argue that *both* groups were using psi.[20]

Dream telepathy only a few years ago was considered by many to be an area of research which would give parapsychology the respect in scientific circles for which parapsychologists have so long yearned. A series of studies at Maimonides Medical Centre in New York were carried out by Montague Ullman and Stanley Krippner (Ullman, Krippner and Vaughan, 1973) and received financial support from the National Institute of Mental Health. When a subject was in the dream state, as determined by electroencephalographic indicators, a "sender" concentrated on a pictorial target randomly chosen from a set of targets. When the subject was awakened, he described his dream. Judges later assessed the correspondence between his dream report and each of the pictures in the set of possible targets, not knowing which target had actually been used. It was concluded that successful telepathy had occurred. No control group of subjects was used, although a control group, for which no sender or no target was used, would appear essential. Subjects who did not know that they were controls, and judges who were equally ignorant of this fact, would provide, through the correspondence of *their* reports to the target used with subjects run in the experimental group, a baseline against which to judge the efficacy of the "telepathic" dream state. (Of course, one could not rule out "precognitive" knowledge of the target which would be the basis for the judgements of the judges!) One could, alternatively, "send" when the subject was not in the dream state, and compare "success" in this case with success in dream state trials.

Greenbank (1973) suggested another type of control, that is, to match subjects' reports not only against the target series used on a given night, but also against targets used months earlier, with the judges being unaware of which targets were which. (Ullman *et al.* (1973) reported that they had done this with *one* subject in one set of tests, and that "pure-chance" results were obtained.)

David Marks and Richard Kammann are New Zealand psychologists who have used "delayed" control groups to evaluate both the judgemental process used in deciding whether or not a "hit" has occurred in a telepathy experiment, and the actual psi behaviour itself. Their results are very revealing. When Uri Geller was touring New Zealand, he was presented during the course of some interviews with three different drawings folded twice and sealed in two white envelopes (Marks and Kammann, 1977). After extensive handling of the envelope in each case, Geller drew a picture indicating what he "perceived" the drawing to be. (In one case, he made twenty-nine tentative drawings before submitting a final one.) Then the same stimuli were given to each of forty-eight experimentally naïve university students who were told that they were in a study of visual perception, and that they would be given five envelopes, each with a drawing inside, which would be folded and placed inside a second envelope. They were told that they could do anything but open the envelope, and they were to try to reproduce the drawing. Then six other experimentally naïve undergraduates compared these subjects' responses to those of Geller. The drawings of the best student were as good or better than those of Geller. In addition, the drawings of Geller, as

[20] Exactly this argument was put to me by self-proclaimed "renegade" clinical psychologist, Dr. Helen Wambach, who does "past-life regressions". Past-life regression is supposedly the recall, under hypnosis, of memories of previous existences or incarnations. When asked if the reports of hypnotically-regressed subjects should not be compared with reports of non-regressed subjects asked to role play, the response was that this had been done, and that the two groups did not differ. The conclusion that was drawn was that one does not need a "regression" procedure, be it hypnosis or whatever, to "access" pastlife material!

well as those of the best students, bore closer relationship to the target as perceived by transmitted light (i.e. the projection of the folded target) than to the unfolded target, and in one case these two differed considerably. The authors concluded that Geller's demonstration showed no evidence of paranormal powers; when normal envelopes are pressed flat and rotated to certain orientations with the light, one can detect faint lines corresponding to the drawing.

In another *post-hoc* "control" study, Marks and Kammann (1978) examined transcripts from the celebrated Stanford Research Institute (SRI) remote-viewing experiments which have been reported in *Nature* (Targ and Puthoff, 1974). In this experiment, one subject waited at the SRI laboratory with an experimenter, and at a preset time tried to describe the location, unknown to him, where a set of two to four other members of the experimenter team were visiting. Nine different locations were used. Following this, judges were given a list of the nine locations as well as the subject's responses. They then visited each location one after the other and assessed which description best fit each location. Each description was then ranked in terms of its accuracy for a given location. Because of the number of matches between descriptions and locations, it was concluded that remote-viewing (via clairvoyance or telepathy or precognition) had occurred.

Marks and Kammann discovered that, although it was not mentioned in the original reports, the experimenters had furnished the judges with a list of targets which were in the *same* sequence as they had been when used with the subject. They found as well that many cues were available in the transcripts of the subject's responses which indicated the position of the response in the series. For example, the experimenter mentioned a specific location (a nature preserve) visited the previous day and commented "Nothing like having three successes behind you", thus telling the judges that the subject is after the fourth target.

Marks and Kammann found that it was easy to match the transcripts up with the correct targets when these cues were present, but when the cues were removed from the transcripts, a pair of judges, both research psychologists, who attempted to replicate the original judgements by visiting each of the nine sites while armed with the edited transcripts judged the correspondence to be only at the chance level. It was concluded that the cues given to the judges led to biased judgements in favour of the psi-hypothesis. Puthoff has since insisted that the cues identified by Marks and Kammann had been edited out of the transcripts before the judges saw them, although Frazier (1978a) noted that this is contrary to what both Puthoff and Targ had earlier told Marks and contrary as well to what they themselves have published.

In an ESP study involving a Ganzfeld, Palmer, Khamashta, and Israelson (1979) also noticed the effect of the judging procedure. While a sender concentrated on a randomly selected photograph for 5 minutes, receivers who were experiencing perceptual deprivation[21] (Ganzfeld) were asked to "think out loud", reporting their thoughts, feelings and images. Following this procedure, each subject was shown four photographs, one of which was the target. His verbal reports were read to him to refresh his memory, and then he was asked to rate each picture on a scale from 0 to 30 according to how closely it corresponded to his imagery. While the subject's judgement of the correspondence between his thoughts and the various photographs indicated no significant "ESP" effect, when

---

[21] Halved ping-pong balls were taped over their eyes. The balls were illuminated by a white light so as to produce a white, uniform visual field. Subjects wore earphones, over which they heard "white" noise, a gentle hissing noise composed of all sound frequencies.

transcripts of the subject's imagery and the sets of photographs were given to two independent judges, a significant "ESP" effect was found. The authors concluded that,

> The reversal of the mean ESP . . . scores when the ratings were contributed by independent judges dramatically illustrates the importance of judging in free-response ESP experiments. ESP scores in such experiments reflect not only the correspondence between the subject's imagery and the target picture but also the judge's skill, *possibly influenced by paranormal processes*. (Palmer *et al.*, 1979, pp. 339–340; italics added.)

The reader is left to judge for himself whether these findings should have led to a more careful study of factors which might have influenced the judges (along the lines followed by Marks and Kammann (1978)) before any suggestion was made about the possibility of the judges using psi.

Romm (1977) argued that a fundamental problem with both the dream telepathy research and the remote viewing tests is that the reports suffer from what she called "shoe-fitting" language; she cited a study in which the sender was installed in a room draped in white fabric and had ice cubes poured down his back. A receiver who reported "white" was immediately judged to have made a "hit" by an independent panel. Yet, as she observed, words such as "miserable", "wet", or "icy" would have been better hits. She suggested a dictionary demonstration: Take every tenth word on a dictionary page and see how well some of the meanings of some of the words are "hits" for whatever subject you had in mind. Again, the obvious need is for a control group. Why are they not used? Is it because that, as Gardner (1975) concluded, when conditions are loose and testing is informal, one gets results, but when controls are imposed, the scoring rates fall?

As one example, consider the research into psychokinesis. Early studies using dice produced what parapsychologists considered to be impressive results. Yet, as procedures were tightened up in response to external criticism, it became more and more difficult to obtain positive results. Rush, in a highly partisan review of problems in psychokinesis research, commented on the problems inherent in research involving the rolling of dice, referring to

> . . . the fact that progressive "cleaning up" of experimental design had coincided with a dwindling harvest of positive results. By 1960 the possibility that further confidence in the occurrence of psychokinesis could be obtained from such experiments seemed unpromising. (1977, p. 40.)

Response bias

Every Sunday evening during several months in 1937, the Zenith Foundation in the United States broadcast a simple telepathy experiment over a nationwide network. At a given signal, listeners were asked to try to determine "telepathically" which of two specified symbols was being concentrated upon by a group of supposedly telepathic senders in the studio. Listeners were asked to respond by mail, and a large number of letters were received. While an analysis of the over one million responses indicated markedly more success than would be expected by chance, Goodfellow (1939) reported that it was not necessary to postulate telepathy to explain the results. The two most important factors accounting for the subjects higher than chance result were found to be: (1) the predisposing influence of subtle suggestions found in the test instructions; and (2) the sequence used by subjects in recording their guesses.

Whenever human beings are asked to choose numbers or colours or words at random, the results are far from random. There is a tendency for many people to give the same response. Consider some examples which have been provided by Marks and Kammann (1980).[22] When subjects were asked to think of any two-digit number, 43 percent gave numbers 11, 12, 13, 21, 22 or 23, while only 7 percent would be expected to do so by chance. When asked to think of two geometric forms, one inside the other, 34 percent responded with a circle– triangle combination. When asked to give a two-digit number between 1 and 50, with both digits odd and not the same, 33 percent responded with 37, with 35 and 39 being next in frequency.

One cannot ignore such response bias. If one happens to use a "popular" number such as 37 in a mass-ESP test, one will discover that many more people will successfully identify it than would be expected "by chance".

A related problem is that of "prediction". As has been mentioned earlier, if a "seer" makes enough predictions, some are likely to turn out to be true by coincidence alone. They also are more likely to be seen as correct if the predictions are vague. Consider this example, reported by Frazier (1980a):

> In December 1978, it was predicted in writing that 46 people would die in an airplane crash on March 11, 1979, outside a major population centre in the Northern Hemisphere, and that the aircraft logo would have red in it. On March 14, 1979, a Royal Jordanian aircraft crashed near Doha, the capital of Qatar on the Persian Gulf. Forty-five people were killed. Royal Jordanian's logo is maroon in colour.

While this prediction may seem amazing in its near accuracy, it was made on the basis of statistical analysis, not paranormal foresight. Richard Newton, a University of Massachusetts student, took the available data for aircrashes over the last 26 years, and calculated that March is the most likely month for crashes, an average of forty-six people were killed in crashes in that month, most crashes occur near major population areas, most flights are in the Northern Hemisphere and 50 percent of all airline logos have red in them. Newton suggested that for well-publicized events such as air crashes, such information may be unconsciously gathered and summarized (recall the discussion of the tacit dimension in Chapter 4), and this may contribute to predictions that psychics and others make. The point to be learned from Newton's demonstration is that people's predictions may be based in part on information that they have unconsciously "collected". If an individual makes a specific prediction without realizing why, he may select time periods and other details which are "probable" based on past information.

Selection of subjects

It has been argued (see Gardner, 1957) that subject selection, operating unconsciously,[23] can affect observed extra-chance scoring. As Gardner said, the effect would be obvious if one began with 100 subjects, took those who scored in the top half in a preliminary test, gave a second test, again eliminated the lower half, and continued on in this manner until there was one who had achieved a long string of successes. However, he added, researchers rarely would make such a crude error, but the error can occur in a more subtle way. If a hundred

---

[22] These tasks were based on requests often made by popular "psychics"; the psychic "reads" the subject's mind after he has chosen a number.

[23] Parapsychologists have even suggested that the choice of subjects might be mediated by the experimenter's own psi, leading to the selection of high-scoring subjects (Weiner and Morrison, 1979).

experimenters test a subject each, and fifty whose subjects fail the first test give up, while the other fifty carry on, 50 percent of these give up following a second test, and so on, eventually one experimenter will have observed high scores in a subject 6 or 7 times in a row. (If the subject does poorly in continued testing, this could be explained as the decline effect.) Since the experimenter and the subject do not know about all the other experiments, their results seem impressive. This is another way of saying that some subjects sooner or later will score at above-chance expectation levels. It is to be expected occasionally.

Subject selection can be created by the subjects themselves. Davis (n.d.) noted that if, over a series of ESP sessions, subjects who do poorly become discouraged and drop out of the testing, and data is eliminated because they did not complete the testing, the average score for the remaining subjects considered as a group will appear to be higher than one would expect by chance. This is a very important point.

Selective publishing

Another related problem is the selective publishing of positive outcomes. Bakan addressed this in saying that, in most instances, people do not bother to publish "non-significant" results, and are rarely successful when they try to do so. Thus, he concluded, "the very publication practices themselves are part and parcel of the probabilistic processes on which we base our conclusion concerning the nature of psychological phenomena" (1966, p. 151). In other words, if 100 studies are run, by chance one would expect that, if H_0 is true, some of them would produce positive results. If only the positive ones are published, then the literature could be filled with studies whose results reflect chance effects. (This is not a problem only in parapsychology.) Parapsychologists (e.g. Thouless, 1963) often argue that given the very low p values associated with the results of some studies (e.g. $p < 10^{-31}$ in the Soal–Goldney experiments) there would have to be an unbelievably large number of unpublished results lying around to justify the belief that those results were due to selective publication. This defense simply belies a lack of understanding of what the p-value means. Recall the discussion of p values: The "$p < 10^{-31}$" refers only to the probability that the results obtained in the particular experiment would be likely to have been obtained if the null hypothesis is true. It does *not* indicate that the "observed non-chance effect is a strong one". It does *not* refer to the likelihood of obtaining the same results in a replication study.

Parapsychologist John Beloff is not taken in by the usual arguments that parapsychologists use:

> Most parapsychologists that I know are just too disheartened and abashed when they fail to get results to have the necessary determination to write up a report on their experiments and submit it for publication. I sometimes wonder how many young hopefuls are drawn each year to parapsychology by the exciting reports they read in the journals, oblivious of this huge silent majority of negative instances. (1973, p. 29).

Recording errors

Whenever data is handled manually, whether in recording, transcription, or calculation, errors are of course possible. Psychologists discovered, by examining studies of recording errors in their own domain, that such errors are more often than not in the direction of the experimenter's expectations or wishes (Rosenthal, 1966; Johnson and Adair, 1972; Silverman, 1977). It is believed that such errors are unconscious, and do not represent deliberate fraud.

Parapsychological research has also suffered from the same problem. Kennedy (1952) discussed several ESP studies in which recording errors were responsible for the results being favourable to the ESP hypothesis.

It makes good sense, then, to ensure that the persons doing the recording in an ESP experiment are not aware of which response is the correct one, and Rhine (1974) reported that this became part of the standard practice in his laboratory at Duke University. Nonetheless, this is yet another pitfall that not all researchers guard against, and recording errors must be taken into consideration as a possibility in the analysis of a given study, unless it is clear that appropriate precautions were taken.

The Schmidt studies

Many parapsychologists appear to be extremely impressed with the research of paraphysicist Helmut Schmidt, who introduced a "quantum mechanical random event generator" into parapsychological research.

Parapsychologist John Randall said,

> In so far as it is humanly possible to prove anything in this uncertain world, the Schmidt experiments provide us with the final proof of the reality of ESP and PK. There is now only one possible escape for the skeptic who wishes to avoid the reality of psi, and that is to believe that Schmidt deliberately falsified the whole of his data. (1975, p. 131.)

In one experiment (Schmidt, 1969a), in which subjects attempted to predict which of four lamps would light on each trial, one subject made 22,569 trials and scored 295.75 hits above chance ("odds against chance": 27,000 to one). Another, out of 26,250 trials, scored 90.5 hits above chance (not considered significant). A third, in 22,247 trials, scored 315 above chance ("odds against chance": 94,000 to one): He believed that he was using PK to make a certain lamp, #4, light, and sure enough, analyses of the data showed that the #4 lamp came on with increasing frequency. (Of course, were it the case that, for whatever reason, #4 came on with increasing frequency without the aid of the subject, we would expect the subject to choose it more often and thus to be correct more often.)

In a second study, (Schmidt, 1969b) subjects were allowed to opt for trying to score high or low; one subject who opted to score high completed 5000 trials and scored 66 above chance; a second performed two tests, opted to score high in the first and scored 123 above chance in 5672 trials, opted to score low in a second and scored 126 below chance in 4328 trials. A third subject, opting to score low, scored 86 below chance out of 5000 trials. Hansel (1980) pointed out that the total number of hits (i.e. trials when a subject correctly predicted which lamp would next light) was only at the chance level. But when *successes* (i.e. a subject's misses when trying to score low, and hits when trying to score high) were considered, the p value was $p < 10^{-10}$!

Although such results may seem impressive, before accepting them at face value, consider the following general problems which have been raised with regard to Schmidt's research:

1. Schmidt works in virtual isolation and does not give others access to his raw data (Frazier, 1979a).

2. Hansel (1980) pointed out that although only meagre detail was provided by Schmidt in his reports, it would appear that the exact numbers and types of trials were not specified in advance, thus allowing for the optional stopping problem.
3. Only a single investigator was involved (Hansel, 1980). This makes experimenter bias (and even the possibility of fraud) more conceivable.
4. Hansel (1980) worried that the equipment itself might not be foolproof. He pointed to certain possible technical problems that might bias its operation. One would want to have independent expert advice about the adequacy of the machine's operation.
5. Only when data were extracted and categorized according to whether the subject was trying to obtain hits or misses did extra-chance effects show up. Hansel (1980) argued that such treatment of the data opens the way for all kinds of errors—recording errors, etc. Hansel lamented that,

The most remarkable feature of Schmidt's experiments is the manner in which, in the majority of cases, his results manage to exclude any safeguards conferred by using a machine. (1980, p. 229.)

With regards to one experiment, Hansel added,

. . . the significance of the result was not revealed by the non-resettable counters inside the machine. . . . The odds of ten thousand million to one, claimed as appertaining to the result of the experiment, apply to data extracted from the machine on the print-out but selected according to whether the subject was trying to secure hits or misses. (1980, p. 224.)

The obvious solution to this problem would be to have all data of interest automatically recorded inside the machine.
6. Another problem with Schmidt's research program is that it consists of a number of one-shot demonstrations. His study of the cat in the cool garden shed was mentioned earlier. When a statistically significant effect was found, rather than studying this in more detail, he went on to study cockroaches and their precognitive ability to avoid shock.
7. Schmidt is quite willing to explain away undesirable evidence. When cockroaches received more shocks than predicted by a chance model, Schmidt (1970) suggested that it was his own psychokinesis which had affected the generator. If it cannot be explained by one psi principle, it can be explained by another. Thus, the claims are non-falsifiable.
8. The total independence of putative PK "success" from the experimental set-up itself is curious. In one study, Schmidt and Pantas (1972) used two different random number generators, each with different circuitry. Half-way through the trials, which were either ESP or PK type for a given subject, a switch was secretly closed by an experimenter to disengage the random number generator that was in use and engage the other machine which was in another room. The subjects apparently scored above chance both before and after the change. Many other studies have also found that the subject's success is not dependent on situational variables. This makes the putative psi remarkable for its ability to function despite such dramatic and unknown (to the subject) changes in the target.

Schmidt concluded that we should not try to understand psychokinesis in terms of some hypothetical mechanism by which the mind interferes with the machine, but that

The fact that the electronic generator was such a complicated system, which none of the subjects fully understood, and the fact that the subjects directed their attention only to the display panel, may suggest that PK works teleologically. It may be goal-oriented in the sense that the psychological appeal of the display is more relevant to the occurrence of PK than the detailed structure of the random generator used. (1971, pp. 757–758.)

This apparent lack of concern with the intermediate steps is another example of how magical thinking creeps into parapsychological explanation.

Parapsychology: The Defense of Statistics

In the early days of experimental parapsychology, critics attacked parapsychologists, often unfairly, about weaknesses in their statistical approach. In response to such attacks, the *Journal of Parapsychology* in 1937 carried the text of a press release issued and signed by the President of the American Institute of Mathematical Statistics, Burton H. Camp:

> Dr. Rhine's investigations have two aspects: experimental and statistical. On the experimental side, mathematicians of course have nothing to say. On the statistical side, however, recent mathematical work has established the fact that, assuming the experiments have been properly performed, the statistical analysis is essentially valid. If the Rhine investigation is to be fairly attacked, it must be on other than mathematical grounds. (Notes, *J. Parapsychology*, 1937.)

That statement has been cited many times since as a "clean bill of health" for the way in which parapsychologists employ statistical analysis.

No one can make a blanket statement about the accuracy of the statistics used without examining *every* study and every statistical test. One cannot separate the evaluation of the statistical techniques employed from an evaluation of the methodology employed. Both must be done in every study. As Hyman commented,

> I don't know who Mr. Camp is or what the Institute of Mathematical Statistics is. But the statement says little more than that Rhine and his co-workers, when they compute the critical ratio, are employing the correct formula and referring to the appropriate probability tables . . . the test is appropriate when it can be safely assumed that all the underlying assumptions have been met. (1977b, p. 48.)

In fact, as Hyman noted, there is considerable variability in the statistical sophistication of researchers in parapsychology; side by side in the same journal are found articles employing very sophisticated techniques and articles with very poor and sloppy techniques.

Another defense made by parapsychologists against attacks made on their use of statistical analysis is by comparison with the techniques used in the discipline which is responsible for most of the critical evaluations of parapsychology, psychology itself. Parapsychologists argue that their use of statistical analysis is every bit as good as that of psychologists. At their best, they may be correct. Unfortunately, psychologists and other social scientists often make many of the same basic errors that are made by parapsychologists. People tend to view the statistical test as though it operates quite independently of any assumptions made by the researchers about the distribution underlying the data, and as though the decisions reached by means of statistical tests are in themselves capable of saying something about the theoretical ideas under test. Consider the words of one parapsychologist, Timm, who argued that because parapsychologists use the same tests as other researchers, this means that any criticism of their use must apply equally to all others who use them;

> As a matter of fact, the generally employed tests of significance (t-test, analysis of variance, correlation methods, and analogous nonparametric statistics) are the same that have been used in

the biosocial sciences for a considerable stretch of time. To criticize these seriously one would have to extend the criticism to every science using these methods, since there is no difference in the formal structure of the experiments between the diverse fields of employment. (1979.)

There are two important points to stress in response: (1) It is not the statistical analysis *per se* which should be at issue. It is the *interpretation* of the statistical decision that is in question. As Epstein noted,

> Indisputably, the statistical evaluations of ESP experiments have been of a quality far beyond the standards of the experiments themselves. As a consequence, the mathematical soundness of the analysis of ESP and PK experiments has been declared to prove the soundness of the experimental procedures. . . . (1967, p. 418.)[24]

(2) Many of the errors made by parapsychologists in their interpretation of their statistical evidence are made, as we have said, in as blatant or as subtle a fashion by some psychologists as well, and to compare oneself to the latter and then claim purity is hardly convincing. The important difference here between psychologists and parapsychologists is that the former (with the exception perhaps of some researchers in the "softer" areas of the field) can interpret their statistical evidence against the background of a broader research context with numerous independent supports for hypotheses and claims.

Concluding Remarks

The statistical case for the paranormal is, to be quite blunt, extremely weak. The presence of statistical "non-chance" effects is hardly surprising given the factors discussed in this chapter—very large numbers of trials, poor experimental control, and so forth. However, most importantly, the statistical evidence does not satisfy Giere's second condition for a good test (see Chapter 6): If psi does not exist, the second condition would require that one would be unlikely to observe the presumed evidence of psi. Yet, there are any number of ways in which error can creep into the design of the study, the methodology, or the analysis and lead to the predicted effects. Thus, there is no way to *falsify* the psi hypothesis, nor is there any way to test it against a competing hypothesis such as "Zeus exists, and tantalizes people by causing departures from statistical expectation". The concept of synchronicity is another hypothesis which could account for observed statistical effects no worse (and no better) than the psi hypothesis.

Suppose for a moment that *all* statistical evidence adduced in support of psi is due to methodological weaknesses, the vagaries of chance, and so forth. In such a case, one might expect to find similar evidence of "psi" in situations which, at least to the skeptic, might appear just a little bit ludicrous. Indeed, if we were to put rocks under a heat lamp controlled by a random-event generator, might we not, some of us at least, find that out of 5000 trials, the rocks were "able" to keep the lamps on (for whatever "reason"), say, 51 percent of the time, enough to generate an impressively small p-value? To my knowledge, this has not been tried with rocks. It has been tried with eggs [Levy (1971) reported that fertilized eggs were able to keep a heat lamp on for a greater proportion of the time than non-fertilized eggs], cockroaches and cats (Schmidt, 1970). Several studies involving nothing but two sets of cards or two sets of random numbers were described earlier. Instead of facing the possibility that it

---

[24] Epstein made this point even though he pointed to several statistical problems. This is not a statistical "clean bill of health" for parapsychology.

may be the method of study and analysis that is spuriously generating "non-chance" results, parapsychologists persist in giving *ad hoc* explanations for each "unreasonable" case of psi. As discussed earlier, explanations for the ESP effect with two sets of random numbers included "retroactive psychokinesis" and "seriality". Why won't parapsychologists, with few exceptions, act as though they are at least prepared to accept the possibility that their statistical evidence is spurious, and even that psi may not exist?

Bridgman (1956) said that if the advocates of ESP were to simply say that "All I mean when I say the event was not chance is that the event was not expected and surprised me", he would have no quarrel (1956, p. 16). Yet, he said, parapsychologists go on to conclude that their non-chance events involve some sort of regularity, with the additional implication that some new unknown faculty of the mind is involved. The only justification for such a conclusion would be the demonstration of some pertinent regularity. However, if one cannot make statements about how to elicit psi, about what conditions are required, and about when psi should *not* be observed, if one cannot *predict* its appearance (as a function of initial conditions) then there is no regularity.

All that statistical evidence could possibly achieve, at its best, is the demonstration that some influence is present which leads to departures from the chance model (if the latter can be shown to be appropriate for the situation). In 1959 Rawcliffe commented,

> Detailed analysis of the reports of psychical research experiments reveals that there is not even a *prima facie* case for the existence of "psi-phenomena", judged from the scientific standpoint. The need for a theory to explain them does not arise. In any event, parapsychological experiments could, by their very nature, establish only one thing, viz., that there was a causal nexus involved which produced the results observed. It would, however, be absurd for any scientist to account for any such causal nexus by the expedient of falling back on metaphysical theories which derive directly from the primitive beliefs and superstitions of his ancestors. (p. 21.)

Nothing has happened in the interim to render Rawcliffe's analysis any less pertinent today.

CHAPTER 8
The Public Debate Continues

I have had contact with some of the most skillful researchers in the field. These include Ed Kelly—author of a lengthy chapter on the use of statistics in ESP research; Julie Eisenbud—regarded as a kind of grand old man of the field by parapsychologists I know; Charles Tart—former national president of a large parapsychology group, author of many books and studies; Hal Puthoff and Russell Targ—authors of government funded studies, the most well-funded parapsychologists of all time. Surely these researchers should know how to avoid the pitfalls and use acceptable methodology. My contact with them has not brought to light any evidence of paranormal phenomena. Instead, I find sincere, dedicated researchers doing sloppy experiments.

Persi Diaconis[1]

. . . the answer to the spurious accusations of fraud and incompetence (as opposed to legitimate scientific criticism) . . . will come not from the researchers, but rather from a new quarter, an informed and sophisticated public, aided by the press, who by and large deal fairly with this area of research.

R. Targ and H. E. Puthoff[2]

PARAPSYCHOLOGY, as formally practiced, appears to be much like any other domain of science. It has the requisite professional groups, professional journals, popular journals, research foundations and institutes, and research grants. However, while on rare occasions parapsychological research projects have been funded by the funding agencies for "normal" scientific research, for the most part parapsychologists have had to count on bequests and donations to support their research activities. For example, in 1972 an Arizona court awarded more than a quarter of a million dollars to the American Society for Psychical Research from the estate of James Kidd, a miner who was missing and declared legally dead. Kidd had specified that his entire estate be given to any person or group that could find evidence of post mortem survival. This bequest is in part responsible for the recent upsurge in research into survival after death. More recently, James McDonnell, chairman of the McDonnell Douglas Aerospace Corporation, awarded a grant of 500,000 dollars to Washington University in St. Louis exclusively for psychic research (Wade, 1979).

While many wealthy people, usually in their later years, have contributed generously to parapsychological research, this money has not always been used as intended. For instance, the late Thomas Stanford willed two sums of money to Stanford University. The first, over a half million dollars, was to be used for psychical or psychological research, and the second, 60,000 dollars, was to be used exclusively for psychical research. While some psychic research was supported by the latter, both sums are now used by the psychology department for non-psychical research. A similar use was put to money left to Harvard University for psychical research (Stevens, 1967).

Parapsychologists, and especially Joseph Banks Rhine, have long sought to establish

---

[1] Diaconis (1979), p. 31.
[2] Targ & Puthoff (1977), p. 87.

parapsychology as a "respectable" venture in the eyes of other scientists. Attempts have been made to create a division of parapsychology within the American Psychological Association, but the possibility of success in this venture appears remote. However, parapsychologists were greatly encouraged when the prestigious *American Association for the Advancement of Science* (A.A.A.S.) finally voted in 1969 to admit the Parapsychology Association to its ranks. The late Margaret Mead was influential in bringing about the admission, arguing forcefully that an open scientific mind required that research be respected whatever its subject matter. The A.A.A.S. decision has been widely publicized by many parapsychologists as an objective demonstration that scientists view parapsychology as a valid and proper domain of scientific inquiry. Recently, however, there have been challenges to the continued membership of the Parapsychology Association in the A.A.A.S. Philosopher Antony Flew (1980) has called for their expulsion, as has theoretical physicist John Wheeler. Following the delivery of a paper at the 1979 annual A.A.A.S. meeting, Wheeler spoke bluntly;

> Every science that is a science has hundreds of hard results; but search fails to turn up a single one in 'parapsychology'. Would it not be fair, for the credit of science, for 'parapsychology' to be required to supply one or two or three battle-tested findings as a condition for membership in the A.A.A.S.? . . .[3]

Parapsychologists' View of Skeptics

Claims of scientific discoveries which seem to be incompatible with currently accepted theory usually generate considerable controversy. Such controversy is healthy (as was discussed in Chapter 6), since it forces those who believe that they have made such discoveries to marshal enough evidence to persuade other scientists to take their claims seriously. This is what is happening with regard to claims of the paranormal. However, while it is easy for a skeptic to consider the cautious and reserved reaction of the scientific community to claims of the paranormal to be quite proper, such reservation often provokes impatience on the part of many parapsychologists.

As was mentioned in Chapter 6, some parapsychologists see skepticism as a sign that parapsychology is part of a new paradigm awaiting a Kuhnian shift. These people believe that parapsychology throws doubt on the basic tenets of normal scientific endeavour, and so is resisted. On the other hand, Targ and Puthoff argued that parapsychological phenomena are *not* inconsistent with the framework of modern physics, but only with laws of physics based on the "naïve realism" of old. An increasing number of physicists are coming to accept parapsychology, they said: "The loyal opposition thus numbers fewer and fewer scientists among its ranks; the physicists by and large are leaving first, the psychologists last." (1977, p. 171) Critics are portrayed as out of date, behind the times. (However, the same comment could have been made during the heyday of spiritualism almost a century ago. Many prominent physicists were convinced that the supposed paranormal powers of mediums were genuine, but these same mediums were ultimately exposed as frauds by Houdini and others.) Targ and Puthoff turned the skeptics' criticisms to the skeptics themselves:

> It is the skeptic, not the [parapsychological] researcher, who is short on rigorous observation and long on theory. It is the hardened skeptic who betrays a strong emotional commitment to an a priori belief structure, being motivated as he is to go out of his way to criticize a field of research

---

[3] Cited by Gardner, 1979b.

about which he has little firsthand data. Furthermore, in these days of gravitational waves, . . . and "quantum interconnectedness", the burden of proof with regard to excluding the possibility of paranormal functioning now lies with the skeptics. (1977, p. 178.)

Joseph Banks Rhine, viewing psychologists as the most intransigent critics, argued that they are not always equipped to evaluate parapsychological research:

The field of parapsychology has long needed better warnings along its borders against the too easy assumption that whoever has a good training in the main field (psychology, of course) should have no difficulty in taking over a project in a new subdivision. This is often a fatal assumption. Sensorimotor methodology and design do not well fit the situation on the psi side of the line. (1968, pp. 126–127, parentheses in original.)

Lawrence LeShan, another prominent parapsychologist, is candid in his view of critics. According to him, many scientists do not understand that the mechanistic view of the universe, from which most objections to ESP were made, is long dead:

. . . many so-called professional scientists are glorified technicians who know nothing about their own fields of science except how to push meter readings and equations around. (1979, p. 8.)

He argued that the claim of insufficient evidence is "ridiculous" and is the result of people not having done their "homework". To the objection of non-replicability, he responded that the same criticism would invalidate geology, astronomy, and the social sciences as sciences. However, LeShan should realize that most social scientists do not claim that their domains have yet achieved the status of "science" and it is even harder to understand why LeShan would mention astronomy and geology in this context. Replicability essentially means that if one duplicates the conditions of the original study, one can observe the original findings for oneself. In astronomy and geology, one does not have replicability in the sense of being able to set up conditions so as to observe an effect. Yet, in both astronomy and geology, everything is *publicly* observable; Halley's predictions about "his" comet were *publicly* confirmed by its reappearance at the time he specified it should reappear. We do not have to accept the word of either astronomers or geologists. We can observe for ourselves.

LeShan commented that one should say this to those who make accusations of fraud in the context of discussing parapsychological research:

This is not an argument in the realm of scientific discourse. It is rather an admission that the possibility is making you anxious. I didn't hear you make that accusation when the evidence for quasars was advanced, or quarks, neutrinos, or DNA. (1979, p. 8.)

LeShan might be well advised to consider that fraud in these other areas would not have long withstood the probings of skeptical scientists.

Another view of skeptics is that they are unwilling to face up to parapsychological facts because of emotional shortcomings. For example, McConnell suggested that,

In the West we have been taught that each of us is a unit of consciousness, isolated from our fellow humans except by sensory-motor pathways. Psi effects suggest otherwise—a philosophically disturbing possibility. (1977b, p. 434.)

Eisenbud (1963) went even further: There is, he said, an unusual degree of irrational skepticism and hostility shown by scientists towards parapsychology. This is because they are emotionally threatened, he argued, and he coined the term "psi reactance" to describe this reaction. Rejdak (1974) was even more accusatory arguing that critics are not open to new ideas. Their attitudes, he says, are the consequence of fear; the field is filled with unknowns and what is observed could lead to mysticism, something that the 'hard core' skeptics cannot handle. Indolence is a factor too, he said; having become masters in a scientific domain, they do not want to have the trouble of learning to think in a new way.

Magicians are often the target of particular abuse from some apologists for the paranormal. They tend to be less easily convinced than some scientists. Adept at the practice of deception, they are quick to assume that others who work wonders are likewise talented. The unmasking of mediums by Houdini and Dunninger, the exposé of Uri Geller and Jean-Paul Girard by James Randi, and other similar dénouements make magicians a special enemy to those who hold the psychic world dear. Magicians tend not to bother with the niceties of academic debate—they openly accuse those they believe to be practicing deception.

A leading parapsychologist, W. E. Cox of the Institute of Parapsychology in Durham North Carolina, stated that magicians can be divided into two groups—those "who palm off imitative ESP as *bona fide* ESP", and those who, whether performing "mentalists" or not, are prejudiced against ESP, treating it as a pseudoscience (Cox, 1974). He criticized magicians' attempts to persuade the public that, because they can duplicate a psychic's feats, the psychic must be practicing deception. Eric Dingwall, who has become preeminent in parapsychological circles, though quite skeptical of most things in parapsychology, is a skilled magician familiar with some of the most outstanding magicians of modern times, *and* a member of the Committee for the Scientific Investigation of Claims of the Paranormal, a group of skeptics. He has commented on Cox's vitriol,

> Mr. Cox seems to have been successfully persuaded to believe that it is the magician who calls the tune while the medium lets the investigator call it. This is surely a delusion. Both call the tune and both try to persuade you that you are calling it. This is much more difficult for the magician than for the medium since the magician is more or less forced to bring off the trick, whereas the medium can always plead that conditions are bad, that vibrations are faulty, or whatever he can think of at the moment. (1974, p. 27.)

> Mr. Cox seems to think that the skepticism of magicians "considerably outstrips that of professional psychologists". Well, of course it does. Professional psychologists as a group know hardly anything about the kind of deception of which competent magicians are adept. (1974, p. 27.)

Parapsychologists over the years (e.g. McConnell, 1977a; Pratt, Rhine, Smith, Stuart, and Greenwood, 1940; Rao, 1979) have responded to the criticisms made by critics. Consider the problem of replicability as one instance: they have argued either that replicability in parapsychology does exist, although not in the sense of being able to produce psi effects on demand (Rao, 1979), or that parapsychology may be dealing with a domain of nature where non-repeatability and non-predictability are the rule (Pratt, 1974). McConnell said in this context: "There has been no revelation from God that all experimental phenomena must be repeatable upon demand" (1977a, p. 203). Critics have not been impressed by such attempts at rebuttal.

A Skeptical Approach

While parapsychologists may view their critics as being behind the times, fearful of threats to their own established world-view, or irrational and hostile, E. G. Boring, himself a critic of parapsychology, viewed the critic's concerns in this manner:

The experimental method, which includes control, was invented and used by the natural philosophers because they mistrusted their own free inductive intuition. Such people are nowadays called scientists . . . they are angered because uncontrolled intuition is what they as scientists are fighting and they see in the way parapsychology transcends its observed data a threat to what is basic in science. They are not angry, I think, because new scientific hypotheses are being proposed, but because they think the parapsychologists transcend their observations, finding mystery more exciting than fact. (1955, p. 115.)

We have seen in the preceding chapters how risky it is to take reports of paranormal happenings, whether they are spontaneous or produced in the laboratory, at face value. These reports are not necessarily less reliable than reports about any other event or experience, but we have no independent way of checking their accuracy. Reports of the "normal" as opposed to the "paranormal" can be judged with the knowledge that, unless the report is about a subjective experience, we can ultimately check on some details to test their accuracy or assess the likelihood of the reported event by comparison with currently accepted theory. If an acquaintance tells us that when he arrived home at his twelfth-story apartment last night, he was surprised to find a live cow in the living room, we would presume that he is joking. If he persists, we would want details about how he dealt with the situation, and these could, in principle, be checked. Further, we can assess the likelihood of the event in light of the framework in which it occurred. However, if he says that he had seen a ghost in his apartment, we are left entirely without recourse to verify his report.[4] So it is with experiments that cannot be replicated—we have to trust both the honesty and skill of the experimenter. We have discussed in past chapters how the research reports of Targ and Puthoff either omitted seemingly unimportant but crucial details, or, as Marks and Kammann (1977) found, described the research as more tightly controlled than it had been. To find possible sources of experimental contamination requires diligence and the good fortune of having access to an accurate and independent account of the original situation. This puts critics in an unenviable position.

Scientists and academics are taught to concern themselves with logical arguments and data, and not with the character or ability of the person responsible for them. Yet, to follow that dictum when dealing with some representatives of parapsychology is to treat their statements, which lack the means of independent verification, on the same basis as statements which can ultimately be checked. If professor X attests that he observed a "psychic" perform levitation under "totally controlled conditions", is it not proper to assess his credentials as an observer? If he has been "taken in" before, should we not be leery of accepting his word this time? Gardner (1977) named several leading parapsychologists who have been "gulled" in the past—Helmut Schmidt, discussed earlier in connection with radioactive decay random-number generators—was much impressed by the psychic ability of Uri Geller, as were Thelma Moss, William Cox, and other prominent parapsychologists. Yet, Geller is now viewed as a fraud even by most parapsychologists. Should we not be extremely cautious the next time that these people attest to someone's psychic powers?

While an *ad hominem* attack is generally and properly disdained in science, it sometimes is important to consider the motivation of the researcher. Even some parapsychologists recognize this (often with reference to the writings of skeptics!); McConnell advised,

---

[4] It is interesting to note that while most people will laugh in disbelief at the "cow" story, the same people will react with curiosity and interest to the story of the ghost. They are confident in assigning a low likelihood to the possibility that the cow story is true.

Whether we are listening to a tale of a ghost in a haunted house or reading the tightly edited *Journal of Experimental Psychology*, we have to concern ourselves with two questions: what is the content of the report and what are the competence and motivation of the observer? (1969, p. 261.)

Is it proper to concern oneself with the belief systems of those who purport to have found evidence of the paranormal in the laboratory? Is it relevant that Soal was once a "competent" automatic writer (Rawcliffe, 1959)? Is it of importance that, among those researchers at the Stanford Research Institute who were involved in research which generated some of the most important claims in modern parapsychology, there are a number of practicing Scientologists (Wilhelm, 1976)? Included among the latter is Harold Puthoff, the chief investigator in the Geller studies who, according to Hyman (1977b), worked his way up to being a Class III Operating Thetan,[5] and who had previously obtained research funds to study the putative paranormal ability of plants to sense the thoughts of humans. Crandall said,

> Questions of objectivity may legitimately be raised when Scientologists, who are committed *theologically* to belief in astral projection and psychokinesis, are performing "successful" experiments involving subjects who are also Scientologists and other who share these beliefs. It is like asking the Vatican to vouch for the authenticity of the miracles at Lourdes. (1977, p. 21.)

Crandall's point is well taken, remembering that, unlike normal scientific experiments, 'successful' paranormal experiments are not replicable, either by skeptics, or even by many believers. Researchers of many religious orientations have made signal contributions to normal science, but always when *replicable* phenomena were involved. When they strayed beyond that, their pronouncements were treated only as beliefs. The late Wilder Penfield provided a major contribution to our understanding of the neurophysiology of the brain, but when in his last book (Penfield, 1975) he argued that his brain research had led him to the conclusion that the soul must exist, neurophysiologists treated this conclusion as a part of Penfield's own metaphysics and not as a serious scientific hypothesis, since there is no way of subjecting it to a test.

The Media and Popular Literature

Anyone who takes a serious interest in the evaluation of parapsychology finds himself confronted with two sets of authorities.[6] The position of the majority of the members of the scientific community is largely one of doubt or outright skepticism, while advocates of parapsychology, many with good scientific/academic credentials, argue forcefully that paranormal phenomena exist and that their existence has been scientifically verified many times. Who should the layperson believe? It seems that personal experience pushes people towards the paranormal camp. The appearance of a dorsal fin above the water's surface can readily convince one of the presence of sharks, whereas the absence of the same does not convince anyone that there are no sharks around, especially if one is predisposed to believe that there might be. In the same way, as was discussed in Chapter 4, most people are likely to have had occasional psi-like experiences. Personal experience combined with the emotional

---

[5] The state of 'Operating Thetan' is one where the 'Thetan' (which is a concept similar to that of a soul) can free itself from the body and use its fantastic powers at will. According to the founder of Scientology, L. Ron Hubbard, the Greek gods, who could use thunder and lightening at their whim, were Operating Thetans (Evans, 1974, p. 115).

[6] Recall Rokeach's discussion of authority, p. 45.

attraction psi phenomena might hold may well be enough to lead the average person to agree with the proponents of the paranormal.

If the layperson wishes to inform himself about what is known about the putatively paranormal, he will seek out books and articles dealing with the subject. However, the media in general give parapsychology a one-sided treatment. Skeptical viewpoints are difficult to find, especially in the "parapsychology and occult" section of most public bookstores.

Great numbers of people believe what they see in black and white in newspapers or magazines. "They would not be allowed to print that if it were not true" is a common response to fabulous reports of the paranormal carried in the media. I was once asked during a lecture on perception in an Introductory Psychology course to comment on ESP. I said that, while parapsychologists claimed to have confirmatory evidence, there was still considerable controversy about the subject. At the next lecture, a student reproached me; I had been misinformed, he said, because during that week he had seen a television interview in which two scientists stated that ESP is real and is accepted as so by scientists. "The network wouldn't run that if it wasn't true", he informed me.

Unfortunately, many people are persuaded on the basis of what they have read that studies of psi have been tightly controlled and the conclusions are highly suggestive of some paranormal force. There has been so much written in the popular press, there have been so many parapsychologists who have proclaimed the evidence for psi to be overwhelming, and there have been so few rebuttals that, to anyone not familiar with the field, it would seem that "something" must be there. "Where there's smoke, there is fire", as the old truism goes. The media for the most part have preferred the sensational and the exciting to more cautious statements about any phenomenon or situation of interest. A report of a flying saucer sighting may receive prominent coverage. A subsequent prosaic explanation for the event is unlikely to be reported at all. With this in mind, it is worthwhile examining some of the more disturbing aspects of media treatment of the paranormal.

The extreme cautiousness of the editors of *Nature* regarding the publication of the Targ and Puthoff studies of remote viewing was discussed earlier. They listed their strong reservations about it in an editorial and took the unusual step of directing readers to the simultaneous publication of a critique of these studies in the *New Scientist*. What did the public hear about it? As one example, consider the story prepared by a leading American wire service,[7] which began,

> Many people may have the ability to receive and send information in a way other than by the known normal senses, two physicists report.

Shortly later in the same report,

> "It may be that remote perceptual ability is widely distributed in the general population, but because the perception is generally below an individual's level of awareness, it is repressed or not noticed" Dr. Harold Puthoff and Russell Targ, of Stanford Research Institute, Menlo Park Calif., wrote in *Nature*, the British Scientific Journal.

There was not a hint of the serious reservations expressed by the editors, nor in the fact that the editors viewed the publication of this article as a way of getting the argument about the paranormal into the open, rather than as an acceptance of the interpretation of the data.

James ("The Amazing") Randi (1977) has also spoken of the irresponsibility of most of the media when dealing with parapsychology. He mentioned as an example North American

---

[7] This Associated Press (AP) report was carried in the *Toronto Star*, November 6, 1974.

and European newspaper and television reports about a Mr. Lee Fried's precognition of an airline disaster. Fried, a Duke University student, deposited a letter with the president of Duke University which, when opened one week later, declared that 583 people would perish in a collision of two 747 jumbo jets. Such an event had occurred in the meantime! Randi found that only one of seventeen newspaper reports that he saw did not "slant" the item by failing to report that in the original press interview Fried had made it clear that he is a performing magician and his prediction contained no element of ESP. He did what many magicians, including Randi, have done over the years; he created the *impression*, through trickery, that he had made an astonishing prediction, and skilfully deceived people into believing that the prediction had been made *before* the event.

Daniel Cohen, a journalist and author who has written frequently and skeptically about the paranormal, observed that there is really very little hard news generated in the field of parapsychology each year. However, he added,

> Rather than having to court the media, like most scientists are forced to do, parapsychologists are often in the position of being courted by the media. Newspapers, magazines and television are hungry for news of parapsychology because they know that is something that their readers and viewers want. The subject sells magazines and books and boosts the rating of TV shows. The result is that journalists are often tempted to inflate a story, making news where none or very little exists. (1971, p. 2.)

With regard to the famous Bridey Murphy reincarnation case,[8] Cohen recounted that

> I can recall a discussion that I once had with one of the editors who helped to bring the Bridey Murphy reincarnation case so dramatically to the attention of the American public in the late 1950's. This man had training as a reporter, and I don't think he ever believed a word of the Bridey Murphy story. He certainly was aware of all the holes in it that were later gleefully pointed out by the critics. His concern was only to make sure that he was not being made part of a deliberate hoax. The fact that he also believed the people involved to be foolish, and the story itself utterly without foundation did not stop him from spreading it to millions of readers. (1971, p. 19.)

Many people think if a respectable publishing house publishes a book as non-fiction, its editors must believe the contents to be factual. Cohen suggested that even respectable publishing houses ask only two questions: "Will the book sell?" and "Will I get sued?". If the answer to these questions are "yes" and "no" respectively, they will publish the book regardless of what they think of its contents.

Authors of critical books on the paranormal often encounter difficulty in finding a publisher. For example, Ernest Taves, who has done considerable critical study of parapsychology and visual perception, and who coauthored a critical book on UFOs with the late Donald Menzel, described his experience in trying to find a publisher for a proposed book on irrational beliefs. He received replies from publishers stating,

> Our experience tells us it is hard enough to sell books which go against one specific fad or superstition . . . when it comes to dealing with practically every superstition at once as you propose . . . people just don't seem to turn to books.

> . . . I'm not personally keen on buying a whole book of knocks, and I wonder how many other buyers would be . . . .

> . . . though we can appreciate your distaste for many of the irrationalities of the time, we feel such a book would have a hard time in the marketplace. (Taves, 1978, pp. 75–76.)

---

[8] The interested reader is referred to Gardner (1957) and Ducasse (1960) for two different viewpoints.

Psychologist Barry Singer (1979) described the difficulty he and George Abell, an astronomy professor, had in finding a publisher for a book about the paranormal which was written from a skeptical perspective.[9] Singer reported that an editor at Prentice-Hall had told him that pro-paranormal books sell better than anti-paranormal books; Prentice-Hall had just released *The Amityville Horror*,[10] which the editor expected would do well despite the probable lack of factual basis for it.

Singer commented,

> While corresponding with prospective contributors, I encountered a good deal of frustration stemming from their previous attempts to publish critical views on the paranormal, and James Randi has documented examples of deliberate media bias. . . . Such practices have always annoyed me, but my balance was recently tipped from annoyance to outrage. It is not so much the actual exploitative media practices that have enraged me, it is the cheerful cynicism with which the exploitation is conducted. (1979, p. 44.)

He also said,

> The "priests" of the paranormal . . . are powerful, affluent individuals who have made a lot of money from their "mystery-makings". My acquaintances among the writers, publishers, and producers of material on the paranormal possess multiple estates, yachts, and luxury automobiles. It is clearly in their interest to continue to issue arcane, exciting mysteries to the public; mysteries that they cheerfully admit in private are fiction. (1979, p. 45.)

Thus, people are led to believe, by a large number of books on the subject, that in a roughly triangular area of ocean in the vicinity of Bermuda, many ships and planes have mysteriously disappeared, suggesting the presence of a strange force, a "timewarp", or alien spaceships. Yet Lawrence Kusche (1975), author of *The Bermuda Triangle mystery–solved*, and the only writer on the subject who took the trouble to examine naval records, found *no* mystery:

> The legend of the Bermuda Triangle is a manufactured mystery. It began because of careless research and was elaborated upon and perpetuated by writers who either purposely or unknowingly made use of misconceptions, faulty reasoning, and sensationalism. It was repeated so many times that it began to take on the aura of truth. (1975, p. 292.)

There have been attempts to generate other "mysteries" of the sea through "non-fiction" books, including the "Limbo of the Lost" in the North Atlantic and even a "Great Lakes Triangle".

We often are told by the media about "psychic sleuths" who have helped police to solve crimes or find lost hunters or locate stolen objects. When it is reported that even the police were amazed by the psychic's accuracy, how is the reader to explain it, if he does not accept that paranormal ability is involved? Hansel (1966) took the time to check into the details surrounding the apparent success in crime-solving of psychic sleuth Dr. W. H. C. Tenhaeff, then Director of the Parapsychology Institute at the University of Utrecht in Holland, and his team of "paragnosts", or clairvoyants. Hansel contacted the police involved in one of Tenhaeff's "successes" and found that Tenhaeff's "paragnosts" had been of no help to the police. Hansel then cited the report of Dr. F. Brink, a Dutch Police Inspector, who had investigated the attempts of parapsychologists to aid the Dutch police. He concluded that the police had not to his knowledge ever obtained help from the putative clairvoyant powers of these psychics. The use of psychics in police investigations was recently studied by

---

[9] It was accepted for publication by Charles Scribner's Sons.
[10] This book was on the best-seller list for *non*-fiction for several months, and has now been turned into a film of the same name. It appears to have been based on a simple hoax (Frazier, 1979b; Morris, 1978).

the Los Angeles Police Department (Resier, Saxe, and Wagner, 1979). Twelve psychics, eight of them "professional", were given information about two unsolved crimes and two solved crimes and asked to give their reactions. The tests proved negative, and it was concluded that "the usefulness of psychics as an aid in criminal investigations has not been validated". Such critical reports are ignored by the media.

Peter Hurkos, also of Dutch origin, has been described as the world's greatest psychic sleuth. He credits himself with having helped to solve murders in seventeen countries. However, closer scrutiny reveals that Hurkos' record is simply not impressive (Christopher, 1975). He incorrectly identified the "Boston Strangler", he incorrectly identified the murderer in a case in Virginia in 1960, and in 1952 he staked "his life and reputation" on the statement that Adolph Hitler was still alive. In 1969 Hurkos was hired by a friend of one of the victims of the "Sharon Tate murders" to find the killers (Sladek, 1973). Hurkos "revealed" that the murderers were three men, that he knew who they were and that he had identified them to the police. In fact, two women and one man committed the murders, with a third woman standing look-out. Hurkos was correct in his prediction that the killer would kill again, for the Manson group did just that, but this prediction is hardly startling given the nature of the Tate murders. The media and the people who follow the media either do not inform themselves of Hurkos' "misses", or they forget his misses and remember his hits.

The popular media have reported that astronaut Edgar Mitchell of the Apollo 14 moon mission, the sixth man to walk on the moon, conducted an unofficial test of ESP from outer space; he tried to send telepathic messages to earthbound friends on four separate occasions. According to Christopher's (1975) account, Mitchell, who had become involved in mysticism and parapsychology several years prior to the Apollo 14 mission, had become friends with Reverend Arthur Ford, the famous medium who was exposed as a fraud shortly after his death in 1971.[11] Ford was excited by the idea of an ESP test conducted from outer space. Mitchell tried to "transmit" a column of twenty-five randomly selected digits ranging from 1 to 5. These were meant to correspond to the five Zener card symbols. The receivers were given a schedule indicating the time periods during which he would "transmit"; all this was done without the knowledge of NASA authorities, who had a year earlier turned down an application from the American Society for Psychical Research to conduct a telepathy experiment. Problems developed, partly because of a 40-minute delay in the launching of Apollo 14. Hence, Mitchell's thought-transmissions, which were carried out during his rest periods, were held 40 minutes later than planned, and 40 minutes after the receivers on earth were expecting the signals. Although Mitchell 'sent' four columns of data, one on each of four occasions, two receivers had written down columns of data on six occasions while two others, for lack of time, had been receivers during two sessions only. Because of the lapse of time between sending and receiving, it was decided to view the test as one of precognition. Would the list of symbols thought of by the astronaut match those of the receivers? Joseph Banks Rhine and his research group were among those who carried out the data analysis, comparing Mitchell's symbol list with those of the two receivers who had received six messages and ignoring the lists provided by the two people who had received on only two occasions each. Fifty-one matches were found, compared with the forty predicted by chance and despite the smallness of the sample and the odd conditions surrounding the data collection and choice of data, this was hailed as a victory (Christopher, 1975). In a further analysis the 300 guesses made at a time closest to the times Mitchell was transmitting were compared with his transmissions. While sixty matches could be expected by chance, only

---

[11] See Spraggett and Rauscher (1973).

thirty-five occurred. These results were also seen as a success for the psi hypothesis as they were interpreted as indicating a significant degree of psi-missing (Mitchell, 1971).

Mitchell described the results without mention of the psi-missing or the haphazard timing and data collection. He said in an article in the *New York Times* that the four receivers guessed the symbols so successfully that the score "could be duplicated by chance [only] in one out of 3,000 experiments" (Christopher, 1975).

Many reports have circulated in the media about astronaut's sightings of UFOs (Oberg, 1978). We are told, in the pages of *Science Digest*, that the Apollo 11 astronauts were followed by a "mass of intelligent energy", and that photographs taken by the astronauts captured a UFO. The NASA photograph taken by the astronauts was published in *Science Digest* and the "UFO" was clearly visible. Yet when Oberg and Sheaffer (1977) examined the *original* NASA photograph, they found that there was an odd-shaped object to the right of the picture (which was readily identified as a piece of torn insulation, "one of hundreds which can be seen on a typical space mission") which was not in the *Science Digest* photograph. More surprising is the fact that the "UFO" at the centre of the *Science Digest* picture does *not* appear in the NASA photograph! The chief editor of *Science Digest* admitted to Oberg and Sheaffer that the insulation fragment had been airbrushed out, so that the reader would not be distracted. He insisted, however, that he did not add the "UFO". Yet all other copies of the NASA photograph show nothing in the spot where the *Science Digest* UFO was. *Science Digest*'s chief editor suggested that NASA had begun to retouch copies of the photo so that the object no longer appears! We are inclined to believe what we read, but more inclined to believe what we see. We do not usually consider the possibility of retouching when examining media reproductions of NASA photographs.

Another prominent example of deception of the public is the popular and widely-acclaimed series of books written by Carlos Castañeda, who claimed to have undertaken a 5-year apprenticeship to a Yaqui Indian Shaman named Don Juan.[12] In what was supposed to be the best anthropological tradition, Castañeda carefully observed and recorded the events of a world totally new to him, a world of "non-ordinary reality". For his work, he was awarded a doctoral degree by the University of California at Los Angeles. His doctoral dissertation was indistinguishable from his book, *Journey to Ixtlan*, which was already in the bookstores (deMille, 1978a, 1978b). DeMille carefully examined Castañeda's writings, uncovered a host of internal contradictions and discrepancies, and concluded that Castañeda's work was a clever hoax. Yet, while he successfully passed off the work as serious ethnography, his exposure as a hoaxer, surprisingly, did not seem to evoke much concern among anthropologists. No move was made to revoke his doctorate, for example. DeMille went so far as to suggest that Castañeda had received his degree *despite* suspicion about his work and because of internal politics among members of the UCLA anthropology department.

Truzzi expressed concern that the public was continuing to be duped by the Castañeda books, which are categorized as non-fiction by the Library of Congress;

> As a member of the American Anthropological Association, I would be pleased if our Association took an interest in the matter and issued a statement for the public on Castañeda's work following the results of their investigation into the truth of these claimed ethnographies that so many people seem to have accepted as representing excellence in anthropological research. (1977b, p. 124.)

---

[12] Castañeda (1968).

The television viewer has learned to separate apparent fact from fiction on the basis of the way material is presented. *Star Trek* is clearly fiction, and so no one believes that the process by which Captain Kirk "beams down" from the Enterprise to a planet's surface is other than fiction. We suspend our disbelief. On the other hand, people have been conditioned to assume that the material in documentary-style programs is carefully researched and factual. Unfortunately, there have been a number of recent films produced in documentary style and presented on television without any disclaimer, giving the viewer no basis to suspect that the subject matter in controversial. One widely shown film on psychic surgery is a case in point. At a time when thousands of North Americans were flocking to the Philippines in the hope of escaping the ravages of fatal diseases through the wonder cures of the "psychic surgeons", this film was presented without any indication that it was other than a documentary. It was one-sided, presenting the testimonies of numerous people who claimed to have been "cured", and interviews with various "scientists" who completely supported the psychic explanation provided an apparent scientific stamp of approval. This is extreme irresponsibility. No mention was made of several critical examinations of psychic surgery which have revealed it to be fraudulent exploitation. Either people in television programming are themselves persuaded by previews of these films that the reports are accurate, or they do not care.

Is it surprising that people are persuaded? In the absence of a source of more skeptical material, why would a person not believe what appears to be the modern scientific viewpoint? After all, the layperson is beguiled by all sorts of technical "mysteries"—lasars, holograms, "curved" space, and so forth. Why not telepathy? Or precognition? It is difficult for the layman to distinguish between what is improbable and what is currently viewed as impossible; if he believes the media, he is likely to be persuaded that psi exists.

Lessons from History

Parapsychology has been around for a long time; formal research has been conducted for over a century. It is worthwhile to recall some of the "well-documented" beliefs of the past which turned out to be false, to make us more cautious about the interpretation of "evidence".

Sheaffer (1977) drew a parallel between many current beliefs—UFOs, ESP, and so on—and the belief in fairies. In the period 1917–1921 there were widespread reports of fairy-sightings, which Sir Arthur Conan Doyle carefully researched and documented. He compiled a list of first-hand sightings from around the world which he described in his book *The coming of the fairies*. In some cases, more than one person had witnessed the fairies. More impressive yet, Conan Doyle obtained a series of five photographs, taken by a 16-year-old girl and her 10-year-old cousin, which clearly showed winged fairies playing in the forest. Photographic experts at Kodak Corporation in England examined the negatives and could find no evidence of fakery.

Sheaffer commented, citing in part Conan Doyle's words:

> Multiple independent witnesses. A series of photographs. Worldwide sightings. Close encounter cases. Certainly Conan Doyle did not exaggerate when he described the evidence for fairies as "overwhelming". As he observed, . . . "these numerous testimonies come from people who are very solid and successful in the affairs of life. . . . To wave aside the evidence of such people on the ground that it does not correspond with our own experience is an act of mental arrogance which no wise man will admit." (1977, pp. 50–51.)

Klass (1977) in turn drew a parallel between belief in UFOs and the case of "N-rays"; his comments are just as applicable to the discussion of ESP. In 1903 Professor R. Blondot, head of the physics department at the University of Nancy in France, discovered a new kind of ray which was different from the recently discovered X-rays and radioactivity. He labelled them N-rays, the N referring to the name of his university. Blondot reported that N-rays are emitted by metal objects and that they enhance vision. If the gas lights were turned down so that one could not quite read a calendar on the wall, and a metal object was pointed at it, one could then read it. Within a year, almost 100 papers confirming the existence of N-rays were published by the French Academy. More and more scientists jumped on the N-ray bandwagon and confirmatory papers were also published by investigators outside France (Squire, 1978). It was discovered that the application of an anesthetic such as ether or chloroform to the metal mysteriously stopped N-ray emission. Researchers ultimately discovered that all materials, animal, human, vegetable or mineral, emitted N-rays, except for one substance—wood. The French Academy announced that it was going to award Blondot a 20,000 franc prize and a gold medal for his discovery. By this time he had built a spectroscope using aluminium lenses and a prism, and reported that he had identified various wave lengths of N-rays.

However, in 1904 Dr. Robert Wood, an American scientist who had been unable to replicate the N-ray findings, visited Blondot's laboratory.[13] At one point during Blondot's demonstration of the identification of N-ray spectral lines using the spectrograph, Wood secretly removed the aluminium prism, making the spectroscope inoperable. Blondot repeated his identification of the lines in the N-ray spectrum as though the prism were still there. This spelled the downfall of N-rays. Although the French Academy did award the prize and medal to Blondot, it stated that the honour was for his life's work as a whole. N-rays were not mentioned.

Incidentally, when Wood told Blondot at one point that the latter's spectroscope was not precise enough to detect the claimed effect, Blondot responded that that in itself was one of the inexplicable properties of N-rays. The N-ray enthusiasts had no "experimenter effect" behind which to hide, but this comment of Blondot's is close to the kind of comments often made by parapsychologists about psi.[14]

Many eyewitnesses attested to the reality of fairies. So too have many people reported that they have experienced ESP. "Scientific" studies of N-rays "demonstrated" their reality. We are told that there is laboratory evidence for ESP. If we are to learn from the past, we will not too quickly accept either testimony or laboratory data without first going to all necessary lengths to test the veracity of the claims. As was shown earlier, human perception and memory is selective and interpretive. Even scientists with training in logical reasoning and empiricism can deceive themselves or be deceived by others when seeking evidence for phenomena in which they have a strong belief.

How should Skeptics Respond?

If it should turn out that parapsychology goes the way of N-rays and fairies, the story of its rise, its heyday, and its fall will make fascinating reading for the student of science. On the

---

[13] For Wood's own account, see Seabrooke (1941).

[14] It is surprising that no one has remarked on the coincidence that *wood* was the only substance not emitting N-rays, and *Wood* was the man who was responsible for the "downfall" of N-rays.

other hand, should psi effects become understood as part of a new physical conception of the universe, it is doubtful whether anything that has been discovered to the present in parapsychology will have been of much importance in bringing about this changed world-view. What have parapsychologists found out, even if we suspend our disbelief and take everything they say as truth? We face the sticky problem, if we believe, of choosing a representative position, for as we have seen parapsychologists vary from believing that no laboratory evidence of psi has been forthcoming to believing that post-mortem survival, the aura, dowsing, astral projection, precognition, and reincarnation have all been given ample empirical support. Who should we believe? We should have to test for ourselves the various claims that have been made, and given the notorious lack of replicability of psi experiments, and the experimenter effect which plagues some believers (and all skeptics), the results would not be clearer than those we have today.

Should the prudent scientist, shunning dogmatism, adopt a wait-and-see, "let us know when you've got something more substantial" position? Or should parapsychology receive more direct encouragement, as when the A.A.A.S. admitted it into the circle of "scientific disciplines"? Is it the responsibility of the scientist to teach the public how to evaluate claims and how to interpret experience so that they might choose other than paranormal explanations? Should he try to communicate better the methods and goals of science to the general public?

It is a thorny issue. If those who are skeptical remain taciturn, the field is left open for those who propagate paranormal beliefs, either in the name of science, or with a direct anti-science bias. The parapsychologists themselves seem disinterested in trying to separate the wheat from the chaff, although many play lip-service to the need for skepticism and critical thinking.

Beloff is one parapsychologist who is concerned by the wave of pseudo-scientific and occult belief that is sweeping society;

> When the universities are no longer peaceful havens of reason and learning, we have a positive duty to restrain the credulity of the young and to counter the mass of misinformation to which they are exposed and to which they are so pathetically vulnerable. (1975, p. 9.)

However, Beloff's view is not representative of parapsychologists in general.

Skeptics should not react to what they consider outrageous, non-scientific or anti-scientific claims by following the example of a group of scientists who threatened to boycott the publishing house that agreed to publish a book by Velikovsky (whose ideas about solar system history contradicted accepted scientific belief). The publisher issued the book, Velikovsky's image as a martyr was enhanced, and the image of the scientific community was tarnished. This is not a solution for anyone dedicated to the pursuit of truth and the free flow of ideas.

In 1975, "Objections to astrology: A statement by 186 leading scientists" was published in *The Humanist*[15] and widely publicized by the media. Among those who signed the statement were eighteen Nobel Laureates. The statement was blunt; it said that astrology not only lacks a verified scientific basis, but there is strong evidence against it. The statement read in part,

> In these uncertain times many long for the comfort of having guidance in making decisions. They would like to believe in a destiny predetermined by astral forces beyond their control. However we must all face the world, and we must realize that our futures lie in ourselves and not in the stars.

---

[15]   1975, **35** (3).

The scientists indicated particular concern with the "continued uncritical dissemination" of astrological forecasts and horoscopes by the media and by otherwise reputable newspapers, magazines, and book publishers:

> This can only contribute to the growth of irrationalism and obscurantism. We believe that the time has come to challenge directly, and forcefully, the pretentious claims of astrological charlatans.

More than 90 percent of the scientists who endorsed the "Objections to astrology" statements were astronomers and astrophysicists, and several of them, including one of the three principal authors of the statement, have written on the subject of astrology and debated with astrologers (Kurtz and Nisbet, 1976).

This unusual direct attack by scientists has had virtually no effect on the public acceptance of astrology, nor on media dissemination of astrological forecasts. For the public, it was a non-event. However, it did stir controversy within the scientific community. Carl Sagan (1976), a noted astronomer and critic of pseudo-science, disapproved of the statement calling it another example of the pretentiousness of scientific orthodoxy. Sociologist Ron Westrum (1976) argued that a person who is an astronomer is not automatically an expert on astrology. He questioned how many of the 186 scientists had the expertise in or knowledge of astrology to dismiss it out of hand, and called attention to a set of studies which he said provided data contradicting the claim that astrology is all nonsense. He also objected to the "take-our-word-for-it" stance of the statement.

While Westrum deserves support in his concern about the use of "authority" to shape people's beliefs, we must remember that proponents of astrology and parapsychology use the "authority" of science whenever they can to back their appeal. The employment of the "modern physics" view is a case in point. Few parapsychologists have more than an inkling about modern physics, and yet many defend their cause by telling the public that in the complexities of modern physics there is support for psi phenomena, and that supporting scientific evidence is coming constantly from laboratories and universities all over the world, and that acceptance of the Parapsychology Association as part of the A.A.A.S. is a sign of recognition from the scientific community.

The skeptics' dilemma is simply this: If one is truly dedicated to the ethic of free inquiry, one does not want to censor ideas, to brand some notions as 'rational' and others as 'irrational', to dictate what is proper speculation and what is sheer silliness. Yet the proliferation of pseudo-science, the apparent shift away from rational evaluation of information, the disillusionment with science itself, the widespread deception of the public, and the profits made from promises of psychic insight or psychic powers or psychic cures, should be of great concern to anyone interested in truth. The parapsychological community has made little or no effort to help protect the public from the wildest of claims and promises. Is the scientific community to sit by and watch others use its name to push such questionable claims? Remember that the public may *expect* scientists to object publicly when they see nonsense dressed up as science. The same feeling that many people express towards the media ("they wouldn't be allowed to print that if it weren't true") may obtain here. In terms of Tversky and Kahneman's availability heuristic, the individual evaluating astrology may recall many cases of "experts" supporting astrology or parapsychology, but few or none opposing it, and he may naturally assume that the scientific world accepts these phenomena.

Should scientists spend their time testing claims? In the field of parapsychology, it seems impossible for skeptics to be taken seriously by parapsychologists. By doing careful tests of "biorhythm theory" do scientists confirm in the public mind that biorhythm, although controversial, merits scientific investigation? Most scientists and academics, with a few exceptions, are more courteous towards parapsychologists than vice versa. They insist on adopting a position that the null hypothesis cannot be proved, but that the alternative is also unsupported: "Perhaps there is something there, but I'm not persuaded at the moment", they say. This is laudable, yet the inquiring layperson, faced with a dogmatic statement of belief by parapsychologists and a "The jury isn't in" stance by the scientists, can hardly be faulted for concluding that "there must be something there".

In 1976 a group of philosophers, psychologists, magicians, natural scientists, writers, and others including myself, drawn together by common concern for the "rising tide of pseudo-science", formed a group called the *Committee for the Scientific Investigation of Claims of the Paranormal* (CSICOP). The aims were: (1) to provide the public with an alternate viewpoint about the paranormal, a view which is unabashedly skeptical yet hopefully not dogmatic; and (2) to test the abilities of psychics under controlled conditions and to investigate other claimed instances of the paranormal.[16] This Committee and its subcommittees in seven other countries include notable scholars such as astronomers George Abell, Bart Bok, and Carl Sagan, psychologists Donald Hebb, Ray Hyman, C. E. M. Hansel and B. F. Skinner, philosophers Brand Blanshard, Mario Bunge, Antony Flew, Sidney Hook, Paul Kurtz and Ernest Nagel, magicians James (The Amazing) Randi, Milbourne Christopher and Henry Gordon, science writers Isacc Asimov and Martin Gardner, and many others. These people are not inelastic in their thinking; all have demonstrated considerable creativity and free-thinking in their respective fields. Yet, the very formation of this organization created discontent, not only from members of the parapsychology community, but also from within mainstream science. Murmurs of "witch hunt" and "heavy-handed authoritarianism" were heard.[17] To be fair, in any such *ad hoc* group there are those who are more outspoken than others and those less tactful than one might wish. The point here is that reaction to the Committee is another example of the ambivalent attitude that scientists have towards the one-sided dissemination of information about the paranormal. There are some who react with concern and try to counter what they see as propaganda which may ultimately weaken the stature of both science and critical thought in society, but many others are loath to speak out, believing that scientists have no right to use their authority as scientists to try to influence people.

Concluding Comments

The general public is by and large being misled by the media with regard to the world of the paranormal. The problem is not that people might begin to believe in telepathy or ghosts or survival of the "soul". The problem is that much of parapsychology, and much of the new wave of Eastern philosophy—religion—psychotherapy, teaches people to abandon critical thought, to consider the scientific method as too restrictive, passé, incapable of reaching

---

[16] As of January 1980, those few willing to submit themselves to test have not demonstrated any evidence of paranormal ability (e.g. see Randi, 1978, 1979a).

[17] John Marshall, a reporter for the Toronto *Globe and Mail*, examined some of the thousands of Scientology documents seized by the U.S. government during its investigation of illegal activities on the part of the Church of Scientology. Among them was a six-page document describing a plan to discredit CSICOP by circulating letters forged on CSICOP letterhead purporting to show that CSICOP was set up by the CIA to quash paranormal research outside the CIA. Such a letter apparently was "leaked" to several prominent people including columnist Jack Anderson (Frazier, 1980b).

ultimate truths, and to view the individual and the world in magical terms.

As parapsychology becomes more "accepted" (and that seems to be happening in contemporary society), its "applications" become a greater concern to those who are skeptical. A major airline admitted using biorhythm analysis as one basis for deciding when its pilots should not fly. An American judge used a convicted person's astrological chart to determine his sentence.[18] An archeologist is employing a psychic to help locate artifacts and interpret their history.[19] A Pentagon task force with an annual budget of six million dollars has been set up to investigate military applications of psychic phenomena and to develop defenses against "psychotronic" weapons.[20] Such examples seem to be on the increase. At what point should we begin to express concern?

Girden, in his review of parapsychology, warned that,

> Perhaps it is time that the establishment stop leaning over backwards in attempting to demonstrate fairness; additional bends, and the cost to science and society, may be enormous before necessary correctives are introduced. (1978, pp. 408–409.)

While it is easy for skeptics to turn a blind eye and a deaf ear to the generally one-sided media coverage of the paranormal, such a reaction leaves the public with no way to learn about the weakness of the paranormal position, no way to weigh the pros and the cons of the arguments on each side. What is required is not shrill denunciation of parapsychology and its advocates, but cool-headed and responsible defense of science and rationality. If we shrink from that task, let us not condescendingly blame the public for their belief in the paranormal. If only parapsychologists speak in the name of science, why should the public doubt them?

---

[18] Frazier, 1978b.
[19] *Toronto Star*, March 11, 1974.
[20] *Discover*, March 1981, p. 15.

CHAPTER 9

Conclusions

> ". . . I would contend that there is no real reason to believe that the supernatural is any more absent or remote from the horizons of everyday life of most people today than it was six thousand years ago. . . ."
>
> A. M. Greeley[1]

W HAT if parapsychologists are correct, what if psi exists and contemporary scientists are ignoring one of the most important potential advancements in knowledge of all time? What would the demonstrated existence of psi mean for the world, especially if as is claimed people can learn to develop psi abilities?

Some parapsychologists and paraphysicists have already given some thought to the matter of application of psi. Physicists Targ and Puthoff (1972) discussed the "peaceful uses of psychic energy" in their book *Mind Reach*, and suggested that psi would be useful in the following ways:

1. Futuristic prediction—precognition could be developed so that future social and political trends could be known in advance.
2. Medical diagnosis—paranormal ability may be useful both in diagnosis and healing.
3. Space exploration—the out-of-body experience or remote viewing (clairvoyance) could provide an effective and inexpensive mode of exploring outer space.
4. Executive ESP—Targ and Puthoff cited evidence of a positive correlation between a company's profits over a 5-year period and its executives' abilities to score above chance in a precognition experiment. Presumably, then, ESP could be harnessed in the corporate boardroom.
5. Stock markets and gambling—Targ and Puthoff argued that psychic functioning is non-analytic in nature, and because of this it would be under only the most unusual conditions that a psychic could use his powers to accurately predict the outcome of a gambling game in a casino, or to predict which stocks will go up in the next day's trading. Yet, they said, there is evidence that an individual can "fool" his psychic ability into giving him the information he requires in such circumstances.

However, Targ and Puthoff have been somewhat conservative in their analysis. If, in fact, people can be cured, information can be transmitted, objects can be influenced, and the future can be foreseen, if a person's essence can travel from the physical body, and if this essence survives bodily death, the implications for our lives are obviously mind-boggling. The blind, by developing their psi-ability, would have no need of eyes to see. Earthquakes, crimes, and accidents could be predicted in time to save lives (although it is a thorny problem to imagine being able to see the future, and then changing present circumstances so that the

---

[1] Greeley (1972) p. 5.

future itself is changed. Surely one would foresee the future as it actually turns out to be.) The psychic skills of millions could be nourished and honed and focused to break up hurricanes and successfully prevent "dying" satellites from falling on populated areas. (A "network" of psychics tried unsuccessfully to keep *Skylab* from falling.)

But what chaos we would have. There would, of course, be no privacy, since by extrasensory perception one could see even into people's minds. Dictators would no longer have to trust the words of their followers; they could "know" their feelings. How would people react if they could catch glimpses of the future? How could the stock market function if traders could use precognition? If most people could foresee the future, how would life be with millions of people all attempting to change present circumstances so as to optimize their personal futures? What would happen when two adversaries each tried to harm the other via PK? The gunfights of the Old American West would probably pale by comparison.

If psi exists, and if the psi-mediated "experimenter effect" is real, never again could scientists be so cavalier as to dismiss theories and claims because they only work for some people. Perpetual-motion machines may indeed work, despite their apparent violation of thermodynamic principles, since they may be driven by the psychokinetic energy of their inventer. The production of such energy may be inhibited by the presence of skeptics, preventing them from seeing the phenomenon for themselves. Any claim made by anyone in any area of science, despite the inability of others to verify it, could be yet another manifestation of psi and its experimenter effect.

Science seeks to separate the truth from fiction, reality from imagination, fact from artifact. Early scientists and pre-scientists, as well as contemporary scientists, have followed many false leads: the search for the Philosopher's Stone by which base metals might be turned to gold; the belief in phlogiston and ether; the attempt to "explain" and describe personality by an analysis of the bumps on the head; the leeching of blood as a tonic or remedy; the removal of frontal lobe tissue to render patients less aggressive (a practice supported by not much more knowledge than that held by primitive man when he practiced "trephination"—the drilling of a small hole in the skull to let spirits escape). However, by presuming the existence of a causal link and seeking it out, by down-playing unsupported speculations in favour of hypotheses backed by objective evidence, science has advanced.

If psi exists, practically *everything* is possible, and science, the very tool that most parapsychologists swear allegiance to in their examination of psi, will be superfluous. It will turn out to have been a gigantic error, since the uncontrolled (and *uncontrollable*) influence of psi, perhaps poorly developed, would have presumably been operating throughout the history of science; scientific laws as we know them may simply be a sort of "psi-consensus": the experimenter effect happened to work in the same direction for all who tried a given experiment. It would seem, then, that "scientific validation of psi" would be a contradiction of terms; if psi exists, science as we know it cannot.

Critics over the years have assailed parapsychologist's seeming lack of concern with conventional scientific rigour, coupled, paradoxically, with their claims that they are using scientific methodology. D. H. Rawcliffe (1959) saw ESP as old metaphysical beliefs dressed up in new quasi-scientific garb, and urged parapsychologists to be concerned with causality, to look for causal links between events that are supposedly paranormally related, rather than simply accepting the paranormal explanation. G. R. Price (1955) emphasized the need for a demonstration of psi that could be repeated by, or at least for, any competent scientist. Girden (1978) concluded that the lack of substantial, replicable data and the absence of appropriate theoretical concepts make parapsychology seem like "a statistic in search of a theory" (p. 408). Moss and Butler, like Rawcliffe, linked ESP to magic.

> ESP . . . does not represent some brave new frontier of human knowledge; it is nothing more than a thinly disguised form of essentialism, a reversion to a pre-scientific religio-mystical tradition. It relates, quite clearly, to the primitive practice of assigning causation to mysterious, impalpable, evanescent inner forces whenever the natural web of causation is not immediately apparent. (1978, p. 1077.)

Among the major weakness of parapsychology which have been identified in this book are the following:[2]

1. There is no experiment or demonstration which can be replicated by or in the presence of a competent, though skeptical, scientist (Chapter 6).[3]
2. The hypotheses put forth about psi are non-falsifiable; there is no way for parapsychologists to learn that psi does not exist (if it does not) since all failures to produce evidence of psi can be explained away. In addition, it cannot be demonstrated that the psi-explanation can uniquely, or even best, account for the results of psi experiments. Researchers take statistical evidence as a manifestation of psi without any justifiable reason for doing so; there is no independent way of demonstrating the existence of psi, apart from the statistical results (Chapters 6 and 7).
3. There is a disorderliness to the phenomena. For example, British and American experimenters seemed to be dealing with strangely different situations: clairvoyance was common in Rhine's subjects, rare among the subjects studied by Soal in England Improvements in experimental control lead to decreases in psi performance (Chapters 6 and 7).
4. After a century or more of formal parapsychological inquiry, there appears to be no increase in either theoretical clarity or objective evidence. It is still impossible to predict when ESP should or will occur (Chapter 6).
5. In the absence of the capacity to independently replicate psi studies, fraud and incompetence are special and significant problems which cannot be swept away simply by righteous indignation (Chapters 6 and 7).
6. The great sensitives and psychics never seem to be able to demonstrate their powers under properly controlled conditions (conditions approved not only by proponents of the paranormal, but also by skeptics). Often there is a reluctance to submit to critical testing by those not already convinced of the existence of psi. This moved C. P. Snow (1978) to write,

> An abnormal number of all reported paranormal phenomena appear to have happened to holy idiots, fools, or crooks. I say this brutally, for a precise reason. We ought to consider how a sensible and intelligent man would actually behave if he believed that he possessed genuine paranormal powers. He would realize that the matter was one of transcendental significance. He would want to establish his powers before persons whose opinions would be trusted by the intellectual world. If he was certain, for example, that his mind could, without any physical agency, lift a heavy table several feet, or his own body even more feet, or could twist a bar of metal, then he would want to prove this beyond, as they say in court, any reasonable doubt.
> What he would not do is set up as a magician or illusionist, and do conjuring tricks. He would desire to prove his case before the most severe enquiry achieveable. It might take a long time

---

[2] As was pointed out earlier, parapsychologists have attempted to respond to such criticisms in the past. Although, in my view, their defense is as weak as the original claims, the interested reader is advised to consider such sources as McConnell (1977a) and Rao (1979).

[3] Chapter reference refers to the original discussion of the problem.

before he was believed. But men with great powers often take a long time for those powers to be believed. If this man had the powers which I am stipulating, it probably wouldn't take him any longer to be accepted than it did Henry Moore to make his name as a sculptor.

Any intelligent man would realize that it was worth all the serious effort in the world. The rewards would be enormous—money would accrue, if he was interested in money, but in fact he would realize that that was trivial besides having the chance to change the thinking of mankind.

At the same time, there are a number of reasons to *expect* people to have experiences and which *seem* to be transcendental/paranormal:

1. Normal perceptual, memory, learning and cognitive processes should be *expected* to produce occasional "anomalous" experiences. Parapsychologists seem singularly uninterested in normal mental functioning. The everyday experiences that are described as "psychic" by many do not *require* a paranormal explanation (Chapter 4).
2. The demonstrated human disinclination to accept coincidence as an explanation predisposes people to see covariation and impute causality where neither exists. People have a very strong propensity to ignore negative instances. We remember the times two salient events occurred closely together, in time, and readily forget the times that one occurred without the other (Chapter 5).
3. Logic and rationality are not innate, but learned, and magical or superstitious beliefs and practices develop in both the individual and society in response to the need for reduction of anxiety or fear. Some beliefs and practices become part of the cultural package that is transmitted to each new generation. Early training in transcendental beliefs makes most people willing to accept transcendental phenomena without the same critical scrutiny that would be applied to more mundane events. The perseveration of such beliefs, reinforced both culturally and individually, is not surprising. If psi or other conceptions of transcendental forces did not exist, other magico-religious beliefs would surely have developed in their place (Chapter 2).
4. Beliefs of a transcendental nature may be so basic (i.e. "primitive", in Rokeach's terms) that they are all but unchangeable. In addition, people tend to select and interpret information in such a way as to maintain consistency with the beliefs they already have. Disconfirmation of strongly held and publicly stated beliefs may, paradoxically, increase the strength of the belief (Chapter 3).

The parallels between psi and magic should not be forgotten. Two quotations from the literature strike me as summations of the debate between believer and skeptic. The first is in the spirit of the skeptical position: belief in psi, in the absence of good evidence, is no different from magic. This comment was made by Sir James Frazer over a half century ago:

> . . . belief in the sympathetic influence exerted on each other by persons or things at a distance is the essence of magic. Whatever doubts science may entertain as to the possibility of action at a distance, magic has none; faith in telepathy is one of its first principles. (1923, p. 25.)

The second statement, made by a parapsychologist (Beynam, 1977), illustrates the believer's willingness to find psi phenomena everywhere. If magical practices exist, he said, they might themselves be instances of psi:

> Since magic, when shorn of all its window dressing, appears to be more or less equivalent to PK, it will be necessary in our treatment of PK to explain the laws of sympathy and homeopathy as well. (1977, p. 323.)

We have seen (Chapter 6) that parapsychology, judged by the Bunge criteria, is clearly pseudo-science. In the same vein, Nobel laureate Irving Langmuir (1953/1968) proposed a list of symptoms of what he called "pathological science" and it is interesting to consider the case of parapsychology in this light:

1. The maximum effect that can be observed is produced by a causative agent of barely detectable intensity, and the magnitude of the effect is substantially independent of the cause.
2. The effect is of a magnitude that remains close to the limits of detectability; or many measurements are necessary because of the very low significance of the results.
3. There are claims of great accuracy.
4. There are fantastic theories contrary to experience.
5. Criticisms are met by *ad hoc* excuses.

Langmuir apparently intended these symptoms to refer, *not* to crackpots and frauds, but to the beliefs of sincere but deluded individuals, among whom are often found respected scientists. He suggested that the presence of one or more of these symptoms should be a warning that careful scrutiny is required.

Parapsychologists often complain they are not taken seriously by orthodox scientists, and that if scientists would give parapsychology a fair chance, they would be persuaded by the "impressive evidence". This defense is unfair. Even within parapsychology there are those, such as Beloff, who have great difficulty obtaining results which might support the psi hypothesis. Thus, one should not expect a stampede of conventional scientists to take up research in this area. Some skeptics have made attempts to detect psi, but have come away with their skepticism intact. Claims that their skepticism inhibited the operation of psi beg the question. There are some who took parapsychology seriously and began with great interest and anticipation, but became disillusioned after they became more familiar with it.[4] Those from orthodox science who have experienced failure to detect psi are seldom heard about; journals are rarely interested in publishing *failures* to replicate.

Parapsychologists argue that orthodox scientists insist on exceptionally tough standards for the evaluation of psi. Skeptics respond that extraordinary claims require extraordinary evidence. However, it is not because of a lack of *extraordinary* evidence that the case of psi is given little attention by the scientific community. The evidence does not support even an *ordinary* claim. Compare the case of parapsychology with that of a researcher who discovers a drug which shows slight but highly significant effects over a large sample of subjects, but fails to produce any effect for researchers who doubt its efficacy. If the developer of the drug neither predicts when it will be effective nor describes the causal mechanism involved, his claim, while *ordinary*, will not win the support of the pharmaceutical/medical community. Extraordinary evidence is not required to rouse the interest of the scientific mainstream. *Ordinary* evidence, other than simple, non-chance effects which are not replicable, would quickly persuade a great many otherwise skeptical scientists to turn to the study of the paranormal.

---

[4] For example, Christopher Evans, Antony Flew, John Taylor.

Fostering Critical Thought

To the extent that existential fears serve to make parapsychology attractive as a kind of surrogate faith, paranormal belief will continue to flourish in one form or another. Yet, as I pointed out in Chapter 2, I do not believe that this is the only or even the major reason for belief in the paranormal. Much of this belief is based either on a negative reaction to the mechanistic view of humankind that science seems to provide, or conversely, on the view that scientific evidence supports the claims for the existence of psi. We can do something about these two factors. Scientists need to educate the public about science. They must show the public that science is not an out-of-control monster, nor is the practice of science cold and heartless as it is sometimes portrayed. Scientists should communicate the elegance of scientific pursuit, and the wonderment engendered by scientific discovery. Jastrow (1935/1962) spoke of wonder as an intellectual emotion on a par with curiosity. The unusual and the exceptional impress us, he said; we are excited by the sight of the world's largest mountain, or the highest waterfall; we are intrigued by the "mystery" of haunted castles. Hebb (1974) suggested that the "far-out" idea can be attractive simply because it is far out; this aspect of human motivation has not been adequately studied, he said. If Jastrow and Hebb are correct, this might explain in part the fascination many people have for stories of the paranormal. A problem arises, not when people give liberty to their ideas and speculations and revel in fascination, but when they mistake what they are doing to be rational. Science is capable of providing just as much fascination as parapsychology for those who turn to it. As astronomer Carl Sagan commented, the findings of modern science are

> far more compelling and exciting than most of the doctrines of pseudoscience. Science is more intricate and subtle, reveals a much richer universe and powerfully evokes our sense of wonder. And it has the additional and important virtue—to whatever extent the word has any meaning—of being true. (1978, p. 232.)

The educational system has a major role to play in this regard. As well as teaching an appreciation of the wonderment of science, we should teach children much more about critical reasoning; they should be taught that suspended judgement is necessary in some situations. Kelly and Crilly (1979) urged that school curricula should, in teaching critical reasoning skills,

1. impress upon the student that the written word is not self-validating;
2. teach students about the aims and objectives of science, and provide guidelines for distinguishing science from pseudo-science (in terms of replicability, falsifiability, etc.);
3. teach students to take the source of information into account (e.g. Is the source doing active scientific research?);
4. teach students to question whether a set of claims fit in with the established structure of science, or exist in isolation;
5. familiarize students with logical fallacies and persuasive techniques of rhetoric.

Children also should be taught to expect that occasionally they will have "anomalous" experiences (e.g. *déjà vu*; another person mentions something that an individual happens to be thinking about, etc.). By teaching them about non-literal perception and memory and the tacit dimension of consciousness, such experiences, which because of their unexpectedness elicit an emotional reaction, may be interpreted as no more important than the common experience of approaching someone that you are sure you recognize, only to find when close that you are mistaken.

Children should be taught not to expect to be able to find ready explanations for everything they experience. School children are given an unreal picture of life; while many situations in real life are fraught with uncertainty, children are taught to expect cut-and-dried answers to cut-and-dried questions. When they are finally confronted with a question without a simple answer, they are baffled and tend to pin their faith on any clue, regardless of how irrelevant it might be (Cohen, 1960). How much better it would be to give them experience in situations of considerable ambiguity, where the outcomes are uncertain and where they learn to compare their own guesses and extrapolations with what later occurs, and to acknowledge and overcome their uncertainties. The school system ideally should teach children about the limitations of their own reasoning, and the propensity for magical thinking in all of us.[5]

Parapsychology is indistinguishable from pseudo-science, and its ideas are essentially those of magic. This does not of course mean that psi does not exist, for one cannot demonstrate the non-existence of psi any more than one can prove the non-existence of Santa Claus. But let there be no mistake about the empirical evidence: There is *no* evidence that would lead the cautious observer to believe that parapsychologists and paraphysicists are on the track of a real phenomenon, a real energy or power that has so far escaped the attention of those people engaged in "normal" science. There is considerable reason, on the other hand, to believe that human desires and human self-delusion are responsible for the durability of parapsychology as a formal endeavour.

Those who believe in psi on the basis of faith alone will hear no argument from me. Those who claim to have scientific evidence for psi, on the other hand, should expect no sympathy. When people march their beliefs into the scientific arena, they must stand prepared to accept the scars of battle. If their ideas contain truth, they will ultimately win out. Parapsychologists, after a century of battle in this arena, refuse to accept defeat. That, of course, is their prerogative. However, scientists should feel no guilt. Justice is being and will be done.

As for the individual, each of us is vulnerable to magical thought; each of us is capable of allowing our interpretations of events to be unduly influenced by our emotional reactions to them. The folklore of our culture, told to us when our rationality was still developing, has left an indelible mark on us all. As Ravensdale and Morgan said,

> If you have never felt your pulse rate rise in an empty house or churchyard; never broken into a nervous jog trot down a dark country lane; never felt hairs prickle on the back of your neck; . . . it may be that you can afford to scoff, for these are the grassroots of belief in magic. . . . We were all children once; we feared the dark and magic and we carried out esoteric little rituals, handed down to us, which seemed to offer some hope of a safer world. (1974, pp. 196–197.)

Our unconscious remains confidently magical to this day.[6]

---

[5] However, it must be recognized that social and even religious pressure works against the kinds of measures advocated above. The school system is limited in what it can accomplish in this regard because of such pressures. Progress comes slowly.

[6] Gilmore (1980).

Bibliography

ABELL, G. O. and GREENSPAN, B. (1979) The moon and the maternity ward. *The Skeptical Inquirer*, III(4), 17–25.

ALBIN, R. and MONTAGNA, D. D. (1977) Mystical aspects of science. *The Humanist*, XXXVII(2), 44–46.

ALCOCK, J. E. (1975) Some correlates of extraordinary belief. Paper presented at the Canadian Psychological Association Annual Conference, Québec.

ALCOCK, J. E. (1977) Extraordinary belief and general credulity. Paper presented at the Canadian Psychological Association Annual Conference, Vancouver.

ALCOCK, J. E. (1979) Psychology and near-death experiences. *The Skeptical Inquirer*, III(3), 25–41.

ALCOCK, J. E. and OTIS, L. P. (1980) Critical thinking and belief in the paranormal. *Psychological Reports*, **46**, 479–482.

ALLPORT, G. W. (1955) *Becoming*. New Haven: Yale University Press.

ANASTASI, A. (1964) Subliminal perception. In A. ANASTASI, *Fields of applied psychology*. New York: McGraw-Hill.

ARGYLE, M. and BEIT-HALLAHMI, B. (1975) *The social psychology of religion*. London: Routledge & Kegan Paul.

ASIMOV, I. (1979) Asimov's corollary. *The Skeptical Inquirer*, III(3), 58–67.

ATKINSON, J. W. (1964) *An introduction to motivation*. Princeton, N. J.: Van Nostrand.

AYEROFF, F. and ABELSON, R. P. (1976) ESP and ESB: Belief in personal success at mental telepathy. *Journal of Personality and Social Psychology*, **34**(2), 240–247.

BACKSTER, C. (1968) Evidence of a primary perception in plant life. *International Journal of Parapsychology*, **X**(4), 329–348.

BACON, F. (1974) *Novum organum*. (J. DEVEY, Ed.) New York: P. F. Collier & Son, 1902 (originally published 1620). Cited by M. SNYDER, E. D. TANKE and E. BERSCHEID, Social perception and interpersonal behaviour: On the self-fulfilling nature of social stereotypes. *Sociometry*, **37**(1), 1–12.

BAKAN, D. (1966) The test of significance in psychological research. *Psychological Bulletin*, **66**(6), 423–437.

BALANOVSKI, E. and TAYLOR, J. G. (1978) Can electromagnetism account for extrasensory phenomena? *Nature*, **276**, 64–67.

BATSON, C. D. (1975) Rational processing or rationalization? The effect of disconfirming information on a stated religious belief. *Journal of Personality and Social Psychology*, **32**(1), 176–184.

BELOFF, J. (1973) *Psychological sciences*. London: Crosby Lockwood Staples.

BELOFF, J. (1975) The study of the paranormal as an educative experience. *Parapsychology Review*, **6**(6), 8–11.

BELOFF, J. (1977) Historical overview. In B. B. WOLMAN (Ed.), *Handbook of parapsychology*, New York: Van Nostrand, pp. 3–24.

BELOFF, J. (1980) Seven evidential experiments. *Zetetic Scholar*, **6**, 91–94.

BELOFF, J. and BATE, D. (1971) An attempt to replicate the Schmidt findings. *Journal of the Society for Psychical Research*, **46**, 21–31.

BENASSI, V. A., SWEENEY, P. D. and DREVNO, G. E. (1979) Mind over matter: Perceived success at psychokinesis. *Journal of Personality and Social Psychology*, **37**(8), 1377–1386.

BENDER, H. (1938) The case of Ilga K: Report of a phenomenon of unusual perception. *Journal of Parapsychology*, **2**(1), 5–22.

BENFORD, G. A., BOOK, D. L. and NEWCOMB, W. A. (1970) The tachyonic antitelephone. *Physical Review*, **2**, 263–265.

BENSON, H. (1975) *The relaxation response*. New York: Avon.

BERGER, P. L. (1970) *A Rumour of angels*. Harmondsworth: Penguin.

BEYNAM, L. M. (1977) Quantum Physics and paranormal events. In J. WHITE and S. KRIPPNER (Eds.), *Future science*, Garden City, New York: Doubleday, pp. 309–336.

BIRGE, R. T. (1966) Science, pseudo-science and parapsychology. AAAS Vice-Presidential Address, Washington, D. C., December, 1958. Cited by Dommeyer (1966), *op. cit.*

BORING, E. G. (1954) The nature and history of experimental control. *American Journal of Psychology*, **67**, 573–589.

BORING, E. G. (1955) The present status of parapsychology. *American Scientist*, **43**, 108–117.

BORING, E. G. (1961) The spirits against bosh. *Contemporary Psychology*, **6**, 149–151.

BORING, E. G. (1966) Paranormal phenomena: Evidence, specification and chance. Introduction to C. E. M. Hansel's *ESP: A scientific evaluation.* New York: Charles Scribner's Sons, pp. xiii–xxi.

BOULDING, K. E. (1980) Science: Our common heritage. *Science*, **207**(4433), 831–836.

BOWKER, J. (1973) *The sense of God.* Oxford: Clarendon Press.

BRAUD, S. E. (1979) The observational theories of parapsychology: a critique. *The Journal of the American Society for Psychical Research*, **73**, 349–366.

BRIDGMAN, P. W. (1956) Probability, logic, and ESP. *Science*, **123**, 15–17.

BROAD, C. D. (1962) *Lectures on psychical research.* London: Routledge & Kegan Paul.

BROUGHTON, R. S. (1979) Repeatability and the experimenter effect. *Parapsychology Review*, **10**(1), 11–15.

BROWN, G. SPENCER (1953) Statistical significance in psychical research. *Nature*, **172**, 154–156.

BROWN, G. SPENCER (1957) *Probability and scientific inference.* London: Longman, Green & Co.

BROWN, H. I. (1977) *Perception, theory and commitment.* Chicago: University of Chicago Press.

BROWN, R. and MCNEILL, D. (1966) The "tip of the tongue" phenomenon. *Journal of Verbal Learning and Verbal Behaviour*, **5**, 325–337.

BRUSH, S. G. (1974) Should the history of science be rated X? *Science*, **183**, 1164–1172.

BUCKHOUT, R. (1974) Eyewitness testimony. *Scientific American*, **231**(6), 23–31.

BUDD, S. (1973) *Sociologists and religion.* London: Collier-MacMillan.

BUGELSKI, B. R. (1951) *Experimental psychology.* New York: Holt

BUGELSKI, B. R. and BUGELSKI, S. (1940) A further attempt to test the role of chance in ESP experiments. *Journal of Parapsychology*, **4**, 142–148.

BUNGE, M. (1959a) *Metascientific queries.* Springfield, Ill.: Charles C. Thomas.

BUNGE, M. (1959b) *Causality.* Cambridge, Mass.: Harvard University Press.

BUNGE, M. (1967) *Scientific research*, Vol. I. New York: Springer-Verlag.

BUNGE, M. (1980) Demarcating science from pseudo-science. Beyond the fringe of science symposium, McGill University, February 19, 1980.

BURDICK, D. S. and KELLY, E. F. (1977) Statistical methods in parapsychological research. In B. B. WOLMAN (Ed.), *Handbook of parapsychology*, New York: Van Nostrand Reinhold, pp. 81–130.

BURDOCK, E. I. (1954) A case of ESP: Critique of "Personal values and ESP scores" by G. R. Schmeidler. *Journal of Abnormal and Social Psychology*, **49**, 314–315.

BURNAM, T. (1975) *The dictionary of misinformation.* New York: Ballantine.

CAPRA, F. (n.d.) Can science explain psychic phenomena? Mimeo.

CAPRA, F. (1975) *The tao of physics.* Suffolk: Wildwood House.

CASTAÑEDA, C. (1968) *The teachings of Don Juan: A Yaqui way of knowledge.* Berkeley: University of California Press.

CAVENDISH, R. (1977) *A history of magic.* New York: Taplinger.

CHAPLIN, J. P. (1976) *Dictionary of the occult and paranormal.* New York: Dell.

CHAPMAN, L. J. (1967) Illusory correlation in observational report. *Journal of Verbal Learning and Verbal Behavior*, **6**, 151–155.

CHAPMAN, L. J. and CHAPMAN, J. P. (1969) Illusory correlation as an obstacle to the use of valid psychodiagnostic signs. *Journal of Abnormal Psychology*, **74**, 271–280.

CHILD, I. (1978) Book review of B. B. Wolman's *Handbook of parapsychology. Parapsychology Review*, **9**(2), 9–13.

CHRISTOPHER, M. (1970) *ESP, seers & psychics.* New York: Thomas Y. Crowell.

CHRISTOPHER, M. (1975) *Mediums, mystics, and the occult.* New York: Thomas Y. Crowell.

CLARK, D. and MURDIN, L. (1979) The rehabilitation of Stephen Grey. *New Scientist*, **82**, 652–655

COE, M. R. Jr. (1958) Fire-walking and related behaviours. *The Journal of the American Society for Psychical Research*, **52**, 85–97.

COHEN, D. (1971) Parapsychology in the mass media. *Parapsychology Review*, **2**(1), 1–20.

COHEN, D. (1973) *ESP: The search beyond the senses.* New York: Harcourt Brace Jovanovich.

COHEN, J. (1960) *Chance, skill and luck*. Harmondsworth: Penguin.

COLLINS, H. M. (1976) Upon the replication of scientific findings: A discussion illuminated by the experiences of researchers into parapsychology. Proceedings of 4 S/ISA International Conference on Social Studies of Science. Cornell University. (mimeo).

COMSTOCK, W. R. (1971) The study of religion and primitive religions. In W. R. COMSTOCK (Ed.) *Religion and man: An introduction*. New York: Harper & Row.

COTGROVE, S. (1973) Anti-science. *New Scientist*, **59**, 82–84.

COX, W. E. (1974) Parapsychology and magicians. *Parapsychology Review*, **5**(3).

CRANDALL, R. (1977) The Scientology connection. Book review of John Wilhelm's *The search for superman*. *The Humanist*, **XXXVII**(3), 21.

CREATION-LIFE publishers. (1977) *Twenty-one scientists who believe in creation*. San Diego, California: Creation-Life Publishers.

CROW, W. B. (1968) *A history of magic, witchcraft and occultism*. Great Britain: The Aquarian Press.

CRUMBAUGH, J. C. (1966) A scientific critique of parapsychology. *International Journal of Neuropsychiatry*, **5**, 521–529.

DAVIS, J. W. (1979) Psi in animals: A review of research. *Parapsychology Review*, **10**(2), 1–9.

DAVIS, J. W. (n.d.) Procedural accuracy in parapsychology: Or . . . how do our friends justify their means? Mimeo.

DAVIS, K. (1949) *Human society*. New York: MacMillan.

DAY, H. (1975) *Occult illustrated dictionary*. New York: Oxford.

DECONCHY, J.-P. (1971) *L'orthodoxie religieuse*. Paris: Les Editions Ouvrières.

DEIKMAN, A. J. (1966) Deautomization and the mystic experience. *Psychiatry*, **29**, 324–338.

DE MILLE, R. (1978a) *Castañeda's journey* (2nd ed.). Santa-Barbara, California: Capra Press.

DE MILLE, R. (1978b) Book review of C. Castañeda's *The second ring of power*. *The Skeptical Inquirer*, **II**(2), 114–116.

D'ESPAGNAT, B. (1979) The quantum theory and reality. *Scientific American*, **241**, 158–181.

DEUTSCH, R. (1979) Personal communication.

DEVOTO, B. (Ed.) (1962) *Mark Twain—Letters from the earth*. New York: Harper & Row.

DIACONIS, P. (1978) Statistical problems in ESP research. *Science*, **201**, 131–136.

DIACONIS, P. (1979) Rejoinder to Edward F. Kelly. *Zetetic Scholar*, **5**, 29–34.

DINGWALL, E. J. (1974) Letter. *Parapsychology Review*, **5**(6), 27–28.

DITTES, J. E. (1973) Justification by faith and the experimental psychologist. In L. B. BROWN (Ed.), *Psychology and religion*. Hardmondsworth: Penguin.

DOBZHANSKY, T. (1972) The ascent of man. *Social Biology*, **19**, 367–378.

DODD, D. H. and WHITE, R. M. Jr. (1980) *Cognition: Mental structures and processes*. Boston: Allyn & Bacon.

DOMMEYER, F. C. (1966) Parapsychology: old delusion or new science? *International Journal of Neuropsychiatry*, **2**(5), 539–555.

DOMMEYER, F. C. (1975) Book review. *Parapsychology Review*, **6**(2), 11–12.

DOXEY, N. (1976) Personal communication.

DOYLE, C. (1965) Psychology, science, and the western democratic tradition. Unpublished doctoral thesis. University of Michigan.

DUCASSE, C. J. (1960) How the case of the *Search for Bridey Murphy* stands today. *Journal of the American Society for Psychical Research*, **LIV**(1), 3–22.

DURKHEIM, E. (n.d.) *The elementary forms of the religious life, a study of religious sociology*. London: George Allen & Unwin. Originally published in 1912.

DUVAL, P. and MONTREDON, E. (1971) ESP experiments with mice. In J. B. RHINE (Ed.), *Progress in parapsychology*. Durham, N.C.: Parapsychology Press.

EHRENWALD, J. (1974) Book review of Laurence LeShan's *The Medium, the mystic and the physicist*. *Parapsychology Review*, **5**(5), 5–6.

EINHORN, H. S. and HOGARTH, R. M. (1978) Confidence in judgement: Persistence of the illusion of validity. *Psychological Review*, **85**(5), 395–416.

EINSTEIN, A. (1950) *Out of my later years*. New York: Philosophical Library.

EINSTEIN, A. (1954) "Motiv des Forchens", cited by Holton (1974), *op. cit.*

EISENBERG, H. (1977) *Inner spaces*. Don Mills, Ontario: Musson.

EISENBUD, J. (1963) Psi and the nature of things. *International Journal of Parapsychology*, **5**, 245–269.

ELIADE, M. (1969) *The quest: History and meaning in religion*. Chicago: University of Chicago Press.

EPSTEIN, R. A. (1967) *The theory of gambling and statistical logic*. New York: Academic Press.

ESTES, W. K. (1976) The cognitive side of probability learning. *Psychological Review*, **83**(1), 37–64.

EVANS, C. (1973) Parapsychology: what the questionnaire revealed. *New Scientist*, **57**(830), 209.

EVANS, C. (1974) *Cults of unreason*. Herts., England: Panther.

EVANS, H. R. (1975) Introduction and history of magic. In A. A. HOPKINS, *Magic* (1897). Reprinted in D. H. Charney, *Magic*. New York: New American Library.

EVANS-PRITCHARD, E. E. (1937) *Witchcraft, oracles and magic among the Azande*. Oxford: Clarendon Press.

FARADAY, M. (1853) Experimental investigation of table-moving. *The Athenaeum* (July), 801–803. Cited by Hansel (1980), *op. cit.*

FEATHER, N. T. (1964) Acceptance and rejection of arguments in relation to attitude strength, critical ability, and intolerance of inconsistency. *Journal of Abnormal and Social Psychology*, **69**, 127–136.

FEHRER, E. and RAAB, D. (1962) Reaction time to stimuli masked by meta-contrast. *Journal of Experimental Psychology*, **63**, 143–147.

FESTINGER, L., RIECKEN, H. W., and SCHACTER, S. (1956) *When prophecy fails*. Minneapolis: University of Minnesota.

FINKE, R. A. (1980) Levels of equivalence in imagery and perception. *Psychological Review*, **87**(2), 113–132.

FIRSOFF, V. A. (1974) Life and quantum physics. *Parapsychology Review*, **5**(6), 11–16.

FISCHER, R. and LANDON, G. M. (1972) On the arousal state-dependent recall of "subconscious" experience: state boundedness. *British Journal of Psychiatry*, **120**, 159–172.

FISCHHOFF, B. and BEYTH, R. (1975) "I knew it would happen". Remembered probabilities of once-future things. *Organizational Behavior and Human Performance*, **13**, 1–16.

FLAVELL, J. H. (1963) *The developmental psychology of Jean Piaget*. New York: Van Nostrand.

FLEW, A. (1976) Parapsychology revisited: Laws, miracles, and repeatability. *The Humanist*, **XXXVI**(3), 28–30.

FLEW, A. (1980) Parapsychology: science or pseudo-science? *Pacific Philosophical Quarterly*, 61, 100–114.

FORER, B. R. (1949) The fallacy of personal validation: A classroom demonstration of gullibility. *Journal of Abnormal and Social Psychology*, **44**, 118–123.

FRANK, J. T. (1977) Nature and function of belief systems. *American Psychologist*, **32**(7), 555–559.

FRANKEL, C. (1973) The nature and sources of irrationalism. *Science*, **180**, 927–931.

FRAZER, JAMES G. (1923) *The golden bough*. London: MacMillan (originally published in 1896).

FRAZIER, K. (1978a) Clues in "remote viewing". *The Skeptical Inquirer*, **III**(2), 3–4.

FRAZIER, K. (1978b) Justice by horoscope. *The Skeptical Inquirer*, **II**(2), 8–9.

FRAZIER, K. (1979a) Schmidt's airing at the APS. *The Skeptical Inquirer*, **III**(4), 2–4.

FRAZIER, K. (1979b) Amityville hokum: The hoax and the hype. *The Skeptical Inquirer*, **IV**(2), 2–4.

FRAZIER, K. (1980a) Prediction, yes. Psychic, No! *The Skeptical Inquirer*, **IV**(3), 13–14.

FRAZIER, K. (1980b) A Scientology "dirty tricks" campaign against CSICOP. *The Skeptical Inquirer*, **IV**(3), 8–10.

FREUD, S. (1928) *The future of an illusion*. London: Hogarth Press.

FROMM, E. (1941) *Escape from freedom*. New York: Holt, Rinehart & Winston.

GALSTON, A. W. and SLAYMAN, C. L. (1979) The not-so-secret life of plants. *American Scientist*, **67**, 337–344.

GARDNER, M. (1957) *Fads and fallacies in the name of science*. New York: Dover.

GARDNER, M. (1972) Mathematical games: Why the long arm of coincidence is usually not as long as it seems. *Scientific American*, **227**(4), 110–112B.

GARDNER, M. (1974) Mathematical games: On the contradictions of time travel. *Scientific American*, **230**(5), 120–125.

GARDNER, M. (1975) Mathematical games: Concerning an effort to demonstrate extrasensory perception by machine. *Scientific American*, **233**, 114–118.

GARDNER, M. (1976a) *The relativity explosion*. New York: Vintage Books.

GARDNER, M. (1976b) Magic and paraphysics. *Technology Review*, **78**(7), 42–51.

GARDNER, M. (1977) A skeptic's view of parapsychology. *The Humanist*, **XXXVII**(6), 45–46.

GARDNER, M. (1979a) Mathematical games: How to be a psychic, even if you are a horse or some other animal. *Scientific American*, **240**(5), 18–25.

GARDNER, M. (1979b) Quantum theory and quack theory. *The New York Review of Books* (May 17), **XXVI**(8), 39–40.

GAUQUELIN, M. and GAUQUELIN, F. (1976) The truth about the Mars Effect on sports champions. *The Humanist*, **XXXVI**, 44–45.

GIBSON, W. (1967) *Secrets of magic*. New York: Grosset & Dunlap.

GIERE, R. N. (1979) *Understanding scientific reasoning*. New York: Holt, Rinehart & Winston.

GILMORE, J. B. (1980) Personal communication.

GILMORE, J. B. (1974) Randomization in experimental settings. Unpublished manuscript.

GIRDEN, E. (1978) Parapsychology. In E. C. CARTERETTE and M. P. FRIEDMAN (Eds.), *Handbook of perception, Vol. X: Perceptual ecology*. New York: Academic Press, pp. 386–412.

GOLDBERG, S. (1979) Is astrology science? *The Humanist*, **XXXIX**(2), 9–16.

GOLDSTEIN, B. R. (1978) Book review of R. R. Newton's *The crime of Claudius Ptolemy. Science*, **199**, 872.

GOODFELLOW, L. D. (1939) A psychological interpretation of the results of the Zenith radio experiments in telepathy. *Journal of Experimental Psychology*, **23**, 601–632.

GOODSTEIN, L. D. and BRAZIS, K. L. (1970) Psychology of scientist: XXX. Credibility of psychologists: an empirical study. *Psychological Reports*, **27**, 835–838.

GREELEY, A. M. (1970) Superstition, ecstasy and tribal consciousness. *Social Research*, **37**(2), 203–211.

GREELEY, A. M. (1972) *Unsecular man*. New York: Schocken Books.

GREELEY, A. M. (1974) *Ecstasy: A way of knowing*. Englewood Cliffs, N.J.: Prentice-Hall.

GREELEY, A. M. (1975) The sociology of the paranormal: A reconnaissance. *Sage Research Papers in the Social Sciences*, series 90-023, **3**.

GREENBANK, R. K. Cited by ULLMAN *et al.* (1973), *op. cit.*, p. 234.

GREENFIELD, P. M. and BRUNER, J. (1969) Culture and cognitive growth. In D. A. GOSLIN, *Handbook of socialization theory and practice*. Chicago: Rand McNally.

GULLIKSON, H. O. (1938) Extra-sensory perception: What is it? *American Journal of Sociology*, **XLIII**(4), 623–631.

HALLAM, A. (1975) Alfred Wegener and the hypothesis of continental drift. *Scientific American*, **232**, 88–97.

HAMMOND, D. (1970) Magic: A problem in semantics. *American Anthropologist*, **72**, 1349–1356.

HANSEL, C. E. M. (1966) *ESP: A scientific evaluation*. New York: Charles Scribner's Sons.

HANSEL, C. E. M. (1971) Parapsychology: the views of a critic. *Parapsychology Review*, **2**, 17–20.

HANSEL, C. E. M. (1980) *ESP and parapsychology: A critical re-evaluation*. Buffalo: Prometheus Books.

HARDY, A., HARVIE, R., and KOESTLER, A. (1973) *The challenge of chance*. London: Hutchinson.

HARRIS, E. E. (1970) *Hypothesis and perception*. London: George Allen & Unwin.

HARRIS, M. (1974) *Cows, pigs, wars & witches*. New York: Random House.

HARRIS, M. (1978) No end of messiahs. *The New York Times*, CXXVIII (November 26) E21.

HARVEY, B. (1978) Cranks and other. *New Scientist* **77**(1094), 739–741.

HAWKING, S. and ELLIS, G. (1973) The large scale curvature of space-time. *Cambridge monographs on mathematical physics*.

HEBB, D. O. (1974) What psychology is about. *American Psychologist*, **29**(2), 71–79.

HEBB, D. O. (1978) Personal communication.

HENSLIN, J. M. (1967) Craps and magic. *American Journal of Sociology*, **73**, 316–330.

HOLTON, G. (1974) On being caught between Dionysians and Apollonians. *Daedalus*, **103**, 65–81.

HONORTON, C. and HARPER, S. (1974) Psi-mediated imagery and ideation in an experimental procedure for regulating perceptual input. *Journal of the American Society for Psychical Research*, **68**, 156–168.

HOOK, S. (1977) The new religiosity. *The Humanist*, **XXXVII**(1), 38–39.

HUNSBERGER, B. (1978) The religiosity of college students: Stability and change over years at university. *Journal for the Scientific Study of Religion*, **17**(2), 159–164.

HUXLEY, A. (1959) *"The doors of perception" and "Heaven and hell"*. Harmondsworth: Penguin.

HYMAN, R. (1977a) "Cold reading": How to convince strangers that you know all about them. *The Zetetic*, **1**(2), 18–37.

HYMAN, R. (1977b) The case against parapsychology. *The Humanist*, **XXXVII**(6), 47–49.

INHELDER, B. and PIAGET, J. (1958) *The growth of logical thinking from childhood to adolescence*. New York: Basic Books.

JAHODA, G. (1968) Scientific training and the persistence of traditional beliefs among West African university students. *Nature*, **220**(5174), 1356.

JAHODA, G. (1969) *The psychology of superstition.* Harmondsworth: Penguin.

JAMES, W. (1956) *The will to believe.* New York: Dover (originally published 1896).

JAMES, W. (1962) *The varieties of religious experience.* New York: Modern Library.

JASTROW, J. (1962) *Error and eccentricity in human belief.* New York: Dover (originally published 1935).

JAWANDA, J. S. (1968) Superstition and personality. *Journal of Psychological Research*, **12**(1), 21–24.

JENKINS, H. M. and WARD, W. C. (1965) Judgement of contingency between responses and outcomes. *Psychological Monographs*, **79**(1).

JOHNSON, R. W. and ADAIR, J. G. (1972) Experimenter expectancy vs. systematic recording errors under automated and nonautomated stimulus presentation. *Journal of Experimental Research in Personality*, **6**, 88–94.

JONES, W. H., RUSSELL, D., and NICKEL, T. W. (1976) Personality and behavioral correlates of superstitious beliefs. Paper presented at the Midwestern Psychological Association conference, Chicago.

JUNG, C. G. (1938) *Psychology and religion.* New Haven: Yale University Press. Jovanouich, Inc. London: Routledge & Kegan Paul.

JUNG, C. G. (1933) *Modern man in search of a soul.* New York: Harcourt, Brace.

JUNG, J. (1971) *The experienter's dilemma.* New York: Harper & Row.

KAHNEMAN, D. and TVERSKY, A. (1973) On the psychology of prediction, *Psychological Review*, **80**, 237–251.

KANTHAMANI, H. and KELLY, E. F. (1974a) Card experiments with a special subject. 1. Single-card clairvoyance. *Journal of Parapsychology*, **38**, 16–26.

KAUFMANN, K. (1973) *Social psychology.* New York: Holt, Rinehart & Winston.

KAUFMAN, L. and ROCK, I. (1962) The moon illusion. *Scientific American*, **207**(1), 120–131.

KELLY, E. F. (1979) Reply to Persi Diaconis. *Zetetic Scholar*, **5**, 20–28.

KELLY, E. F. and KANTHAMANI, B. K. (1972) A subject's efforts toward voluntary control. *Journal of Parapsychology*, **36**, 185–197.

KELLY, E. F., KANTHAMANI, H., CHILD, I. L., and YOUNG, F. W. (1975) On the relation between visual and ESP confusion structures in an exceptional ESP subject. *Journal of the American Society for Psychical Research*, **69**, 1–31.

KELLY, I. W. (1979) Astrology and science: A critical examination. *Psychological Reports*, **44**, 1231–1240.

KELLY, I. and CRILLY, K. (1979) Critical thinking and the analysis of pseudoscience in the schools. *Alberta Science Education Journal*, **XVII**(3), 12–15.

KENNEDY, J. L. (1952) An evaluation of extra-sensory perception. *Proceedings of the American Philosophical Society*, **96**, 513–518.

KLASS, P. J. (1974) *UFOs explained.* New York: Random House.

KLASS, P. J. (1977) N-rays and UFOs: Are they related? *The Skeptical Inquirer*, **II**(1), 57–61.

KLASS, P. J. (1978) NASA, the White House and UFOs. *The Skeptical Inquirer*, **II**(2), 72–81.

KLECK, R. E. and WHEATON, J. (1967) Dogmatism and responses to opinion-consistent and opinion-inconsistent information. *Journal of Personality and Social Psychology*, **5**(2), 249–252.

KLEINKE, C. L. (1978) *Self-perception.* San Francisco: W. H. Freeman.

KLERMAN, G. L. (1979) The age of melancholy. *Psychology Today*, **12**(1), 36–42, 88.

KLUVER, H. (1966) *Mescal and mechanisms of hallucinations.* Chicago: University of Chicago Press. Cited by Siegel (1977), *op. cit.*

KOESTLER, A. (1971) *The case of the midwife toad.* New York: Random House.

KOESTLER, A. (1972) *The roots of coincidence.* London: Hutchinson.

KOESTLER, A. (1974) Comment. *Impact of Science on Society* (Unesco), **XXIV**(4), 271–284.

KREPS, B. (1979) Hypnotic regression. *Homemaker's Magazine*, **14**(6), 18–38.

KRIPPNER, S. (1977) *Advances in parapsychological research I: Psychokinesis.* New York: Plenum.

KROEBER, A. L. (1963) *Anthropology: Culture patterns and processes.* New York: Harcourt, Brace & World.

KUHN, T. S. (1970) *The structure of scientific revolutions* (2nd ed.). Chicago: University of Chicago Press.

KURTZ, P. (1978) Is parapsychology a science? *The Skeptical Inquirer*, **III**(2), 14–32.

KURTZ, P. and NISBET, L. (1976) Are astronomers and astrophysicists qualified to criticize astrology? *The Zetetic*, **1**(1), 47–52.

KURTZ, R. M. and GARFIELD, S. L. (1978) Illusory correlation: A further exploration of Chapman's paradigm. *Journal of Consulting and Clinical Psychology*, **46**, 1009–1015.

KUSCHE, L. D. (1975) *The Bermuda Triangle mystery–solved*. New York: Warner.

LAMBERT, W. W., TRIANDIS, L. M., and WOLF, M. (1959) Some correlates of belief in the malevolence and benevolence of supernatural beings: A cross-societal study. *Journal of Abnormal and Social Psychology*, **58**, 162–169.

LANGER, E. J. (1975) The illusion of control. *Journal of Personality and Social Psychology*, **32**(2), 311–328.

LANGER, E. J. and ROTH, J. (1975) Heads I win, tails it's chance: The illusion of control as a function of the sequence of outcomes in a purely chance task. *Journal of Personality and Social Psychology*, **32**(6), 951–955.

LANGMUIR, I. (1953/1968) Colloquium given at the Knolls Research Laboratory, December 18, 1953. Transcribed and edited by R. N. Hall. Report No. 68–C–035, General Electric Research and Development Centre, Schenectady, New York, April 1968.

LAYTON, B. D. and TURNBULL, B. (1975) Belief, evaluation, and performance on an ESP task. *Journal of Experimental Social Psychology*, **11**(2), 166–180.

LEDOUX, J. E., WILSON, D. H., and GAZZANIGA, M. S. (1979) Beyond commissurotomy: clues to consciousness. In M. S. GAZZANIGA (Ed.), *Handbook of Behavioral Neurobiology*. Volume 2: *Neuropsychology*. New York: Plenum, pp. 543–554.

LEE, P. R. and PETROCELLI, F. (1971) Can consciousness make a difference? In P. R. LEE, R. E. ORNSTERN, D. GALEN, A. DEIKMAN, and C. T. TART, *Symposium on consciousness*. Harmondsworth: Penguin, pp. 1–18.

LE SHAN, L. (1978) Psi and altered states of consciousness: Necessary methods in physics and parapsychology. *Parapsychology Review*, **9**(3), 13–17.

LE SHAN, L. (1979) On dealing with our critics. *Parapsychology Review*, **10**(1), 7–8.

LEUBA, C. (1939) An experiment to test the role of chance in ESP research. *Journal of Parapsychology*, **2**, 217–221.

LEUBA, J. H. (1925) *The psychology of religious mysticism*. London: Routledge & Kegan Paul.

LEUBA, J. H. (1934) Religious beliefs of American scientists. *Harper's Magazine*, **169**, 297.

LEVINE, S. V. (1979) Role of psychiatry in the phenomenon of cults. *Canadian Journal of Psychiatry*, **24**, 593–603.

LEVY, W. J. (1971) Possible PK by chicken embryos to obtain warmth. *Journal of Parapsychology*, **35**, 321–322.

LÉVY-BRUHL, L. (1926) *How natives think*. London: Allen.

LEWIN, K. (1931) The conflict between Aristotelian and Galileian modes of thought in contemporary psychology. *Journal of General Psychology*, **5**, 141–177.

LEWINSOHN, R. (1961) *Science, prophecy and prediction*. New York: Harper & Row.

LEWIS, I. M. (1971) *Ecstatic religion*. Harmondsworth, England: Penguin.

LOFTUS, E. F. and PALMER, J. C. (1974) Reconstruction of automobile destruction: An example of the interaction between language and memory. *Journal of Verbal Learning and Verbal Behavior*, **13**(5), 585–589.

LORD, C. G., ROSS, L., and LEPPER, M. R. (1979) Biased assimilation and attitude polarization: The effects of prior theories on subsequently considered evidence. *Journal of Personality and Social Psychology*, **37**(11), 2098–2109.

LUDWIG, A. M. (1966) Altered states of consciousness. *Archives of General Psychiatry*, **15**, 225–234.

LYKKEN, D. T. (1968) Statistical significance in psychological research. *Psychological Bulletin*, **70**(3), 151–159.

LYNCH, J. J. (1973) Biofeedback: Some reflections on modern behavioural science. In L. BIRK (Ed.), *Biofeedback: Behavioral medicine*. New York: Grune & Stratton, 191–203.

MCBURNEY, D. H. (1976) ESP in the psychology curriculum. *Teaching of Psychology*, **3**(2), 66–69.

MCCONNELL, R. A. (1969) ESP and credibility in Science. *American Psychologist*, **24**, 531–538.

McConnell, R. A. (1977a) The resolution of conflicting beliefs about the ESP evidence. *Journal of Parapsychology*, **41**, 198–214.

McConnell, R. A. (1977b) A parapsychological dialogue. *Journal of the American Society for Psychical Research*, **71**, 429–435.

MacDougall, C. (1940) *Hoaxes*. New York: Dover.

McDougall, W. (1938/1973) *Body and mind* (8th ed.). London: Methuen, 1938. Cited by Vetter, G. B. *Magic and religion*. New York: Philosophical Library, 1973.

MacKenzie, A. (1980) Personal communication.

McKown, D. B. (1979) Close encounters of the ominous kind: Science and religion in contemporary America. *The Humanist*, **XXXIX**(1), 4–7.

McVaugh, M. R. and Mauskopf, S. H. (1974) Historical perspectives and parapsychology. *The Journal of Parapsychology*, **38**(3), 312–323.

McWhirter, N. and McWhirter, W. (1969) *Dunlop illustrated encyclopedia of facts*. New York: Bantam.

Maddi, S. R. (1971) The search for meaning. *Nebraska symposium on motivation, 1970*. Lincoln, Nebraska: University of Nebraska Press, 131–186.

Mahoney, M. (1976a) *The scientist: Anatomy of the truth merchant*. Cambridge, Massachusets: Ballinger.

Mahoney, M. (1976b) The truth seekers. *Psychology Today*, **9**(11), 60–65.

Maier, N. R. F. (1931) Reasoning in humans: II. The solution of a problem and its appearance in consciousness. *Journal of Comparative Psychology*, **12**, 181–194.

Malinowski, B. (1948) *Magic, science and religion and other essays*. New York: Free Press.

Marks, D. and Kammann, R. (1977) The nonpsychic powers of Uri Geller. *The Zetetic*, **1**(2), 9–17.

Marks, D. and Kammann, R. (1978) Information transmission in remote viewing experiments. *Nature*, **274**, 680–681.

Marks, D. and Kammann, R. (1980) *The psychology of the psychic*. Buffalo: Prometheus Books.

Marwick, M. (1974) Is science a form of witchcraft? *New Scientist*, **63**, 578–581.

Maslow, A. H. (1959) Condition of being in the peak experience. *Journal of Genetic Psychology*, **94**, 43–66.

Massad, C. M., Hubbard, M., and Newtson, D. (1979) Selective perception of events. *Journal of Experimental Social Psychology*, **15**, 513–532.

Mead, M. (1977) Introduction to R. Targ & H. E. Puthoff, *Mind-reach*. Delacorte Press, pp. xv-xxii.

Medhurst, R. G. (1971) The origin of the "prepared random numbers" used in the Shackleton experiments. *Journal of the Society for Psychical Research*, **46**, 39–55.

Meehl, P. E. and Scriven, M. (1956) Compatibility of science and ESP. *Science*, **123**, 14–15.

Melzack, R. (1973) *The puzzle of pain*. New York: Basic Books.

Menzel, D. H. and Taves, E. H. (1977) *The UFO enigma*, Garden City: Doubleday.

Messadie, G. (1978a) Le mystère du triangle des Bouches-du-Rhone. *Science & Vie*, **CXXIX**(727), 24–25.

Messadie, G. (1978b) Le triangle des Bouches-du-Rhone: Comment on monte une mystification. *Science & Vie*, **CXXIX**(729), 34–35.

Michotte, J. (1946) *La perception de la causalité*, Paris.

Miller, G. A. (1962) *Psychology: The science of mental life*. New York: Harper & Row.

Mitchell, E. D. (1971) An ESP test from Apollo 14. *The Journal of Parapsychology*, **35**(2), 89–107.

Mitroff, I. (1974) *The subjective side of science*, Amsterdam: Elsevier.

Mitroff, I. (1976) Passionate scientists. *Society*, **13**(6), pp. 51–57.

Monte, C. F. (1975) *Psychology's scientific endeavour*, New York: Praeger.

Moody, R. A. (1975) *Life after life*. New York: Bantam Books.

Moody, R. A. (1977) *Reflections on life after life*. New York: Bantam Books.

Moore, L. (1977) *In search of white crows*. New York: Oxford University Press.

Moore, T. E. (1980) Subliminal advertising: What you see is what you get. Unpublished manuscript.

Morris, R. L. (1977) Parapsychology, biology and anpsi. In B. B. Wolman (Ed.), *Handbook of parapsychology*. New York: Van Nostrand Reinhold, 687–715.

Morris, R. L. (1978) Book Review of Jay Anson's *The Amityville Horror*. *The Skeptical Inquirer*, **II**(2), 95–101.

Moss, S. and Butler, D. C. (1978) The scientific credibility of ESP. *Perceptual and Motor Skills*, **46**, 1063–1079.

Mulhulland, J. (1938) *Beware familiar spirits*. New York: Scribner's.

Mundle, C. W. K. (1976) On the 'psychic' powers of non-human animals. In S. C. Thakur (Ed.), *Philosophy and psychical research*. London: George Allen & Unwin.

Mundle, C. W. K. (1973) The Soal—Goldney experiments, *Nature*, **245**, 54.

Murphy, G. (1971) The problem of repeatability in psychical research. *Journal of the American Society for Psychical Research*, **65**, 3–16.

Neisser, U. (1968) The processes of vision. *Scientific American*, **219**(3), 204–214.

Newton, R. R. (1977) The crime of Claudius Ptolemy. Baltimore: Johns Hopkins University Press.

Nicol, J. E. (1955) The design of experiments in psychokinesis. *Journal of the Society for Psychical Research*, **38**, 72–73.

Nicol, J. E. (1961) Keeping up with the Joneses. Book review of S. G. Soal's and H. T. Bowden's *The mind readers. Tomorrow Magazine*, **1**, 58–66.

Nisbett, R. E. and Wilson, T. D. (1977) Telling more than we can know: Verbal reports on mental processes. *Psychological Review*, **84**(3), 231–259.

Nixon, H. K. (1925) Popular answers to some psychological questions. *American Journal of Psychology*, **36**, 418–423.

Nunnally, J. (1960) The place of statistics in psychology. *Education and Psychological Measurement*, **20**, 641–650. Cited by Bakan (1966), *op. cit.*

Oberg, J. (1978) Astronaut "UFO" sightings. *The Skeptical Inquirer*, **III**(1), 39–46.

Oberg, J. and Sheaffer, R. (1977) Pseudo-science at *Science Digest. The Skeptical Inquirer*, **II**(1), 41–44.

O'Brien, J. T. (1976) Examining experimenter effects. *Parapsychology Review*, **7**(5), 25–28.

Offir, C. W. (1975) Flaundering in fallacy: Seven quick ways to kid yourself. *Psychology Today*, **8**(11), 66–68.

Oram, A. T. (1954) An experiment with random numbers. *Journal of the Society for Psychical Research*, **37**, 369–377.

Ornstein, R. E. (1976) The techniques of meditation and their implications for modern psychology. In C. Naranjo and R. E. Ornstein, *On the psychology of meditation*. New York: Viking Penguin.

Osis, K. and Haraldsson, E. (1977) *At the hour of death*. New York: Avon.

Otis, L. P. (1979) A survey of extraordinary beliefs. York University Master of Arts thesis.

Otis, L. P. and Alcock, J. E. (1979) Factors affecting extraordinary belief. Unpublished manuscript.

Pahnke, W. N. and Richards, W. A. (1969) Implications of LSD and experimental mysticism. In C. W. Tart (Ed.), *Altered states of consciousness*. New York: Wiley.

Palmer, J. (1978) Extrasensory perception: Research findings. In S. Krippner (Ed.), *Advances in parapsychological research 2: Extrasensory perception*. New York: Plenum.

Palmer, J., Khamashta, K., and Israelson, K. (1979) An ESP Ganzfeld experiment with transcendental meditators. *Journal of the American Society for Psychical Research*, **73**(4), 333–348.

Panati, C. (1975a) Precognition and time. *Parapsychology Review*. **6**(4), 1–4.

Panati, C. (1975b) Psi symposium at AAAS meeting. *Parapsychology Review*, **6**(3), 1–3.

Parker, A. (1978) A holistic methodology in psi research. *Parapsychology Review*, **9**(2), 1–6.

Pasachoff, J. M., Cohen, R. J., and Pasachoff, N. W. (1970) Belief in the supernatural among Harvard and West African university students. *Nature*, **227**, 971–972.

Penfield, W. (1975) *The mystery of the mind*. Princeton: Princeton University Press.

Persinger, M. A. (1976) The problems of human verbal behavior: The final reference for measuring ostensible psi phenomena. *The Journal of Research in Psi Phenomena*, **1**(1), 72–90.

Phillips, P. (1979a) Some traps in dealing with our critics. *Parapsychology Review*, **10**(4), 7–8.

Phillips, P. (1979b) Correspondence. *Parapsychology Review*, **10**(6), 25–26.

Piaget, J. (1929) *The child's conception of the world*. London: Kegan Paul.

Piaget, J. (1954) *The construction of reality in the child*. New York: Basic Books.

Platt, J. R. (1964) Strong inference. *Science*, **146**, 347–353.

Polanyi, M. (1958) *Personal knowledge: Towards a post-critical philosophy*. Chicago: University of Chicago Press.

Polanyi, M. (1963) The potential theory of adsorption. *Science*, **141**, 1010–1013.

POLANYI, M. (1967) *The tacit dimension*. London: Routledge & Kegan Paul.

POPPER, K. R. (1959) *The logic of scientific discovery*. Toronto: University of Toronto Press (original edition, 1935).

PRATT, J. G. (1974) In search of a consistent scorer. In J. BELOFF (Ed.), *New directions in parapsychology*. London: Elek Science.

PRATT, J. G., RHINE, J. B., SMITH, B. M., STUART, C. E., and GREENWOOD, J. A. (1966) *Extra-sensory perception after sixty years*. Boston: Bruce Humphries, (originally published 1940).

PRATT, J. G. and WOODRUFF, J. C. (1939) Size of stimulus symbols in extrasensory perception. *Journal of Parapsychology*, **III**, 121–158.

PRICE, G. R. (1955) Science and the supernatural. *Science*, **122**, 359–367.

QUINE, W. V. and ULLIAN, J. S. (1970) *The web of belief*. New York: Random House.

RANDALL, J. L. (1974) Biological aspects of PSI. In J. BELOFF (Ed.), *New directions in parapsychology*. London: Elek Science, 77–94.

RANDALL, J. L. (1975) *Parapsychology and the nature of life*. London: Souvenir Press.

RANDI, J. (1975) *The magic of Uri Geller*. New York: Ballantine.

RANDI, J. (1977) The media and reports on the paranormal. *The Humanist*, **XXXVII**(4), 45–47.

RANDI, J. (1978) Tests and investigations of three "psychics". *The Skeptical Inquirer*, **II**(2), 25–39.

RANDI, J. (1979a) Examination of the claims of Suzie Cottrell. *The Skeptical Inquirer*, **III**(3), 16–21.

RANDI, J. (1979b) A controlled test of dowsing abilities. *The Skeptical Inquirer*, **IV**(1), 16–20.

RAO, K. R. (1978) Psi: Its place in nature. *Journal of Parapsychology*, **42**, 276–303.

RAO, K. R. (1979) On "The scientific credibility of ESP". *Perceptual and Motor Skills*, **49**, 415–429.

RAVENSDALE, T. and MORGAN, J. (1974) *The psychology of witchcraft*. New York: Arco.

RAWCLIFFE, D. H. (1959) *Occult and supernatural phenomena*. New York: Dover.

REED, G. (1972) *The psychology of anomalous experience*. London: Hutchinson & Co.

REJDAK, Z. (1974) Psychotronics: the state of the art. *Impact of science on society* (Unesco), **XXIV**(4), 285–290.

RESIER, M. SAXE, S., and WAGNER, C. (1979) *Police science and administration*. Cited by K. Frazier, *The Skeptical Inquirer*, **III**(4), 7.

RHINE, J. B. (1953). *New world of the mind*. New York: William Sloane Associates.

RHINE, J. B. (1956) *A brief introduction to parapsychology*. Durham, N.C.: Duke University Press.

RHINE, J. B. (1964) Special motivation in some exceptional ESP performances. *Journal of Parapsychology*, **28**, 42–50.

RHINE, J. B. (1968) Psi and parapsychology: Conflict and solution. *Journal of Parapsychology*, **XXXII**, 101–128.

RHINE, J. B. (Ed.) (1971) *Progress in parapsychology*. Durham, N.C.: Parapsychology Press, Appendix A.

RHINE, J. B. (1974a) Telepathy and other untestable hypotheses. *Journal of Parapsychology*, **38**, 137–153.

RHINE, J. B. (1974b) Comments: "A new case of experimenter unreliability". *Journal of Parapsychology*, **38**(1), 215–225.

RHINE, J. B. (1977) History of experimental studies. In B. B. WOLMAN (Ed.), *Handbook of parapsychology*. New York: Van Nostrand Reinhold, 25–47.

RHINE, J. B. and RHINE, L. E. (1929) An investigation of a "mind-reading" horse. *Journal of Abnormal and Social Psychology*, **23**, 449–466.

ROBINSON, A.L. (1980) Nuclear evidence that neutrinos have mass. *Science*, **208**, 697.

ROE, A. (1951a) A psychological study of physical scientists. *Genetic Psychology Monographs*, **43**, 121–125.

ROE, A. (1951b) A psychological study of eminent biologists. *Psychology monographs*, **65**(14), 1–68.

ROE, A. (1953) A psychological study of eminent psychologists and anthropologists and a comparison with biological and physical scientists. *Psychological monographs*, **67**(2), 1–55.

ROGO, D. S. (1972) The crisis in experimental parapsychology. *Parapsychology Review*, **3**(4), 5–7.

ROGO, D. S. (1975) *Parapsychology: A century of inquiry*. New York: Dell.

ROGO, D. S. (1976) *In search of the unknown*. New York: Taplinger.

ROGO, D. S. (1977a) Parapsychology and the genesis of doubt. *Parapsychology Review*, **8**(6), 20–22.

ROGO, D. S. (1977b) The case for parapsychology. *The Humanist*, **XXXVII**(6), 40–44.

ROGO, D. S. (1980) Carl Sagan vs. the paranormal. *Fate*, April 1, 73–81.

ROKEACH, M. (1960) *The open and closed mind.* New York: Basic Books.
ROKEACH, M. (1968)*Beliefs, attitudes and values.* San Francisco: Jossey-Bass.
ROLL, W. G. (1977) Poltergeists. In B. B. WOLMAN(Ed.), *Handbook of parapsychology.* New York: Van Nostrand Reinhold, pp. 382–413.
ROMM, E. G. (1977) When you give a closet occultist a Ph.D., what kind of research can you expect? *The Humanist,* **XXXVII**(3), 12–15.
ROSENTHAL, R. (1966) *Experimenter effects in behavioral research.* New York: Appleton-Century-Crofts.
ROSS, L. (1977) The intuitive psychologist and his shortcomings: Distortions in the attribution process. In L. BERKOWITZ (Ed.), *Advances in Experimental Social Psychology,* vol. 10, New York: Academic Press.
ROTHMAN, M. A. (1970) Response to McCONNELL. *American Psychologist,* **25,** 280–281.
ROTHMAN, R. A. (1978) The new perpetual motion. *The Humanist,* **XXXVIII**(4), 42–45.
ROTTER, J. B. (1972) Beliefs, social attitudes and behavior: A social learning analysis. In J. B. ROTTER, J. E. CHANCE, and E. J. PHARES (Eds.), *Applications of a social-learning theory of personality.* New York: Holt, Rinehart & Winston.
RUSH, J. H. (1977) Problems and methods in psychokinesis research. In S. KRIPPNER (Ed.), *Advances in parapsychological research I: Psychokinesis.* New York: Plenum.
RUSSELL, D. and JONES, W. H. (1980) When superstition fails: Reactions to disconfirmation of paranormal beliefs. *Personality and Social Psychology Bulletin,* **6**(1), 83–88.
SACHS, R. G. (1972) Time reversal. *Science,* **176,** 587–597.
SAGAN, C. (1976) Correspondence. *The Humanist,* **XXXVI**(1), 2.
SAGAN, C. (1978) Astral projection and the horse that could count. *Playboy,* **25**(July), 82–86, 226–232.
SAGAN, C. (1979) *Broca's brain.* New York: Random House.
SALES, S. M. (1972) Economic threat as a determinant of conversion rates in authoritarian and unauthoritarian churches. *Journal of Personality and Social Psychology,* **23**(3), 420–428.
SALTER, C. A. and ROUTLEDGE, L. M. (1971) Supernatural beliefs among graduate students at the University of Pennsylvania. *Nature,* **232,** 278–279.
SARBIN, T. R., TAFT, R., and BAILEY, D. E. (1960) *Clinical inference and cognitive theory.* New York: Holt, Rinehart & Winston.
SARGANT, W. (1973) *The mind possessed.* London: Heinemann.
SCHEIBE, K. E. (1970) *Beliefs and values.* New York: Holt, Rinehart & Winston.
SCHMEIDLER, G. R. (1952) Personal values and ESP scores. *Journal of Abnormal and Social Psychology,* **47,** 757–761.
SCHMEIDLER, G. R. (1977) Methods for controlled research on ESP and PK. In B. B. WOLMAN (Ed.), *Handbook of parapsychology.* New York: Van Nostrand Reinhold, 131–162.
SCHMEIDLER, G. R. and McCONNELL, R. A. (1958) *ESP and personality patterns.* New Haven: Yale University Press.
SCHMIDT, H. (1969a) *Anomalous prediction of quantum processes by some human subjects.* Boeing Scientific Research Laboratories Document D1-82-0821, Plasma Physics Laboratory, February 1969. Cited by Hansel (1980), *op. cit.*
SCHMIDT, H. (1969b) Precognition of a quantum process. *Journal of Parapsychology,* **33,** 99–108.
SCHMIDT, H. (1970) PK experiments with animals as subjects. *Journal of parapsychology,* **34,** 255–261.
SCHMIDT, H. (1971). Mental influences on random events. *New Scientist,* **50,** 757–758.
SCHMIDT, H. (1973) PK tests with a high-speed random number generator. *Journal of Parapsychology,* **37,** 105–118.
SCHMIDT, H. (1974) Psychokinesis. In E.D. MITCHELL, *Psychic exploration: A challenge for science.* New York: G.P. Putnam's Sons.
SCHMIDT, H. (1975) Toward a mathematical theory of psi. *Journal of the American Society for Psychical Research,* **69,** 301–319.
SCHMIDT, H. (1978) Can an effect precede its cause? A model of the non-causal world. *Foundations of Physics,* **8,** 463–480.
SCHMIDT, H. and PANTAS, L. (1972) PSI tests with internally different machines. *Journal of Parapsychology,* **36**(3), 222–232.

Scott, C. (1958) Spencer Brown and probability. *Journal of the Society for Psychical Research*, **39**, 217–234.

Scott, C. and Goldney, K. M. (1960) The Jones boys and the ultrasonic whistle. *Journal of the Society for Psychical Research*, **40**, 249–260.

Scott, C. and Haskell, P. (1973) "Normal" explanation of the Soal–Goldney Experiments in extrasensory perception. *Nature*, **245**, 52–54.

Seabrook, W. (1941) *Dr. Wood, modern wizard of the laboratory.* New York: Harcourt, Brace.

Sebeok, T. A. and Umiker-Sebeok, J. (1979) Performing animals: Secrets of the trade. *Psychology Today*, **13**(6), 78–83.

Segal, S. J. (1970) Imagery and reality: Can they be distinguished? In W. Keup (Ed.), *Origin and mechanisms of hallucinations.* New York: Plenum.

Seligman, K. (1948) *Magic, supernaturalism and religion.* New York: Pantheon Books.

Seligman, M. E. P. and Hager, J. L. (1972) Biological boundaries of learning (the sauce-Béarnaise syndrome). *Psychology Today*, **6**(3), 59–61.

Sheaffer, R. (1977) Do fairies exist? *The Skeptical Inquirer*, **II**(1), 45–52.

Sherif, M. A. (1935) A study of some social factors in perception. *Archiva Psychologia*, **2**(187).

Shweder, R. A. (1977) Likeness and likelihood in everyday thought: Magical thinking in judgements about personality. *Current Anthropology*, **18**(4), 637–658.

Siegel, R. K. (1977) Hallucinations. *Scientific American*, **237**, 132–140.

Signorelli, A. (1974) Statistics—tool or master of the psychologist? *American Psychologist*, **29**, pp. 774–777.

Silverman, I. (1977) *The human subject in the psychological laboratory.* New York: Pergamon.

Singer, B. (1979) McDonald's and the occult. *The Humanist*, **XXXIX**(3), 44–45.

Skinner, B. F. (1948a) Superstition in the pigeon. *Journal of Experimental Psychology*, **38**, 168–172.

Skinner, B. F. (1948b) Card-guessing experiments. *American Scientist*, **36**, 456–462.

Skinner, B. F. (1953) *Science and human behavior.* New York: Free Press.

Sladek, J. (1973) *The new apocrypha*, New York: Stein & Day.

Slovic, P., Fischhoff, B., and Lichtenstein, S. (1977) Behavioural decision theory. In M. R. Rosenzweig and L. W. Porter (Eds.), *Annual Review of Psychology*, **28**, 1–39.

Smedslund, J. (1963) The concept of correlation in adults. *Scandinavian Journal of Psychology*, **4**, 165–173.

Snow, C. P. (1978) Passing beyond belief. A review of Brian Inglis' *Natural and Supernatural: A History of the Paranormal. Financial Times*, London, January 28, 1978.

Snyder, C. R. and Shenkel, R. J. (1975) The P. T. Barnum effect. *Psychology Today*, **8**(10), 52–55.

Spiro, M. E. (1966) Religion: Problems of definition and explanation. In M. Banton (Ed.), *Anthropological approaches to the study of religion.* London: Tavistock.

Spraggett, A., with Rauscher, W. L. (1973) *Arthur Ford: The man who talked with the dead.* New York: New American Library.

Sprinthall, R. C. and Lubetkin, B. S. (1965) ESP: Motivation as a factor in ability. *Journal of Psychology*, **60**, 313–318.

Squire, W. (1978) Correspondence. *The Skeptical Inquirer*, **II**(2), 142.

Stanford, R. G. (1977) Experimental psychokinesis: A review from diverse perspectives. In B. B. Wolman (Ed.), *Handbook of parapsychology.* New York: Van Nostrand Reinhold, pp. 324–381.

Staude, J. R. (1972) Alienated youth and the cult of the occult. In M. M. Medley and J. E. Conyers (Eds.), *Sociology for the seventies.* New York: Wiley.

Stent, G. S. (1972) Prematurity and uniqueness in scientific discovery. *Scientific American*, **227**(6), 84–93.

Stevens, S. S. (1967) The market for miracles. *Contemporary Psychology*, **12**, 1–3.

Strickland, L. H., Lewicki, R. J., and Katz, A. M. (1966) Temporal orientation and perceived control as determinants of risk-taking. *Journal of Experimental Social Psychology*, **2**(2), 143–151.

Swanson, G. E. (1960) *The birth of the gods.* Ann Arbor: University of Michigan Press.

Targ, R. and Puthoff, H. (1974) Information transfer under conditions of sensory shielding. *Nature*, **251**, 602–607.

Targ, R. and Puthoff, H. (1977) *Mind-reach.* Delacorte Press.

Tart, C. T. (1968) A psychophysiological study of out-of-the-body experiences in a selected subject. *Journal of the American Society for Psychical Research*, **62**, 3–27.

TART, C. T. (1977) *PSI: Scientific studies of the psychic realm.* New York: E. P. Dutton.

TART, C. T. (1980) Letter to *New Scientist,* **85,** 184–185.

TAVES, E. H. (1978) Correspondence. *The Skeptical Inquirer,* **III**(1), 75–76.

TAYLOR, J. G. (1975) *Superminds.* New York: Viking Press.

TAYLOR, J. G. and BALANOVSKI, E. (1979) Is there any scientific explanation of the paranormal? *Nature,* **279,** 631–633.

TERMAN, L. M. (1955) Are scientists different? *Scientific American,* **192**(1), 25–29.

THAKUR, S. C. (1976) Telepathy, evolution and dualism. In S. C. THAKUR (Ed.), *Philosophy and psychical research.* London: George Allen & Unwin.

THOMAS, K. (1971) *Religion and the decline of magic.* Harmondsworth: Penguin.

THOULESS, R. H. (1923) *An introduction to the psychology of religion.* Cambridge: Cambridge University Press.

THOULESS, R. H. (1963) *Experimental psychical research.* Harmondsworth: Penguin.

THOULESS, R. H. (1972) *From anecdote to experiment in psychical research.* London: Routledge & Kegan Paul.

TIMM, U. (1979) [On the statistical evaluation of parapsychological experiments: A personal rejoinder to the article published by Krengel and Liese.] *Zeitschrift für Parapsychologie und Grenzgebiete der psychologie,* **21,** 73–75. (Abstract, *Journal of Parapsychology,* 1979, **43**(3), 263.)

TINBERGEN, N. (1965) *Animal Behaviour.* Cited by Mundle (1976), *op. cit.*

TIRYAKIAN, E. A. (1972) Toward the sociology of esoteric culture. *American Journal of Sociology,* **78**(3), 491–512.

TOULMIN, S. (1972) *Human Understanding,* Vol. I. Oxford: Clarendon Press.

TRUEBLOOD, D. E. (1942) *The logic of belief.* New York: Harper.

TRUZZI, M. (1977a) From the editor. *The Zetetic,* 1(2), 3–8.

TRUZZI, M. (1977b) Correspondence. *The Zetetic,* **II**(1), 123–124.

TRUZZI, M. (1979) Quoteworthy. *Zetetic Scholar,* **3** and **4,** 26.

TVERSKY, A. and KAHNEMAN, D. (1973) Availability: A heuristic for judging frequency and probability. *Cognitive Psychology,* **5,** 207–232.

TVERSKY, A. and KAHNEMAN, D. (1974) Judgement under uncertainty: Heuristics and biases. *Science,* **185**(4157), 1124–1131.

TYLER, H. (1977) The unsinkable Jeane Dixon. *The Humanist,* **XXXVII**(3), 6–9.

TYLOR, E. B. (1958) *The origins of culture.* New York: Harper Torchbook. Originally published 1871.

ULLMAN, M., KRIPPNER, S., and VAUGHAN, A. (1973) *Dream telepathy.* Baltimore: Penguin.

ULRICH, R. E., STACHNIK, T. J., and STAINTON, N. R. (1966) Student acceptance of generalized personality interpretation. In R. ULRICH, T. STACHNIK, and J. MABRY (Eds.), *Control of human behavior* (Vol. 1). Glenview, Illinois: Scott, Foresman, pp. 259–260.

UNDERWOOD, P. (1979) *Dictionary of the occult & supernatural.* London: Fontana.

VAN DE CASTLE, R. L. (1977) Parapsychology and anthropology. In B. B. WOLMAN (Ed.), *Handbook of parapsychology.* New York: Van Nostrand Reinhold, pp. 667–686.

VENN, J. (1876) *The logic of chance.* London: Macmillan (2nd ed.). Cited by COHEN (1960), *op. cit.*

VETTER, G. B. (1973) *Magic and religion.* New York: Philosophical Library.

VIDULICH, R. W. and KAIMAN, I. P. (1961) The effects of information source status and dogmatism upon conformity behavior. *Journal of Abnormal and Social Psychology,* **63,** 639–642.

VOGT, E. Z. and HYMAN, R. (1959) *Waterwitching USA.* Chicago: University of Chicago Press.

WADE, N. (1977) Scandal in the heavens: Renowned astronomer accused of fraud. *Science,* **198,** 707–708.

WADE, N. (1979) Airplane magnate donates $500,000 for psi research. *Science,* **205,** 1359.

WAGNER, M. H. and MONNET, M. (1979) Attitudes of college professors toward extrasensory perception. *Zetetic Scholar,* **5,** 7–16.

WALKER, E. H. (1975) Foundations of paraphysical and parapsychological phenomena. In L. OTERI (Ed.), *Quantum physics and parapsychology.* New York: Parapsychology Foundation, pp. 1–53.

WARD, W. (1979) Randomness effects in a simulated ESP card-guessing experiment. *Journal of the Society for Psychical Research,* **50,** 108–13.

WARD, W. C. and JENKINS, H. M. (1965) The display of information and the judgement of contingency. *Canadian Journal of Psychology,* **19,** 231–241.

WARNER, L. (1952) A second survey of psychological opinion on ESP. *Journal of Parapsychology,* **16,** 284–295.

WARNER, L. and CLARK, C. C. (1938) A survey of psychological opinion on ESP. *Journal of Parapsychology*, **2**, 296–301.

WATSON, G. and GLASER, E. M. (1964) *Critical thinking appraisal*. New York: Harcourt, Brace & World.

WEAVER, W. (1963) *Lady luck: The theory of probability*. Garden City, New York: Doubleday.

WEINER, D. H. and MORRISON, M. (1979) A preliminary survey of research practices in parapsychology. Paper read at Southeastern Regional Parapsychological Association Conference, Campbell College, Buies Creek, N.C., February 9–10, 1979.

WERNER, H. (1935) Studies in contour: I. Qualitative analyses. *American Journal of Psychology*, **47**, 40–60.

WEST, D. J. (1966) The strength and weakness of the available evidence for extrasensory perception. In G. E. W. WOLSTENHOLME and E. C. P. MILLAR (Eds.), *Extrasensory perception*. New York: Citadel Press, pp. 14–23.

WEST, D. J. (1971) Reasons for continuing doubt about the existence of psychic phenomena. *Parapsychology Review*, **2**(2), 23–25.

WESTFALL, R. S. (1973) Newton and the fudge factor. *Science*, **179**, 751–758.

WESTRUM, R. (1976) Scientists as experts: Observations on "objections to astrology". *The Zetetic*, **1**(1), 34–46.

WHITEMAN, J. H. M. (1977) Parapsychology and physics. In B. B. WOLMAN (Ed.), *Handbook of parapsychology*. New York: Van Nostrand Reinhold.

WILHELM, J. L. (1976) *The search for superman*. New York: Pocket Books.

WILKENING, H. E. (1973) *The psychology almanac: A handbook for students*. Monterey, California: Brooks-Cole.

WILSON, J. D. and PATTERSON, J. R. (1970) *The conservatism scale*. Windsor, England: NFER Publishing Co.

WILSON, W. R. (1964) Do parapsychologists really believe in ESP? *Journal of Social Psychology*, **64**, 379–389.

WINDHOLZ, G. and DIAMANT, L. (1974) Some personality traits of believers in extraordinary phenomena. *Bulletin of the Psychonomic Society*, **3**(2), 125–126.

WOLMAN, B. B. (Ed.) (1977) *Handbook of parapsychology*. New York: Van Nostrand.

WUTHNOW, R. and GLOCK, C. Y. (1974) God in the gut. *Psychology Today*, **8**(6), 131–136.

Suggested Readings

Viewpoints critical of parapsychology

CHRISTOPHER, M. *ESP, seers and psychics*. New York: Thomas Y. Crowell, 1970.
CHRISTOPHER, M. *Mediums, mystics and the occult*. New York: Thomas Y. Crowell, 1975.
GARDNER, M. *Fads and fallacies in the name of science*. New York: Dover, 1957.
HANSEL, C.E.M. *ESP: A scientific evaluation*. New York: Charles Scribner's Sons, 1966.
HANSEL, C. E. M. *ESP and parapsychology: A critical re-evaluation*. Buffalo: Prometheus Books, 1980.
MARKS, D. and KAMMANN, R. *The psychology of the psychic*. Buffalo: Prometheus Books, 1980.
MOORE, L. *In search of white crows*. New York: Oxford, 1977.
RANDI, J. *The magic of Uri Geller*. New York: Ballantine, 1975.
REED, G. *The psychology of anomalous experience*. London: Hutchinson & Co., 1972.

The following periodicals are highly recommended:

The Skeptical Inquirer (The Committee for the Scientific Investigation of Claims of the Paranormal, Box 29, Kensington Station, Buffalo, N.Y. 14215, U.S.A.)
Zetetic Scholar (Marcello Truzzi, Editor, Department of Sociology, Eastern Michigan University, Ypsilanti, Michigan, 48197, U.S.A.)

Viewpoints sympathetic towards parapsychology

BELOFF, J. *Psychological sciences*. London: Crosby, Lockwood, Staples, 1973 (see Chapter 8: "Parapsychology").
BELOFF, J. *New directions in parapsychology*. London: Elek Science, 1974.
KRIPPNER, S. (Ed.) *Advances in parapsychological research. 1. Psychokinesis*. New York: Plenum, 1977.
KRIPPNER, S. (Ed.) *Advances in parapsychological research. 2. Extrasensory perception*. New York: Plenum, 1978.
RANDALL, J. L. *Parapsychology and the nature of life*. London: Souvenir Press, 1975.
ROGO, D. S. *Parapsychology: A century of inquiry*. New York: Dell, 1975.
TART, C. *Psi: Scientific studies of the psychic realm*. New York: E. P. Dutton, 1977.
THAKUR, S. (Ed.) *Philosophy and psychical research*. London: George Allen & Unwin, 1976.
WOLMAN, B.B. (Ed.) *Handbook of parapsychology*. New York: Van Nostrand, 1977.

These journals are devoted to experimental parapsychology:

The Journal of the American Society for Psychical Research (The American Society for Psychical Research, 5 West 73rd Street, New York, N.Y., 10023, U.S.A.)
The Journal of Parapsychology (The Parapsychology Press, College Station, Durham, N.C. 27708, U.S.A.)
Journal of the Society for Psychical Research (British Society for Psychical Research, 1 Adam and Eve Mews, London W. 8)
The Journal of Research in Psi Phenomena (Kingston Association for Research in Psi Phenomena, Box 141, Kingston, Ontario, K7L 4V6, Canada)
Parapsychology Review (Parapsychology Foundation, Inc., 29 West 57th Street, New York, N.Y., 10019)

Index of Names

(Names also appearing in the Bibliography are in Roman type; the others are in italics)

213

Subject Index